MARCHING TO GLORY

Marching to Glory

THE HISTORY OF THE SALVATION ARMY IN THE UNITED STATES OF AMERICA, 1880–1980

EDWARD H. McKINLEY

1817

HARPER & ROW, PUBLISHERS

SAN FRANCISCO

Cambridge   London
Hagerstown   Mexico City
Philadelphia São Paulo
New York   Sydney

Marching to Glory
dedicated to
The Salvation Army Student Fellowship Band
of Asbury College

MARCHING TO GLORY: *The History of The Salvation Army in the United States of America, 1880–1980.* Copyright © 1980 by The Salvation Army. All rights reserved. Printed in the United States of America. No part of this book may be used or reproduced in any manner whatsoever without written permission except in the case of brief quotations embodied in critical articles and reviews. For information address Harper & Row, Publishers, Inc., 10 East 53rd Street, New York, NY 10022. Published simultaneously in Canada by Fitzhenry & Whiteside Limited, Toronto.

FIRST EDITION

Designed by Jim Mennick

Library of Congress Cataloging in Publication Data
McKinley, Edward H.
MARCHING TO GLORY.

Bibliography: p. 230
Includes index.
1. Salvation Army—United States—History.
I. Title.
BX9716.M32   1980   267'.15'0973   79-2997
ISBN 0-06-65538-0

80 81 82 83 84 10 9 8 7 6 5 4 3 2 1

Shout aloud salvation, and we'll have another
 song;
Sing it with a spirit that will start the world along;
Sing it as our comrades sang it many a thousand
 strong,

   As they were marching to Glory.

   March on, march on! we bring the Jubilee;
   Fight on, fight on! salvation makes us free;
   We'll shout our Saviour's praises over every
     land and sea
   As we go marching to Glory!

How the anxious shout it when they hear the joyful
 sound!
How the weakest conquer when the Saviour they
 have found!
How our grand battalions with triumphant power
 abound,

   As we go marching to Glory.

So we'll make a thoroughfare for Jesus and His
 train;
All the world shall hear us as fresh converts still we
 gain;
Sin shall fly before us for resistance is in vain,

   As we go marching to Glory.

       —words by GEORGE SCOTT RAILTON, 1880;
   to be sung to the tune *"Marching through Georgia,"*
           music by HENRY C. WORK, 1865.

Many hands, many hearts, many heads have toiled and prayed and planned to bring the Army where it now is. History will record but a small part of the events, and many of the actors will be completely forgotten, but from God's history, on the Great Muster day, every heartache, every tear, every agonizing prayer, every day and night of toil will be read out and credited to the proper persons. God won the victory, and to Him we give the glory. It was not an uninteresting fight.

> —*The War Cry*, Pacific Coast edition,
> July 16, 1892, on the ninth anniversary of
> The Salvation Army in California.

Contents

$\mathcal{P}$reface

In anticipation of the celebration of the 100th anniversary of The Salvation Army in the United States of America, The Salvation Army commissioners' conference commissioned Dr. Edward McKinley, professor of history at Asbury College, Wilmore, Kentucky, to write the fascinating story of the religious and charitable movement throughout its first century of service in America.

As National Commander of this organization that has grown from its small beginnings in 1880 to a dynamic movement with 9,450 units of service in all fifty states, I am pleased to present this dramatic story. More than a mere description of events or a recounting of facts, it is an accurate, lively, intriguing, and moving account of people whose lives have been strangely and wonderfully bonded to Jesus Christ, to each other, and to The Salvation Army. Tribute is paid to the thousands of devoted Salvationists and friends of the Army whose commitment to its ideals and spiritual foundations has built and preserved for us this "Army of God." Modern-day Salvationists value the noble heritage that encourages them to serve the present age without sacrificing the ideals and purposes on which the organization was founded.

Marching to Glory is real, not a fairy tale: it is a saga of actual events; a record of the interplay of dominant personalities; a story of controversy and its resolution; and a reminder of an eternal and faithful God, who works through frail human personality to accomplish His purposes.

Dr. McKinley's knowledge as a historian, his skill as a researcher and writer, his meticulous dedication to truth, and his devotion to God and

The Salvation Army have enabled him to produce this book, which I commend to all readers.

COMMISSIONER ERNEST W. HOLZ
NATIONAL COMMANDER

October 1979

Foreword

This volume is offered to the reader as part of the national commemoration of the one hundredth anniversary of The Salvation Army in the United States. It is unlikely that any literate American is wholly unaware of the Army; nor are many completely indifferent to it. Some vague image of the organization is impressed on nearly every mind. The fact that the Army is benevolent, traditionally a worthy object of charity, is so well known as to require no demonstration: the name of the movement alone is sufficient to draw encouragement and support from a generous and grateful public.

Yet The Salvation Army is both more and less than most people suppose it to be. The Army is more than vaguely beneficial, more than a mere charity. It is a religious crusade, an evangelical Christian denomination the sole purpose of which is to secure the redemption of lost sinners through faith in the Atonement of Christ. The Salvation Army believes, however, that some people—those who are hungry or lonesome, helpless or frightened, sick or poor, or too old or too young for others to care much about—must first be given practical assurance that God and His children love them and will not leave them in their want and despair, before they can be told of His grace and love. Nevertheless the Army is fiercely evangelical, and about nothing is it less vague than its commitment to its Biblical doctrines.

The Salvation Army is not a legion of angels, nor martyrs, nor saints who have given themselves so completely to comforting the poor and saving souls that they have no thought for their own happiness. The

Salvation Army has always been made up of quite ordinary human beings, admittedly willing to do the most extraordinary things, but even the most zealous are neighborly, hard-working, common sort of people. The officers are the ministers, the soldiers are the members, but much of their lives is spent outside of Army service in the commonplace activities of life in America. Salvationists like to eat, and to sleep on Sunday afternoon. They enjoy their youth, they tell jokes, play softball, and work on their cars. They like music, they love and are loved; they grow old, and would prefer to grow older still. They die at last, of the ordinary afflictions that carry us all off sooner or later.

They are set apart from their fellows not by unnatural saintliness, by visions, or by hopeless asceticism, but by the recognition that in giving many hours of the week, a bit of courage, and a large amount of very human energy to the service of God in The Salvation Army, they are allowing God to endow their lives with the only meaning those lives will ever have, to be in their brief day on earth the embodiment of the supreme truth that Christianity is love in action, and to be in eternity the products of that love.

The fact that The Salvation Army is well regarded in the United States makes its history an attractive subject. The fact that the Army is a crusade for Christ makes its history important. The fact that its members are such ordinary people makes its history inspiring. The story of The Salvation Army proves that there is something good in the hearts of the American people that no amount of cynicism and national self-doubt has yet spoiled; it also proves that there is a God after all, and that anyone at all can serve Him well.

Acknowledgments

The preparation of the volume now before the reader has required the active cooperation of a large number of persons, both within and outside of The Salvation Army. The author is glad to acknowledge that he has been given not only the fullest cooperation in his work, but a great amount of kindness, encouragement, advice, and hospitality as well. For these boons he could offer no adequate payment, nor can he now, except to state that he is, and shall always remain, profoundly grateful for them.

Without casting the contributions of hundreds of helpful persons into a shadow, the author feels bound in gratitude to acknowledge in a special way those whose assistance was particularly beneficial.

Mr Douglas H. McMahon, Jr, and Professor Robert Rood Moore invested many hours in reading the rough drafts with great care, and made many corrections and suggestions that were invaluable. The literary department at the Army's Eastern territory has carried the main responsibility for coordinating the publication of this book; Major Dorothy Breen, the literary secretary, has given the project her hearty cooperation and kindly encouragement, without which it would have been difficult to finish the work within the time limit that circumstances imposed upon it. Brigadier Christine McMillan and Colonel Dorothy Phillips read the manuscript with close attention and made many helpful suggestions; the former, an officer with a long memory for illuminating details and a great love for the Army's past, made a valuable contribution to the work. The new Salvation Army Archives and Research

Center, under Mr Thomas Wilsted, offered the author every courtesy; the prompt and very helpful cooperation of Mr Tyrone G. Butler, assistant archivist, was especially welcome in the last, hectic stages of preparing the manuscript.

Colonel Paul D. Seiler of Ocean Grove, New Jersey, very generously opened his extensive collection of Salvation Army memorabilia, papers and books to the author. His is the largest personal collection of its kind in the United States, and the Colonel's kindness in providing the author with full access to it was warmly appreciated. Commissioner Ernest W. Holz and Major John Busby of Atlanta were likewise generous in opening their own large private collections of correspondence and papers to the author, as was Mr Harry Sparks of Los Angeles. Dr Louis Marchiafava, assistant archivist at the Houston Metropolitan Research Center, and his staff courteously guided the author through the large Milsaps collection.

The long hours of advance research and correspondence of Lt.–Colonel Eric Newbould, and his daily attendance when the author arrived, made the research trip to the Salvation Army's Western territorial headquarters at Rancho Palos Verdes, California, one of the author's most fruitful periods of investigation. Commissioner Richard E. Holz, the territorial commander, and Colonel Will Pratt, the chief secretary, gave the author much of their time and knowledge and offered him their kindness and hospitality in welcome abundance. Lt.–Colonel Donald V. Barry and Dorothy Gilkey of the Western territorial personnel department, the training principal, Major Ken Hodder and his assistant, Major Don Pack, and Major Leroy Pedersen of the Los Angeles divisional staff were kind and helpful in many important ways.

Commissioner Ernest W. Holz, who became National Commander in 1979, and Colonel John Paton, the Southern territorial leaders, virtually placed the records of headquarters at the author's disposal, spent many hours with him in interview and made every arrangement that courtesy and genuine interest in the author's work could suggest. Major Fred Ruth, the principal, and Major John Busby, the general secretary, very helpfully gave the author the use of the School for Officers' Training library and museum in Atlanta.

The Eastern territorial staff likewise opened their files and gave much of their time to the author. Commissioner W.R.H. Goodier, Colonel Albert Scott, and Lt.-Colonel Charles Southwood, the personnel secretary, gave assistance and advice of special value. Major and Mrs Gordon Sharp kindly lent the use of the extensive education department library. Lt.-Colonel David Baxendale kindly arranged for the author to use the very valuable and comprehensive collections in the library and museum at the School for Officers' Training at Suffern, New York. The author was kindly received there by Brigadier Bernard Ditmer, the general secretary, and aided in many ways by the librarian, Major Lorraine Sacks, and her staff.

Commissioner Paul J. Kaiser, the national commander (1977–1979) and Colonel Orval Taylor, the national chief secretary (1978–1979), were generous with their time and provided the author with much valuable information.

The many persons whom the author interviewed provided helpful, and often inspiring, pieces of information, many of which were incorporated into the finished text. Certain officers were particularly helpful, investing considerable time and effort in the author's work, offering advice, opening personal papers, and arranging further interviews. First among these was Colonel William Maltby of Asbury Park, New Jersey, without whose active assistance and kind interest the author would have missed a great deal of precious information. Lt.-Colonel William Bearchell, Colonel Florence Turkington and Mrs Colonel Edmund C. Hoffman of Asbury Park, Colonel and Mrs. C. Stanley Staiger of Ocean Grove, Colonel Bertram Rodda of Oakland, California, Brigadier Masahide Imai of Santa Clara, and Everald Knudsen Crowell of Los Angeles. Lt.-Colonel Edward Laity and Mrs Colonel Lillian Hansen Noble of Atlanta were likewise so generous and helpful that their contributions call for special note. In connection with the author's many visits to the Retired Officers' Residence in Asbury Park, the cooperation and hospitality of the manager, Major James Watson, was greatly appreciated. The author offers special thanks to Mr and Mrs Douglas McMahon, Sr, of Ocean Grove, and Captain and Mrs James Farrell of Atlanta, for regularly opening their homes to him during research trips.

The Faculty Research and Development Committee of Asbury College, chaired by Dr Howard Barnett, kindly provided the author with a work-leave in the spring quarter of 1979.

The following is a list of those who made a direct contribution to the collection of information for the present book. The author is solely responsible for any errors in or omissions from the text.

Brigadier Evelyn Allison
Major Harold Anderson
Lt.–Colonel Cyril Barnes
Colonel Giles Barrett
Lt.–Colonel Donald V. Barry
Lt.–Colonel David Baxendale
Brigadier and Mrs Ernest Baxendale
Lt.–Colonel William Bearchell
Sr.–Major and Mrs Carl W. Blied
Lt.–Colonel and Mrs Wesley Bouterse
Major Dorothy Breen
Lt.–Colonel William Burrows
Major John Busby
Mr Tyrone G. Butler
Mrs Lt.–Colonel William Carlson
Brigadier Lawrence Castagna
Mr Ralph Chamberlain
Commissioner William E. Chamberlain
Mr Philip Collier
Brigadier Ruth Cox, RN
Brigadier Fred Crossley
Professor James E. Curnow
Brigadier Bernard Ditmer
Brigadier Henry Dries
Brigadier Emma Ellegard
Major Houston Ellis
Mrs Peter R. Falbee
Lieutenant William Francis
Captain and Mrs Warren Fulton
Lieutenant Marshall Gesner

Dorothy Gilkey
Commissioner W.R.H. Goodier
Professor Roger Green
Colonel Frank Guldenschuh
Mrs Brigadier Elsie Henderson
Major Harold Hinson
Major Kenneth Hodder
Mr Kenneth G. Hodder
Mrs Colonel Edmund C. Hoffman
Lt.–Colonel Peter Hofman
Commissioner Ernest W. Holz
Commissioner Richard E. Holz
Brigadier Diana Houghton
Brigadier and Mrs Masahide Imai
Major Stanley Jaynes
Lt.–Colonel Edward Johnson
Commissioner Paul J. Kaiser
Lt.–Colonel and Mrs. Edward Laity
Major B. T. Lewis
Lt.–Colonel Olof Lundgren
Mr Kenneth E. Luyk, Jr
Colonel William Maltby
Dr Louis Marchiafava
Brigadier Olive McKeown
Mr Tom McMahon
Brigadier Christine McMillan
Colonel Andrew S. Miller
Lt.–Colonel Ernest A. Miller
Lt.–Colonel David W. Moulton
Commissioner John D. Needham
Captain Phil Needham
Colonel C. Emil Nelson
Lt.–Colonel Eric Newbould
Mrs Colonel Lillian Hansen Noble
Major James Pappas
Colonel John Paton

Major Leroy Pedersen
Colonel Dorothy D. Phillips
Colonel Will Pratt
Lt.–Colonel Lyell Rader
Mrs Colonel William Range
Lt.–Colonel R. Eugene Rice
Colonel Bertram Rodda
Brigadier Ron Rowland
Major Lorraine Sacks
Sr.–Major Charles A. Schuerholz
Colonel Albert Scott
Colonel and Mrs Paul D. Seiler
Sr.–Major Bertha Shadick
Major and Mrs Gordon Sharp
Brigadier Lloyd Smith
Sr.–Major Magna Sorenson
Lt.–Colonel Charles Southwood
Mr Harry Sparks
Sr.–Major and Mrs F. Railton Sprake
Colonel and Mrs C. Stanley Staiger '
Lt.–Colonel Ray Steadman-Allen
Mr James T. Stillwell
Bandmaster Alfred V. Swenarton
Lt.–Colonel and Mrs Chester O. Taylor
Colonel Orval Taylor
Colonel Florence Turkington
Major James Watson
Mrs Sr.–Major George Watt
Brigadier James Watt
Major Charles Wikle
Lt.–Colonel Norman Winterbottom
Miss T. E. Wood
Miriam Zeigler

CHAPTER I

1880~1890

"All the world shall hear us . . ."

They came to launch a great crusade. By all odds, they should have failed on the spot, outright and finally. Led by an amiable eccentric, as single-minded as an arrow in flight (but who proved in the end to be as ill-fitted to this grand endeavor as he was to many smaller ones), were seven women so graceless that their leader referred to them affectionately as "half-a-dozen ignoramuses." This was the pioneer party of The Salvation Army. They struggled with a flag, luggage, and the other passengers down the gangplank of the steamer *Australia* at Castle Garden, New York City, on March 10, 1880, to claim America for God.[1]

George Scott Railton, the leader of the "splendid seven," was a pioneer in more ways than one. His arrival in New York made him the first officially-authorized Salvation Army missionary, the first sent by General William Booth to carry the gospel of this his militant, rapidly growing East London crusade beyond the confines of its native Britain. Railton, thirty years old and a bachelor, had been responsible for many of the innovations that led to the creation of the new Army. The orphan child of Wesleyan missionaries who had gallantly perished nursing the sick during a fever epidemic in Antigua, Railton had been a zealous Christian since the age of ten. In 1868, at age nineteen, revolted by the tedium and the many small compromises that made up the daily life of business—Railton was a clerk—he resolved to lose himself in a larger cause: world evangelism. He acquired a huge banner inscribed with "Repentance–Faith–Holiness!" and thus armed, threw himself, penniless, ignorant, and unafraid, into an abortive one-man campaign to win Morocco for Christ.

Victorian evangelicals found this charming, and Railton was encouraged to become a full-fledged minister. He was drawn to the Reverend William Booth by the twin allurements of a pamphlet entitled "How to Reach the Masses with the Gospel" and the knowledge that Booth, the author, was searching for an assistant to organize his Christian Mission, a flourishing evangelical crusade he had started among the working class and poor of East London in 1865.

The genesis of The Salvation Army in the land of its birth is well-known, one of the cherished fixtures of Victorian history. Yet however often told the tale, it must be told again: not even a casual understanding of the work of the Army in America is possible without a knowledge of its beginning in the experience, personality, and theology of William Booth and those closest to him in his work.

Born in 1829 in Nottingham, the son of a bankrupt, small-scale building contractor, Booth was forced from childhood onward into a mean and lonely life. His one solace was religion. Converted at the age of fifteen and soon a member of the hospitable Wesleyan Church, Booth gave all the time he could spare from his detested employment as a pawnbroker's apprentice to lay preaching and street evangelism. He moved to London and resolved to escape from the pawnshop trade altogether, to give himself entirely to evangelism. In this attempt he was aided by a small salary provided for him by a sympathetic Christian with the unlikely name of Rabbits.

The crusades of the youthful preacher were crowned with success upon success. Booth himself was far more than a mere zealot: he was a colorful and fervent speaker, with a sense of the effectiveness of the carefully-chosen phrase. Well-informed from his own experience as to the despair and poverty of those who listened to him, indoors and outdoors, he could explain the promises of Christ in a manner that was compelling. Striking in appearance, with piercing eyes and a face—even as a young man—like that of an Old Testament prophet, Booth adopted out of sincere conviction a doctrine that was itself highly attractive: the doctrine of holiness. This theology, which is associated with John Wesley but not exclusive to him, is posited on two basic premises: one, the absolute and inescapable necessity of conversion—of accepting in faith that man is born under the power of original sin and can escape from its consequences only by accepting that the grace of Christ on the Cross alone is the sovereign cure—and two, that after conversion sinful tendencies remain, but that God offers His children a kind of perfection in grace whereby His love, and theirs for Him and for each other, purges the last traces of selfishness, self-will, and pride. However vague some of Booth's growing army of converts may have been on theological details, the compulsion to win others to Christ and to live lives of holy love were the twin mainstays of his London mission, and later of The Salvation Army (see Appendix III for the complete doctrines of The Salvation Army).

Railton found in The Christian Mission the cause to which he could at last surrender himself in delicious abandon. In the Founder's wife, Catherine, he found the perfect collaborator. Since her marriage to William Booth in 1855, she had exercised an influence over her husband that was entirely in keeping with her strength of character and her sterling qualities. For Catherine Booth was that rarest of historical beings: a legend that survives scrutiny. As devoted as her husband to the salvation of souls—whom she, like Booth, visualized as perishing in droves in sinful ignorance—Catherine was far more interested than the practical William in theology and social causes, such as the elevation of women to places of responsibility and usefulness in Christian endeavor. High minded and noble—she was first attracted to her future husband during his recitation of that timeless temperance classic, "The Grog-Seller's Dream"—Catherine was also prudent, patient, kindhearted and sensitive, mother and tutor to seven remarkable children, and an efficient organizer of people and money. Booth was quite correctly amazed at his excellent wife, touchingly devoted to her throughout their thirty-five years of marriage, with a childlike love that was one of his truly endearing qualities.

Guided by the Booths, Railton, and increasingly the Booths' eldest son Bramwell, the work of the Mission progressed swiftly. The single-minded leaders never allowed the movement to stray from its soul-saving purpose. They were willing, even eager, to experiment with new means to the great end. Sometimes these changes reflected the personal inclinations of the guiding personalities as to the best way to organize the work. The Booths and Railton, and most of the remaining leaders, favored an autocratic structure as opposed to the democratic control of groups like the Methodist New Connexion, the denomination from which William and Catherine had recently departed over a vote that denied them the privilege of full-time evangelism. Drawn almost from the beginning to the urban crowds—the working-class poor, desperate people struggling to gain and hold a place for themselves among the respectably employed, orphans, the helpless, pensionless aged, prostitutes, the clods and cast-offs, broken-wheels, and ne'er-do-wells of Victorian England—Booth carried the gospel of redemption.

Booth and his fellow workers were convinced that God was blessing this work, because when Booth began, as the truest expression of the gospel of love, to provide the poor with the rudimentary little charities of cheap, wholesome food and shelter, the Christian Mission was flooded with converts and volunteer helpers. Threatened with inundation and unable to coordinate his burgeoning spiritual empire without stern organization, which he in any case found congenial, Booth and his closest confederates were prompted—inspired, judging by the results—to transform their volunteer army into a real one. In 1878 they sallied forth in their new guise— The Salvation Army was born. Within a year, the now-familiar accoutrements of the "Great Salvation War" began to be added piecemeal: church halls became corps, flags, ceremonials, military badges, ranks, brass bands, and the rudiments of uniform were added with wildly encouraging results. Thus could an Army pioneer write of this vital year: "Guided, doubtless, by Providence, and prompted by the Spirit of God, one new departure had succeeded another, until the Mission had become what it was ultimately designated —an Army."[2]

Even before these inspired and profitable transformation took place in their affairs, Booth's converts had been remarkably loyal to him and to the principles upon which his Mission was based. Leaving the mother country behind did not dampen their zeal—and in that great age of immigration from the British Isles, many Mission converts did leave. As early as 1872 a determined Christian Missioner named James Jermy all on his own planted a seedling from the mother plant in Cleveland, Ohio, although the work withered and died when Jermy returned to England in 1876. In December of that year, another Mission associate wrote from New Jersey, pleading with Booth to send emissaries to start the great work in America. In fact, the dramatic effect of Railton's beachhead landing might have been diluted—as it was in his own estimation if not in the more sober eye of history—by the fact that the "Pioneer Party" was met in New York by Salvationists and supporters of the work, which had been established in Philadelphia by a family named Shirley six months earlier.[3]

American Salvationists rightly venerate the name of Eliza Shirley and her parents Amos and Annie, who unofficially commenced Salvation Army operations in the United States in 1879. They faced obstacles that would have daunted cooler heads—and cooler hearts. Convinced, however, that they were the agents of God's sovereign will, that America needed an organization like The Salvation Army, and unable to find anything even remotely similiar to their beloved work, which they sorely missed, they prepared to attack. Annie recalled later that they started the Army in America because "we could not live without it."[4]

Eliza Shirley was an early convert, won by the fledgling Army in 1878 at the age of sixteen. Her zeal for souls was sufficient preparation to enter the work on a full-time basis; she was commissioned a lieutenant and sent to join the great crusade as an assistant officer during a period of rapid expansion. In April of that year her father Amos, also a Salvation Army convert, left the family at home in Coventry and sailed for America, holding forth to his wife and daughter the allure of better times in the new world. A skilled silk worker, he secured a position as foreman in the firm of Adams & Company, silk manufacturers in Kensington, a suburb of Philadelphia. He promptly sent for his wife and Eliza, urging them to join him in order to begin The Salvation Army in America. Whatever his motives had been for going to the new world, Shirley had been inspired on the scene by a vision of what the Army could do for the Christless masses in Philadelphia. Eliza and Annie were naturally anxious to go. But when the seventeen-year old lieutenant asked William Booth—now General Booth—for a transfer to Philadelphia, of all places, he was not unnaturally surprised. He demurred and tried to dissuade her, flourishing the girl's vows, the great need for workers in England, and as the trump, Matthew 10:37: that whosoever loveth mother and father more than Christ is not worthy of Him. Still, he could not stand in the way of the family's reunion. Encouraged by Eliza's zeal, Booth relented: if the girl was determined to go, she might start a work in Philadelphia along Salvation Army lines. "If it is a success," he added, "we may see our way clear to take it over." Then the General hesitated again: his poetic and charming son Herbert was dispatched to try to dissuade the Shirley women, but in vain. At last Lieutenant Shirley and her mother were given a regulation Salvation Army send-off from Coventry. No doubt filled with gratitude by the General's last and greatest concession—that they might actually name their new work in America after the parent body—the women sailed. They were told to report any successes to headquarters. The family joined hands in August, and true to their word, set to work at once to redeem the General's grudging confidence in them. They did not fail.

While Amos spent his working hours at the silk factory, Annie and Eliza searched the poor neighborhoods of Philadelphia for a hall they could afford to rent. They finally located an abandoned chair factory between Fifth and Sixth on Oxford Street, large enough and cheap, but filthy, floorless, unfurnished, with picturesque holes in the roof. The ever-cheerful Eliza compared it favorably to the Manger of Bethlehem, and the women attempted to close the deal on the spot. The owner, not surprisingly, had never heard of The Salvation Army and expressed misgivings about the reliability of rent payments, to say nothing of his shock at being addressed by two "female preachers." Amos arrived with a month's rent in advance, drawn from his wages, and the hall was secured.

The family worked late into the night for weeks, preparing their fort for the first assault on Satan and his minions. The walls were whitewashed, sawdust was strewn on the dirt floor, and a platform was built of low-grade, unplaned lumber. With the family's small savings entirely expended in these endeavors, the Shirleys in perfect faith petitioned the Lord for the exact sum necessary to purchase lumber to build benches for the expected crowds to sit upon. When a man arrived with the very sum in hand—he informed the rejoicing Shirleys that God had told him while at prayer to carry such a sum to this address—the cheerful militants naturally took this extraordinary development as further proof of the righteousness of their crusade. Nothing could stop them now!

Sunday, October 5, 1879, was set for the opening of the new work. Amos had plastered the neighborhood with posters announcing that "Two Hallelujah Females"—neither "women" nor "lassies" sat well with Father Shirley—would "speak and sing in behalf of God and Precious Souls." The heading ran, in large and florid type: "Salvation Army," and the times and location of the meetings were given. "Rich and Poor, Come in Crowds."

The great day dawned, and the heroic trio marched out with hearts full of high promise. On the way to the "Salvation Factory," the Shirleys held a short service on the corner of Fourth and Oxford, singing, "We are bound for the land of the pure and the holy." Reminiscing about the event forty-six years later, Eliza could not recall if anyone stopped to listen to them. Thus do great events, those much sought-after turning points and watersheds in human affairs, pass unnoticed. For this gallant little scene surely was a great event: the first Salvation Army street-corner meeting in American history. No unprejudiced observer can fail to be touched by it: these obscure and unimportant people, favored by nothing in this life, unknown and unsupported even by their distant comrades, possessed of nothing but a love for God and their fellow sinners, held up the Cross of Christ over the manure and cobblestones of a Philadelphia gutter in 1879.

The indoor meeting was, alas, an anticlimax after such a courageous beginning. Not even the plucky Eliza could make a "crowd" out of the twelve persons waiting on the platform for the service to begin; the more so as these were "Christian friends" who had taken an interest in the Shirley's pioneer work and offered to help them conduct the first official meeting. Undaunted, the Shirleys were convinced, as were later pioneer officers, that multitudes secretly hungered for the gospel and had only to be confronted with their peril without it to embrace its saving grace. Clearly, another street meeting was required. This time the Shirleys took up their stand at Five Points, a cheerless but crowded intersection of five slum streets. The sound of "We are going to wear a crown, to wear a starry crown" emptied the nearby saloons, much to the joy of the missionaries. But when they tried to deliver a message to the gathered crowd, it dispersed in a cloud of oaths and jibes. The Shirleys gamely announced that they would return to the same corner at 7:00 P.M.: they were greeted by many of the same crowd with a shower of insults, mud, and garbage. The audience gathered inside the hall for the evening service was again small, and consisted of sympathetic Christians.

Confused and discouraged, especially by the perilous developments at Five Points, the Shirleys asked the mayor for protection. In what was to become a pattern in early Salvation Army history in the United States, city officials revealed themselves to be unsympathetic to the Army's outdoor evangelism. The Shirleys were told that any disturbance caused by their work was entirely due to its eccentric and annoying character. They were ordered to hold forth in the future in some place other than the public streets. The pioneers were finally reduced to trudging eight blocks from their hall to hold their open-air services in a vacant lot, where not a soul listened to them. In the meantime, the interest of the few "Christian friends" had dwindled, and even the indoor services were held in an empty hall. Four weeks passed, with the Shirleys' hopes for the future of their mission sinking daily lower. Penniless, friendless, and discouraged, they prayed for some sign from the

Heavenly Commander that He favored their dying crusade, and would yet bless it.

Arriving at their dark and lonesome lot one evening, the trio were amazed to find flames, smoke, noise, and—most dazzling of all prospects to their hungry hearts—a crowd! Several boys had set fire to a barrel of tar in the Shirleys' lot, and the horse-drawn fire engines had arrived promptly. Fire was a desperate threat in the crowded, wooden, gas-lit cities of the late nineteenth century; fear, along with the self-important clang and bustle of fire engines, always drew large crowds to fires. The Shirleys were certain the fire was providential, and threw themselves on the startled crowd with thankful hearts, singing, "Traveller, whither art thou going, Heedless of the clouds that form?" Their curiosity naturally aroused, the crowd stayed to listen to Amos' brief, simple homily on the grace of Christ. At the end of it, a drunken, rumpled man, who proved later to be a notorious local known only as "Reddie," struggled forward to ask, in his bewilderment, if such Good News could be for the likes of *him?* Tearfully the Shirleys assured him that it was, and embraced the man, bearing him off in triumph to the Salvation Factory, "ten thousand hallelujahs" in their hearts. The crowd, now thoroughly amazed, followed the quartet into the hall. Reddie was allowed to sleep while the Shirleys sang, prayed, and spoke to the crowd, which now occupied all the seats and filled the hall to overflowing. Reddie was revived, and in the presence of the large and enthusiastic crowd—Eliza later remembered the number to have been over eight hundred—he was soundly converted. Sobered by his experience, Reddie promised to come again the next day to explain in his own words what had happened to him—giving his "testimony," an act the Army encourages to this very day. Many in the crowd had been deeply affected by all that happened —that Reddie was suddenly a changed man none could deny—and they promised to return to hear him. The Shirleys took up a collection and raised enough to carry on for a few more weeks. Though exhausted, they were overjoyed: the work was saved. The Salvation Army had been launched in the United States after all.[5]

At least, it was launched so far as the Shirleys were concerned. The Salvation Army in Britain as yet knew nothing of these momentous events. Spreading rapidly in that country amid hurricanes of controversy and with every resource stretched to the thinnest possible point, the movement took no thought of the departed Eliza Shirley and her mission to the new world. But the movement did not remain unaware of the work in Philadelphia for long. With the Salvation Factory an assured success, to which crowds—and far better, converts—repaired in ever larger numbers, Amos and Annie sent Eliza in January, 1880, to open a second mission station—or corps, to use the new military terminology coming into use—on Forty-Second and Market Streets. Delighted at their success, the Shirleys collected newspaper clippings about the new mission and sent them triumphantly to General Booth, along with letters requesting him to officially take command of The Salvation Army in America.

Booth was naturally pleased, and resolved after the first batch of good reports to promote Eliza Shirley to the rank of Captain. But the Shirleys' continued importunities presented the General with a dilemma: he knew that the press of demands on the swelling Army in England made it almost impossible to spare any qualified officer to go to America. It would be a time-consuming and expensive trip to a country of which most Englishmen, the General included, knew little. On the other hand, if he did *not* act to graft this spontaneous American offshoot back onto the mother Army, he would lose control over it altogether. And Eliza *had* gone out with something like his promise that he would look at whatever she was able to start.

The influence of George Scott Railton was crucial at this juncture. His motives for pressing himself on Booth as the leader of an American expedition were complex. Railton was a visionary, for whom merely practical considerations like time and money meant nothing. He would throw himself on the American shore as he had on the Moroccan, his innocence untarnished by knowledge of the country. Railton was undeniably touched, as were William and Catherine, by the fact that the "war" had "broken out" in America as a consequence of the "unconquerable, unalterable essence of its nature"; it was "like a plant of God's own sowing." To deny it the sustenance that only headquarters could provide would be sinful and irresponsible. The Scriptures demanded a zeal for souls that transcended natural boundaries. In addition, Railton was increasingly frustrated in his role as Booth's secretary: as the Army adopted an ever more consistent and inflexible military structure, the duties of the second-in-command to William Booth shifted from Railton, General Secretary of the Christian Mission, to Bramwell Booth, newly-installed Chief of the Staff of The Salvation Army.[6]

Railton had a powerful ally in Catherine. The two had much in common: both were fond of theology—the practical-minded General regarded them both as bookish—both were zealously loyal to the General and his mission, which they had done so much to organize and guide, and both were committed to a variety of social reforms, which at first did not command a large part of the General's interest. First among these was the advancement of women into positions of usefulness and leadership in religious work. From the beginning the Army had attracted women in large numbers, and many were pressed into service as officers. Railton now hit upon the idea of offering to make up the American expedition entirely of women, with himself as leader. This would show what women could do, and it would ensure, through the simple fact of the marriages he confidently expected each to arrange for herself on the other shore, that the Army in America would be *American*. It is also likely that the kindly Catherine, sensing a clash between Railton and Bramwell, found a solution in an independent command for Railton away from London. Railton's arguments, Catherine's endorsement, and the plain fact of the Shirleys' success carried the General. Whether or not Booth was "forced by circumstances," as Railton wrote later, the decision was made: America for God and the Army![7]

The preparations for the send-off of Railton and the "Hallelujah Seven" were characteristically flamboyant. Collecting the lucky seven had been dramatic enough. Railton selected sturdy, stable women, with a ten-year veteran of the war, Captain Emma Westbrook, to lead them. The first telegram she had ever received—a memorable event in itself —informed her of her appointment "to America," and instructed her to send in her measurement "for a uniform." Westbrook thought she was having a hallucination: she had never heard of wearing a uniform, and had no certain notion where America even was, let alone why she should *go* there. The first of several farewells held for the departing pioneers was no more reassuring: the speaker prayed for God to "drown 'em" on the way if they were going to fail Him when they got there! As there were several other meetings in the same spirit, the ladies could at least be grateful that the arrangements for their departure were quickly concluded. Notices of the Shirleys' success and the departure of the new American expedition appeared within two weeks of each other, on January 31 and February 14, 1880.[8]

The "Farewell Celebration" at Army headquarters in Whitechapel was historic in more ways than one. Over a period of time the Booths had resolved to clothe their Army in military uniform. The details of the uniform had yet to be settled, and in fact have been changed many times since—Salvationists have appeared in a bewildering array of ranks, stars, crests, frogs, cords, and colors over the years. The principle of uniform-wearing, however, had great merit: Salvationists would thus declare to the world their Christian witness and loyalty to the great cause, and the many soldiers too poor to purchase decent clothing would suffer no invidious self-reproach. All were equal in the Great Salvation War. At the Whitechapel farewell, Railton was the first officer to appear in full uniform. He was also the first man to bear the exalted rank of Commissioner, specially created for the American expedition (as was an exquisitely formal oath of loyalty to Booth and the Army which Railton, who was nothing if not a good sport, gamely recited on the eve of his departure). To cap the testimonies and speeches, Catherine handed Railton two new Salvation Army flags: one for the Shirleys in Philadelphia, and one for the "Blood & Fire New York No. 1," which as yet existed only in hope. The party sailed on the Anchor Liner *Australia* on February 14, 1880, after a march to the dock, which—as usual—stopped traffic. Railton looked "as happy as an angel" on the deck. His heart soared at the prospect ahead. As the ship prepared to drop her pilot at Dover, Railton scribbled a last note to the General: "The fact is we are so thoroughly satisfied that Filled with God, we'll shake America that all that lies between us and that result is marvellously insignificant."[9]

The pioneer party rejoiced at the sight of the scene of their future triumphs as the *Australia* berthed at Castle Garden on March 10, 1880. But then, mused Railton in the first American *War Cry* in January, 1881, *any* country would have looked inviting after "four weeks' tossing" on the sea. The trip had been unusually eventful, even for heroes. The seven women promptly collapsed with seasickness, their agonies punctuated by storms and a cracked cylinder in the engine that nearly caused the ship to turn back. Then there were unsettling rumors that the first-class passengers regarded Railton, who was holding services all over the ship, as a lunatic (while the steerage passengers—"card-playing Germans"—didn't regard him at all.) The high point of the voyage had been the Commissioner's attempts to cheer the ladies by singing hymns through their cabin door. The pioneers were glad to see the new world at last.[10]

March 10, 1880. That subsequent events made it a day of significance no one, even a hundred years later, can deny. Railton and the "seven sisters" were determined to make their arrival in the United States significant without waiting for subsequent events. They marched down the gangplank, holding one of their Salvation Army flags—to which a small American flag had been affixed in the union corner—aloft. The Commissioner and the women were in their new uniforms, he in "dark blue suit, cutaway coat and a high peaked hat," the ladies in short blue dresses, blue coats trimmed in yellow, and "Derby hats." Each hat carried a red band upon which "The Salvation Army" had been worked in gilt letters. Their walk down the gangplank had been a bit unsteady, but the pioneers literally leapt from the bottom step into action. The Army flag was planted with dramatic postures, and the country was claimed for God and the Army. They began to sing. The first hymn—which is still in The Salvation Army *Songbook*—was characteristically to the point: "With a sorrow for sin, let repentance begin." Not surprisingly, a "curious throng" formed around the little group: the general impression that this was some kind of "travelling concert troop" was dispelled by the singing of another hymn, "You must be a lover of the Lord, or you won't go to Heaven when you die." This "drill" was cut short by the arrival of Amos Shirley, who had come from Philadelphia to meet the official party, and who now hurried forward to greet Railton. The historian notes sadly that their remarks were neither recorded nor remembered, although a reporter who was on the scene noted that, oddly enough, Railton treated Shirley "rather coldly." The pioneers were likewise greeted by Rev. and Mrs James Ervine; the latter had written to the General in 1876 asking for missionaries. These people, who like the Shirleys were overjoyed at the long-awaited arrival of Army emissaries, had come to take them to their home in Jersey City.[11]

But not before Railton had spied the reporters. With an instinct that served the Army well, Railton began to converse with several newspaper reporters who happened to be present. Just as the Ervines and the "Christian friends" who helped the Shirleys with their first meetings demonstrate that the Army has never had to go it *entirely* alone, so Railton's eagerness to discourse at length to the reporters, who to his happy surprise were all around, shows that the Army recognized from the beginning the value of publicity—especially newspaper publicity, which was free. Reporters in those days had the habit of showing up at Castle Garden to watch the steamers unload their colorful and often newsworthy immigrant cargos, and the novel arrival of The Salvation Army was an unexpected boon to the New York press. Railton was delighted: "The press took us up with characteristic energy." The Commissioner pleasantly remarked to one wondering reporter that The Salvation Army, "did not consist of wild and thoughtless fanatics and that its members had no idea of making a mockery of religion. On the contrary, it consisted of pure men and women, who were devoted to Christ and who had agreed to sacrifice their lives to making converts." He invited other reporters to look them up again when they had a meeting hall. Captain Westbrook triumphantly reeled off statistics— another shadow cast back from the future—that demonstrated the success of the Army in England. Before leaving the dock area with the welcome party, Railton made inquiries as to whether there were any printing shops nearby that would produce free posters for the new arrivals.[12]

Exhausted from these endeavors, the eight Salvationists gratefully repaired to the Ervine home in Jersey City. Railton, however, could not rest: he was anxious to return to New York City to find a hall to rent. Ervine brought him to a group of Christian businessmen and ministers who held a weekly prayer breakfast on Fulton Street. These kindly men were touched by Railton's passion for lost souls, and offered him the use of various churches. He refused. Railton was determined to carry the gospel to the unchurched masses: the Army, like The Christian Mission from which it developed, was at this stage wholly given over to evangelism, most of it on street corners and in music halls. The Commissioner intended to do the same in America. So when the newspaper accounts of the landing brought an invitation from the enterprising Harry Hill, owner of a concert saloon, to "do a turn" on Sunday—which horrified the Fulton Street churchmen—Railton jumped at it. He had seen the Booths use the stage effectively in London. The audience was certain to be just the sort of people the Army was after. Harry Hill's Variety, which stood at the corner of Houston and Crosby Streets, a block east of Broadway, thus gained a kind of immortal glory. There, amid the chipped gilt, stale beer, and gas lights, The Salvation Army held its first official meeting in the United States. The circumstances were not auspicious—Hill and most of the audience regarded the Army as a joke—and the meeting closed without visible results. Yet a beginning had been made, and in the right place. The only regrets that Railton ever had about the meeting were that he had refused the manager's offer of money and that he had asked the men in the audience not to smoke during the service: it only made them uncomfortable. It was clear to him that a standing rule against tobacco in Army meetings might repel from the doors the very sort of men the Army was after.[13]

The details of that first meeting, which was held on Sunday, March 14, 1880, are well known. The service was well attended by the Variety's usual clientele and—again—by the Army's "Christian friends," who were "drawn thither by a decent mingling of curiosity and sympathy." It was also well-reported. The New York *World* called it "A Peculiar People amid Queer Surroundings." The first hymn was "Lover of the Lord," which had saved the day at Castle Garden. After each song— "Will you go to the Eden above?" was applauded—Railton would exhort the crowd, then kneel to pray. His female assistants surrounded him in "various and curious positions." When the lieutenants delivered their testimonies, which were obviously memorized, the crowd grew restless. Railton circulated among the crowd and put his arm around several of the men, which embarrassed them. For the Variety regulars, the novelty of the Salvation Army act had passed. After a fruitless invitation to repentance, the crusaders and those who had come to hear them left together.[14]

The next morning, at the Fulton Street prayer breakfast, Railton was greeted with condescension. Predictions were confirmed: the Variety "turn" had been a humiliating fiasco. But the bread thus cast upon the waters did not sink. One of the group had been blessed by the Army's zeal. Mr Richard Owens offered the pioneers the free use of his own Hudson River Hall, at Ninth Avenue and Twenty-Ninth Street, for a month. And that very night Railton's party secured their first convert. Ash-Barrel Jimmy (or "Jemmy," as he was sometimes called) was a homeless, hopeless drunkard, who had earned his nickname when he was found by a policeman dead drunk in a barrel, his hair frozen to the bottom, and was dragged thus embarrelled to the police court. The magistrate was in a jocular mood: he ordered James Kemp to attend The Salvation Army act at the Variety. Ash-Barrel lacked the twenty-five cents admission, but he dutifully—and drunkenly—found his way to the Hudson River Hall the next night. After making several efforts to get past the policeman patrolling in front of the hall, Ash-barrel was finally gathered up in Railton's loving arms and carried over the threshold. Kemp was soundly converted: a turning point in more lives than his own. Ash-Barrel was a well-known local hard case, and word of his "getting saved" brought crowds. Enough money was collected by the Army pioneers to rent a hall of their own, the Grand Union on Seventh Avenue, which became the "Blood & Fire New York No. 1" corps for which Catherine Booth's flag had been destined.[15]

The chronology of these first few days is difficult to trace. Even in a settled command, with regular procedures, Railton took a cavalier view of record-keeping. Now a pioneer with ten things to do at once, flying around the city like some wild evangelical bird, he kept no records at all. Nor did his lieutenants, stalwart women with great hearts but little ability. None of them were even skillful readers, and they had no interest in details. Fortunately, some knowledge of events can be gleaned from reminiscences, contemporary newspapers, and a handful of fragmentary records. The meeting at Hill's gave the Army publicity among a small but earnest group of clergymen and lay Christians who were inspired to carry the gospel to the urban poor. Owens' loan of the Hudson River Hall reflected this concern. Other missions opened their doors to The Salvation Army. On March 15 Railton held one of several meetings in a converted brothel at 44 Baxter Street, in a desperate slum. The floor was spattered with tobacco spittle, and the place was crammed with "the refuse of the Fourth Ward dance cellars," stinking, smoke-filled, and noisy—"a yellow fever pest house could not have been less attractive." The Army "did not seem to mind" and held a full service. Other halls may have been used as well. There is even confusion as to where Ash-Barrel Jimmy was actually rescued. It is certain, however, that large crowds attended Army meetings. It is also certain that Railton traveled beyond New York City, renting halls and theaters to "open fire" on the lost cities of New Jersey. The Great Salvation War was launched in Newark in the Odeon Theater on March 21; Camden and Atlantic City were opened later in that same month.[16]

This was success beyond hope, but it presented Railton with a problem: the halls could not hold the crowds, and police were forced to bar the doors for fear of suffocation or fire. Railton quite sensibly decided to take the good news to the street corners. The corner outside the Hudson River Hall would be perfect: there would be no limitations on space there, and plenty of potential converts right at hand. Mayor Edward Cooper thought otherwise: city law allowed only ordained clergymen to hold religious services on the public streets, and then only by special permit. Railton exploded. Cast down in an instant from ecstatic heights, never a lamb except in love, the Commissioner delivered an ultimatum in the form of a proclamation on the City Hall steps. It contained a dire threat: if the authorities would not relent on this position—Railton considered it no more than "etiquette"—he would remove his "headquarters" to another, friendlier city. Unmoved, Cooper refused again. Railton's statement that the "entire Salvation Army in America" would pray Cooper around likewise failed to produce anything but a cartoon in the New York *Graphic,* which portrayed the Mayor sitting in a circle of praying lassies, with the caption, "Past Praying For!" Even though another permanent convert—Louis Pertain, a man who remained faithful for forty-two years—was saved the night before Railton's departure, the matter was decided: if the Army "could not develop in perfect liberty that line of action which more than any other has made and will make this Army a delivery force for the multitudes," the Army would go to Philadelphia. And after scattering the seeds of salvation on the fruitful soil of New Jersey, to Philadelphia the Army went.[17]

The Commissioner arrived in his new headquarters city on March 24, 1880. The Shirleys had not been idle since their first gallant little open-air meeting nearly six months before. When Railton presented Amos and Eliza with the Salvation Army flag he had brought to them from Catherine Booth, there were two hundred cheering soldiers present, each with a Salvation Army hat band. Railton was stunned: it seemed to him the "biggest meeting of my life." Fifteen hundred people crowded into the hall hired for the festivities. Philadelphia was clearly a center of lively interest in the Army; in fact, it was the center of Army activity in the United States for another year. In May, when Railton reported to the General that there were eight corps in America, six of them were in Philadelphia: the two Shirley corps were mined to provide leadership for four more. Convinced by these events that this hospitable city was the ideal place for national headquarters, Railton opened one —the first ever in America—at 45 South Third Street. A large sign hung across the front announced to the world that this was "The Headquarters for The Salvation Army in America." The actual office was in the basement, dank and dirty, and it was here that Railton lived and worked.[18]

The summer of 1880 was an odyssey in the Homeric style for the Army pioneers. Railton was indefatigable, and he loved the United States. The heat of the summer and the vast size of the country (which combined to stupefy most English officers), the variety of races, languages, climates, and scenes all stimulated his energies to new levels. His vision was global—Scandinavians, Germans, blacks, all would be drawn in by the Army net: "If I can get the Americans, Germans, and Africans all fairly started, I hope by stirring such up to hearty rivalry to keep them all at full gallop."[19]

A newspaper, *The Salvation News*, was started on July 3, 1880. By chance, a copy of the entire second number (July 10) and a fragment of the third survive. The first edition was sold out in a few hours, but Railton admitted he could not offer "any regular terms" for the *News:* it was "merely a pioneer of our American *War Cry,*" soon to appear. The *News* is nonetheless an historical gem. It contains a hymn by Amos Shirley; news of the valiant fight being waged by "brave Captain Westbrook," who had been left to command New York No. 1 on Seventh Avenue, where she preached the gospel and collared roughnecks; advertisements of Army books written by Catherine Booth; and little snatches regarding several Fourth of July picnics, marches, and the testimonies of various converts.[20]

Railton embarked on long train trips to find likely places upon which to "open fire." He traveled light and left almost no record; he probably visited many cities of which we know nothing. Meanwhile, the hectic pace and the heat were proving too much for the pioneer women: three of them collapsed and returned to England. Other English officers were sent to replace them, and American officers—the first was Lieutenant Jennie Dickinson of Philadelphia in March—arose to join the ranks. The first "officers' councils" were held by Railton in Philadelphia and New York in May, to encourage the staff and plan strategy. Although the staff in New York was entirely prostrated by the heat, Railton judged the councils a huge success. Penniless, often in the face of active physical hostility, jeered at and mimicked, the Army advanced through that exciting summer. By the fall there were twelve corps in the United States, and fifteen hundred souls had been saved. Franklin, Pennsylvania, was opened as the "7th Pennsylvania," and in October two converts traveled on their own to "open fire" on Baltimore. It was the first anniversary of the Shirleys' street-corner service in Philadelphia.[21]

Clearly, the Commissioner had moved wisely in joining the Shirley forces and consolidating the success in Philadelphia. Railton, however, was not a practical man: for reasons that remain somewhat obscure, he decided in November to transfer headquarters to St. Louis! He had traveled widely in the summer, covering 4200 miles speaking eighty times, "living a real soldier life" scouting the terrain for future attacks. St. Louis was the gateway to the West, and Railton was not alone in believing that this was where the future greatness of the country lay. The city would be the perfect headquarters for a western campaign. The fact that The Salvation Army was unknown in the city, that the savage midwestern winter was rapidly descending, and that he had advanced 959 railroad miles from the rest of his troops, did not trouble Railton —in fact, he does not seem to have been absolutely certain *where* his troops were. Baltimore had opened spontaneously the month before, and the war seemed to be spreading out of control. Railton loved it. In January, 1881, he wrote from St. Louis that he would "welcome the War news from any quarter and shall be thankful to strangers in any State, who are actually carrying on aggressive efforts, quite as much as to any of our own people, who may visit us with information." In St. Louis, as in so many other places where Railton opened fire, he found encouragement and support, and gladly acknowledged these "good folk" and "sympathizers."22

But he still did most of the work by himself: he remembered St. Louis as "the place where I learnt most to fight alone." He was penniless, and would have suffered actual want if a Mr and Mrs George Parker had not taken him in for the winter simply because he was a Christian worker. After his first meeting he could not rent a hall for weeks: the crowd had spit tobacco on the floor, and the owner would not have Railton back, despite his offer—now clearly repentant of his misjudgment at the Variety meeting—to provide spittoons. There were rumors of broken benches. One of the major obstacles that early-day officers had to overcome was the fact that few would rent or loan them meeting halls: the crowds they collected for their indoor meetings tended to be drunks and rough customers who amused themselves by smashing the rented furniture when they lost interest in the proceedings. Railton spent all of November and December searching for a hall to rent. He succeeded, of course, but not before New Year's day, 1881. On January 1, he opened his crusade at Sturgeon Market Hall, with a program advertised like a train excursion: "the Old Reliable Repentance, Faith and Holiness Line." Crowds were small—in Railton's language, "not large"—and there was no money.23

There was never enough money. Even when he didn't eat, and if he slept on old newspapers at headquarters, there was not enough to pay for posters, rent halls, and launch the American version of *The War Cry*. This last project he had cherished since July; but when an edition finally appeared on January 15, 1881, it was only on an "irregular" basis, like *The Salvation News* it replaced. And if hostility and poverty were not enough, the city authorities refused to allow the Army to preach on the streets of St. Louis. Railton was undaunted through it all: "difficulties are created by the devil and his helpers solely." Reasoning that the mayor had "no power over the iced Mississippi, especially on the Illinois side," Railton went out on a Sunday to speak "plainly" to the skaters. He reported that it was "quite a novelty to have a congregation come skating around." There have been few men more zealous for Christ, more willing to suffer loneliness and humiliation for Him, than George Scott Railton, whose short but seminal sojourn in American history was now at an end. On January 1, 1881, he was ordered to return to London. His abilities as an organizer of advance-guard attacks were needed there: the home front was advancing rapidly, and outposts had been thrown open in France and Australia.[24]

Railton had protested the order when it first came. He loved the United States, despite the weather, which he now privately admitted to be subject to discouragingly un-English extremes. He had applied to become a naturalized citizen at Independence Hall almost as soon as he arrived in Philadelphia. He was concerned for the future of the American Army, filled with visions of the destined greatness of the country and of the Army if he could only stay to catch the rising tide. His missionary project had only just begun: surely the General would relent. Surely not: the second cable said simply, "Come along."[25]

Professor Herbert Wisbey suggests that an ability to remain deaf to the pleas of those dearest to him was one of Booth's strengths. Perhaps, but it is certain that the loss of Railton to the pioneer work eventually had serious consequences. An immediate effect was the disappearance of the Army from St. Louis; Railton's work left not a trace. When the Army reopened in St. Louis in 1887, the officers thought they were making a "first appearance." Another scholar states that the "recall of Railton, a man of great ability, threw the organization into complete confusion for five years." It is also certain that William Booth's ability to remain deaf to the pleas of those nearest to him would be at least partially responsible for two major crises in the affairs of The Salvation Army in America.[26]

At first, however, the dramatic speed with which the Army spread throughout the country—seemingly springing up in a half-dozen places at once—obscured the departure of Railton from the public eye. Frederick Booth-Tucker, himself a national commander in years to come, correctly assessed Railton's singular year: the "foundations" had been laid; the work was carried on after Railton left with "signal success." The departing Commissioner left Captain Amos Shirley in charge, pending the arrival of a new leader from London. It was to be the only recognition that the pioneer Captain ever received. When Major Thomas E. Moore arrived to take command in June, he made Shirley his aide-de-camp as a kindness, but Shirley quarreled with Moore, for reasons now unknown, and resigned after a month. His wife, however, remained an active officer. Amos drowned in the sea at Asbury Park, New Jersey, on August 12, 1884—"wafted home on a wave of the Sea," was the cheerful way *The War Cry* reported it. The courageous Eliza, who left the United States in 1881 for a rest from her pioneering labors, married Captain Philip Symmonds while in England. They returned to America in 1885. Widowed early, she remained an active and successful officer the rest of her long and happy life, and left behind her children, grandchildren, and great-grandchildren who are to this day loyal soldiers in the crusade that she once launched on a dirty Philadelphia street corner.[27]

With or without these pioneers, the Great Salvation War went forward on several fronts. When Railton's party arrived in 1880, *Harper's Weekly* dryly observed that they had a "gigantic and ambitious scheme of travelling all through this country, and establishing branches of their organization in every city and town." It did not remain a "scheme" for long: even critics of the Army and its ways were amazed at its "earnest zeal." 1881 was admittedly a year of consolidation. In 1882, however, a bridgehead was thrown into Ohio, and the Blood-and-Fire flag flew over fallen Steubenville. The crusade spread into Brooklyn, the "City of Churches," where four corps opened in rapid-fire order. Encouraged by this hospitality, Major Moore transferred national headquarters to Brooklyn in July, in the newly rented, soon-to-be famous Lyceum. In 1883 the Army extended its operations to Connecticut and California (where the Army had blossomed forth spontaneously) and then to Kentucky, Indiana, Michigan, Massachusetts, and West Virginia. The rockbound coast of Maine came under fire in 1884; in December of that year Akron opened as "Ohio No. 10." By January, 1885, Columbus became the "15th Ohio."[28]

The year 1885 was especially auspicious. In February Captain William Evans, his wife, and a lieutenant began operations on a Chicago street corner with a drum and a concertina. Despite "storms of violence," the city took to the Army, and Chicago became the greatest center of Salvationist activity in the country. Washington, D.C., was opened; and Janesville, Wisconsin, was attacked singlehandedly by sixteen-year old Lieutenant Edward Parker. Five other states were "pioneered" in 1885. (Early officers were casual grammarians; the Army used several nouns as verbs: "pioneer" is one, "farewell" is another.) Corps were proliferating: the Army abandoned its practice of numbering them by state (as in "Ohio No. 10") and began numbering them by city ("Brooklyn No. 2," "Chicago No. 13," etc.).[29]

By the end of the decade The Salvation Army was triumphantly operating its evangelical crusade—and the beginnings of a social welfare program—in forty-three states. Increases were being reported so rapidly that national headquarters could no longer maintain effective direct control of the field. In 1884 eight "divisions" were created and put into the charge of divisional officers, in order to more effectively supervise the burgeoning spiritual empire. These officers were themselves eventually swamped by a rising tide of converts, and in 1890 it was decided that henceforth the field officer—the person actually operating the individual corps—would have the privilege (hitherto reserved to the divisional officer), of swearing in the new recruits as soldiers.[30]

The Salvation Army arose in the far west in a manner that confirmed the General's confidence in extending the war to America. All the elements of the dramatic were present in the California story: colorful personalities, Herculean energies, obstacles that would have chilled the heart of a dragon, sweeping conversions, and—espe cially cherished by Army leaders—spontaneity. The Army burst forth on the Golden Shore almost of its own volition, like a wild plant growing up from a forgotten seed carried far away on the wind. Railton would have loved it.

San Francisco is a city that lives in a fog of nostalgia. It seems always to have basked in a golden sunset, which casts beneficent rays upon a charming mixture of Victorian row houses, reeling seagulls, and cable cars. The truth, alas, is less golden. In the 1880s, San Francisco was as nasty a place as thugs, derelicts, and prostitutes could produce on short notice. Before the Gold Rush of 1849, the site had been a Spanish townlet. Gold had created the city, and gold kept it alive. The rich lived on Nob Hill in an opulence that still seems dazzling. Although many prospered in various levels of honest endeavor, others were shipwrecked on the Golden Shore, driven to desperation, begging, prostitution, even violence, to extend their lives a day at a time, like stray dogs or cockroaches. Old San Francisco, for all its gilding and sterling, was cruel and sordid. Yet zealous Christians believe that where need is great, God's grace is greater. The spirit of compassion was not entirely extinguished:

a few persons endeavored to bring the gospel of love to the streets of San Francisco.

In the summer of 1882 a group of Bay Area "Holiness men," already convinced that their theology of love demanded action on behalf of the lost and dying on every hand, were galvanized by the blessings of a camp meeting in Oakland and the fortuitous appearance of one copy of the London *War Cry*. Thus encouraged, the Pacific Coast Holiness Association promptly transformed themselves by unanimous vote into the "Salvation Army." George Newton was chosen as "Commander," and meetings were held—the first on the first Friday in October, 1882. The little group held nightly street meetings in San Francisco, on Kearney Street on the Barbary Coast, and published four issues of a *War Cry* of their own, edited by J.B. Knight. The first edition in November predicted ten thousand recruits in thirty days and asked for musicians to form a brass band, which was already regarded as a characteristic feature of the street warfare they had read about elsewhere. So far the group could only muster a drum and a triangle, but nothing daunted, they marched out in a long single file, carrying torches and a "transparency"—a sign painted on gauze stretched over a frame, illuminated from within by a kerosene flame—and singing gospel songs. This activity attracted the attention of a young Christian, John Milsaps, who began attending the indoor meetings held on Eddy Street in the Children's Hall (loaned by a group of Adventists on condition that the "Army" pay the gas bill). Here Milsaps learned that this "Army" was an imitation of one in England, conducted by a man named Booth and that the San Francisco branch "sprang at a moment of enthusiasm" from the now defunct Holiness Association. Milsaps felt a strong conviction to join this little group; struggle as he might, he was hooked: on January 15, 1883, he was enrolled as a soldier.[31]

Milsaps was like many early Salvationists. Until he joined the Army —even this rump version—he had found no outlet for the wellspring of energy and devotion hidden within him. Hitherto a drifter and a sport, he found in the Army a long-sought channel for a life of service and purpose. Already a nominal Christian, he found no difficulty in becoming a wholehearted one. Milsaps set to work at once, cleaning the hall, testifying in the street-corner circle, and serving as secretary to Commander Newton, for which service he was soon promoted to "sergeant." He showed warm enthusiasm for his new crusade. Outposts were opened in Oakland across the Bay, and San Jose to the south. The leaders were former church people. The editor, Knight, was a Baptist, and the "Captain" in San Jose was the son of William Taylor, the Methodist missionary bishop to Africa. Few actual reprobates were saved; San Francisco remained the new Sodom. Enthusiasm began to flag, in the face not only of dwindling returns, but of poverty, ridicule, and threats.[32]

By July, 1883, the original forty members had been reduced to thirteen; Sergeant Milsaps remained among the faithful. Commander Newton felt called to other, more promising fields. He wrote to General Booth not once but several times over a period of time offering him the command of all Salvation Army forces on the Pacific Coast. To Newton this seemed only fitting; to Booth, it was the call of Heaven—again. This time he did not hesitate: he accepted Newton's offer as soon as a suitable officer could be selected and sent. The problem was to find a man who was able, aggressive, and replaceable. The General finally settled on a young Captain, Alfred Wells, whom he astounded with a promotion to Major and orders to open the war in California.[33]

Wells arrived in San Francisco on July 21, 1883, after a meandering trip across the country from New York during which he conferred official flags on two new outposts in Louisville, Kentucky, and New Albany, Indiana, and was offered a flourishing rescue mission in Chicago if he would take it over for The Salvation Army. The new commander was soon joined in California by reinforcements from England: volunteering for America was becoming less terrifying among Booth's officers. In October, Captain Harry Stillwell arrived; a year later, both Wells' and Stillwell's fiancees followed. Thus strengthened, and with the still shrinking remnant of the Holiness group in hand, the Army began a vigorous campaign. The first official corps was opened in Oakland. Although California No. 1 did not always have regular officers in the early months, Oakland Citadel Corps quickly became—and remains to this day—a vibrant center of Army activity on the west coast. The corps moved amidst great jubilation, hallelujahs, and horn-honks into its own newly-built wooden "Salvation Castle" on Eighth and Webster in December, 1885. Because it was the most handsome Salvation Army facility west of Chicago, California Divisional Headquarters promptly moved in with the Oakland soldiers.[34]

The more feeble San Francisco operation seems to have languished for a while, but not before Sergeant Milsaps won his most notable convert, an Armenian shoemaker named Joseph Garabed (or Garabedian), known to his friends and to Salvation Army history as Joe the Turk. A volatile eccentric, Joe served for two years as "doorkeeper" —a combination of head usher and bouncer—for San Francisco No. 1 corps until he became an officer himself. Wells promoted Milsaps to Captain and sent him to pioneer Stockton, while Stillwell took over the corps in San Jose, where he "had a hard rub but never flinched." In November 1883 a struggling western version of the official *War Cry* appeared for the first time. It became a monthly in March 1884, but wasn't a weekly like the eastern edition until November 1889. Milsaps, whose highly colorful accounts of the war had become expected features of the new paper, was made editor in December 1886.[35]

The Army in New York continued, with a fine disregard for geography, to list two "divisions": America and California. National headquarters rejoiced over reports of "California salvation gold dust," and in 1885 noted that the work on the Pacific coast "never looked so well as at present." Unconnected to the rest of the American Army, reporting directly to General Booth in London, The Salvation Army in California struggled on. Progress was slow, against "terrible difficulties." California was so wicked that the air seemed "filled with devils." In July, 1884, on the first anniversary of The Salvation Army out west, there were only four corps; in 1886 there were eight, four of these barely flickering.[36]

A welcome development came when the Pacific Coast Division was taken under the mantle of national headquarters. Major Wells left for England in May, 1886, leaving Captain Stillwell—the root of a still flourishing Army family tree—in charge. In August, Mrs. Stillwell traveled north to open the work in Portland, Oregon. Major J.H. Britton arrived in October from New York to take command, so that Stillwell was able to join his wife in Oregon in December, when a new division was organized there. The war gained more ground once the Army was unified. On May 8, 1887, two officers—one of them Happy Joe, the Turk—opened fire on Los Angeles, in a tent in a lot on the corner of Fort and Temple Streets. In June, Salt Lake City was taken by assault; the first Salvation Army officer to die in the west, Cadet J.M. Burns of Oakland, died in Salt Lake in November of typhoid fever. By July Seattle had a corps, in August Boise, Idaho, in July, 1888, Helena, Montana, and in September, 1889, Reno fell to a Blood-and-Fire squadron. By 1890 there were forty-two corps in the West, and "several hundred soldiers."[37]

Meanwhile, there had been triumph and tragedy back east: a disastrous secession of officers and soldiers from which the Army recovered only slowly and through a sequence of events that even the cynical must call miraculous. The principal agent in the crisis, Major Thomas E. Moore, was an unlikely villain. Moore, sent to replace Railton in June, 1880, was a devoted and enthusiastic officer. A cockney, formerly a divisional officer in charge of the corps in London, Moore was flattered by his selection to "command American forces." He was determined to carry the Salvation War to the farthest corners of this benighted land. He was an indefatigable traveler, opening new corps, encouraging the embattled hosts, and sending cheerful messages to places like California that were too distant to visit at once. A man whose motto seems to have been summed up in one of his several original songs, "Victory or Death," Moore was popular and respected by his officers. He was colorful, obviously sincere, and a successful evangelist, under whose ministry many were converted. Railton, always the gadfly, tried to be fair even during Moore's later official disgrace at international headquarters: Moore had "certainly pushed the war forward with all diligence."[38]

Unfortunately, Major Moore had two defects—one minor, the other catastrophic—in his equipment for the post of national commander. The minor defect was that Moore had little ability, and no interest, in the practical side of administration. First and last an evangelist, he cared little for fund raising and bookkeeping, which he seems to have mostly ignored. The major defect was that Moore never understood the mind of General Booth, who regarded The Salvation Army as a living entity encircling the globe, and his own authority over it as sacred and inviolable. These potential rubs became real at a logical point: the material wealth of the Army and the question of who owned it.

Under American law in the 1880s, someone—a "person"—had to hold legal title to everything of value. The courts had speeded the process of industrial consolidation by even defining corporations as "persons" entitled to "own" property. The difficulty was, however, as far as General Booth (and British law) was concerned, that all property given or deeded to The Salvation Army was owned by General Booth. As fate would have it, American state laws differed widely on the matter of the ownership of property by foreign citizens; it was difficult and complicated to the point of impossibility for one foreign citizen to own property throughout the United States. Thus Major Moore, who became a naturalized citizen for this very purpose, held legal title to all properties given to or purchased by The Salvation Army in the United States, and all funds collected by it. He did this solely as the agent of General Booth, as far as the Army was concerned; but in the eyes of the law, the Army's wealth and property, which showed early signs of becoming considerable, belonged outright to Major Thomas E. Moore. And so did the liabilities that might accrue against those properties: only corporations offer limited liability to their investors and agents; no such thing as limited liability existed for persons like Moore.

It is clear now, and ought to have been clear to everybody at the time, that the Army had to be incorporated in the United States, most logically under the state laws of New York, site of national headquarters. It was clear to Moore, who began as early as 1882 to try to convince the General, to whom it was unclear. In July, 1883, the Major filed a preliminary petition for incorporation under the statutes of New York. This was partly to protect headquarters against the novel project of the corps in New Brunswick, New Jersey, to incorporate itself under the generous corporation laws of that hospitable state. The corps leaders wished to avoid charges, which had become public, that money being raised by the "5th New Jersey" to build a new hall was going to Moore personally, or to Booth in London. These charges and the resultant incorporation of the corps alarmed Moore, and with good reason: as an incorporated body, the 5th New Jersey could demand the funds already collected and deposited in the regulation way in the headquarters corps account. Should the demand of the "rebel" leaders be refused, as it surely would be, Moore was liable to arrest for civil suit any time he happened into New Jersey—which, considering the furious pace of the Great Salvation War along the Jersey Shore, was inevitable. The Major, Captain Westbrook, and another veteran officer sailed for England to urge the case for incorporation on the General. Unfortunately, it remained unclear to Booth, and the three returned in defeat. Then the inevitable happened: Major Moore was arrested in December, 1883, while holding a preaching service in the corps at Rahway, New Jersey.

Moore was driven to drastic action by the events of 1884. The loyalty to international headquarters of many in the ranks was becoming clouded. American Salvationists were disappointed when neither General Booth nor Bramwell came to the gala fourth anniversary festivities in Brooklyn. Eliza Shirley Symmonds recalled that the failure of the Booths to expose themselves to an American Army that knew nothing of them personally, and of whom they seemed to have known almost as little, was a major cause for the widespread support given to Moore in the October crisis. This conclusion seems to be warranted by contemporary facts. Two staff-captains sent by the General in July to give him a first-hand report on the situation in Brooklyn managed to throw oil on the embers. They discovered to their chagrin that The Salvation Army in America did not yet command sufficient popular support to enable it to apply for special legislation with any hope of success; and under existing laws of incorporation in New York, any act obtained would place full control of all assets in the hands of the local trustees. The auditors therefore suggested that Moore retain legal title to all Army property, but that these properties be mortgaged to William Booth for more than their market value (thus giving Booth first and full claim—in effect, ownership—to any property that was the object of a suit). This subterfuge was unlikely to deceive anyone for long, and once discovered would bring humiliating publicity down on the heads of the American Army leaders. At the same time, the visiting officers gratuitously reported that Moore was not adept at business matters generally, and even putting aside the incorporation heresy his accounts were "in confusion." Several of the eight new divisional officers created that very summer joined their complaints about this side of Moore's leadership to the report of the two emissaries.[39]

In July, 1884, *The War Cry* carried a "notarized statement" from the General, reaffirming that the legal foundation of the Army—the Deed Poll of 1878—vested "control and direction" of the organization solely in the person of William Booth, that all properties of the Army were to be "conveyed to, and held by, the General," that Moore was his appointed commissioner to direct all Salvation Army activities in the United States, "including the State of New Jersey," and that Moore would be "acting unfaithfully to his high trust" if he handed over one cent to "certain persons in the city of New Brunswick." Moore was neatly caught: "faithfulness" to the General meant jail in New Jersey. But Moore was not left dangling between extremes for long. Convinced by the report of his auditors that Moore was a bungler, and certain after the Rahway arrest (to which another, in Newburgh New York, had been added) that the Major was going to incorporate the Army despite his orders, Booth decided to transfer Moore to South Africa.[40]

Moore still did not wish an open rupture with the General. He was convinced that incorporation was essential for the salvation of the Army, and that given time—and a *fait accompli*—the General would come to accept this fact. A rupture, however, was hard to avoid. Sensing rebellion, Booth ordered the commander of the newly-created Canadian territory, Major Thomas B. Coombs, to hasten to Brooklyn to relieve Moore of his command. Refused admittance at headquarters, Coombs telegraphed the American field that Moore was deposed and he, Coombs, in charge. Moore wired soon after with orders to disregard communications from Coombs. Interest among officers was understandably aroused by these events. When Moore called a conference at headquarters in October to explain his position, as many as were able to disentangle themselves from their work flocked to attend the meeting —from which Moore had taken the precaution of excluding Coombs and the discontented divisional officers who had joined their complaints to those of the staff–captains in July. Moore declared himself willing to accept any assignment, even South Africa (which he regarded as an undeserved demotion) once the General accepted the necessity of incorporation. Even if the officers present voted to approve incorporation, and Moore proceeded with it, he assured his listeners that General Booth would still be in absolute spiritual command of the American Army. The vote was 121 to four for incorporation, and The Salvation Army was incorporated on October 24, 1884. In a rare burst of business acumen, Moore also registered all Salvation Army insignia, including the crest, and copyrighted *The War Cry*. [41]

The resulting confusion, which lasted for five years, caused serious difficulties for Salvationists and sympathizers alike. The General, outraged at Moore's treason, dispatched Major Frank Smith to take command of the Army in the United States. Smith was a man of ability, like Moore an experienced divisional officer in London, loyal to the General, and an effective public speaker. He was keenly interested in social problems and a politically-minded man, which was rare for an officer. His appointment was nevertheless a mistake: Smith was fiercely zealous, and lacked tact and patience. Setting up a rival "loyal" headquarters near Battery Park, issuing a "loyal" *War Cry*, the new Commissioner peremptorily dismissed as rebels the large majority of officers who still innocently believed Moore to be in charge, or who chose to follow him because of principle. Officers like Richard E. Holz, a German-American convert who was to become one of America's distinguished officers and founder of a long line of such, was one of many who sought Smith out for advice and information only to be rebuffed as a dupe and a traitor. Ignoring Moore's very real contribution to the war effort, Smith stated that his rival had incorporated the Army only to cover his "mismanagement and insubordination." Five of the eight divisional officers and seventeen corps, several of them desperately poor in soldiers and funds, declared their loyalty to Booth and the international Army in response to Smith's demand for "full surrender"; the rest remained with Moore or faded away as public sympathy—at first surprised, then amused, and finally bored at the prospect of two Salvation Armies struggling over the same ground—dwindled and cooled.[42]

Major Smith was not, however, merely a booby. He regarded it as his duty to represent the General's viewpoint exactly, and he did so consistently. Booth believed that The Salvation Army was a living whole, one movement, above local laws and international boundaries. He believed that he had been called by God to organize this crusade, which God was surely blessing; Booth could not in conscience lay aside this sacred trust by sharing authority or allowing subordinate parts of the "world-wide Army," as he liked to call it, secure autonomy on any point, however minor. The General was absolutely sincere. Everything William Booth did, he did for the Great Salvation War. He gave his every moment to it, he sacrificed his children to it, and—old, blind, dying—he gave his last, and most noble, public statement to it. In a series of open letters in the American *War Cry*, Booth pleaded with wavering soldiers to rally to him—everything must be for "the ONE Salvation Army," every book and chair (and heart and mind) must be "nailed to the one Salvation Army flag." Smith himself, who has been slighted in official Army histories, made a considerable contribution towards regaining some of the immense ground lost in the secession. A man of social compassion —he later pioneered the Army's social welfare program in England— Smith planned various campaigns to win the poor and neglected, and began several abortive schemes to reach urban blacks. He clearly misjudged the character of the would-be prodigals whom he rebuffed without a hearing, yet he wore himself out in a ceaseless campaign to advance the cause of the loyal Army. In this endeavor, despite all, he largely succeeded.[43]

The "Salvation Army of America," which "General" Moore called his forces, started with many advantages. Many of his officers were noble souls, zealous for Christ. "Moore's Army" had its annals of heartbreak and victory, as the editions of his *War Cry* and the scattered surviving reports and private papers of his officers can attest. But slowly, inexorably, the Salvation Army of America withered and died. There were several reasons for this failure. Despite initial hard work and sacrifice, most of Moore's officers did not attract sufficient funds or converts to survive. The loyalists were convinced that God had raised up The Salvation Army for His own purposes, which were not yet fulfilled. Though both groups propagated similar doctrines, used the same techniques, sang the same songs, and appeared almost identical, Booth's Army marching under a new crest cleverly crowned with a gallant eagle (which really represented the wings on which the redeemed shall mount up, but which Americans found gratifyingly patriotic anyway) grew and prospered while Moore's Army languished.[44]

The excitement caused by the secession seems to have been localized, and in many places, brief. Even in 1884, at the height of the controversy, the young convert Adam Gifford in McKeesport, Pennsylvania, never heard of Moore or Coombs. The Army in the West, an area of vast potential, was unaffected by the secession. The Pacific Coast Division was simply informed by wire that Commissioner Frank Smith was their new commander. Chicago was opened in February, 1885, by Captain William Evans, who had come with Smith from England along with several dozen other "reinforcements." Evans was an able and attractive officer, and the Army in Chicago grew rapidly, amidst scenes of great excitement. Every convert was a loyalist.[45]

A major factor in the Booth triumph was Booth himself. Effective in print—his *War Cry* letters were widely read—the General was overpowering in person. His first trip outside the British Isles came in the fall of 1886 when he arrived in America, via Canada, to survey this distant front and to encourage the loyalists. The Army was not only encouraged: it was delirious. The General's visit became a triumphal course, amidst explosions of tambourine rattlings, the East Liverpool brass band, and "Hurrah[s] for Jesus." The pandemonium in Chicago in the newly captured Rink was broken only by Commissioner Smith repeatedly blowing on a police whistle. Everywhere the General went he spoke lovingly of Christ, the sinner's Friend, and of his own vision of the redemption of the world through the self-sacrifice and loyalty of The Salvation Army. From Danbury, Connecticut, in November (where he was in town at the same time as his fading rival, General Moore), to that Elysium of piety, Ocean Grove, New Jersey, in January 1887, William Booth was cheered, adored, quoted—and believed. The decline of Moore's troops became precipitate.[46]

Moore's own lack of administrative skill played a part in his army's decline. His self-elevation to stellar rank had not made him a financial wizard. Money dried up, the rent on his headquarters was not paid, and in December, 1888, the Board of Trustees—Moore shortsightedly made his army more democratic than Booth's—asked him to resign. When he indignantly refused, they deposed him in January 1889. The command was offered to another, who refused, then to Colonel Holz, who accepted reluctantly, only as a means to his long-cherished goal of reconciliation with the world-wide Army; for this reason Holz did not accept the rank of General with his new command, but remained a Colonel. He promptly opened informal negotiations with the genial Evans, fresh from his Chicago triumphs and now installed as Chief of the Staff to the new national commander, the sparkling Ballington Booth. Major Smith, worn to the thread by his labors, had returned to England in 1887 to be replaced by the General's second son. Ballington was conciliatory towards the Moore rebels from the beginning; he made reconciliation not only possible but inviting. He invited Holz to share public platforms with him and acted as though Holz were already restored. Many of Holz' officers, rebuffed by Smith, hesitantly came forward now, asking Holz to inquire as to whether they might be taken back as well. All was speedily arranged. On October 17, 1889, in Saratoga, New York, Holz and thirty other officers, including that doughty pioneer Captain Emma Westbrook, were restored to The Salvation Army in a tearful and "powerful" public meeting. Holz (taken back as a Major) was promptly appointed divisional officer for the New York State Division. Other officers followed Holz' lead, and returned to the Booth ranks. The Army had weathered its first real crisis.[47]

CHAPTER II

1880-1900

"Come, join our Army, to battle we go."

—WILLIAM PEARSON, 1879

The Great Salvation War advanced steadily in the last two decades of the nineteenth century. Progress was often dramatic. The Army opened in Chicago in February 1885: within the first year 547 separate conversions were reported in *The War Cry*—and this figure represents only thirty-six weekly reports; at the same rate for fifty-two weeks, there would have been eight hundred converts. When Commissioner Frank Smith visited Chicago in January 1886, he claimed that a thousand souls had been saved in the Army's meetings since it had opened fire on the city. There were many critics of The Salvation Army in the early years, but no one could deny that it was succeeding in attracting large numbers of people to its services, and that many of these were being "rescued from sin."[1]

The reasons for this were complex; any attempt to explain the rapid growth of The Salvation Army in these years must proceed carefully. It is never possible for believers to entirely separate the direct work of God from the many effects for which there is a purely natural explanation. Army officers operated on the old adage that men should act as though everything depended on them, and pray as though it all depended on God. Salvationists certainly knew human nature, and used that knowledge in shrewd and effective ways: yet they were convinced that every advance was led only by God, that every convert was a "Trophy of Grace." The songs of the era declared these beliefs to the world: "Jesus is our Captain," "God leads the dear Army along;" Salvationists were "Soldiers of Jesus" in the "Army of the Lord."[2]

The General and his leading officers were certain that God was the prime mover in their success: it was His reward to the Army for preaching the true Gospel to all who would listen. The Army had, in fact, very definite doctrinal views, a fact which many contemporary observers discounted. Recent studies by Leicester Longden, Philip D. Needham, and Roger Green, however, demonstrate that William Booth had a thorough knowledge of orthodox Wesleyan doctrine. All three studies suggest that Booth's concept of the Army and its mission sprang directly from his theological beliefs.[3]

Salvationists were convinced that their doctrines were based solely on the Bible: Ballington Booth, national commander from 1887 to 1896, wrote that the Army preached "a plain and simple revival of the teachings of Christ and His Apostles," while his wife Maud spoke of "no new doctrines" but those of Paul, Luther, and Wesley. The Army believed that the people of the world lived under the curse of sin. Every person who was not made to recognize that fact and claim the forgiveness and salvation that God offered through Christ was cast, when he died, into eternal torment. Salvationists were driven by a sense of responsibility almost too awesome to bear: the energy and fervor with which they preached touched the hearts of pathetic and lonely people who were all too aware of the price mankind paid for sin and who, apprised at last of a cure, flocked forward, outdoors and in, to be "washed in the Blood of the Lamb."[4]

Once rescued, the new convert was immediately pressed into the war for souls, as a testifier and supporter if not as a soldier. "We are a salvation people," William Booth wrote in 1879; "this is our specialty —getting saved and keeping saved and then getting somebody else saved." The life of converts was given new meaning—the highest possible meaning: they were not only saved, but given the privilege of saving others. Here was the world's great cause, and these new "blood-washed warriors," lonely and obscure no longer, were given a part to play in it. Professor Green makes an additional suggestion: the fact that Booth was a "post-Millennialist" further explains the abandon with which the Army threw itself into its work. If Christ would come again in glory only after the Millennium—the reign of the saints on earth—then the sooner the Army had won the world for Christ, the sooner He could come again to claim His own; Booth went so far in 1890 as to refer to the Millennium as "the ultimate triumph of Salvation Army principles."[5]

And there was more: after salvation, converts were urged to dedicate their hearts to Christ without reservation, so that His love poured in and purged all selfishness and pride. The "sanctified" soldiers could then shed the love of God abroad in an ever more brightly burning desire to save souls, to share love, and to provide some kind of physical or emotional comfort to the miserable and desperate people they daily encountered. This was the doctrine of "holiness" upon which the Army was founded from the beginning. It was not without pitfalls—several pioneer officers withdrew, for instance, after seeking in vain for the gift of "sinless perfection," a quest based on the odd idea that the love of God in the heart removes one's capacity to commit sin—but officers quickly learned to steer their converts to a practical holiness, couched in terms of zeal and compassion, which was eagerly accepted. Many friends of the Army, no less than Booth and his officers, attributed the success of The Salvation Army to its direct and earnest preaching of this gospel of salvation and love: an organization that had been created and controlled from the beginning by a "conception of life as an opportunity to save souls for heaven" and by "a basic sympathy for all men that suffer" could not fail.[6]

For many years the Army's leading, and still most famous, exponent of practical holiness was Samuel Logan Brengle, a graduate of Boston Theological Seminary who became an officer in 1887. Severely injured in Boston by a drunk who tried to kill him with a paving stone, Brengle spent his long convalescence writing articles on holiness for *The War Cry*. These articles, which were later collected together in *Helps to Holiness* (part of the "Red Hot Library" of devotional classics personally selected by General Booth), established Brengle's reputation as the Army's leading exponent of the doctrine. Brengle was a kindly man, easily approached, eloquent, still remembered as a flesh-and-blood saint who faced real problems. He explained holiness in terms of Scripture and his own experiences; his preaching and his writing—which ran to many volumes—were in a straightforward, conversational style, anecdotal, and full of stories and analogies to which the average Salvationist could relate. Generations of them found blessed relief in Brengle's homey explanations:

> There are people who fail to get the blessing, because they are seeking something altogether distinct from Holiness. They want a vision of Heaven, of balls of fire, of some angel; or they want an experience that will save them from all trials and temptations, and from all possible mistakes and infirmities;

or they want a power that will make sinners fall like dead men when they speak. They overlook the verse which declares that "the end of the commandment is love out of a pure heart, and of a good conscience, and of faith unfeigned"; which teaches us that Holiness is nothing more than a pure heart, filled with perfect love, a clear conscience toward God and man, which comes from a faithful discharge of duty and simple faith without hypocrisy.[7]

A large part of the motive and the success of the pioneer Army can thus be explained in terms of doctrine: yet contemporaries spoke condescendingly of the Army's "singularly meagre 'theology.' " The explanation for this paradox lies in the fact that officers themselves spoke slightingly of "mere" theories, and boasted with Catherine Booth that they were "not very intellectual" or "learned." The General and his officers had no time for idle disputations: life was a struggle, and the Christian religion was a perpetual and bitter warfare. Railton dismissed "theory" in the first American *War Cry:* "The world has ten thousand times too much of that already. Let us force war." The Great Salvation War was no mere metaphor to the Army. Booth adapted his creed to the "exigencies of the soul-saving task," and, according to a scholarly analysis by Captain Philip Needham, it was this rather than any lack of mental powers in Army leaders that explained the directness and simplicity of official theology. Anything that stood in the way of a universal call to repentance was eliminated. The Army abandoned the practice of sacraments once Booth, strongly influenced by Catherine and Railton, came to believe that participation in sacraments is not essential to salvation. It was easy enough to be convinced that these practices were confusing to the ignorant, and in the form of Communion wine were a dangerous temptation to the salvaged drunkard. The Army insisted repeatedly that the only real religion was that which was believed heartily and lived out daily: "Christ in the heart," declared *The War Cry* in 1881, "is worth more than a world full of theories." Ballington Booth proposed substituting "heartology" for the dread word "theology." An image of itself cherished by the Army in these years was that of a refuge in a rising tide of sin, in which thousands were drowning on every side. The Army was variously an island, a lighthouse, or a lifeboat: in every case Salvationists, dry and secure, were shown bending to the work of saving the lost, tossing out ropes and nets. The Salvation Army used hymns like "Throw out the Lifeline" and "Rescue the Perishing" so often in street services that these became almost symbolic of its outdoor crusade.[8]

It is small wonder, then, that persons already disposed to be critical of the Army would regard its theological resources as thin. Pioneer officers sometimes added credence to the charges. Most early officers were recent converts who knew little of theological matters. Men and women were pressed into duty as officers with no preparation, commissioned on the spot by enthusiastic divisional officers and sent off to command a station. Although Mrs Ballington Booth took pains to refute allegations that Salvationists were "not Bible-students" by stating that "nowhere in the world are there such Bible-readers as the Army has made of its converts," the truth often fell short of her claim. Many officers displayed little knowledge of the Scriptures, memorizing or quoting Bible texts only as a means to convince sinners that all was lost without Christ.[9]

No matter how important or attractive the Army's doctrines were, however, they were not self-propagating. Theology alone cannot account for the rapid spread of the Army over the face of the land. The exuberance of the soldiers, the very joy they found in fighting, won attention for them. "Other sects have professed cheerfulness," observed one magazine, "but none have so openly embraced the spirit of jollity." The hallelujah battalions advanced to sprightly tunes that told the world there was "joy in The Salvation Army: 'Tis Blood and Fire give the Army joy, And victory all the way." The Army was a "living protest against all mere formal religion, all mere ceremonies, creeds, or professions which have no life in them." If The Salvation Army had anything, it had life: a contagious, bumptious vitality that filled the streets of America with "loud joyful songs of praise."[10]

The pioneer Salvationists had discovered with Railton that "there is no cause so hopeless as one without enthusiasm." Officers were not so much enthusiastic as they were impassioned: only a high level of excitement could have produced the prodigies of work that were required to push the constant expansion of the war front. The first thing the Louisville *Courier Journal* noted about the Salvationists who opened fire there in April 1883 was that they were "indefatigable and wonderfully zealous." Similar tributes appeared in scores of contemporary newspapers. Captain Stillwell and his "Hallelujah wife" announced from Oakland: "My wife and I are fully saved, and mean to leave this city better than we found it; if hard work and holy living can do anything much will be done." In New Brunswick the 5th New Jersey braced itself for "incessant war," holding services "every night without a break." Officers sometimes conducted fifteen meetings each week, indoors and outdoors; preaching a dozen times a week was not uncommon, although the record of young Captain Harry Ironside was more nearly typical for the officer of the early 1890s: in his first year as an officer in California, he preached four hundred sermons. The quality of some of these homilies must have been dubious: the officer's daily schedule, which called for hours on the street selling *The War Cry*, collecting money, paying encouraging visits to the soldiery, and doing a host of other undramatic things left little time for sermon preparation. The General warned his troops in 1885 that the work was not all glamour: "Be a Salvation Plod" he ordered. Still, the soldiers who had to listen to almost as many sermons as the officer delivered had to be considered; officers were transferred every few weeks or months so that their stock of sermons would always seem fresh to their listeners. Ironside, for instance, commanded three successive corps in his first year, and Brengle served at Danbury, Connecticut, for just three weeks in 1888.[11]

It is hardly surprising that a number of pioneer Salvationists worked themselves into a state of collapse. So many persons of all ranks fainted in Army meetings because of "exhaustion or starvation" that in 1892 Maud Booth wrote an article in *The War Cry* explaining to her officers how to tell "sham faints" from the real item ("the patient always changes color . . ."). The Army was inspired to open special "homes of rest" for its sagging warriors, one on a hillside in Sausalito, California, in 1890, the other in North Long Branch, New Jersey, in 1891. To many pioneers, however, the idea of taking a vacation while sinners perished was too selfish for contemplation. Officers refused to leave their posts to avail themselves of the new rest homes until they were in an advanced state of exhaustion. Headquarters was forced in June, 1891, to order every officer to take at least twelve days vacation ("furlough") during each year, in order to prevent "serious break-downs of health." The demands on an officer's time and energy remained unrelenting: Headquarters regretfully registered many resignations due to "failing health" during the twenty years after 1880.[12]

The Army's greatest task in these years, and the one into which officers channeled most of their strength, was opening new corps. In the summer of 1880 there were eight corps in the United States, six of them in Philadelphia: in the summer of 1890 there were 410 corps in thirty-five states. These figures represent human effort on a Herculean scale. The process by which the Army opened fire on a place, refreshingly straightforward in theory, was often hair-raising, and always exhausting, in practice.[13]

The attacking party wasted no time in attracting as much public attention as possible: there could be no sneak attacks on the devil and all his works; as his triumph had been public, so must his ruin be. Besides, had Christ not warned His soldiers that whosoever denied Him before men, the same would be denied before His Father? No sooner had lodgings been secured—a cheap rooming house or a pew in a friendly church—than the Blood-and-Fire flag was unfurled, literally. The Army attacked *en masse* wherever possible. The officers actually sent to open a place would be reinforced for the first few days by a group of officers and soldiers from nearby corps or divisional headquarters. The party would march, playing musical instruments if they had them, singing if they had none, banging a drum and tambourines, to some conspicuous spot such as a busy intersection or the town square. The arrival of The Salvation Army would be announced, along with warnings directed to listening sinners to repent, after which a barrage of songs and prayers would be laid down. The group would then disperse to find a hall to rent, which would then serve as a meeting place and sleeping quarters. If the place were heated by a stove, as most were, simple meals—usually coffee, fried potatoes and bread—could be prepared; otherwise the militants ate where they could: often in cheap boarding houses, sometimes on stale bakery goods or unsold left-over portions from restaurants, sold to them for a pittance. One pioneer was forced to live for weeks on eggs, wild strawberries, and limburger cheese; another had nothing more to eat than week-old crackers thrown into an empty kerosene box at the back of the hall.[14]

Even securing the hall was not always easy. It was often difficult for pioneer officers to rent furnished halls: the risk to gaslight fixtures, chairs, and other breakables was so well known to prospective landlords that officers sometimes went in disguise to rent halls. Unfurnished meeting rooms were more generally available, and cheaper, but taking such a place meant the added burden of collecting money, mostly from indifferent passersby, to buy lumber to build benches and a platform. The halls were usually on the second floor of business establishments, very often at the back, with windows looking out on a backyard or alley: the Army's frontage on the street was only the door at the foot of the stairs, although audacious officers sometimes paid extra for the privilege of painting the name of their organization in bold letters across the front of the building. Suitable meeting halls were not always available, furnished or not. Any large indoor room could be pressed into service. Soldiers were asked to watch for "buildings likely to suit" as "barracks." Philadelphia No. 1 opened in an abandoned chair factory, Newark in a theater, Peoria over a livery stable, Danbury in a skating rink. Once the fortress had been secured, and regular meetings announced, most of the attack party returned to their regular duties, leaving the appointed officers—sometimes a man or woman alone, more often a matched pair —on their own to carry on the salvation war.[15]

The energies expended in proliferating corps are not the only explanation for the rapid spread of the Army. The organization's military structure itself was novel and appealing. The Salvation Army evolved slowly in England: it was the gradual production of William Booth's powerful and autocratic personality; of his militant redemptive theology, which viewed all of life as a struggle, a "holy war"; of the fact that he received "more practical help from the regulations of the British Army than . . . from all the methods of the churches" in organizing his Mission followers into an effective fighting force. In America the transforming process by which The Christian Mission became The Salvation Army mattered not in the least. In America the Army arrived full blown, freshly sprung from the forehead of Zeus—and in America, it worked Everything about it appealed to someone.[16]

Everybody loves a parade, especially if he's in it. The appeal of special uniforms, of identifying in dramatic and visible ways with a popular crusade, is universal, transcending class lines. For those who have little else in life, the appeal is irresistible. To take up the poor and forgotten, dress them in handsome blue uniforms—often the first suit of clothes they had ever owned that gave them pride—promote them to a colorful variety of different kinds of sergeant, in a crusade in which victory is divinely assured, is not only compassionate: it reveals a remarkable knowledge of human nature. Maud Ballington Booth, writing in 1889, proudly admitted that the Army drew on what was common to human nature.

A very interesting suggestion was made by a friend at Washington, D.C., with reference to our military nomenclature and customs which will bear repeating. His theory is that it satisfies the military instinct that almost every race possesses, that inborn enjoyment of marching movements, music, uniform, processions, and all the "Pomp, pride and circumstance of war," without injury or bloodshed; in point of fact, bringing peace instead of war. Perhaps the motive of the Army could not be better expressed: To take man's natural instincts and pleasures which have been perverted, and to gratify them in a manner which will bless and not curse the race, and will glorify, not dishonor God, has been from the first the aim and method of the work.[17]

The Army adapted to militancy with characteristic thoroughness. Salvationists of all ranks were expected to be in uniform every time they were on duty, which for the soldiers meant fifteen times per week, and for the officers meant always, by official order in 1889. At first the traditional highcollar blue tunic for men and women was not regulation uniform: the faithful appeared in an exotic collection of makeshift and multi-colored apparel that was consistent only in being eye-catching. The first Salvationist that young Adam Gifford saw on the streets of Pittsburgh wore a "fireman's leather helmet, with a band for trimming, on which were the words, 'Prepare to meet thy God!' " At first the Army did not operate a special department to supply uniforms: in 1886 a new officer like Lieutenant Edward Parker simply purchased some trim in (nearly) the correct color at a dry goods store and sewed it on his civilian jacket; other pioneers had uniforms made locally.

Even when the Trade Department for uniforms was established at Army headquarters, the matter of ranks and trims was never permanently settled. The basic Army colors were adopted early: blue for purity, red for the Blood of Christ, yellow for the fire of the Holy Spirit. Uniforms were generally blue and hat trim generally red, recalling that day in 1880 when Railton appeared in the first official uniform on the eve of his departure for America. But against that somber background a rainbow of colors have played over the years, to accompany a bewildering array of ranks and titles which in their brief day were the cynosure of many Army eyes. The black straw bonnet for women appeared in 1880, the invention of Catherine Booth, and was widely worn from the earliest years. Cheap, durable, protective, and solidly unworldly, the bonnet with its red band and huge bow and ribbons became a symbol of the Great Salvation War. Men continued much longer to display a certain perverse individuality on their heads. Pith helmets, toppers, cowboy hats, derbies, sailor hats, and discarded military band helmets proudly appeared, each with its Army hatband, until 1891 when a stern rebuke from headquarters brought the troops under regulation caps, one style for officers, another for soldiers.[18]

Of such things as Army ranks, of course, the public knew and cared little. Salvationists were urged to wear their uniforms, not to display rank, but to be "outwardly known when passing among worldlings." *The War Cry* declared in 1885 that a uniform was of great value in "standing out for Jesus." Salvationists were proud of their uniforms, proud to be associated with the great crusade for which the uniform stood. Partly because of this pride, and partly because of economic necessity, many soldiers wore their uniforms even when not on Salvation Army duty— anywhere formal clothing would be expected: school commencements, neighborhood weddings and funerals, the visit of relatives. One old comrade in the 1890s slept in his uniform so that if death came in the night he would be found "in the uniform he loved so well."[19]

Every aspect of the soldier's life and work was displayed in battle array. The one book, beside the Bible, that every soldier was expected to read was the *Soldier's Manual*. It was full of the "true war spirit." "There has been plenty of preaching, talking, and praying, but none of these ever won a battle, unless backed home by a real, practical activity in the holy war." Birth was the arrival of "reinforcements," death was "promotion to Glory." Daily devotional readings were "rations," prayer was "knee drill." To interject an "Amen" into a service was to "fire a volley." The soldier's weekly contribution in money was a "cartridge," which was not paid but "fired." Short, snappy testimonies in the meetings were "small shot", the Army's weekly newspaper was *The War Cry*, a series of planned revival meetings was a "siege," the officer's home was called "quarters," and vacations became "furloughs." A new convert was a "captive" and officers were judged by their superiors not on the basis of Sunday school attendance or funds raised, but on the "number of prisoners captured." The devil was no abstraction: he was the enemy commander, as real as sin and death. A jubilant report from Oakland in 1884 declared, "We are learning how to load and fire hot shot and are bringing down some of Satan's best soldiers." Jubilance was indeed the tonic chord. However serious the business at hand, the Great Salvation War was never joyless. Victory was assured, with palms and crowns laid up on high for those who did not falter. So with "charges upon enemy ground," volleys, hot shot, and small shot, the happy Army advanced, "marching on with the flag unfurled," and a brass band playing.[20]

Especially with a brass band—or with such bits and pieces of a band as the pioneers could gather together. Never did an organization become more closely identified by the public with one part of its activity than did The Salvation Army with its street-meeting bands. And with good reason: no other part of the Body of Christ in history has demonstrated with more dramatic certainty the effectiveness of music in winning converts and holding them.

The Army had learned the value of bands in England in 1878, when four sympathetic military bandsmen named Fry joined a beleagured street corner service in Salisbury. Even in the absence of the British workingman's penchant for bands, the lesson learned in Salisbury transferred easily to America, where band instruments served the Army's purposes ideally. With zeal, even the least adept convert could produce a sound, and with practice, a melody. This was especially true of percussion instruments, the use of which conveniently spared the convert, eager to join the fray, the necessity of practice. With instruments it was possible to carry the sound of a street service over the rattles and clops of horse-drawn traffic. Bands were military, and added a brave and stirring note to the street marches that preceded every evening service, and charged the singing indoors to new heights of enthusiasm. Playing an instrument gave the soldier a feeling of belonging, of fulfilling a role in the great salvation crusade: the alto horn or valve trombone was his badge of merit, visible proof to the world that he was no longer a poor and lonely drudge, but a bandsman in The Salvation Army, a person of consequence at last. In addition, it was fun—a fact the Army gladly emphasized. In 1893 officers were instructed to tell their young people that a crusade planned for that year would be "better than football. Saving is exciting work."[21]

As a movement struggling for whatever support came to hand, the Army was glad to have any instruments at all in the early days. When Major Moore staged a third anniversary parade to the New York City Hall in 1883, the Army band consisted of two kettle drums, a bass drum and a fife, none of which—alas—played together during any part of the march. Saco, Maine, fell in 1884 to a hallelujah onslaught led by four drums, five triangles, and twelve tambourines. The high musical standards of a later day were notably absent in the 1880s, and there is uncertainty as to when the first actual Salvation Army band—the kind with instruments other than drums—was formed in America. Colonel Brindley Boon states in an authorized history of Salvation Army bands that the first official Army band in the United States was the National Staff Band, made up of headquarters officers and employees; it played for the first time on June 18, 1887, at the Brooklyn Lyceum. In fact, in 1885 Oakland Citadel had a fourteen-piece band, Danbury had a "new brass band," and East Liverpool, Ohio, sported a full band, which played the next year at the dedication of the new Chicago Temple and filled the air "with angels' whispers." Most corps had to struggle along with considerably less: even New York No. 1 had no regular band until 1888. Typical accounts told of meetings and marches accompanied by a trombone, bass drum, and snare drum, or a cornet, drum, and pair of cymbals. Banjos, guitars, a "picalo," concertinas, "clarionets," violins, autoharps, and cowbells all were pressed into service. An 1895 service in southern California was led by Comrade Comstock and his "famous fife," which he had played at the capture of Vicksburg. The Army offered a set of the traditional instruments for an all-brass band for sale as early as 1888—the year that Chicago acquired its first Army band— but it was well into the twentieth century before woodwinds and strings ceased to appear in Army bands. Massachusetts even had a "Divisional Orchestra" in 1891.[22]

Proficiency in these pioneer aggregations counted for less than zeal and holy living. "If a man is not right in his soul, or is not loyal to the Army, or is not a true Blood-and-Fire Soldier, he must not be a Bandsman, whatever his musical abilities may be." Officers were strictly warned to watch "against professionalism" in their bands. There seems to have been little danger. When Captain Edward Parker was appointed bandmaster of the new Illinois Divisional Band in 1889, he could not read a note of music. And in San Francisco in 1891, the No. 3 Corps' band sallied forth after one week of practice to astonish the world with its rendition of "Rescue the Perishing." Small wonder that a Chicago band produced a "delirious uproar" in 1891, or that two years later an Army band in Portland, Oregon, was described as "a sort of little German band affair." The musical reputation thus gathered to The Salvation Army lingered for years, and became part of the stock-in-trade of American humorists. The pioneer Army cared little for that. Let the world laugh: people were attracted by the music, souls were won. Sympathetic observers agreed: "Honest success of such gigantic dimensions is sublime," declared one writer in *Scribner's Magazine* in 1896, "won though it may be to an accompaniment of ill-blown trombones and kettle-drums off the key."[23]

Part of the appeal of Army music lay in its popular nature. Booth loved the traditional hymns of the church and they were never abandoned, but they were soon joined by songs set either to sprightly tunes of original Army composition or to popular secular melodies which the Army shamelessly expropriated. The General brushed aside objections with Charles Wesley's question: "Why should the devil have all the good tunes?" The idea was simple: join some lines of religious verse (preferably "snappy" or "red-hot," although the words of many traditional hymns were also used) to a tune already well-known to the audience, so they could sing along without feeling awkward or self-conscious. For this purpose, "any serviceable tune" would suffice. If this combination touched the hearts of the people, who could gainsay its use? If it did not, the Army would try another—there were plenty of tunes from which to pick. The range of airs and melodies employed by the Army in its pioneer adventures was amazing: everything from "She's in the Asylum Now" to the Cornell University *alma mater*. Railton was particularly fond of American Civil War songs, but barroom ballads, love songs, vaudeville, and minstrel tunes were no less eagerly adopted. Small wonder that critics and friends alike expressed the conviction that The Salvation Army was certain to be mistaken for a circus parade—as indeed it was when Railton and the heroic seven landed at Battery Park in 1880. Identification of course can be double-edged: when a circus parade rode into Danbury in 1885, local drunks mistakenly attacked with a "shower of rotten apples."[24]

Striking as the effect of bands must have been, music was not the only arrow in the Army's quiver. The devil had more reason than one to tremble: there was very little in the way of the dramatic or comical that pioneer Salvationists would not do to attract a crowd to hear the gospel. Respectable people might quail before this avalanche of "clap-trap" and "rowdyism": the Army sniffed at their opinion; what did it matter if the Army complied with established customs, so long as the Army attracted sinners. Let the newspapers ridicule them: all the better—it was free publicity. Everything was explained by the "first necessity of the movement, which is TO ATTRACT ATTENTION!" It is difficult to imagine how the Army could have failed with such devices as burning the devil in effigy in front of national headquarters (after dissecting its various body parts, including a huge red tongue marked "gossip"); or parading down San Francisco's Market Street, dressed entirely in sheets and pillowcases, singing "A Robe of White, a Crown of Gold"; or marching forty bridesmaids down a Chicago street dressed in star-spangled sashes and red liberty caps (complete with Army hatbands), preceded by a torchlight parade! Then there were the umbrellas with red-hot gospel mottos on every section; announcements painted on the sides of wagons, upon which were lassies perched precariously, beating drums or ringing handbells; the huge palm fans, sandwich signs, transparencies, giant boxes, bottles and barrels, messages on the outside, hardy Salvationists on the inside, dancing along the street. The variations were endless, the effect the same. To quote one who observed the San Francisco sheet-and-pillowcase parade, people were "desperately interested." Not surprisingly.[25]

The religious meetings to which these allurements pointed were hardly less energetic. The same principles held for all meetings, outdoors or indoors: "Everything short, sharp, striking, vigorous." The order of service varied considerably, but lively and enthusiastic singing with much hand-clapping and volley-firing, a gospel message and testimonies were a part of every service. This last was regarded as the most important part of the meeting. Testimonies from the soldiers and converts advertised the power of grace in a manner more effective than any other; converts were encouraged by the experiences of their new friends, and sinners were made to hope. The testimonies of converted reprobates, especially those who were well-known locally, caused crowds to gather at street-corner meetings and fill Army halls. One sympathetic and perceptive writer commented in 1884 on the appeal of testimonies, which she regarded as accounting "in a good measure for the Army's success . . . But the great charm of these meetings and that, indeed, which secure for them the perpetual freshness and attractiveness, keeping their halls filled, night after night, is contained in the personal testimonies of the converts as to the joy and strength which they have received in the 'great salvation' from sin and its bondage."[26]

Some of the stories of these early-day trophies of grace would have melted hearts of stone. Maude A. Harris, the "Saved Bare-Back Rider," had been raised as an orphan in a circus, with only an elephant for a friend. After a flashy, sordid life as a bareback rider, professional baseball player, rower, and jockey, she was converted at age nineteen at the Army in Albany, and became an officer. Another convert had been drunk so long on the night he was saved that he no longer owned a shirt, and there was not enough food in his room "for two mice." Wife-beaters, cheats and bullies, prostitutes, boys who had stolen the family food money, unfaithful husbands, burglars, and teamsters who had been cruel to their horses stood for their brief and glorious moments in the limelight of grace. Then there were the more colorful characters, those trophies who became regular features at Army meetings: Captain John O'Brine, the "Saved Seal" (showman), "Orange Box George," the "Dutch Volcano," "Hell Fire Jack," the "Welsh Hallelujah Midget," the "Hallelujah Baggageman," and a host of assorted and long-forgotten "devil-drivers" who now reign with Christ in glory.[27]

Beyond the standard use of songs, message, and testimonies, the content of Army meetings varied. The Army, which produced a regulation governing practically every other aspect of its work, placed no limits on its religious meetings. Officers were, on the contrary, encouraged to experiment. Imaginations thus stimulated produced remarkable results. Adjutant Wallace Winchell subpoenaed the devil to a mock trial in Chicago in 1894, while Staff–Captain Thomas launched a revival at Los Angeles No. 1 in 1896 by preaching on eternity while standing before an open, empty coffin. Both of these techniques became Army favorites. One successful innovation stimulated many others: officers wore prison garb in the pulpit, rode horses onto the platform, or released flocks of canaries in the meetings. The use of the "stereopticon"—a kind of lantern-show with slides of Bible verses and dramatic scenes—was so popular that headquarters had to issue an order in 1897 that only "approved" slides could be used. Staff–Captain John Milsaps intoduced the "phonograph service" to the Pacific coast in 1897, a novelty item which soon had national appeal. Special books of instruction were prepared for drills with flags, tambourines, and Chinese lanterns.[28]

Despite these entertaining diversions, The Salvation Army laid down the gospel with what Catherine Booth called "unerring accuracy." The meetings were conducted for one purpose only: the conversion of sinners, or their growth in grace. However bizarre the attraction or enjoyable the service—and the Army was fun—no one came away without knowing that Jesus was the sinner's hope. Not only regular services, but special ceremonies, such as the dedication of infants, weddings, and funerals, ended with a period of invitation—the "altar call," during which people who wished religious counseling were asked to come forward to kneel at the "mercy seat," a special rail or bench set aside for that purpose. Dramatic transformations were often the result; occasionally a repentant would leave the symbol of his former sin at the altar: jewelry, tobacco, bottles—even weapons. Brengle collected a dagger, a revolver, and a tomahawk during the course of his career as a revivalist for the Army. The great majority of converts left nothing more wonderful at the altar than their broken lives and blasted dreams, now gilded with hope.[29]

Salvationists were convinced that their message was universal. They did not cavil at the command of their Heavenly Captain to take the gospel to all the world. They were encouraged to discover that in America sizable portions of all the world were conveniently at hand, and more were arriving every day. Uprooted from all that was cherished and familiar, jammed into unhealthy tenements, ignorant of the language and confused by the manners of their new homeland, many immigrants sought an enhanced religious commitment to preserve some sense of ethnic identity. Into these teeming waters the Army threw its nets. The Salvation Army was actively committed to attracting members of foreign-language populations from its earliest days in this country. The "Foreign Department" produced some of the Army's great saints, and —particularly in the Scandinavian division of the work—traditions that have remained alive and beloved well past the mid-twentieth century.[30]

The mission to Scandinavian immigrants began in a characteristically spontaneous way. In the winter of 1887 four Swedish laundresses, soldiers at Brooklyn No. 1, began holding services in their native language after the regular services were over. When these Swedish services became popular among churchless and lonely Scandinavian domestics and sailors, the women rented a storefront on Atlantic Avenue. As these still-unofficial meetings grew daily larger, two Swedish-American officers, Annie and Mary Hartelius, arrived—or rather, re-arrived—on the scene. These two sisters had been converted at a street service in Brooklyn in 1882 and had shortly volunteered to return to their native Sweden as missionary officers in 1883. Thus crowned as the first Salvation Army missionaries to be sent abroad from the United States, the Hartelius sisters returned in time to throw themselves into the burgeoning Swedish mission in Brooklyn, which by now had hopelessly outgrown the resources of the valiant but exhausted laundresses. Ballington Booth appointed the sisters to command the new corps, Brooklyn No. 3, which opened on December 23, 1887. The work progressed with amazing rapidity; clearly *The War Cry* was right in boasting that the Swedes were "a nationality peculiarly affected by our methods and doctrines."[31]

The "Saved Swedes" of Brooklyn No. 3 soon had company. Other cities with large Swedish populations promptly opened missions among them. The first west of New York was in Minneapolis, in April, 1888; then St. Paul, and Chicago, where Scandinavian work prospered as nowhere else. *The War Cry* began printing a column and songs in Swedish as a prelude to a full-fledged Swedish edition, the *Stridsropet*, which was launched in February 1891. The next year the already flourishing Swedish work was stimulated to a new outburst of energy by the arrival of Commissioner Hanna Ouchterlony, the heroic officer who had pioneered in Sweden a few months before the Hartelius sisters had arrived to help her. The Commissioner held two hundred meetings, to which Swedish people came in large numbers. Her services in Chicago were particularly successful: by 1894, there were six Swedish corps in that city, crowned by the famous Chicago No. 13. On the tenth anniversary of the opening of Brooklyn No.3 (which by now was a kind of shrine to Swedish Salvationists, revered among them as *Osterns stjarne:*—the "Star of the East"), there were forty-nine corps, 103 officers, twelve brass bands, and a special training garrison in Chicago to prepare officers— all in the Scandinavian branch of the work. The Scandinavian ministry was extended to the Pacific Coast on February 26, 1899, when a mission was opened in San Francisco to reach Swedish sailors.[32]

The success of the Scandinavian work was partly due to factors unique to the Swedes. The Salvation Army had made many converts in Sweden, and thousands of these joined the tide of immigration to the United States. Many were delighted to find here their beloved *Frälsingsarmen*, the one familiar thing in a new and alien world. In addition, a large number of the Swedish immigrants were single women, many of whom found employment as domestic servants. Trapped in a dull and lonesome occupation, they delighted to hasten at night to the gay and hearty fellowship of the Army corps. The other large group touched by the Army's Scandinavian ministry consisted of Swedish and Norwegian sailors, who came ashore in port cities like Brooklyn, San Francisco, and Seattle for periods ranging from overnight to several weeks. These men were grateful for company in their native language and looked forward to seeing the Army women, enjoying the singing, and eating the enormous quantities of food that became characteristic of the Scandinavian corps in their heyday.[33]

Work among other ethnic groups was launched with equal fervor, but failed to gain similar ground. Railton had a peculiarly strong affinity for Germany and Germans, and entertained great hopes for the results of Army work among them. He went after them at once, wiring the General on the latter's twenty-fifth wedding anniversary in June, 1880: "American Army salutes you. First German battery opened New York on Sunday. Gloriously grand celebration." This was premature, like all Railton's pronouncements on the Germans. Two days later he wrote to Booth that he hoped to "get the Americans, Germans, and Africans all fairly started." Success eluded the pioneers. Moore's *War Cry* offered a column for the *Deutschen Kameraden,* written by Staff-Captain Richard Holz, but it wasn't until 1887 that the loyal Army opened a German corps. Railton, by then territorial commander in Germany, sent stirring accounts of conversions there to readers of the American *War Cry,* urging his comrades to start German corps among the millions of Germans in America. An occasional German *War Cry* was offered first in October, 1892, but permanent corps failed to materialize. At the Columbian Congress in 1893, the perpetually optimistic Railton as guest of honor spoke in German, mostly about his work in the Fatherland, and once again announced that the Army planned to start German corps in America. Patience was rewarded suddenly, but in the end, only briefly. A German corps was opened in Buffalo in 1893, and then a second in New York. Within five years there were twenty-one German corps in America, located in cities with large German populations like Buffalo, Hoboken, Cleveland, Cincinnati, Milwaukee, and San Francisco.[34]

The German Salvationists, however, proved to be different from the Swedish in several basic ways. For one thing, despite Railton's abiding affection for all things German, the Army did not prosper in the Fatherland as it had in Sweden: few of the German immigrants who came to America were Salvationists; most were Roman Catholic. In addition, German-Americans did not cling to their native language with the tenacity of the Swede. The few German converts secured by the Army preferred to attend English-speaking corps in order to learn the new language. Half the soldiers in Cincinnati's two flourishing American corps spoke or understood German in 1894, for instance, while the two small German corps languished. Finally, it was difficult to convince Germans to become officers in sufficient numbers to sustain the German corps work. The attrition rate among the few Germans who did become officers was high. The one German-American who became a successful and prominent officer was Richard E. Holz; he developed a following among German Salvationists, who followed him into and out of the ill-fated Moore Army. In 1896 Holz was placed in charge of the "Scandinavian, German and Italian Department" set up by the new commander, Booth-Tucker, to coordinate all foreign language work. The German work declined rapidly, however, and the Italian work consisted of a single family of three Italian converts named Natino working valiantly, and in the long run unsuccessfully, against great odds at 201 Hester Street in Mulberry Bend. In 1897 the second-in-command for Sweden, Colonel George Sowton, replaced Holz, and the Army's foreign language work came to center on Scandinavians.[35]

On the Pacific coast, Salvationists likewise looked upon the hordes of Chinese immigrants as fields white unto harvest. Attempts were made from the beginning to "save the Chinaman." The Army's hopes were boundless: not only would California have her "Chinese Division of The Salvation Army," but the Army would train Chinese officers to "attack China's four hundred millions" in their homeland. The first Chinese convert, Wong Ock, thought to be saved in 1884 in San Francisco, caught this vision. After several months of fruitless street preaching Wong, the "hallelujah Chinaman," decided to go to London to prepare himself to lead an invasion force to China. He departed in full Chinese costume, sailing for London on April 18, 1885. Alas, he returned not to China, but to San Francisco, where it was reported in 1887 that he was still valiantly preaching to indifferent crowds in Chinatown.

Fong Foo Sec was converted in Sacramento in 1889, and became an officer. He agitated for permission to open fire on his fellow Chinese in San Francisco. In 1896 he was promoted to Ensign, the first Chinese in the world to be raised to staff rank in The Salvation Army (and, sad to say, at that time one of the few ever to have heard of the Army). Fong apparently had staff or clerical duties, because when a Chinese corps was finally opened later the same year, the pioneer officer was Captain May Jackson. With its gaslights, two "little dragon flags," and John 3:16 in Chinese characters on the wall, the Chinese corps was a triumph from the start; by the end of the year thirty-six Chinese had been saved, and a second Chinese corps opened in San Jose. Prominent Army visitors to San Francisco always wanted to visit its exotic Oriental outpost: Booth-Tucker, who loved going about in disguise, once showed up at the corps in full Chinese regalia! A Chinese *War Cry* was started in 1896 as well, designed to explain basic Christian truths to the Chinese. Fong, long revered by Chinese Salvationists, finally returned to China and became English language editor of the Shanghai *Commercial Press,* but not before the Chinese corps was permanently established in San Francisco.[36]

The story of the Army's repeated efforts to draw blacks into the ranks during these years is a touching one. To the many obstacles that stood in the way of Army work generally was added the insurmountable fact of racial antipathy, against which even God's grace was not proof. James Jermy, the Christian Missioner who began an abortive work in Cleveland in 1872, often preached to small black or racially-mixed congregations. Railton hoped from the beginning to get the "Africans . . . fairly started," but found the few blacks he encountered indifferent to his appeals. No details are known. Major Frank Smith was as zealous as Railton had been in believing that the Army should be the "first Christian community in America" that would "faithfully and wholly break down the wall of partition" separating the races; but unlike Railton, Smith laid definite plans to reach blacks, and attempted to carry them out.[37]

Major Smith was an officer with a heightened sense of social responsibility; his commitment to evangelizing the "Freedmen," as he called them, was prompt and genuine. It is to the credit of his troops that he secured the cooperation of so many of them for a campaign that was certain to be long, difficult, and unpopular among the poor and working-class whites who formed the great bulk of Army supporters. He announced the opening of the Army's "first colored station" in Baltimore in November, 1884, but nothing came of it. The following summer, however, Smith launched the "Great Colored Campaign and Combined Attack upon the South." A black officer had arrived providentially to take command of the expedition. Captain W.S. Braithwaite, a Methodist pastor from British Guiana, had been saved from a backslidden life at a Salvation Army service in Asbury Park, New Jersey. Special meetings were held in New York, New England, and Michigan to secure funds, volunteers, and prayers for the work: all who believed that "the colored race settled in our midst" were "possessed of immortal souls" were asked to donate. Considerable momentum must have been generated, because when Braithwaite was dismissed in November after the Army had investigated mysterious "circumstances and charges," the "Great Colored Campaign" did not falter. Fredericksburg, Virginia, was opened in November, 1885, as the 1st Virginia (actually it was the second: Alexandria had been open for three months). Two of the four pioneer officers were black: Captain Johnson, described in *The War Cry* as a "bright mulatto" born in Maine, and Lieutenant Minor, "a handsome colored woman" who had been born a slave in Virginia. The majority of the persons in the congregations at their first meetings, indoors and out, were black. This was encouraging. Ambitious plans were laid to open black corps in Washington, Frederick, Richmond, and Norfolk. The Army tried to enlist more volunteers with what it called "colored skins and white hearts" in the crusade. All went well at first. A visiting officer found a mixed crowd of five hundred at Fredericksburg in January, 1886. When General Booth visited the "colored corps" in 1887 there were forty "Blood-and-Fire Soldiers," mostly in uniform, hundreds on the platform, and a packed hall.[38]

Black converts were welcomed throughout the Army, and were often featured in the meetings as testifiers and entertainers. The black soldiers were popular as "specials" and were enthusastically received by congregations. "Special George," a black soldier who played cornet, harmonica and guitar, was popular in eastern cities, while groups called "colored jubilee singers" sang and testified at Chicago No. 1 in 1889 and in all three Los Angeles corps in 1896. Other black soldiers did valiant service for the cross in their local corps, often enduring the misunderstanding and indifference of both races. Isaac Smith, converted in 1885, became the Color Sergeant at New York No. 3 and did not miss a single open-air meeting for the next fifteen years. When Brengle was in Danbury a black soldier named George Washington was one of only two who were willing to accompany him to street services—the other was a crippled child. It is true, of course, that the Army's major interest in blacks was in converting them: the same was true of its major interest in everyone. It is also true that the black "specials" were often made to appear comical, and *The War Cry* printed poems in "darkie dialect." Yet the magazine also printed many straightforward testimonies from the "colored comrades." The Army's attack on race prejudice was genuine, if somewhat hampered by stereotypical thinking and massive social inertia.[39]

Certainly Ballington Booth's motive in taking five blacks as part of the American delegation to the Army's international congress in England in 1894 was at least partly to demonstrate official endorsement of evangelism among blacks. The men themselves were certainly sincere, and held a spontaneous revival meeting on the ship. The next year the Army took a courageous stand, both on the spot and, later, officially, against the rising tide of lynching that disfigured the decade of the nineties in the South. In 1895 the two white officers in command of Frederick, Maryland, now a forlorn relic of the "colored campaign" of earlier days, threw themselves into a valiant but fruitless attempt to rescue a black man from a lynch mob, following and pleading with the mob all the way from the jail to the tree. In the end, hoping to shame the men into a change of heart, the officers asked to pray with the doomed man. All in vain: the mob respectfully uncovered their heads for the prayer, then hanged the man. "Salvation Army, be quick!" stormed *The War Cry:* the "Lynching craze" must stop. The victims of black crime were to be pitied, certainly—but black men were "also victims of terrible cruelties and assaults." Lynching was "horrible . . . atrocious."[40]

The solution to these problems was clear: all men of all races must be saved. The Army must step up its campaign to redeem the South. "The Children for God! There must be no Distinction of Color or Class!" declared a *War Cry* cover in July, 1894, which portrayed a crowd of black, asiatic, and rich and poor white children reaching up to the General. The Army was as good as its word—or tried to be: in 1894, and again in 1896, expeditions were announced to extend "Salvation Army work among the colored population of the Southern States." These proved abortive. Meanwhile the original black stations languished. Funds could not be raised, black officers were not available, the white officers delegated to lead these campaigns through their initial stages were called to other assignments that headquarters considered more urgent. The Army's commitment to spreading its work among blacks remained official policy, but the actual results were largely in the realm of hope. Perhaps that was enough to win the gratitude of blacks for whom even hope was encouraging: Booker T. Washington wrote in 1896, "I have always had the greatest respect for the work of the Salvation Army, especially because I have noted that it draws no color line in religion."[41]

The Salvation Army clearly took a broad view of its function in America. Salvationists were convinced that they were called to preach a universal gospel, that all must be saved, and that any means that would work to that great end ought to be tried. They likewise believed with their General that theirs was the particular destiny to carry the word of redemption to the masses of churchless, Christless urban poor. It was inevitable that an organization of practical minded zealots, propagating a gospel of universal love to large numbers of broken and desperate people, would be drawn to recognize one supreme fact: there is no true religion that is not acted out in compassion for the real problems of real people—there is no piety without love, and love that is merely abstract is not love at all, but sentiment. The gospel message must be accompanied by expressions of love so unmistakable that no potential convert could miss them; then only would the good news of God's grace seem real. The Army's evangelical heart was warmed, while its practical heart was stimulated. It was only half enough to declare that God is love: The Salvation Army would *show* that He was.

Pioneer officers were little concerned with theories of social justice: they knew only that their Heavenly Commander had ordered His soldiers to take in strangers, visit the sick and imprisoned, offer drink to the thirsty, and food to the hungry; they also knew that there were souls dying all around, and that the first step in saving some of them was to lift them up so they could hear that such a thing as salvation existed. Social welfare was both Biblical and practical: Salvationists needed no more elaborate arguments than these. The Army never offered a developed theory for its social welfare program. Each part evolved piecemeal, over the years, in response to immediate practical needs that were uncovered in the course of the evangelical crusade.[42]

A variety of small-scale relief operations—more like little kindnesses —must have begun in many corps almost from the day they opened. It is almost certain that "much genuine and wholly fruitful . . . work" was done for unwed mothers and rescued prostitutes in the corps officers' private quarters long before formal "rescue work" was launched. The first recorded and official social program in the Army came in 1885, when the Chaplain of the Hartford jail asked the local corps to hold a meeting for the prisoners: he correctly reasoned that his charges would be encouraged by the testimonies of several former inmates, now saved and serving in the Army. In Sacramento, California, soldiers began holding services in the jail in August 1886; by March of the following year, two officers were "conducting meetings regularly in the Stockton jail." Other beneficial programs developed spontaneously. In April 1887, the officer at Danbury invited seventy-five poor children off the street for a hot meal, served up by the beaming ladies of the corps.[43]

A major program—and the one which came to be the Army's most beloved and successful—was inaugurated in October 1886, in Brooklyn. *The War Cry* carried a front-page announcement: "Rescue Home for Fallen and Homeless Girls. The Salvation Army to the Rescue." Operated on a shoestring (donations of food, old clothes, cast-off furniture, and a used sewing machine were gratefully recorded over several months) and without experienced supervisors, "Morris Cottage" was nonetheless a Godsend. Pregnant women who could not secure a husband in time faced desperate alternatives in the Victorian era: certain and ruinous scandal, an almost certainly suicidal abortion, or flight, alone and penniless. Likewise a young woman, pregnant or not, who wished to escape from a life of prostitution had to have a place to live until she could acquire more honorable work, a place in which she would be safe from the very real danger of being murdered by her disgruntled former employers. The gilding on the good old days wasn't very deep. A rescue home was therefore an indispensable adjunct to street-corner evangelism in the slums. Such homes spread inevitably with the expansion of the Army's religious ministry. "Beulah" opened in Oakland in February 1887. The house was small, and soon overcrowded. The usual gifts of small change, old shoes, and a jar of preserves were acknowledged. The young women threw themselves into the spirit of their new haven by making three Army flags for the officer pioneers to Oregon. Refuges opened in Grand Rapids in 1888 (helped along by the gift of a box of live chickens), and in Los Angeles in 1890. The rescue home ministry was placed on a more certain footing in 1892 when an experienced English officer, Captain Denison, opened new homes in Cleveland and in New York, on 123rd Street, where a "training garrison" was established to train women for rescue work.[44]

The great charm in these enterprises lay in the fact that they were absolutely practical, and provided a service made infinitely more welcome by the absence of any alternative. The same was true for all early-day Army welfare. In 1889 the Army opened a "creche" on Cherry Street in New York, to provide care for infants whose mothers were forced to work, were in jail for short terms, or who had simply neglected them. The babies were placed in shoe boxes for cribs. This original day-care center operated, like the rescue homes, on pennies and donated baby clothes, farina, and rice.[45] A remarkable and equally practical ministry began the same year when Captain Emma J. Bown first sent her "Slum Sisters" in pairs into the streets of New York. These girls simply did whatever came to hand: their sole ministry was to be helpful and speak of Christ when asked their motive. Stroke victims, pathetic and alone, were bathed and fed, the extra baby or two in a crowded flat was washed and cuddled, meals were cooked, beds made, clothing patched, floors scrubbed, returning drunks bundled into bed, the dead washed and dressed for the undertaker (who simply delivered a coffin, took the cash for it, and left.) The slum sisters wore no Army uniform, but passed unobtrusively among their beneficiaries dressed in faded nondescript. Even the Army's worst critics fell silent before this ministry, which the many more sympathetic observers regarded as close to angelic.[46]

While the Army's social work in America was still in fledgling stage, and still confined to women and children, it received an enormous boost and a new dimension by the arrival in 1890 of William Booth's long-awaited statement on Army relief policy. The General's book, *In Darkest England and the Way Out,* caught the American public attention as much for the novelty that still attached to his movement as for the simple force of his arguments. Booth's purpose, as usual, was the salvation of souls; his premise was the "Cab-Horse Charter: . . . When he is down he is helped up, and while he lives he has food, shelter and work;" and his solution was the "Social Scheme." This last consisted of three connected parts: the first was the City Colony, where men and women from the "submerged tenth" of industrial society could be housed, trained, and helped upwards to honorable and useful lives; the second step in redemption was the Farm Colony, where those who wished to do so could be strengthened and trained for agricultural work in the third and ultimate part of the scheme, the Over-Seas Colony, envisioned as large, self-supporting Christian farming communities in South Africa, Canada, or Australia. Booth's "Social Scheme," audacious and in the long run impracticable, praised and criticized, generated widespread public interest in The Salvation Army. The City Colony, and later the Farm Colony, were implemented by officers who never ceased to regard the arrival of *Darkest England* as the major turning point in the development of an Army social program in the United States. This was especially true for the City Colony plan, which aimed directly at relieving the destitution of the large urban population of homeless, penniless men, mostly mendicants and drunkards, a problem of desperate proporations which America had long ceased to be able to ignore.[47]

The first relief work among homeless or drunken men was as practical as the rescue homes and the creche. The Salvation Army's original "Cheap Food and Shelter Depot" opened on December 23, 1891, on the corner of Downing and Bedford Streets in New York, on the first floor of the building shared with the No.2 corps. The depot provided sixty box-beds and a restaurant that offered wholesome meals, all offered at very low prices, which were strictly collected: the Army believed that simple "charity" was degrading; men who paid even a few pennies received the benefit and retained their pride. An immediate difficulty was that many men had no pennies at all. The straightforward Army solution was to provide work for these men. When the second "Lighthouse"—as such depots were soon renamed—was opened in San Francisco December, 1892, Captain Joseph McFee asked the men to collect discarded corks from saloons to make pillows, which could also serve as life preservers. The next year saw the enterprising McFee, pressed for funds, borrow a waterfront crab pot and tripod and ask passersby to "Keep the Pot Boiling!"—an enduring legacy. A far more common means of financing the lighthouses and providing work at the same time was the woodyard. Men who received food and lodging were asked to saw and split wood, and "put it up" in baskets and barrels for delivery at low prices—five cents a basket, twenty-five cents a barrel—to poor families who burned it in stoves to cook and keep warm.[48]

It was an easy, natural step from the woodyards to the "Salvage Brigades." The idea of collecting old clothes and discards, hiring the poor to repair them, and then selling the improved results to other needy persons was not original with the Army; but the Army was the first agency to employ it on a large scale and to bring it to public attention. The salvage brigades began in New Jersey in 1896; refuse was collected in handcarts. In Chicago the salvage project grew directly out of the cheap hostels; in exchange for lodging men were asked to sort out junk and rags given by local businessmen. Occasionally, items were uncovered that could still be useful to slum families; these were rescued and sold for a pittance, so that the recipient, like the worker, retained self-respect: the buyer was a customer, not a beggar. A full-fledged salvage program was in operation in Chicago by mid-1897. The work blossomed; by 1899 there were nineteen such institutions in the United States, with a total of over five thousand beds. The glossy dark-green and Julian red wagons with "The Salvation Army Industrial Department" in gilt letters on the side became as much a fixture of American city life as the Army's parades and street bands. Many an officer's son got his first taste of the thrill of warfare on a daily round of collections, driving a freshly-washed wagon, proudly yet gingerly trying to keep the rear wheels out of streetcar tracks, which could jam the wheel and cause a spill.[49]

Soon the Army couldn't do enough. No sooner had a start been made on meeting one desperate need than another was uncovered, and officers were sent or volunteered to deal with it. Soon there was the "Prison Gate

Brigade" to offer salvation to prisoners, and lodging and help in securing employment for those who were released. The multiplying Rescue Homes for Fallen Women claimed that seventy to eighty-five percent of "these daughters of sorrow" were "restored to lives of virtue." Many programs were launched on a small scale, which would expand mightily in the early years of the next century: Thanksgiving and Christmas dinners for the poor; the "cheap ice" ministry for the sweltering slums, and coal for the winter; steamboat excursions for needy families trapped for years within tenement walls; employment bureaus; secure, cheap, and respectable hotels for single working girls; "fresh-air camps," and special projects to reach the "inebriate classes." These programs were relatively easy to begin; officers, after all, lived on a pittance, and most materials used or given away in social projects had been donated. The only limit on new projects was ingenuity, a quality that men who marched in pillowcases and preached from coffins did not lack. Headquarters was finally forced to act in 1897: "In view of the rapid development of the Social Work . . . no new shelter, Prison Gate or other Social scheme" was to be "promised or commenced" without the national commander's consent.[50]

The country was in a receptive mood. The revelations of reformers and journalists made it increasingly difficult for middle-class city dwellers to ignore the poverty and vice all around them. Painters and photographers, poets and novelists began to portray the alienation and degradation of city life. Many of those who were indifferent or hostile to the Army's religious message and its means of propagating it now expressed sympathy with its program of social amelioration. Many of these people were disappointed later when the Army did not adopt distinctly political or economic solutions to the problems it attempted to solve. Among religious thinkers there was a similar reaction to the Army. The years in which The Salvation Army was coming to public attention were years in which many religious and educational leaders, horrified by the now all too obvious ghastly effects of rapid industrialization, were beginning to question certain traditional Christian beliefs, such as a reliance on individual salvation, as being too facile. "Higher criticism" of biblical texts and Darwinism added to their anxiety. These men developed an alternative to strict orthodoxy, the "Social Gospel," based on the conviction that Christ had come to bring what the influential Walter Rauschenbusch called "social restoration and moral salvage." The leaders of the Social Gospel movement were at first sympathetic to The Salvation

Army, seeing it as a stirring rebuke to conventional religious indifference. They were touched by the earnestness and kindliness of Salvationists working in the slums. Later these leaders were chilled by the Army's biblical literalism and its insistence that salvation was the ultimate cure-all; they became convinced that, for the problems of urban society, the Army could offer no solution worthy of the name. The writings of the Social Gospel movement nonetheless helped the Army: as the journalists and reformers had made social awareness popular, now the Social Gospel made it intellectually fashionable. Both helped to prepare a broader reception for the Army's requests for public support for its own practical programs.[51]

Army officers were fully aware that theirs was not the only solution to the problems of industrialization. Living on the street, their ministry mostly among the working class and poor, Salvationists were witness to the swell of labor unrest that marked the last twenty years of the nineteenth century. The Salvation Army never varied from its insistence that personal salvation was the only ultimate remedy for all human misery; it had little interest in merely economic and political solutions, and took a neutral position on such issues. Its energetic goodwill was offered freely to all in need, and people of almost all persuasions came to trust its evenhandedness. When a group of respectable Chicagoans wanted to distribute food to the families left destitute in the autumn of 1893 (primarily due to a sharp reduction in employment caused by the closing of the Chicago World's Fair, and the national financial panic of that year), the *Chicago Mail* selected the Army to conduct the business, commending its "thoroughly equipped corps of charity workers." In the Pullman Strike of the next year, The Salvation Army threw its small resources into action to relieve the suffering of the strikers, who faced the very real possibility of starvation. Governor John P. Altgeld accepted Staff–Captain Winchell's offer to collect and distribute food. Amid the bloodshed and riot of that terrible summer, the Army reaffirmed its lofty independent view that both employer and employee needed the "salvation of Jesus Christ," while its borrowed wagons carried food through the police lines.[52]

The Army's official position on the labor movement was certainly neutral. Leading officers were more ambiguous: labor leaders found reasons both to praise and to condemn the movement. In an age when the working classes were alienated from most Protestant denominations, the Army's appeal to the working poor was almost unique. When a strike occurred in the mines of western Pennsylvania in 1888, the divisional officer referred to the strikers as "our class of people." The Salvation Army was cheered by labor unions when both groups marched in Fourth of July parades. In 1897 the Army issued a special "Labor Day" number of *The War Cry*, in which there appeared very warm endorsements from the United Mine Workers, who praised the movement for the "interest taken in the working people," and from Eugene V. Debs, leader of the Pullman strikers, who called the Army "Christianity in action." On the other hand, some officers were critical of labor agitation. Officers declared that businessmen ought to support the Army because it improved the work force by transforming the men into honest, sober, and cooperative citizens. On his first visit to San Francisco in 1895, General Booth told two Salvationist employees of the Army printing plant—who approached him to request that the plant be operated according to union rules—that they had to resign from either the Army or the typographical union. The next issue of the *Pacific Union Printer* called the Army a "rat institution" and blacklisted *The War Cry*. "Abusive pamphlets" condemning the Army were distributed for several years by local socialists throughout the western states.[53]

Socialists had reason for concern: there was little in the official posture of the Army to comfort those who advocated radical reform of the American economic system; although, as in the case of attitudes towards labor, some officers were ambiguous in their attitudes towards the wealthy. Major Smith issued a daring statement in 1886 condemning the "overshadowing inequities, the gross selfishness, the hard un-Christian spirit" of the rich—daring, but far from typical: Smith later resigned from the Army to devote his considerable energies entirely to socialist politics in England. The Pacific coast *War Cry* frequently carried cartoons in the nineties that personified sin and portrayed the devil as an imp in top hat and tails, and in other ways ridiculed the fashionable dress and habits of the rich. Generally, however, officers took the economic order as they found it. And how they found it was in the hands of the rich, to whom they increasingly had to turn for large sums of money necessary to operate the Army's ever-expanding social program.[54]

Field officers were expected to finance their own corps by whatever means came to hand: selling *The War Cry* (which produced over half the Army's total income in the mid 1880s), collections taken at every indoor and outdoor meeting, and simple begging. Such means could not begin to produce sufficient funds to finance the Army's burgeoning relief projects, which at first showed no profit. The answer was the Auxiliary League, which after several false starts—it was launched in 1883 for a slightly different purpose but languished during the secession crisis—was revived in 1887 as a means of enlisting the support of the fashionable for the Army's "social wing," without at the same time expecting an endorsement of the Army's religious doctrines and evangelical techniques. Some officers regarded it as a serious misjudgment, if not something worse, that the Army was willing to distinguish between its social and spiritual selves, and to appeal for funds solely for the former. It was an argument that lingered; but for the time being, all objections were carried before the triumphs of Maud Ballington Booth, who galvanized the Auxiliary League when she assumed command of it in 1887. A woman of passionate sincerity, charming, quick-witted and graceful, Mrs Ballington Booth presided over the drawing-room meetings of the League in an elegant uniform "of fine material and neatly made" and a bonnet "trimmed with broad silk ribbon," sometimes alone, sometimes with a slum officer, a singer, or an instrumentalist. Women were so affected by her accounts of the Army's "great work of reclaiming drunkards, rescuing the fallen, and saving the lost" that they wept, opened their purses, and even donated their rings and jewelry on the spot. The Auxiliary League became fashionable, and spread to the Pacific coast. The two types of Auxiliaries—"subscribing," who agreed to donate five dollars per month (a considerable sum in those days) and "collecting," who agreed to collect at least $2.50 per month—numbered six thousand by 1896.[55]

Auxiliaries were expected to support the Army not only with money, but in word and print as well. Among the thousands who agreed to these things and who carried the "small leather ticket bearing the official recognition of headquarters" were some of the richest and most influential people in the United States. President Cleveland received Smith and a delegation at the White House on the sixth anniversary of Railton's landing, and President Harrison sent a noncommittal endorsement to be read at the Army's huge Columbian Congress in New York in December 1892. The support of William McKinley, both as candidate and as President, went beyond the merely formal: a kindly, religious man, McKinley gave the Army his warm and genuine sympathy. Bouyed by the support of the rich and the powerful, the Army had arrived socially.[56]

Yet this story of public acceptance has an ironic, darker side. The years that saw The Salvation Army wafted into the drawing rooms of America on wings of praise also saw it advance into the dives and gutters against a tornado of abuse. This was the time of the Army's trial by fire. The catalogue of hostile acts committed against the Army from 1880 to 1896 is depressingly long, and some of it makes grim reading. At least five Salvationists were martyred (in Colorado Springs, San Francisco, Spokane, St. Louis, and Pittsburgh); a mob tried to lynch young Captain Adam Gifford in Rockville, Connecticut; officers in Leadville, Colorado, and Los Angeles were shot at repeatedly; several soldiers in Brooklyn had their arms broken in 1885; and at least three officers were struck full in the head with bricks thrown at short range: Richard Holz and Captain Mary Powell in Brooklyn in 1885, Samuel Brengle in Boston in 1888. A young girl officer in Portland, Maine, permanently lost her hearing after being knocked unconscious by a large chunk of ice. Many crusaders were badly cut and bruised by direct assaults; several were burned deliberately with cigars and firecrackers. A mob rushed into a meeting at the Chicago No. 3 corps, upset the wood stove, and rushed back outside and locked the door in an attempt to burn the hall and soldiers alike. Attempts were made to burn the corps in Sacramento and a shelter in Los Angeles, and in 1886 a crowd wearing hoods succeeded in burning down the Army hall in Bristol, Connecticut. In Napa, California, the officers were warned to leave town before somebody blew them and their work into atoms with "Dina might."[57]

The large majority of assaults were not aimed at killing or crippling Salvationists or burning down their halls, but their effect on the victims was unpleasant enough. Young Captain Harry Stillwell came to the end of his first meeting at the San Francisco No. 2 corps covered with tobacco spit. William Brewer, the divisional officer in Boston, was accosted while strolling with his infant son in his arms by a man who slapped the baby in the face! Attacks on parades and street-corner meetings were widespread and frequent. The weapons varied: stones, bits of broken brick, old bottles, mud, hard green Bartlett pears, apples, tomatoes, eggs of different ages, garbage, small dead animals, horse manure, and water collected from handy barrels and horse-troughs, or dispensed from the occasional accommodating fire engine. Indoor meetings were hardly more secure: windows, lamps, chairs, and pictures were smashed, flags and banners torn down—the last usually not without stiff resistance: the corps flag was sacred. There were odd variations on the disruptive theme. In San Francisco enemies dumped pepper over the floor; in Buffalo they smuggled pigeons into the hall and released them during the meeting; in Napa dead cats and rotten eggs were pitched into the meeting hall through open windows; in Newark skittle balls were rolled over the floor of the Music Academy above the Army hall. Meetings outdoors or indoors that were not physically attacked were jeered and mimicked, which was often harder to bear: Railton never forgot "the clever and biting sarcasm of the United States, in which all classes and professions can more or less unite."[58]

The intensity of this vituperation, and the fact that it so often issued in actual physical violence, requires several explanations. For one thing, not all respectable and fashionable opinion supported the Army, even in the palmy days of the Auxiliary League. The pioneer Army with its hallelujah hoopla offended many church leaders; many of these later accepted the Army's bizarre antics as well-suited to reach the urban poor, but the initial negative reactions lingered for years and provided encouragement to those whose dislike of the Army was less principled. Ministers declared from the pulpit and the press that the Army made a "mockery" out of sacred things and degraded the heritage of Christianity. Many others did not agree with the Army's fundamentalist doctrines, regardless of its method of presenting them: there were, after all, many Roman Catholics and Jews on the sidewalks. Then, too, no one likes to be preached at, especially outside of church; many people, then as now, regarded religion as a personal matter, or a matter of no real importance, and did not care to be upbraided on the street about it. Many idle, irresponsible men and boys were about, with no regular employment, bored and hopeless, drifting along on the permeable edge of actual criminality, often drunk. To these persons, an attack on a Salvation Army parade was a welcome diversion, a kind of cruel sport they could excuse as harmless fun if nobody actually died. Lower down the social scale were those who found the Army threatening: men whose livlihood depended on the drinking, gambling, and whore-mongering of others. Saloon keepers were particularly liable to feel the adverse effects of the Army's street-corner revival. It is a mistake to suppose that most taverns in the 'nineties were elaborate and well-endowed places with long mahogany bars, gas chandeliers, and cornet, piano, and violin trios. In fact, most were shoestring operations with little in the way of furniture and no music, dark, smoky places for hard drinking on a small margin; the loss of a half-dozen faithfuls brought financial ruin to these places. The same was true for the madams and procurers who lived on the collected earnings of their female charges. The conversion of a prostitute or two, with subsequent flight to a Rescue Home, meant disaster. The Salvation Army's doctrines would have meant little to such people, had the Army been content to dispense them in fashionable churches. But no: the Army gave out the call for repentance—with flags, posters and a brass band—on the street corner, the very doorstep of those it was trying to ruin.

In many cases, its enemies could attack The Salvation Army with impunity. Many American cities had few police, and none at all in the worst districts after dusk. Even when the police were present they often offered the Army little protection, or joined in the attack by arresting the Salvationists for disturbing the peace or blocking the sidewalk—or when all else failed, for violating any one of a series of hastily-enacted ordinances against marching, playing band instruments, or beating drums without a license. In larger cities, mayors and police commissioners simply forbade the Army the privilege of holding services outdoors. Official persecution was not a universal problem, nor did it last long. Many police officers were sympathetic from the first; generally, the police offered the Army security when they were asked, and public opinion and the courts did not abide blatantly discriminatory legislation forever. But where law enforcement officials were indifferent or hostile, or actually in league with the saloon-keepers whose businesses were the mainstay of big-city machine politics, the Army faced a severe trial. Salvationists were convinced that police persecution was caused almost entirely by pressure from liquor dealers with political connections. For awhile, arrests were common. Many Army meetings were broken up by police, many officers arrested—some of them many times.[59]

It was as the "Hallelujah Jail Bird" that Joe the Turk earned his niche in Salvation Army history. A pugnacious, fearless man with little administrative or spiritual ability, Joe was called as much to flamboyance as to religion. Dressed in his "full Turkish costume," he became a kind of happy wanderer, traveling around the country challenging anti-Army statutes, being arrested, and demanding a jury trial. The Turk (actually an Armenian) had discovered early that juries of respectable persons, many of them churchgoers, were more sympathetic to Salvationists than to dive keepers and lowlife plaintiffs. He was usually acquitted, whereupon the statute ceased to have practical effect. Even when convicted and sent to jail for a few days or weeks in lieu of fine (which he always refused to pay, however small the sum), Joe triumphed. He held revival services in his cell, sang, prayed aloud, and decorated the walls, sheets, and the other prisoners' clothing with his special "Jesus Saves" rubber stamp. Once, in the Portland, Oregon, jail in 1890, Joe amplified his motto-stamping ministry; having brought his cellmate to Christ, he discovered to his great joy that the man was a sign painter. The two worked through the night, emblazoning the walls of the cell, which shone forth in the morning with "Jesus is the Drunkard's Friend" and "Where Will You Spend Eternity?" Not all arresting officers and jailors were gentle, and several times he was stoned by mobs. The work of this odd, vexatious man required courage, and brought great benefit to The Salvation Army. The publicity that resulted from his escapades made it difficult to take the offending statutes seriously.[60]

The wave of persecution crested in the late 1880s and began to ebb. By 1892 Ballington Booth was encouraged by the changed attitude of the press and the public, and warned of the "dangers attending the universal well-speaking of all men." Congratulations and statements of support poured into the Army "from Pulpit and Press, from President and Policeman." Persecution had accomplished little even in immediate terms, and nothing permanent. The opposite had been the effect in many places: the Army grew stronger. Touched by the courage of the beleagured Salvationists, angry and embarrassed by discoveries of special statutes and police persecution, public opinion became ever more favorable to the Army. For this reason, and because they regarded opposition as good for the soul and proof that the devil and his stooges were worried, leading officers welcomed persecution. Commissioner Smith added a practical note in 1885 by reminding the troops in Newark that it was better to have a crowd to pelt them than no crowd at all.[61]

Encouraged by approval and strengthened by adversity, the Army broadened its war front. Out West, a mounted branch was formed in June 1892 and thrown into the war. Dressed in top-boots, red shirts, "mouse-colored corduroy inexpressibles," under sombreros with hatbands in Army colors, the "Salvation Army Cavalry" hit the trail in California. The "Mounted Foes of Satan" consisted of Major Philip Kyle and ten young bandsmen (including Lieutenant Fong Foo Sec as cook and bass drummer). They would ride, camp, mount up, instruments more or less at the ready, and "storm the town." In between camping and storming, the cavalrymen painted uplifting mottos on large rocks and enjoyed miraculous cliff-hanger escapes, which enthralled the readers of their weekly dispatches to *The War Cry*.

The results of this endeavor were very encouraging—total success, however, eluded the valiants because none of them could ride a horse. The next two summers an old concord coach and six horses were enlisted, and the group set out again as the "Charioteers." The efforts of these "twelve godly musicians" led by Ensign Sam Wood were crowned with glory: eighty-seven souls were saved the first summer out. One of these was a young Jewish storekeeper, Julius Abrams, who was brought to Christ at a Charioteer open-air meeting in a Mojave desert mining town. Abrams spent thirty years as an officer and Army evangelist. Thus graced by the blessing of God, the old stagecoach was kept in San Francisco as a souvenir and driven in parades. Army visitors from "back East" were thrilled to see the "War Chariot" waiting for them at the ferry slip. Nor did cavalrymen and charioteers exhaust the possibilities: a regular series of circuit-riders was established, called "Outriders." These heroic officers traveled alone or in pairs and carried the salvation war into the back country of California.[62]

Well might the famed artist of the Old West, Charles M. Russell, lament that Dame Progress and Father Time were consigning his beloved gamblers and bushwhackers to oblivion—and not without help! An 1898 pen drawing of Russell's showed Progress and Time lording it over a dispirited crowd of doomed heros—but in the background, under a "Salvation" flag, the lead woman is clearly carrying a *War Cry*. The Old West was dying indeed, and the Army was doing all that valor could ask to minimize the number of souls that died with it.[63]

The prospects were bright before these soldiers of Christ in the waning years of the last century. The plantation owners who ruled the Hawaiian republic invited the Army to send an advance guard in 1894, to evangelize the pineapple workers untouched by the respectable churches. Convinced that their "enlivening methods" would create "a wonderful stir" in the islands, a pioneer party of five officers, led by the indefatigable Staff–Captain Milsaps, landed in Honolulu in September. The party was kindly received by their hosts, introduced to the editors of the three newspapers in town, and provided with a large hall equipped with electric lights and seven hundred seats. President Sanford P. Dole invited the pioneers to the Palace and set upon their brows the seal of official approval, which did not dim when the short-lived republic was annexed to the United States in 1898.[64]

Those were the years in which the Army offered its first, tentative, spiritual overtures to men in the ranks of the American military. National headquarters was concerned that Salvationists who joined the US Army or Navy would lose contact with the vivifying fellowship of their "Blood-washed comrades" and be lost. In the case of the Salvationist crew of a US Revenue Cutter stationed at New Bern, North Carolina, in 1888, there seemed to be little to fear: the crew conducted Army meetings wherever the ship cruised or docked. With Salvationists who found themselves alone, or with only another comrade or two in a regiment or ship, the case was far different. Shortly after their arrival, the Honolulu pioneers went aboard the USS *Charleston* to seek out Salvationists (and to sell *War Cries*, sixty-three of them). In 1896 an official Naval and Military League was established at New York headquarters, under Brigadier Alice Lewis: its primary purpose was to locate Salvationist military men and establish contact with them by letters and visits, and by holding special services for them on their base or ship, or at the nearest corps. Such services were of course broadly evangelical, and men were converted. In 1896 two converted sailors on the USS *Adams* asked to be enrolled as Salvationists on the deck—and were, in the presence of the entire crew.[65]

The Spanish-American War, which began in April 1898, caused a rapid and enormous expansion of American military forces; many Salvationists were among the volunteers. The one-woman Naval and Military League was suddenly hard-pressed to perform its duties, and many officers were enlisted for the duration. The Salvation Army was, in fact, enthusiastic about the spiritual possibilities of the war: in the summer of 1898 *The War Cry* produced a "War Special," in which the cover picture was captioned "The Battleship 'Salvation' Opens Fire on Fort Sin." After bureaucratic objections were smoothed by the kindly intervention of the wife of President McKinley, Brigadier Lewis, with a woman officer to help her, was sent to minister to the troops assembling at Tampa and Key West for the invasion of Cuba. The women were received gallantly, their meetings greatly enlivened by the superb playing of the band of the 9th US Cavalry, a black regiment whose band was said to be the finest in the Army. Thus encouraged, the Salvationists petitioned in vain to follow the troops to Cuba. Meanwhile, Salvation Army detachments went to the new camps at Peekskill and Hempstead; out in California three officers held services in a tent for the fifty Salvationists among the troops waiting to leave San Francisco for the

Philippines; and in Sacramento, the Army joined the Red Cross in handing out a loaf of bread and a mug of coffee to each of five thousand men in training there.[66]

Troops on the Pacific coast were being collected and dispatched in such large numbers that the government facilities were swamped; The Salvation Army likewise could not hope to establish any sort of helpful contact with members of this enormous and transient mass. Many men, like those on the flagship *Olympia* who wired that they were holding Army meetings on their own aboard ship, were already out of reach, reduced to such spiritual resources as they could provide for themselves. Clearly, an officer would have to accompany the troops to the Far East if the "spiritual welfare of all Salvationists serving as soldiers in the Army" was to be attended to properly. Staff–Captain Milsaps was again selected. Major General Wesley Merritt, commanding the Philippine expedition, agreed to allow Milsaps free transportation on the troopship *Newport*, but he was on his own for everything else, including food on board and facilities for his work in the Philippines. Although Milsaps was not a military officer, nor in any legal sense a chaplain, he was regarded as such by himself and The Salvation Army.[67]

Nor was Milsaps a missionary to the Philippines, which he reached in July 1898. His work during the twenty months he stayed in Manila was entirely among American servicemen, almost all of them Salvationists, although he did send to San Francisco for some of the new Chinese *War Cry*, as he apparently hoped to begin some sort of work among the Chinese in Manila. Whatever he was doing, he received little official encouragement; after a full day of walking and asking permission to begin his work, Milsaps and a friendly Salvationist sergeant from Oregon held an impromptu open-air meeting on the old walls of Cavite, singing and testifying to one hundred men as the setting sun gilded the wreck of the Spanish flagship *Reina Christina* in Manila harbor. Milsaps soon opened a "Soldiers' and Sailors' Reading Room" in the city, a place where soldiers could meet, read Salvation Army literature (funds were in short supply), and avail themselves of free stationery and ink. Salvation Army services were held regularly with eight Salvationists who visited Milsaps faithfully. While the Army operated a resting station in New York for convalescent veterans of the Cuban expedition now gloriously concluded, Milsaps remained with his little band of soldiers in Manila, uncertain as to what, if any, the Army's long-range plans were for the Philippines. In fact, the Army had no plans for the Philippines, but that lack did not detract from the official conviction that Milsaps' Philippine expedition had been a complete success, further proof to headquarters that The Salvation Army was an agency through which God was changing the world. Milsaps' return in March 1900 was the occasion for a tremendous rally in San Francisco, one more tribute to the nineteenth century, which had ended so full of promise for The Salvation Army. For had not the Army grown wonderfully? And, even more wonderful, had it not survived, through the good Providence of God, its greatest defection, a secession even more lamentable than Moore's, and passed on to greater things?[68]

CHAPTER III

1896-1914

"How the weakest conquer. . . ."

By the mid-1890s The Salvation Army was a familiar sight on
the streets of America. The open-air ministry remained at the heart of
the Great Salvation War. The Army's formidable arsenal of weapons
could not be wielded with maximum effectiveness inside its own halls,
where the devil hardly dared to venture. The Army's commitment to the
"method of Christ and the Apostles" did not depend on brass bands for
fulfillment—Ensign J.C. Ludgate offered detailed instructions on carrying on a street meeting singlehandedly—but a band was employed
wherever one could be mustered. These were the years that saw the
beginning of the long and still-revered era of the street parade: there
were few commuters hurrying home on the streetcar, few tenement
dwellers strolling the sidewalks to escape the fetid darkness of a window-
less room who did not hear the joyful thump and blare of The Salvation
Army out for the evening march. This remained, according to an official
statement, the Army's first means of attack—"by holding meetings out
of doors, and marching singing through the streets, in harmony with law
and order." When law and order ceased to offer their vain resistance,
and the Army had added its charitable programs of relief and uplift, the
movement became not only familiar, but popular.[1]

The Army continued to offer the world an encouraging set of statistics. Critics who had predicted that it would be a transient fad were
abashed, while soldiers and supporters swelled with pride at repeated
proofs of the blessing of God: every new tally revealed an increase, and
growth was often phenomenal. In 1892 Marshal Ballington Booth, the
national commander, enrolled the fifteen hundredth officer in the

United States; three years later there were two thousand soldiers serving in six hundred corps and twenty-four slum and rescue stations. The precise meaning of these figures, it was true, was somewhat cloudy to all but the most sanguine view. There was, for instance, no easy way to determine how many people were reached by the Army's ministry, nor in what way they were helped; it is certain that only a small percentage of those rescued by the Army ever joined its ranks or offered financial support to the war. Few corps were supported by the contributions of their own members. Nevertheless there were increases, clearly and unmistakably, in the number of officers and stations, and these facts alone were enough to stimulate the Marshal to fresh outbursts of enthusiasm: in 1895 he ordered a one third increase in every statistic.[2]

The Army still owned little real property; most corps sallied forth to war from rented barracks. The one major exception to this gypsy maneuverability—and a symbol of the Army's new prestige—was the National Headquarters building at 120 West Fourteenth Street, New York City. This "imposing if not . . . beautiful structure" was Ballington's pride and joy. He and his wife had expended every energy to raise the huge sums necessary to secure the lot—$160,000—and to raise the eight-story structure—another $200,000. The Army had not yet developed any systematic means of raising large sums of money. The support of the six thousand Auxiliaries was consumed by the rapidly spreading social work, and the many new corps programs were hard-pressed to find the pennies and nickels necessary to survive. For three years the Marshal diverted part or all of the annual "Self-Denial" funds towards the new building. Based on a special voluntary levy raised by the soldiers in addition to their weekly "cartridges," the Self-Denial fund represented a large sacrifice for most Salvationists. The fund ordinarily went toward some special evangelistic project, such as supporting the Army's overseas missionaries. In any case, the new building was finished and opened in June 1895. Complete with crenelated towers, a mock-Gothic battlement frieze, draped with flags, its eight stories glowered over Fourteenth Street like a fortress, its presence periodically reconfirmed for startled pedestrians by the firing of a signal cannon on the roof.[3]

The life of an officer on the field remained hard, full of labor under trying and humiliating circumstances. The soldiers in the corps were too few and too poor to support the work financially, so that officers were reduced to begging in one form or another to keep the doors open. The officers had no claim on the Army even for their penurious allowances:

they could draw their salaries out of the meager collections only after all other outstanding debts were paid. Many officers lived without complaint in grinding poverty: when Emma Westbrook and two cadets opened a corps in Haverstraw, New York, the three carried all they owned in a single peach basket. And when young Adam Gifford's infant son died, Gifford had to dress and bury the child himself, in a donated grave. In addition to the poverty they endured, officers were circumscribed by a web of regulations that controlled every part of their lives, including whom they could marry (another officer) and when (with permission, granted only after the couple had endured a long period of separation and reflection.) These valiants, many of whom were barely literate, threw themselves with high hearts into the struggle after a brief exposure to the rigors of a "training garrison," which consisted almost entirely of scrubbing the floors, memorizing selected passages from the Bible, and selling *The War Cry*. From dawn—the cadets in New York were awakened by a slide trombone at 6:30 A.M.—until the gaslights were turned down late at night, the emphasis was on "practical training in field service." Nothing, not the zeal of youth nor the new hope of the redeemed, prepared these warriors for the months and years of heartbreak and lonely toil that awaited them as officers. Many fell by the wayside. Many did not, and it is to those long-forgotten captains and ensigns and adjutants who gave up their obscure lives, which is all they had to give, in the service of Christ and His Kingdom that history shall give credit for all that The Salvation Army was enabled to accomplish for its Lord. Modern-day Salvationists look on these pioneers gratefully, as they stare out in formal piety from faded photographs. From their lips ascended the clouds of prayers, from their eyes flowed the ocean of tears, from which the Army drew its strength for the Great Salvation War.[4]

By 1896 the Army had reached the point at which its growth no longer depended exclusively on national headquarters. The Army was no longer a tender seedling requiring constant careful attention from New York or London; its roots had gone deep into American soil, its branches grew daily stronger. Leadership was important in 1896, but it was no longer so nearly indispensable as it had been in 1884, when the defection of Major Moore had almost destroyed the Army. These changed conditions were the background against which the next—and happily, the last —major crisis in the leadership of The Salvation Army in the United States took place: the resignation of Marshal and Mrs Ballington Booth as national commanders in January, 1896.

The news came as a complete surprise to the Salvationists in the American field. The commander and his wife, Maud Charlesworth Booth (she often added "Ballington" to her last name), seemed to be highly successful leaders: they were certainly well-liked. Both were officers of exceptional ability, whose administration was marked by advances that the rank-and-file were eager to attribute to their leadership: the reconciliation of Colonel Holz and most of the remnant of the Moore rebels; the construction of the new national headquarters on Fourteenth Street; the rejuvenation of the Auxiliaries, who formed the first stage of the massive public support upon which the Army's social programs would inevitably depend; and the origin, by Maud, of a range of activities designed to convert the convict and to help him into an honest and useful life when he was released. The Booths were powerful public speakers who could electrify large crowds, holding a jammed auditorium almost motionless for an hour, or alternatively convulsing it with laughter, tears and applause. They were the first of the Army's national leaders to be well received outside the ranks. It was as a speaker to ladies of fashion that Maud became fashionable herself, while Ballington edified Chautauqua audiences and charmed the dowager saints of Ocean Grove, New Jersey, on a regular basis.[5]

As effective in print as on the platform, the Booths were prolific writers. In addition to the much-treasured *Soldier's Manual* and several jointly authored books, manifestos, articles, and songs (including "We Shall Win America" and "The cross is not greater than His Grace," which is still sung often in the Army), each wrote weekly columns for *The War Cry.* Hers was winningly entitled "Sunbeams from Mother's Office," and contained helpful and practical hints for her "precious and faithful" women officers; his column was likewise practical: a sermon outline offered to help the hard-pressed officer over at least one of the week's obstacles. Nor did these writers confine themselves to print: both were indefatigable correspondents. Maud wrote regularly, personally, to every woman officer in the country, at the same time that reams of friendly and encouraging letters went to officers over Ballington's florid signature.[6]

Ballington and Maud were clearly an engaging pair. Devoted to the Army's evangelical mission—Ballington once described himself as one "who daily yearns for the Salvation of the worst of our great cities"— both were dramatic and whimsical, which further endeared them to Salvationists, who took it as evidence that their courageous leaders were not concerned for their own reputations. Ballington spent weeks during the winter of 1890–1891 flitting about New York in disguise, collecting impressions for a series of lurid articles he produced for the *Herald,* by which he privately hoped to stimulate contributions to the Army's new social relief program. He also did eccentric things with the long-suffering National Staff Band, which trailed after him on his speaking tours. The band must have dreaded the Marshal's semi-annual expeditions to Ocean Grove: he ordered them out of the train to play on the platform at every stop down the North Jersey Shore route. Although a spellbinder as a speaker, Ballington was a fidgeter on the platform and often preferred more active forms of warfare, like parades (day and night—with torches) mass rallies, and "All-Night for Jesus" meetings. Maud was equally colorful, dividing her copious energies between melting the hearts of the rich with her tales of the life of a slum sister and riding five hundred miles in the cab of a locomotive, gathering material for a special Army ministry she proposed to launch among railroad engineers and firemen (an occupation she felt had been too long neglected). Yet all was not well with the Marshal and Mrs Booth.[7]

The difficulties that overtook them in 1896 sprang from several sources. Minor problems included Ballington's reservations about the official rejection by the Army of sacramental observances, and his inclination to dwell in his mind on the benefits that ordination would bring to Army officers. A few officers were also uneasy about sacraments: Colonel J.J. Keppel, who resigned in 1898, called the Army's position "shifty and unexplainable." Some of Ballington's prestigious clerical friends were still detectably condescending toward the Army on these points.[8]

There were other, more profound problems. If the ancient Greeks were right, tragedies are not accidental, but inevitable: there are situations in life which, given the conditions, cannot but turn out badly, regardless of the character and motives of the principals. Sophocles' *Antigone* is a tragedy in the classical sense: the Salvation Army crisis of 1896 is another. A family quarrel, patriotism, and the high-minded stubbornness that is characteristic of power struggles within religious institutions were joined in an unhappy mixture. The results were predictably disastrous.

General Booth promoted his remarkable children to positions of authority within the Army, and decorated them with special princely ranks —Ballington, for instance, was the "Marshal"—but his motives for doing so were not merely dynastic. The General was a visionary, convinced that God had given him a large part to play in the redemption of the world. With the zealot's sense of urgency, he had little time when selecting officers for high command to gratify the ambitions of the headquarters staff, nor to concern himself with their merely human feelings. He turned naturally to his children: they were an exceptional brood, energetic and clever; they knew his mind. They had been raised in the hothouse spiritual environment of Catherine's household, and had absorbed the Army from infancy. They were loyal to him as General and father, in that order, and could be counted on. Booth relied especially on his oldest son Bramwell, whom he elevated to a position in the Army second only to his own. The thought that his other children, no less zealous and full of ideas than Bramwell, might resent their brother's very real eminence over them does not seem to have occurred to the General.

The seeds of discord thus sown among these high-strung siblings were nurtured with every year, as Bramwell's ascendancy over the others became military and absolute. The General spent more and more time traveling over the world, surveying his vast spiritual domain, and inspiring the troops with his presence; during his long absences from London he left the detailed administration of the Army in Bramwell's loyal and capable hands. This was especially true after 1890, the year that Catherine Booth died of cancer, for which the medicine of the day could offer neither cure nor relief, while William watched in helpless desperation. His grief at her death was sovereign. He never fully recovered from the loss of the one who was the daystar of his life. Booth plunged into an ever more hectic and unrelenting round of tours and meetings, while the Chief's domination of the organizational structure of The Salvation Army became perfect.

Upon no one did these developments press with more galling constancy than upon Ballington Booth. As the triumphant years in America lengthened, the Marshal became suspicious, then convinced, that his elder brother was not prepared to give him the proper credit—or, as it turned out, any credit—for the wonderful progress of the Army in the United States. Little of an encouraging nature came from the General, while the London headquarters seemed to display an alarming lack of knowledge of the United States and the triumphs of the Army here. By 1894, Ballington had come to regard the increasing isolation between New York and London as the one cloud upon his otherwise golden horizon. He arranged a gala visit to the United States for his father, which would serve a double purpose: the General would see how splendidly the war was going in America, and the two men could reestablish the properly warm relationship beyond the interference of Bramwell, whom Ballington regarded in an uncharitable light.[9]

These hopes proved vain: General Booth's Jubilee Tour of September 1894 to February 1895, was a disaster for Ballington and his wife. In public, all went well: the General was lionized, and his trip across the country was a triumphal progress accompanied by the usual thunders of tambourines, volleys, and hallelujahs. Booth was a captivating speaker, but he never played up to a crowd: he was always the General addressing his troops, no matter who the audience was; for his final series of meetings in Carnegie Hall he had a sign of his own design hung from the pulpit, which warned people not to leave while he was speaking. The crowd loved him the more for it, half-convinced that his military gruffness was an act. Privately, in small groups of officers, things were far different. The General was morose and difficult to please, a fussy, faddish eater who suffered from chronic indigestion. Booth was a difficult guest. More importantly to some, he seemed to have developed an aversion to the "Americanization" of the Army in general and to Ballington in particular, which the latter was unable to charm away. The General was not reconciled to that legacy of the Moore secession, the eagle-topped version of the Army crest, used only in the United States. He disliked the use of the American flag beside the Army colors in street parades—a tactic Ballington himself had introduced shortly after his arrival in 1887, in order to offset the charges being hurled by the still-active Moore army that the loyalists were British toadies. The General looked upon The Salvation Army as a worldwide, organic unity, above mere national boundaries; he wrote to his daughter Emma that he was "disgusted" by "all the 'Yankee Doodleism' " he found in the American branch of the Army.[10]

Ballington, Maud, and the General had several private conferences, but these exchanges did not justify the younger man's high hopes for them. Nothing was settled. The General was convinced that Ballington had lost the vision of the worldwide Army and had become too entrenched in the affections of the American people. He regarded it as somehow sinister that his son had become an American citizen, even though the General must have known that Ballington could not hold title to Army property otherwise. The General professed to believe that his childrens' success in securing the support of the Auxiliaries was a base denial of all the Army stood for—a kind of playing-up to the rich. And when he learned how thoroughly Ballington resented the Chief, the General was horrified, denouncing it as practically treason to the flag. He spoke of dividing the American territory into three parts, each joined to a part of Canada, or of mortgaging all Army property in America to finance missions elsewhere. This was not the approach likely to soothe the inflamed sensibilities of the Ballington Booths, fresh from the plaudits of the crowds, which both they and the General knew had been as much for them as for him. Still, all might not have been lost: Ballington was no fool, and was usually blessed in addition with a sensitive and compassionate heart. He might have reflected that the General was very tired, a chronically uncomfortable, grief-stricken old man, his own father, whose blazing passion for the lost souls of the world—a passion which had consumed his entire energy for fifty years—excused a large amount of snappish behavior on the sidelines. The General had always been a crusty old bird, and he counted on his loyal, loving children to forgive him, as no one knew better than Ballington. Better counsel, however, did not prevail on either side, nor was the Spirit allowed to heal the wounded hearts. The General departed in February 1895, unreconciled to the Ballington Booths.[11]

The order relieving them of the American command reached Ballington and Maud on January 6, 1896. It could not have come as a complete surprise: they had had six months, unrelieved by a single word from the General, in which to contemplate the expected blow. Nor were they alone in receiving "farewell" orders: twenty territorial commanders, including all the Booth children (except Bramwell) were being transferred in a general shuffle. Nevertheless, the commanders prepared to resist, first writing to Bramwell (over whose name, unfortunately, the transfer orders had gone out) asking for a reconsideration, then writing again stating that they planned to "quietly retire" rather than accept a transfer out of the United States. Whether this was a bluff, or whether Bramwell used all the patience and tact that common sense suggested to reconcile the Ballingtons, caused speculation that remains unresolved. Three important peace emissaries were sent to New York on behalf of the General: two of them were his children Commandant Herbert Booth and Field–Commissioner Eva Booth, along with Colonel Alexander Nicol. Apparently the presence of his brother and sister chilled all thought of reconciliation in Ballington: he had asked especially when he resigned that no member of the family be sent to speak to him. Meetings were held between these three and the Ballington Booths. What passed between the principals is unknown.[12]

Many leading American officers were saddened and alarmed by these developments, fearing that the public would turn against the Army if it could be made to appear that Ballington's transfer reflected an anti-American attitude on the part of headquarters. By unhappy coincidence, a controversy then raging between Britain and the United States over a border dispute between British Guiana and Venezuela, whose side America championed even at the risk of war, lent credence to these fears. There were public rallies sponsored by the loyal Auxiliaries, anxious to retain the charming Booths. The press gave considerable coverage to these events, which included several suitably dramatic moments: Eva trying to persuade a crowd of confused staff officers to remain loyal to her father, and again at her first public appearance, silencing an unruly crowd at the Cooper Union by waving an American flag.[13]

Following these colorful incidents, the debate declined in quality. After the first three weeks of the crisis both sides abandoned all serious effort to convince the other, and each turned its energies toward drawing public opinion to its side. This period of mutual vituperation, which lasted several months, accomplished nothing except to confuse and sadden the ranks of humble Salvationists who regarded their commander, the Chief, and the General as models of piety and zeal. The affair dragged to its inevitable conclusion. Despite the pleas of officers like Gifford, Brengle, and even the Turk, Ballington resigned in the end, regretfully and with many backward glances, and formed a new organization in March, 1896, called the Volunteers of America. It was much like the Army in military style, but with a more democratic form of government. It also provided for sacramental observances and the ordination of its officers. The Volunteers offered a range of social relief programs something like the Army's, but with a special emphasis on the kind of prison ministry so lovingly nurtured by Maud while still in the Army.[14]

Thus ended a tragic episode, which cost The Salvation Army in America its two most popular officers, and which proved nothing. No real principle was resolved. Attempts to make the General appear as a tyrant, willing to sacrifice even his own son to order to maintain his authority, fell down in the face of Ballington's own well-known autocracy, which many subordinate officers had felt. The issue of British control was a false one, and clouded the real elements in the controversy.

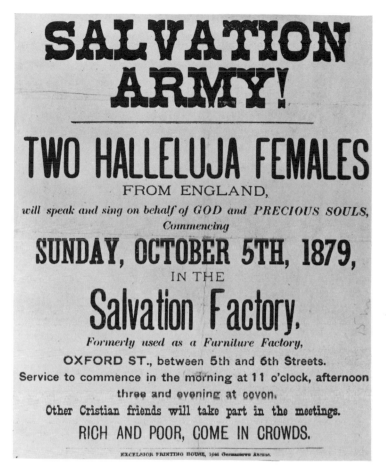

SALVATION ARMY!

TWO HALLELUJA FEMALES

FROM ENGLAND,

will speak and sing on behalf of GOD and PRECIOUS SOULS,
Commencing

SUNDAY, OCTOBER 5TH, 1879,

IN THE

Salvation Factory.

Formerly used as a Furniture Factory,

OXFORD ST., between 5th and 6th Streets.

Service to commence in the morning at 11 o'clock, afternoon
three and evening at seven.

Other Cristian friends will take part in the meetings.

RICH AND POOR, COME IN CROWDS.

EXCELSIOR PRINTING HOUSE, 1646 Germantown Avenue.

Poster advertising the first Philadelphia meeting held by Salvationists Amos, Annie, and Eliza Shirley on October 5, 1879. (Source: The Salvation Army National Information Service.)

Commissioner and Mrs George Scott Railton. In 1880, as a single officer, Railton was sent to the United States as the Army's first missionary. (Source: The Salvation Army Archives and Research Center.)

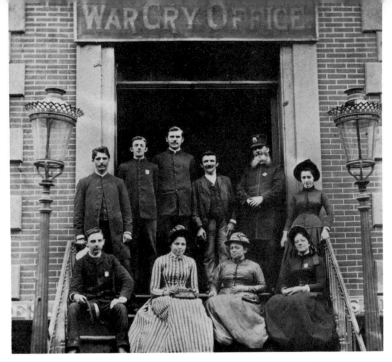

A **War Cry** office (c. 1882) located on State Street, New York City.
Richard Holz is in top row, third from left; "Ashbarrel Jimmy," fourth from
left; and Thomas Moore, fifth from left. (Photo: Joseph Guthorn, New York
City; source: The Salvation Army Archives and Research Center.)

Frederick St George
de Lautour Booth-
Tucker, National
Commander from
1896 – 1904.
(Source: The
Salvation Army
Archives and
Research Center.)

The first national headquarters of The Salvation Army, on Fourteenth Street in New York City (built while Ballington Booth was National Commander) was officially opened in June, 1895. (Source: The Salvation Army Archives and Research Center.)

"Joe the Turk" spending "twenty-five days in jail for Jesus." (Photo: Watson of Portland, Oregon; source: The Museum at the Salvation Army School for Officers' Training, Atlanta, Georgia.)

Lytton Springs Boys' Home, California, at the turn of the century. (Photo: Lothers & Young Studios, San Francisco; source: Property Department, Territorial Headquarters, Western Territory.)

USA Salvationists on board the S.S. Carpathia bound for the 1904 International Congress in London. (Source: The Salvation Army Archives and Research Center.)

General William Booth with his daughter Evangeline, when she was National Commander in 1907. (Photo: Falk Studios, New York City; source: Mr Tom McMahon, Ocean Grove, New Jersey.)

An Industrial Home Wagon, 1908. (Source: Lt.-Colonel Peter J. Hofman, Asbury Park, New Jersey.)

Commandant Eliza Shirley Symmonds, 1908. As a young single girl, in 1879 Eliza Shirley and her family conducted the first unofficial Salvation Army meeting in the United States. (Source: Mrs Everald Knudsen Crowell, granddaughter.)

Mexican Corps No. 2 of El Paso, Texas, was an early corps in which Spanish was spoken. (Source: Property Department, Territorial Headquarters, Western Territory.)

Salvation Army lassies serve coffee and doughnuts to American soldiers in France during World War I. (Source: The Salvation Army National Information Service, New York City.)

Cadet William Maltby leads singing in an open-air meeting held by cadets in 1921. (Source: Colonel William Maltby [R].)

Ballington and his wife had repeatedly maintained before 1896 that The Salvation Army in The United States was an American operation, and that London allowed the American commander great latitude in making decisions. That the General should eventually wish to transfer his son to another post raised no basic question of principle: Ballington's tenure in America was already exceptionally long by 1896; it was inevitable that he would be transferred. The truth is that Ballington had no wish to go, no wish to leave a place where he and his wife had been happy and successful, especially in response to what they unfairly regarded as the whim of the ungrateful old General, who in any case was being manipulated by Bramwell. Ballington had no important disagreement with the Army; he had nothing to say against its system until he was transferred. His love for The Salvation Army was, and remained, genuine; there is evidence in the recollection of elderly retired officers that Ballington occasionally regretted his decision to resign. It is certain that during the crisis of 1896 he consistently urged officers to stand by the General and the flag. The only officer with major administrative responsibilities who followed Ballington out of the ranks at once was Brigadier Edward Fielding, the chief divisional officer in Chicago, a fine officer who resigned in April along with some of the staff. Of the few who trickled out in later years the most noteworthy was Colonel J.J. Keppel, chief divisional officer in Minneapolis, who joined the Volunteers in 1898. Despite the official hostility with which he was regarded by the Army after his resignation, Ballington tried to maintain courteous, if formal, relations with his old comrades. Colonel Richard Holz, for one, never ceased to recall Ballington with gratitude and fondness.[15]

When Ballington first arrived in 1887 to replace the ailing Frank Smith, *The War Cry* declared that "the old chariot, after but a moment's pause for change of drivers, has resumed its rapid journey and is hurriedly rattling along." Now, in 1896, the old chariot suffered more than a "momentary pause:" for a few weeks, work was almost halted. Most officers and soldiers were confused; many wavered as to whom to follow, especially in Chicago. Army leaders averted disaster by following the inspired course of ignoring the schism and pursuing with redoubled zeal their old objective of winning the salvation war. Eva Booth, left in command during the few days before the new commanders could be sent, confined herself to purely religious themes when she addressed Army meetings open to the public, making only an occasional oblique allusion to "this time of sorrows." In places where corps officers resigned, officers from large, loyal corps or from staff positions were rushed to the scene to carry on the work until more permanent replacements could be secured. These officers, too, spoke only of Christ and His redemption, refusing to gratify local reporters with more than general statements about Army discipline and loyalty. Samuel Brengle was typical of many loyal officers during the first tense weeks after Ballington's new movement had been launched. Appointed as general secretary—assistant divisional officer—in the newly reformed Chicago divisional staff, Brengle used his energies almost entirely in speaking and writing on spiritual themes and counseling with wavering officers. His theme was constant throughout the crisis: concentrate on the work God has given the Army —the salvation of the lost. Without ever referring specifically to Ballington, Brengle raised in a hundred ways the question as to how it could matter greatly who the national commander was, or why he refused his orders, when souls were dying all around for want of someone to speak to them. His messages and *War Cry* articles on the theme of single-minded dedication to evangelism were influential in holding many waverers in the ranks. These materials later joined the little shelf of Brengle's red-bound books as *The Soul-Winner's Secret.*

> The soul-winner, then, must once and for all abandon himself to the Lord and to the Lord's work, and having put his hand to the plough must not look back, if he would succeed in his mighty business; and if he continues faithful in this way, "he shall conquer though he die."
>
> He must love his Lord and love his work, and stick to it through all difficulties, perplexities, and discouragements, and not be given to change, for there is no discharge in this war.[16]

The new national commanders were on the scene by April 1: Frederick St George de Lautour Booth-Tucker and his wife Emma—the "Consul"—second daughter of the General. The imperious old Founder was unwilling to see his daughters merely absorbed in marriage: he insisted on the hyphenated name for the three who married and gave the girls rank and authority independent of, and only grudgingly subordinate to, that of their husbands. Frederick Booth-Tucker, the son of a British colonial official in India, was an officer of education, ability, and experience; having spent nine dramatic years as the Army pioneer in India, he came to the American command from London, where he had served since 1894 as the Foreign Secretary, supervising the details of administering the Army's now imperial domain. The new commander tried to be flamboyant, and certainly was zealous; given to thinking in short, intense, and infrequent spurts, he had a particular penchant, almost a mania, for catchy phrases. Essentially a practical man, he had an odd, other-worldly air about him, and lacked Ballington's warmth. He was something of a health faddist, and was never as popular with the public and rank-and-file Salvationists. Yet he was kindhearted, and set a precedent by showing an especial interest in the young cadets. He was much admired by the officers on his staff. Booth-Tucker was greatly assisted in regaining the support of American officers by the new chief secretary, Colonel Edward Higgins, an industrious and generous-spirited officer. The Consul, Emma, was a warm, approachable woman who had taken her role as "mother" of the London training garrison as a kind of divine commission, and continued to regard her new role as national commander in the same maternal way. Far plainer than Maud in appearance and manner, the Consul offered a quiet earnestness and an adaptable intellect among her resources.[17]

The Booth-Tuckers arrived at a critical time in Army history. The defection of Ballington and Maud did not itself endanger the ultimate success of the Army's work, which depended on the hard work and sacrifice of the officers and soldiers; yet the mistaken ideas that gained circulation at the departure of the Booths from headquarters, and resentment against "British autocracy," caused some resignations among these very people so essential to the success of the Army's work, and financial contributions from the general public had dwindled during the confusion. First impressions of the new commanders were thus important. Some waverers stood by the new commanders when it was learned that their infant son, whom they had been forced to leave behind in the care of a servant to recover from a fever, had died while they were on the ocean. The Booth-Tuckers regarded the matter as personal, and won sympathy by their stoic acceptance of the loss. Then, to the relief of American staff officers, both the Booth-Tuckers proved to be competent public speakers. Their first large meeting in Carnegie Hall was a success. The new commanders professed themselves eager to become American citizens, to thunders of applause. They made various other welcome announcements: that they wished to hold out the hand of reconciliation to Ballington and his followers, that the General himself would shortly visit the United States for the same purpose. Personal correspondence indicates that the General continued to hope for a reconciliation through the summer of 1896. There were further encouraging signs from the new commanders: Booth-Tucker's practical-mindedness appealed to hardheaded politicians and businessmen, as Ballington's charm had appealed to socialites. The Army's cause gained prestige when Emma and Booth-Tucker secured the support of Cleveland millionaire Myron T. Herrick, then of Senator Mark Hanna of Ohio, through whom they gained access to the newly-elected President McKinley, a genial, thorough-going Christian who sincerely endorsed the Army.[18]

The Booth-Tuckers were never entirely successful in reconciling the dissidents, nor even of winning the affection of all the loyalists. The Consul's maternal instincts, so appealing to the girls at the London training garrison, impressed some Americans as tiresome condescension. The Booth-Tuckers' eccentricities lost the engaging quality that novelty had bestowed upon them. Resentments against British paternalism, even of the General's nepotism, were voiced in the field, and are preserved in letters and diaries. Yet some of the officers who expressed these feelings were among the hardest working and most willing to sacrifice themselves to the rigors of the war. The Army rallied, with some grumbling, around the new commanders. They embarked at once on national tours, with important results, especially in Chicago—a hotbed of secessionist sentiment—and San Francisco. There were few resignations after 1898. The Army continued to ignore the Volunteers. The Great Salvation War was pushed into new areas; social programs were launched, and at the same time some old difficulties were at last eliminated.[19]

There was no more talk about mortgaging the Army's property in America to finance international projects, nor of dividing the American command jointly with segments of Canada. Moreover, headquarters was willing to make the ultimate concession to strengthen the position of the new commanders and allow the Army to incorporate itself in the United States. The Chief of the Staff must have shuddered when he reflected upon the ease with which his brother, now officially listed as "deserted," could have bankrupted The Salvation Army when he left it in 1896. As an American citizen and the sole trustee of a foreign corporation, Ballington was the outright legal owner of every atom of Army property in the United States, and could have decamped with everything as Moore had done in 1884. Booth-Tucker was instructed to proceed rapidly in the matter. He found the situation "very propitious": The Salvation Army was famous, and could request a special act of incorporation of the New York legislature with some prospect of success. (A corporate charter granted by one state is valid in all states, and the location of national headquarters in Manhattan made it necessary to secure incorporation in the state of New York.) Booth-Tucker privately regarded the legislators with whom he had to deal as a collection of cheats and grafters; still, one takes the world as one finds it, and "even the worst of the boodlers respect The Salvation Army:"

The Army secured the services of a prestigious and influential law firm headed by Benjamin F. Tracy, a distinguished former Secretary of the Navy. The Governor, Theodore Roosevelt, was known to smile upon the Army's militant and aggressive variety of evangelism. On April 28, 1899, The Salvation Army was incorporated in the state of New York under Chapter 468 of the laws of that year. The Salvation Army (the capitalized article became part of the official title) was defined as a "religious and charitable corporation" governed by a Board of Trustees competent to hold and control all the temporalities and property, real and personal, belonging to that corporation, the purposes of which were stated with crusading frankness: "For the spiritual, moral and physical reformation of the working classes; for the reclamation of the vicious, criminal, dissolute and degraded; for visitation among the poor and low and the sick; for the preaching of the Gospel and the dissemination of Christian truth by means of open-air and indoor meetings."[20]

The Army remained a "protest against the conventional methods of the churches," and the salvation war continued to rage unabated. It was curtailed only briefly by the desertion of Ballington, nor was it stimulated by incorporation, of which most soldiers knew nothing more than the brief, glowing accounts in *The War Cry* and cared less. The hallelujah jesters still cavorted in the streets, making captives for Jesus. Major Brengle was released from staff duties and allowed to spend the rest of his career as a preacher and writer of the message of holiness. Major Ludgate produced a new version of his classic instruction for conducting open-air meetings singlehandedly: it was really quite simple; one climbed on a chair, beat a drum, and sang songs from *The War Cry*, prepared to exhort the crowd that would certainly form. The long transition from horse-car to trolley, from gaslight to electricity, offered no new obstacles to parades and street meetings. The Army eagerly adapted every new fad to the great work. After the stereopticon and the phonograph came the bicycle, which became so popular in mobilizing the forces that formal uniform was going into "declension": the commanders had to issue a stern warning to the peddlers that bicycle hats could be worn *only* "when actually bicycling." *The War Cry* still edified

its readers with testimonies like "The Confessions of a Crib-Cracker.
. . . How I Burgled Alderman Beasley's Plate." Indoor meetings were
as fervent as ever: "From the start," read one gloating report, "stiffness
departed and formality was laid on the high shelf." Crusades, revivals
and "sieges" followed one upon another, from the commander's "Century Advance" plan of 1899 to the "Red Crusade," which the Consul
launched in 1903, dressed in a flaming red costume and preaching before
an open coffin—a technique that she was certain "would be calculated
to awaken the careless and make them think of eternity." The General's
third visit to the United States intervened in 1898. The tour was a
coast-to-coast success in every respect save one: the old man met Ballington in Montclair, New Jersey, to effect a reconciliation: his account of
the sad, futile encounter was brief: "We met and prayed and parted"
—forever.[21]

The Booth-Tuckers were essentially practical people, with an eye for
easy solutions. The Consul was a skillful publicist, decisive and clever,
her one ambition to advance the Army. Booth-Tucker was able, despite
his authentic eccentricity, to convey an impression of common sense
ingenuity that men of affairs found reassuring. The commander established rewarding contacts with business and political leaders. At the
same time, the work of scores of slum sisters and rescue officers was
bearing fruit at last: the social wing of the Army was producing a return
in souls harvested, in operating revenue, and in public prestige. Booth-
Tucker sprinkled the social programs with helpful suggestions and directives that strengthened parts of the program. Indeed, the flow of official
minutes on all subjects from headquarters was only briefly interrupted
by the schism of 1896.[22]

There was a major expansion of the salvage operation. Cheap, safe,
and convenient hotels were opened for the needy working woman—
"only women of thoroughly respectable character are received." Some
of the rescue homes were gradually transformed into regulation maternity hospitals, while those that retained the old status were given a
comfortable, homey look and made less institutional for the residents.
The "Penny Ice Philanthropy" reached its peak in 1901, when five tons
of the "precious crystal" were given away in New York City, and the
same amount every day in Chicago through the summer; benefaction
on that scale proved too costly, even with the assistance of the Knicker-
bocker Ice Company, and ice donations on these levels were never
repeated in Chicago. The Army's "Cheap Coal for the Multitudes"

given away or sold for a pittance in bushel baskets was a boon for the poor, but as with the ice ministry the enormous amounts of material that were needed put a strain on the Army's resources: during the peak year of the coal ministry, which bracketed the severe winter of 1903, the Army gave out one thousand tons of coal in each of three frozen cities: New York, Chicago, and Boston. The prison ministry grew and prospered. An outpost opened in San Quentin prison by Oakland Salvationists at the request of a few prisoners who had read *The War Cry* became a full-fledged Salvation Army corps with thirty soldiers in 1897. Booth-Tucker, Emma, and Brengle all visited the corps; the former was so touched by a bouquet of flowers given to him by the convicts that he dried the flowers and kept them. The Consul was strongly drawn to prison work as well, and became famous for her interest in it. She was riding one day in a streetcar when a policeman handcuffed to a prisoner got on. In a flash Emma was at the captive's side, only to learn to her delight that he had recognized her, and had hoped she would speak to him. Adjutant McFee and Brigadier Keppel opened a small but innovative hostel for discharged prisoners in San Ramon, California, in 1900.[23]

The Army enjoyed other major advances as the nineteenth century gave way to the twentieth. After twenty years, the Army was acquiring a second generation. Just as veterans' sleeve stripes (one for each five years in the fight) became necessary with the passing years, so too did organized activities for young people. At first children were simply ignored, partly on the strength of the still-current Victorian theory that children were tiny adults and could sit through adult programs, and partly because the ferocious evangelism of the pioneers left little time and energy to devise extra activities to interest children. The pioneers sometimes turned in reports from the "Little Forts," testimonies of the "real saved little Soldiers," but the emphasis in these reports was on how similar to adults the children were in their courage and zeal. Even this amount of interest apparently fluctuated: in 1887 *The War Cry* lamented that interest in the children of the corps had waned. Occasionally, young people more eager than most would ask for religious services that they could understand and enjoy: they were rebuffed, kindly but firmly. Yet young people were drawn to the Army by its life and color. When these young converts were joined by the increasing numbers of soldiers' children who began to attend the corps, the lack of programs for young people became too obvious to overlook.[24]

In 1891 headquarters ordered that each corps conduct two meetings for young people per week, on Sunday afternoons and Wednesday evenings. These were called "company meetings" and were instructional in nature, to prepare the children in doctrine, singing, and the Army's methods of warfare. After a period of preparation, the young people signed an affirmation of the Army's eleven doctrines and joined the ranks as "junior soldiers." In 1894 the "Band of Love" was added, to provide for children drawn to the Army from non-Salvationist families. The Band was designed to be a magnet for erring youth: it offered useful instruction in things that appealed to the children of the nineties, like "overhead scarf drills" and the proper use of the double hoop, while it exacted from the little trainees a pledge of good living, which included a promise to be kind to animals. Some of the children became quite zealous, tottering down the street laden with buckets of water for overheated draught horses, endangering life and limb to climb trees in order to rescue stranded kittens, orphaned birds, and the occasional escaped canary.

These programs were a good beginning, but in many places youth work languished for lack of the interested and qualified adult leadership upon which headquarters vainly insisted. In 1898 headquarters announced that "the irregularity of the past must be improved upon," and ordered each division to appoint a "Junior Soldier Staff Secretary" to oversee the work of the "junior corps" in that division. In addition, there was to be a special non-commissioned officer in each corps, called the "Young People's Sergeant–Major" (YPSM), to take charge of the youthful recruits. The pattern of two youth meetings per week was continued, as the minimum standard. Those among the young soldiers who felt inspired to offer themselves as officers in the Army were expected to enroll for further instruction as "Corps Cadets." The local sergeants placed in charge of these programs often lacked experience—when Mrs Helen Hoffman asked for help in preparing herself to serve as a YPSM in the late 1890s, she was told that "God will help: Pray to Him!"— but zeal and consistency seemed at last to have overcome other difficulties. By the turn of the century, Army youth work was well established: *The War Cry* reported 396 regularly organized junior corps in June 1899.[25]

The Army extended its operations to include children other than those who came to its meetings. The first home for orphans—"these little atoms of human wreckage"—was opened on Washington's Birthday, 1897, in Fordham, a suburb of New York City, but was soon moved to Rutherford, New Jersey. The opening date suggested the name, the Cherry Tree Home, an inspiration conveyed to the Consul by the young wife of President Cleveland. The home was small—thirty small, single bedrooms—but at that it was a burden on badly strained Army finance because it produced no income whatsoever. From all accounts it was a cheery place, despite the haphazard manner in which it, like the rescue homes, was financed, mostly by donations in kind. In the case of Cherry Tree, the staff could fall back on local ladies who invited the children to home-cooked suppers, and on the profits from the desultory sale of the Army's own brand of tea. Cherry Tree was eventually eclipsed by the Army's other orphanage, at Lytton Springs, California. The western home became a regular community, with its own classroom (decorated with encouraging mottos like "Try Again!"), dairy, chicken farm, and a brass band. Nor are the annals of the children's work without their true heroism. The Army had of course operated several small day-care centers since the beginning of the slum work in the eighties. In October 1900, there was a fire in the Salvation Army Children's Shelter in Cincinnati. The two officer-matrons, Staff–Captain Selma Erickson and Captain Bertha Anderson, gave up their lives in a vain attempt to rescue their five little charges. All seven were buried together in a common grave, over which the city government has maintained an Army flag for eighty years.[26]

Not everything in the Army showed change or improvement during those years. There were still a few arrests, from which not even the commander was exempt. In fact, Booth-Tucker was arrested twice, a distinction no other national commander earned even once. In 1896 he was arrested for skulking about New York at night disguised in his "slum toggery"; although this was practically the traditional Army way to learn more about slum conditions, it was technically against the law. In 1897 he was hauled into court for disturbing the peace—and convicted: a hallelujah "All-Night for Jesus" at national headquarters had been heard "all over the Ninth Ward," banishing sleep and the devil together. There were other problems. A chronic shortage of officers was the major obstacle to effective expansion in the late 1890s; the Corps Cadet Brigade, which numbered five hundred by 1900, was designed to prepare youth to fill this need in the future. Attrition among officers varied, but it may have been high. Some of those who remained were not entirely consumed with zeal: there were officers who groused about filling in statistical forms for headquarters, and others who relished the rumors about impending transfers and promotions that filled the air every few months.[27]

Finance remained a serious problem. In 1899 the Army's main sources of income were still collections taken at every meeting, the "donations of friends," and profits from the sale of *The War Cry*, books, and uniforms. Collections were often dismal, even at large meetings: a collection among three hundred Salvationists at San Francisco No. 1 in November, 1897, yielded an even five dollars. Various innovations were introduced to supplement these meager resources. Ballington and Maud Booth's Auxiliaries had been one such attempt, and the Auxiliaries were maintained by subsequent national commanders, although the membership fee was reduced to five dollars per year in order to maintain the number of members at a high level. (Many Auxiliaries had supported Ballington during the secession.) Booth-Tucker tried "Mercy Boxes," which sympathizers could take into their homes to receive a weekly donation of a penny. The "Merchant's League Box" was designed to stand invitingly on a store counter. The rich were approached directly with requests for outright gifts, loans, or bequests. Local corps often took up these ideas for their own use: the enterprising Adjutant Maltby in Meadville, Pennsylvania, launched his own "Helpers' League" in 1900.[28]

The national staff was determined to secure a balance of income against expense while maintaining the expansion of the salvation war at its current gratifying rate. There were two ways the budget could be balanced: by raising income in every category, or by requiring that the social programs, like the corps work, become self-supporting. Eventually both of these developments occurred, but the immediate result of the campaign to balance Army accounts was the farm colony scheme, which had various other things to commend it as well. The purpose of the farm colony was to provide a refuge in the country for the worthy poor of the cities, a place to which entire families could repair together, the father learning an honest, useful, and healthful trade as a farm worker while mother and the children fed chickens, chopped kindling, and basked in the pleasures of country life. The farm colony was, it will be remembered, a central part of General Booth's "Darkest England" scheme, where men and families were to be trained for life in an "oversea colony." The farm colonies, in a modified form, became Booth-Tucker's pet project.[29]

The Salvation Army shared the idea, almost universal among late nineteenth century reformers, that there was a vital distinction between the "worthy" and "unworthy" poor: the former were the decent and willing who were unable to find honest employment, or the truly help-less, like severe invalids and children; the "unworthy poor" were the vicious and lazy, the prodigals, idlers, and tramps who sought to main-tain themselves by crime, begging, or as inert recipients of charity. This is not to suggest that the Army refused help to anyone, or that officers believed that anyone who wanted work could find it: rather, the Army would offer work to all who came for relief; if there were no other work, the Army would manufacture jobs in its own shops and woodyards. Thus even those too poor to pay the few cents that the Army asked for its ministrations would be spared the humiliation of "pauperization." When the editor of *The War Cry* went in disguise to the lighthouse in New York, he pretended not to have the seven cents that was asked of him for food and lodging: he was lectured on the "evils of indiscriminate charity" and told he could have a meal and stay overnight only if he agreed to saw wood in the morning. The farm colonies were designed to provide more systematic relief for "worthy" poor men and their families.[30]

The General and many leading officers—the Booth-Tuckers emphati-cally among them—believed that city life was inherently unnatural and corrupting. This was a popular notion in the late nineteenth century; part of the appeal of Populism and William Jennings Bryan stemmed from distrust of city life. That this essentially romantic notion should have lingered so long in the minds of officers otherwise so practical will not seem so strange when one reflects on the fact that Salvationists found little to quarrel with in the political and economic systems of the countries in which they served. They believed individual salvation was the sovereign cure for all social evils. These officers did not confront the fact that urban life on a massive scale was here to stay: to them no merely human system was here to stay. If it were easier for a man to be saved outside of the crowded city with its evil influences, then removing him from the city, rejuvenating him in the country, and capturing him for Jesus would hasten the day when cities and evil influences would cease altogether. The goal was escape and salvation, not reform. For the purpose of redemption, the country offered many advantages: families could be rescued together, and the problems of mass unemployment and urban congestion solved at a stroke. In addition, the colonies would solve all the Army's financial problems practically overnight: the farms would be self-supporting from the first, and would soon generate surplus income.[31]

Booth-Tucker was fond of pithy sayings of his own invention; his favorite motto summarized the colony scheme: "The Landless Man to the Manless Land." Both he and the Consul became increasingly enamored of the idea, until by 1903 they were devoting most of their time to the farm colony enterprise. The commanders became rustic, knowledgeable about crop yields and irrigation, possessed of reams of production statistics that they unloaded on dazed Army audiences. Booth-Tucker liked to think of himself as "The Man Behind the Plow," as a *War Cry* cover portrayed him—in full uniform—in 1900. This enthusiasm for redemption through agriculture was so great that the Army toyed briefly with the idea of opening tiny farms on downtown vacant lots, to provide work and food for those among the worthy poor who did not seek a complete escape from city life. This idea was originally put forth by Mayor Hazen S. "Potato Patch" Pingree of Detroit, who turned the patches over to the Army in 1897 when destiny called him to the governor's office. This project, and others to "Pingreeize" Chicago and the Bronx, were on a modest scale compared to the farm colonies proper, which were launched with considerable fanfare at a huge meeting in Carnegie Hall in December 1897.[32]

There were three colonies: Fort Herrick, on land twenty miles from Cleveland given by the banker-politician for whom it was named; Fort Amity, in eastern Colorado; and Fort Romie, near Monterey Bay in California. Administered by the "National Colonization Department" under Colonel Thomas Holland, who also served as manager at Amity, the three farms together housed about five hundred persons on three thousand acres at the height of their moderate and short-lived prosperity. Headquarters was convinced that the farms would be a "practical, commonsense-business-like venture," and early developments encouraged the wildest optimism. The Army received "thousands of applications" at the special farm colony recruitment offices it opened in several large cities. No one was turned away because of "religion, caste, or sex or nationality." There were one thousand applicants in New York City alone, almost five thousand from Chicago. Many prominent persons, including the governors of New York, Colorado, and Michigan and the Mayors of Boston, Denver, and San Francisco publicly endorsed the scheme. The Sixth Annual National Irrigation Congress in Lincoln, Nebraska, called it a "grand, noble and patriotic work." At the height of the crusade in 1904, Senator Hanna agreed to Booth-Tucker's request to prepare a bill to launch farm colonies on a federal scale; after Hanna's untimely death, the bill (S.5126) was introduced into the Senate by Senator George Hoar of Massachusetts. Unfortunately, public enthusiasm failed to take into account the practical problems that beset the colonies from the outset and eventually caused the Army to abandon them.[33]

Amity was located on 1,830 acres in the well-watered Arkansas river valley in eastern Colorado, on the main line of the Santa Fe railroad. Most of the sixty original colonists were from Chicago, unemployed and so poor the Army had to pay their fare to the site and give them something to eat on the train, but they were brave and willing enough. The Army provided ten acres and supplies, the cost of which the colonists were to repay. A range of crops were planted and harvested, and the population swelled to 450. A town with several stores, a post office, Salvation Army corps, and depot grew up. In 1902 the Cherry Tree home was transferred from New Jersey to a new stone structure at Amity, the finest building in the county. The rigors of the first years passed. Amity became comfortable, almost restful. Major Stillwell, the California pioneer, was sent there to recover his strength after he had collapsed from overwork. Yet there were snakes in Eden: the orphanage could not operate without medical and school facilities nearby, and there were few employment or adoption prospects for children so isolated. In 1905 the orphans returned to New Jersey and the stone building became a tuberculosis sanitarium, which failed almost at once. There were grave financial difficulties: the Army confidently advanced large sums on the hope of a return, and these sums it had to borrow at the then-ruinous rate of six percent. Worst of all, the river backed up and alkali seepage poisoned the soil. The colony went into an irreversible decline, and was sold at a loss in 1909.[34]

Booth-Tucker opened Fort Herrick with a brass band and a mass rally in September, 1898, but it was a failure from the start. The 288 acres near Cleveland sold to the Army by Herrick at a bargain rate were surrounded by land that was far too valuable for the Army to purchase: expansion of the colony was therefore impossible, and the original farm was too small to support the eight or nine impoverished families who had moved there. The Army attempted to raise livestock that required a small space, like pigeons, bees, chickens, and rabbits. Unhappily, these activities required experienced workers, which the colony lacked; a good part of the breeder stock simply flew away. When Colonel Holz visited the colony in March 1899, he discovered a "good deal of grumbling and dissatisfaction" among the few colonists, occasioned no doubt by the fact that all the houses had been shoddily built on low ground and had three inches of water in them. He suggested starting all over with new houses, new families, and a new manager. Instead the Army converted the colony into an "Inebriates' Home" under the redoubtable Major McFee, for drunkards rescued by the Army in Cleveland. This likewise proved too costly to operate, and Fort Herrick became a "fresh air camp" for slum children in 1909.[35]

The beginnings in California were no less auspicious, and no less certainly doomed, at least as a means of redeeming the poor. Enthusiasm for the project was especially high in the West, and many prominent San Franciscans supported the Army's idea of a colony. Fort Romie contained 520 acres near Soledad, about 150 miles south of San Francisco. Purchased with the help of the San Francisco Chamber of Commerce in 1898, Romie was actually the first piece of property acquired by the Army for a colony. It was to form "the first link forged in the chain of colonies" which were "to girdle our continent and constitute our Salvation Army Workingman's Paradise." The eighteen indigent families selected from among the Bay Area "worthy poor" departed from Oakland in two wagons decorated with banners: "Ho for the Salvation Army Colony!" Difficulties awaited. The land was rich and loamy, but required irrigation even in the best of times—which the next three years, alas, were not: a drought brought "utter failure" to the colony. The Army was undaunted. In 1901 a steam pump was installed to carry water from the Salinas River to the colony, which was redivided into 20-acre tracts and offered to local families at one hundred dollars per acre on a twenty-year mortgage, with encouraging terms for stock and supplies. Many families, "practically destitute" but with some farming experience, hurried forth to seize upon this opportunity. The little farms prospered, but officers' delight was short-lived: the colonists made so much money on their farms that they all paid off their mortgages by 1905, and the colony ceased to exist. The Army made $12,000 net profit and many grateful friends in Romie, but Romie had failed as an experiment in uplifting the urban poor through farming.[36]

The Army's farm colonies failed, not out of any lack of zeal for the project, nor because the distinction between "worthy" and "idle" poor was in later years to be subjected to criticism, nor even because the belief in the salutary effects of country living was romantic nonsense. The colonies failed because successful farming required skill and experience that the unemployed urban poor, worthy or not, did not possess. The colonies did nothing to relieve the causes of urban poverty, nor did they assist its worst victims. Critics of the colony scheme stated that none of the Army's colonists had ever really been desperate, their families had not been in danger of breaking apart, and none of them had been the objects of charity when the project began. These facts were true; in fact, five of the twenty-eight colonists at Romie were former Salvation Army officers who had resigned because of exhaustion or ill-health. The problems of city poverty had to be solved in the city, or not at all. Even had a sufficient number of poor families come forward endowed with enough agricultural skill to make a farm colony work, the Army lacked the financial resources to acquire large enough tracts of land to provide for more than a handful of the city poor as yeomen farmers—nor could the local agricultural markets support them.[37]

Frederick Booth-Tucker's interest in farm colonies evaporated before their failure to achieve their purpose was finally revealed. The Consul was returning from an inspection trip to Amity when she was killed in a train wreck on October 28, 1903, at Dean Lake, Missouri. She was the only fatality. The commander was unconsolable, barely able to struggle through the several mass memorial meetings and the enormous public funeral that Army tradition demanded. The latter, held at national headquarters in New York, was a memorable affair, the hall closely packed, the tight air hung with solemn band tunes, the open coffin at the foot of the podium, from which Booth-Tucker, most memorable of all, sang his own truly noble testimony:

> Thou knowest all things, my heart Thou canst read;
> Master, Thou knowest I love Thee indeed.
> Ask what Thou wilt my devotion to test,
> I will surrender the dearest and best.

Salvationist families treasured the little funeral programs, trimmed in mournful purple, for years. And in London the General, his grief-stricken heart plunged lower still by the loss of his beloved daughter, experienced a new—and lasting—wave of affection for the country that was to be her home forever: "Indeed, as the Comrade of the Commander, she won a place for herself and The Army in the confidence and appreciation of all that was noblest and best in that great nation."[38]

Exhausted by grief and by the round of meetings and tours into which he plunged in vain to escape from grief, harried by six young children, distraught and dispirited, Frederick Booth-Tucker continued as national commander only a few months longer. In August 1904 *The War Cry* announced his farewell, and in November he left. To replace him, the General selected his fourth daughter, Eva. Unknowingly, his choice bestowed upon The Salvation Army in the United States its most colorful, controversial, and exciting commander, and certainly its most durable one. Christened Eveline and called Eva by her father, a dramatic impulse caused her to select a more euphonious name, and it was as Evangeline Cory Booth that she reigned—no other word will do—over the American Army for an even thirty years.[39]

That the General had succumbed to a certain inclination to nepotism could, by 1904, no longer be denied. Some American officers privately registered their dismay at what seemed to be an almost dynastic succession at national headquarters. Miss Booth was English, thirty-nine years of age, and unmarried, known in this country only from her brief and not altogether successful role in the Ballington schism. Yet Eva had enjoyed considerable experience before coming to America to command: harassed and battered in the Army's pioneer combat days in Britain, she had superintended the training garrison in London; then, as the "Field Commissioner," all of Army work in London for four years; and from 1896 to 1904 she had been national commander in Canada. Her Canadian command had been punctuated by three dramatic trips to the Klondike, whither the Canadian branch of the Army had sent an advance guard to rescue some of the thousands of men who were drawn by the gold rush and were otherwise certain to fall into the clutches of the loose women and publicans who had likewise flocked to the mining camps.

Evangeline Booth proved to be an exceptionally complicated woman. Raised as a kind of junior princess in her father's hectic household court, she was allowed—even encouraged—to abandon herself to her strong, inherited dramatic impulses. The young woman was placed in positions of authority over thousands, in which she was responsible to no one save God and her father (who usually left her to the Former). Thus it is natural that at age thirty-nine Evangeline was imperious and condescending. She was also vain of her appearance, which in fact was pleasantly unexceptional, impetuous, given to emotional flourishes, and something of a poseur. Eva arranged to be surrounded by a staff of officers who were little more than aides and servants. Chief of these was her private secretary, Major Richard Griffiths, a discreet bachelor who came with her from Canada and spent his life in her personal service. She was at the same time a compassionate soul, thoughtful, full of little kindnesses, genuinely sympathetic with the poor and lonely in their sufferings, and a dedicated, fearless evangelical. A clever administrator, well-informed, decisive, with a good eye for details, she gave her subordinates considerable latitude. Above all else, Evangeline was an exceptionally effective public speaker, who could hold large audiences spellbound for hours. Nor did her abilities as a publicist end on the platform: she was particularly adept at charming large fortunes for the Army out of rich men. Into the bargain she played the harp well, and wrote creditable music. Take her for what she was in fact and in fancy, Eva Booth was a phenomenon of historic proportions.

The commission issued to Eveline Cory Booth on November 9, 1904, by the General gave her the rank of commissioner and the title of Commander. Her authority, subject only to his interposition, was absolute—"subject nevertheless at all times to my direction countermand qualification and veto absolute command and control over all Officers and Soldiers in the Salvation Army in the said United States of America. . . ." Her first official meeting as Commander took place at Carnegie Hall on December 6. The faithful and curious alike jammed the hall, and were suitably transfixed by the latest Booth, bracketed by flags, flowers, and a brass band, and buoyed up by volleys and hallelujahs. Settled into her office, she made her appointment personal at once by writing a note to every staff-rank officer in the United States. Eva did well to lay a firm foundation for her administration, although her first few months were necessarily tentative, partly because her appointment coincided with a major change in the administrative structure of the Army. Eva's predecessors had been married men, and shared major responsibilities with their wives. The General felt that Eva, too, required a partner in command, albeit a junior one. The United States was divided administratively at Chicago, and a deputy commander was appointed whose primary responsibility was to serve as territorial commander of the West. The new commissioner, George Kilbey, was directly responsible to the Commander, but there was considerable uncertainty among Salvationists as to his authority to make important decisions in his new territory, decisions which traditionally had been within the disposition of national headquarters.[40]

The public, of course, did not share the Army's concern with these matters. In many ways, in fact, the Army that Eva inherited had ceased to be controversial at all. The press had been friendly since the late 1890s, and Army leaders moved comfortably in the highest circles almost as a matter of course. When the General paid his fourth visit to the United States in 1902–1903 to inspect the still-promising farm colonies, he opened the US Senate in prayer, lunched with President Roosevelt, and spent a memorable afternoon at the Arlington Hotel with Senators Hanna and Hoar, the Vice President, and the Speaker of the House. Who could doubt, an officer asked the delegates to the Army's first Western Territorial Congress in 1906, that God had "blessed and prospered" the Army in its "effort to help the weak. No! It is no longer an experiment." The public's acceptance was largely due to the Army's social program, which expanded steadily, its way smoothed by a generous public and accommodating civic officials. The Army even worked out an uneasy peace with grafters and ward-heelers: one of Chicago's slum posts was on South Clark Street, right across the street from Alderman McKenna's "Hinky-Dink Saloon."[41]

The "workingman's hotels" prospered and spread. When Brigadier Edward J. Parker was appointed National Metropole and Relief Secretary in October 1903, little had been accomplished. Parker knew only that "the Army was forging ahead" with this work, providing decent lodging at low rates for underpaid urban workers and the temporarily unemployed. In five years there were over seventy such hotels, and four for women, with nearly eighty-seven hundred beds. The capstone in this arch was the new Boston People's Palace, a five-story grey brick building opened in 1906 with almost three hundred single rooms, a swimming pool, labor bureau, library,—and on the ground floor a soon-to-be famous Army corps. Social work spread into the Scandinavian branch of the Army when the Scandinavian Sailors' Home was opened in Brooklyn in 1902; by 1905 it was flourishing, flanked by Brooklyn No.6 corps in a converted theatre. Labor bureaus were set up in several headquarters as part of the now obligatory "relief departments" that formed a regular activity at every divisional and territorial office. The "rescue homes for fallen women," now supplemented by maternity services, continued to do beneficent work, made more so by the Army's continued insistence that the refuges be small, comfortable, "homey." Even the sharpest critics of the Army social program called the rescue homes the most effective of their kind in the country, so that public support was forthcoming for an innovation: in 1914 the Army opened a small general hospital in Covington, Kentucky, a suburb of Cincinnati, in order to offer the local population a service and to train nurses for the thirty-one Army rescue homes. The credit for the success of the rescue work went to the indefatigable matrons; the day-to-day operation of a rescue home was backbreaking and heartbreaking at the same time. There were many touching stories tucked away in the admission files of these rescue homes. In Chicago in 1910 a young woman who had somehow been duped by a department store employment agency into becoming a prostitute fled from her madam as the two strolled past an Army street service, threw herself into the ring of Salvationists, and implored their protection. She was taken up lovingly and borne away, but died later under medical treatment.[42]

Perhaps the most engaging aspect of the Army's expanded relief work in the years before the first world war was its ministry to children. The days were now long past when a young person had to beg to be allowed to become a convert. Officers now threw themselves into the work of reaching and uplifting poor and helpless children from the slums. A great day in the lives of many children, and a scene forever fixed in the memories of the few surviving octogenarians who saw it, was the annual Salvation Army excursion. Across Long Island Sound, Chesapeake Bay, and Lake Michigan, up the Hudson, down the Monongahela, steamed the white painted side wheelers, an Army flag at the jackstaff, a band on the hurricane deck, hundreds of cheering "little slummers" leaning over the triple railings, hair tossing, faces damp in the mist of the bow waves. One day in every year in the sun and salt spray, with a box lunch and lemonade thrown in, was no small thing for children who spent months in the noisome dark of back alley flats and dingy schoolrooms. And there were variations on this happy theme: in 1908 Colonel Holz sent out eleven thousand mail appeal letters to finance a grand all-day trip for fifteen hundred Cleveland poor children, who filled seven chartered streetcars for the trip to Euclid Beach, where an amusement park, lunch, movies, ice cream and, a game with the encouraging name of "bun-eating" awaited them. In Chicago, an even more innovative Colonel George French, "a boy among the boys," acquired the loan of fourteen automobiles—which in those days were still regarded by most average people as expensive, exciting novelties—filled thirteen of them with 225 poor slum children and one with the new Chicago Staff Band, and proceeded, with much backfiring, flag-waving, cheering, and unevenly played march music, to a nearby camp for the day. Not to be outdone, the corps officer in Meriden, Connecticut, tried the same thing a month later, with thirty cars and two hundred children.[43]

Army efforts to redeem the lives of the children of the poor were not confined, of course, to day trips. It was clearly necessary to expose them to the sacred truths of Christianity in a more relaxed and unhurried setting. Despite the inexorable decline of the farm colonies that followed the departure in 1904 of Booth-Tucker, their only remaining champion, the Army remained of the opinion that country life was in every respect superior to life in the city. With the colony zealot gone, it was possible to concentrate on more practical forms of sylvan relief. It was only natural that officers would begin to perceive the benefits of children's camps. It is not certain which was the first official Salvation Army summer camp; the best evidence gives the honor to the "Fresh Air Camp" pitched in twenty tents in Kansas City's Fairmont Park in the summer of 1897, the brainchild of the divisional officer, the ubiquitous Harry Stillwell. The Chicago auxiliaries donated the beautiful lakeside acreage at Camp Lake, Wisconsin, in 1904; it remains in Army hands, as the oldest continuing Army camp in the country. The Army's last farm colony, Fort Herrick, after a brief interlude as an inebriates' refuge, became a fresh air camp for Cleveland slum children in 1909. Nor was fresh air the only stimulant offered to young hearts: weekly programs for the young people of the corps were developed through these years as well, culminating in the first "Young People's Councils," held in Chicago in 1913; called "an original plan," the Councils offered three days of rallies and lectures for corps people responsible for youth work. Their young charges attended as well.[44]

In the front lines—the corps themselves—the Great Salvation War made uneven progress. The initial excitement of a pioneer crusade had waned; by the time Evangeline Booth assumed command, The Salvation Army had been in the United States for a quarter of a century. Officers boasted that the Army was no longer an experiment—more to the point with regard to corps work, it was no longer a novelty. After the initial ferment had dissipated, converts were no longer added by hundreds or dozens in a few weeks, but by ones and twos at long intervals. For the large, well-established corps, this tranquil period before the first world war was not ruinous; it provided a needed interval for the soldiers and their families to become rooted and grounded in their faith. A few corps, like Flint, Michigan, grew at a handsome rate due to immigration of

Salvationist workingmen into a local job market. In 1909 Flint acquired an entire brass band through the agency of Bandmaster Beacraft, who was also—conveniently—the manager of the Buick Motor Company. The growth that most large corps experienced was due to the prodigies of effort expended by the officers and soldiers; the weekly schedule of a corps like Chicago No.1, Boston Palace, Flint, or Oakland was staggering. In May 1906, for instance, a week's activities for the band of Chicago No.1 included five open-air meetings, five indoor services, three musical programs for bandless neighboring corps, and two practices. An extra obligation for that month only was a weekly three-hour concert on State Street to raise money for the victims of the San Francisco earthquake. Nor did bad weather stay soldiers from their duty: in January 1904, Chicago No.8 held thirty-nine outdoor services. Any corps capable of meeting the regulation schedule, which called for an indoor meeting every night of the week and three on Sunday (all but two of them preceded by an open-air meeting and a march), was expected to do so; the officer who merely "kept things together" without bringing the corps at least "slightly up" received mediocre marks from his superiors.[45]

With many corps—the majority—the case was far different from what it was for the large ones. The early growth registered at these small stations in pioneer days did not last. Many of those whom the Army rescued were part of a transient population, moving from job to job, place to place, in an endless quest for a better life. A survey of seven officers taken in 1906 revealed that, together, they had seen seven hundred souls saved, of whom 136 became soldiers—roughly one in five. Brigadier Walter Jenkins, who reported this phenomenon, considered that the major cause of it was the transient nature of the converts. In 1908 Colonel Richard Holz surveyed his vast provincial command, which ran from Cleveland to Key West, and concluded that the Army's failure to build up its soldiery was due to the "migratory character of the working people" that were drawn to its services. The result was often small, undermanned corps, which in itself worked against growth: Brigadier Jenkins cited as another cause for the reluctance of converts to join the ranks "the smallness of our corps and consequent disinclination to stand with it."[46]

The small corps was doubly crippled. The Army did not accept inactive membership. Officers depended upon their soldiers, who were expected to take on the rigors of warfare without hesitation, and to abandon job, home, and family if these stood in the way of total consecration to God and the Army. The Army was built on such soldiers, and on the field officers: all advance depended on them, only indirectly on the staff, not at all on the convert who shrank, however understandably, from the sacrifices that warfare required. Soldiers were given special passes, depending on their support of open-air meetings and knee drills. These passes were highly prized: without one a soldier could not attend the weekly soldiers' meeting at which corps problems were discussed and war strategy planned. Officers were warned that the Army could not long survive if it did not make more of its converts into soldiers. Getting people saved was no longer enough: the Army must reach "the people who are more fixed in their abode and habits." The need for soldiers did not cease with the need for warriors. Soldiers not only pushed the war, they financed it, with their cartridges, their hawking of *The War Cry*, and their faithful support of the open-air services at which money was collected. A corps with only a few soldiers not only was too weak in personnel to advance the war: it was in constant, desperate financial difficulty. Officers commanding such places—and there were hundreds of them—faced poverty that was little short of absolute.[47]

The key to the problem was clearly to attract into the ranks what the old General called "the better sort of mankind." But beyond that the Army had to build a second generation, the families of its recruits had to be secured as well, if the Army were to have a future. The many innovations in youth work that characterized these years recognized this fact. Whole families had drawn together and into the ranks. Officers began to undertake rudimentary family counseling, and corps offered small-scale relief designed to hold corps families together, like small loans or a short-term job with the Army to keep a father from going on the road to find work. Sometimes these fledgling family services required courage: when Lt.–Colonel William Bearchell was a small child in 1910 he saw a man shoot his wife and then himself after Bearchell's father, the corps officer in Huntington, West Virginia, had failed to reconcile the couple. Yet the benefits of securing entire families were far too obvious to be set aside because of a few setbacks. In 1908 Major John Bouterse built Asheville, North Carolina, into a large and active corps by making soldiers out of entire families attracted to the Army by an all-winter revival in the Spirit. The Salvation Army launched a new program to reach wives and mothers on a national basis in the years 1913 through 1915, when the Home League began. The League, the first of

which was probably at Pen Argyl, Pennsylvania, offered Christian fellowship, useful household instruction, and was a success from the beginning. In 1915 Chicago's first Home League was officially commissioned
at No.5 corps by the wife of the Territorial Commander of the West,
Mrs Commissioner Thomas Estill.[48]

Despite the discouragement of small corps, from which even the
saintly Brengle was not immune—"I felt I could have had larger crowds
in a church, but I should not have had needier souls"—the Army's
crusading zeal did not entirely disappear during these years of slowed
advance in the field. The Army continued, for instance, to offer plans
to win the black population of the South. General Booth had visited
Mobile in February 1903, during his farm-colony tour; while there, he
spoke at the largest black church in town. His old heart had melted at
the sight of the "weeping penitents," which reminded him of his first
experiences as a revivalist in Cornwall. The Army declared its continuing
interest in Southern blacks, but urged patience. Plans for an "advance"
were "not quite ready." The Army had almost no black officers, even
in the North. There were two black officers working in the New York
rescue home in the early 1900s: "Sisters in Race, Sisters in Grace," they
had both been saved at open-air meetings (in Manchester, New Hamp-
shire, and St. Louis), and both had served briefly as slum sisters in
Philadelphia. In the south there was no progress in making black officers,
and very little success in recruiting black soldiers. In 1908 the provincial
officer stated flatly that "Our work is exclusively among the white population, we do not touch the colored element. This of course limits our
scope for Soldier-making etc. . . ." The difficulty was "the strong antagonistic feeling between the two races," so that the Army found it "practically impossible to do anything among the colored people there." Rescue
homes were segregated, and in Greenville and Birmingham there were
facilities only for white women. Given the legal and social structure of
Southern life seventy years ago, the Army had no option to segregating
its facilities other than closing them altogether and withdrawing from
the region. Official hope for an evangelical advance among blacks remained high despite the many obstacles. In 1912 a black corps was
opened in Washington, D.C., and the next year Colonel Holz, now in
command of the Atlantic Coast Province (which included much of the
South), announced that once again the time was "deemed ripe for The
Salvation Army to start a regularly organized work among the hundreds
of thousands of colored people" of the Southern states.[49]

Nor did the Army's ill-fated black crusades exhaust its interest in the South. The state of Kentucky exerted a powerful allure, despite several false starts (when officers "invaded" Kentucky in 1894, opening in Newport and Louisville, they imagined themselves to be pioneers: in fact Louisville had been "pioneered" twice before, in 1883 and 1887.) Once permanently installed in the Blue Grass State, however, the Army did all in its power to make good its claim that "Kentucky shall be won for God!" The Army was invited to hold meetings in 1895 and 1896 at the camp meeting grounds at High Bridge, south of Lexington. Specials and musicians were gathered from several states, with gratifying results: the local congregation, who had never seen the Army before, regarded it as a "revelation." In the fall of 1903 a more daring invasion was launched. Colonel Holz and eight others, mounted and clad in special khaki uniforms, braved flying shot to bring the gospel to the feuding hills of eastern Kentucky. The hill people, solidly religious, were friendly and hospitable, and open-airs were held along the roads and in court house squares in perfect safety: once the Salvationists held forth on Beaver Creek to a group of operating moonshiners, who listened politely. The Army found it difficult, however, to get more than a bare toehold on the Kentucky beachhead: the people were "Hardshell Baptist of long and approved standing," and a state whose main sources of income were bourbon whiskey, horseracing and tobacco was not fertile ground for The Salvation Army.[50]

Other areas were more congenial. The Scandinavian work continued to flourish: the first decades of the twentieth century were a period not of mere consolidation, but of continual advance. The number of Scandinavian immigrants neared three-quarters of a million persons in the years between 1900 and 1917, greater by almost a hundred thousand than the number who arrived here in the years between 1887, when the Scandinavian work began, and 1900. Secure in its burgeoning nests—New York No. 2 corps was the largest Scandinavian corps outside of Sweden by the end of the first world war—the Scandinavian work advanced across the country, nurtured by the enthusiasm of its cheerful and well-fed minions and guided by such leaders as the sweet-spirited Colonel Ben Nelson, who commanded Scandinavian operations in the Territory of the West from 1908 to 1920. The Scandinavians had their heros, too. On February 11, 1907, the steamer *Larchmont,* en route from Providence to New York City, was struck by a coal schooner in rough weather in Long Island Sound. Aboard were ten Scandinavian Salvationists sailing to a mass rally in New York. When it became clear that the ship would sink before all the lifeboats could be lowered into the water, the soldiers calmly knelt in a ring on the listing deck, urging their terrified fellow passengers to prepare to meet God and singing "Jesus, Lover of my soul, Let me to Thy bosom fly" as the waves closed over their heads. All ten were drowned, but not in vain. The testimony of their faith caused a revival to sweep the Scandinavian ranks, and the funeral at New York No. 2 for the three bodies recovered from the sea turned into a hallelujah free-for-all at which many souls were saved.[51]

Another disaster—the San Francisco earthquake and fire in April 1906—brought the Army into the news as well, and provided the first opportunity for large-scale and systematic emergency relief, upon which the public came in later years to depend. The Army's earliest connection to public emergencies may have been the dauntless George Elliott, a Chicago convert, who in 1889 hastened to fires carrying drinking water to the thirsty firemen and directing the attention of the crowd to the flames as a sample of what awaited the unconverted soul. More temporal measures were taken as well. In 1900 national headquarters offered first aid instruction to officers and soldiers for use in case they might be called upon to offer physical as well as spiritual rescue as they went their rounds in busy streets and back alleys. That same year a hurricane drove a flood over the town of Galveston, and the Army literally threw out the lifeline. "Mother" Thomas, a Houston Salvationist, traveled to the scene to care for the "storm refugees" who had fled to the outskirts of the city. Booth-Tucker quickly sent after her a relief expedition of twelve officers under Brigadier Stillwell and Major Galley, the first aid instructor. These set up tents for the homeless in Texas City, and helped to clean, feed, and shelter some of the thousands of refugees who flocked there.[52]

These helpful activities served as a kind of prelude to the Army's participation in the massive relief operations in California. On April 18, 1906, the San Andreas fault shifted, causing severe earthquakes along part of the California coast. The Army was badly hit by the effects. The Beulah rescue home in Oakland was wrecked, the Lytton orphanage severely damaged, and the Santa Rosa corps hall collapsed—fortunately, Ensign and Mrs Jensen were able to extricate themselves from the rubble. Mrs Anna Butler, the Salvationist matron of the orphanage who was in San Francisco on business, was not so fortunate, and died in the ruins. The city of San Francisco was damaged in the quake, but what destroyed the city—and, temporarily, the Army's various religious and industrial activities in it—was the fire. The "City of the Argonauts" was still illuminated by kerosene and gas in 1906: spilled lamps and broken chimney pipes caused numerous fires, which spread unchecked over the splintered wreckage. The fire department could do nothing: all the city water mains had broken in the quake. When the fires were over three days later, the better part of a city that once housed 400,000 persons had disappeared.[53]

With nothing material left on the scene—the industrial home, light-house, and the corps were gone, and all that remained of California provincial headquarters was a safe and part of a cornet (melted)—The Salvation Army limped into the breach. The Army had no organized plan for disaster relief: most of what was done was spontaneous and very practical. While Commissioner Kilbey announced from Chicago a terri-tory-wide campaign to raise funds and collect food and bedding, Oak-land Salvationists opened the citadel (which had lost its plaster ceiling in the quake) and the Beulah Park camp meeting grounds to refugees, who streamed by the tens of thousands across the Bay to safety. Chinese refugees were given their own little corner of the camp, and proved so receptive to the Army's ministry that several were converted—enough to open a Chinese corps in Oakland in 1907. Eventually, most of the San Francisco Army arrived in Oakland, and the Citadel became tempo-rary headquarters for relief operations. The San Francisco soldiery had already performed one heroic service, during the worst of the fire, by rescuing hundreds of injured persons who had been placed for safekeep-ing in the Mechanics' Pavilion, a large hall supposedly well away from danger. By the time it became clear that this building, like most of the rest of the city, would eventually burn, the wounded there had been forgotten except by their panic-stricken relations. The Army came to the rescue with its small fleet of industrial home wagons. But once this heroic endeavor was over and the injured safely aboard an Oakland ferry, the military government of the city took all the Army's horses for its own supply wagons. Temporarily disconcerted by this development, most Salvationists repaired to Oakland to formulate new plans. They had not long to wait: the military governor detailed all willing Salvationists to help in refugee camps and emergency hospitals. In addition, the military assumed part of the duties of maintaining Beulah camp, freeing more Salvationists for service in San Francisco. The soldiers streamed back across the Bay and into action.[54]

Meanwhile the Commander herself, not content with staging a mass fund-raising rally in Union Square in New York, nor with channeling to Oakland the hundreds of letters and telegrams of prayer and support that daily poured in upon national headquarters, decided to hasten to the scene in person as a surprise to her hard-pressed western troops. The delight in her visit was reciprocal: her pleasure at all that had been done was unfeigned; almost thirty thousand persons had been fed, over nine thousand given beds, a new one-story wooden provincial headquarters already erected on the old site, and the Army was singing and testifying in the refugee camps every night. For their part, San Francisco's soldiers beamed with pride as Evangeline, at the top of her form, charmed the city and captivated a mass meeting on May 30 in Golden Gate Park. Thus rejuvenated, the Army continued its relief efforts through the summer. A party of volunteers arrived in June from Los Angeles, sponsored by William Randolph Hearst, the eccentric millionaire publisher; the party turned down many volunteers, but included all nine Salvationists who had offered themselves. By the fall of the year the city was functioning again, rubble was cleared away, and the Army relief operations were closed down. By the summer of 1907 The Salvation Army, like the rest of the city, was conducting its old business at the old stands: the industrial home wagons plying neighborhood streets, the band of San Francisco No. 1 marching nightly through the newly-restored Barbary Coast, almost as if nothing had happened.[55]

The Army's work in the California disaster received considerable attention in the press, and helped no doubt in reinforcing the image of the movement as an agency for good. The Great Salvation War, the direct assault on Satan and all his works, was thus indirectly aided in the last years before the First World War. There were more direct and straightforward advances as well. The old General paid two visits to the United States in 1907: in March a "flying visit" while en route to Canada and thence to Japan, and an official American tour in the fall. Obviously failing in health, almost certainly making his last trip to the United States, the General was lionized, greeted everywhere by enraptured crowds. He and Eva were received in state by President and Mrs Roosevelt at the White House. The President was genial, and chuckled his approval of the Army's street ministry: "I thoroughly believe in a brass band." These sunny remarks, which covered the range of Army work, failed somehow to dispel the gloom into which November's falling leaves had plunged the General. So many old friends had passed from the American scene—his old friend Mark Hanna, President McKinley, then poor Mrs McKinley, who had just given a memorial stained glass window portraying her husband to the corps in Canton, Ohio. Eva could not charm him out of this mood in the White House, and was concerned. But on the platform, as the apostle of the poor and lost, Booth still flamed forth, the old giant a giant still. At his last address in New York, he commended Eva to the United States as one whose "only ambition is to see you a holy, happy and useful people, one of the strongest, bravest and most effective wings of this great organization" and departed for England amid a tornado of volleys and cheers.[56]

The effect of the General was always electric. The Army redoubled its attack on sin in the streets, with an increasing percentage of the hot-shot being fired at the "drink traffic." Since the eighties the Army had supported the principle of legal prohibition of all alcoholic beverages, but deliberately avoided a public commitment to any political party —including the Prohibition Party itself, which canvassed in vain for Salvationist support. The Army's traditional view was that Christ alone was its Candidate, Who alone could solve the problems of the world; any more mundane advocacy would only alienate one or another part of the public. The Army preferred to attack Demon Rum by direct assault.[57]

The great attack opened on Thanksgiving Day, 1909, with a parade in New York City. The general idea seems to have sprung spontaneously from several minds, but the details of what was guilelessly called the "Boozers' Convention" were devised by the provincial officer, Colonel William McIntyre, a well-spring of novelties, aided in this case by Major G.W. Baillie. The double-deck buses that were to grace Fifth Avenue for many years had just come into service; some of these the Army borrowed and filled with drunkards and idlers collected off the city streets. A parade was formed of these buses, led by a municipal water wagon to which were chained "bona fide bums," a ten-foot papier-mâché whiskey bottle, and five brass bands, all of which arrived at headquarters for a free dinner and an evangelical meeting addressed by notable saved drunkards from all the New York corps. The Boozers' Convention became an annual event, and spread to other cities. In 1910 this straightforward technique netted a particularly noteworthy captive. Henry Milans, former editor of the New York *Daily Mercury*, had become an alcoholic, which ruined his career. Discharged from Bellevue in 1908 with the judgment that he was a "hopeless incurable," Milans fell literally into the gutter, where the Army found him. He was powerfully converted, purged by sovereign grace of his taste for drink, and went forth as a glorious Trophy of Grace, whose testimony in meetings and in print became a mainstay of the Army's growing temperance crusade. It was joined in the arsenal by a variety of pamphlets portraying the effects of drink on body, mind, and soul, parade floats depicting "The Drunkard's Home" (suitably forlorn), and thousands of broadside song sheets, whose homespun truth touched many hearts: "The pail that holds the milk, sir, he used to fill with beer."[58]

To the public, The Salvation Army must have seemed like its old self, the zeal and dedication—even the hallelujah buffoonery—much the same. Certainly the Commander did all that lay within her nearly inexhaustible dramatic powers to inspire the troops. She developed a series of memorized, illustrated lectures—more like tableaux with gestures and music—which held large crowds transfixed. Of these "The Commander in Rags," loosely based on her pioneer experiences in London slums, and later "The World's Greatest Romance" were public favorites. Her zeal for the old Army never waned; she even kept alive the Victorian Army's penchant for being photographed. Her enwreathed picture graced the Christmas *War Cry*, and the fine portrait of Eva kneeling beside her father, taken at the Falk Studio in New York on his last visit in 1907, justly became an Army classic. Yet the passing years brought change to the Army, subtle, yet unnerving. The failure of many corps to grow was part of the cause of a malaise that settled over many officers.[59]

Another source of uneasiness for many Salvationists, at the same time it was an occasion for official pride, was the acquisition of permanent property. The purchase of land and the construction or purchase of corps buildings and social institutions represented a major change in Army policy. The pioneer Army owned no real estate. Army halls were rented, seldom for long. Officers felt that the ownership of property would tie the troops down, imperil the crusade's vital mobility: in 1885 the national commander wrote that "much of the Army's future achievements for good" would be "found in its ability to form flying columns, and to deliver sharp and rapid strokes upon the slumbering consciences of one city after another." The flexibility that halls rented for the month conferred on the Army was cherished. With the single major exception of the national headquarters building on Fourteenth Street, the Army acquired almost no buildings through the administrations of Ballington and the

Booth-Tuckers. This changed during the first two decades of the twentieth century.[60]

There were several causes. For one thing, the General's policy that all bequests to The Salvation Army be used in some permanent manner, as a memorial rather than as operating funds, had resulted by 1905 in a large accumulation of money. The Army decided that these funds should be spent on corps buildings. Many soldiers in big city corps registered dismay at the gypsy-like wandering around town that was a part of their service in the Army. These persons—who were not always a majority—felt that such an organization was "insecure and impermanent" and craved the comfortable assurance of a fixed spiritual home. The large numbers attending Army meetings in the early days had necessitated renting large halls; as the numbers fell off the soldier remnant made their demands for regular meetings halls felt. Finally, several aggressive officers came into positions of authority during the years when sentiment was building to replace rented halls with corps buildings. These men became convinced that the procurement of property was an essential step, upon which the future progress of the Army as a stable and respected force for good in American life depended. This became official Army policy, and in 1907 *The War Cry* declared that the fact that the Army was gaining properties was a sign of "the lofty pedestal of public confidence upon which we stand today." Colonel McIntyre and Colonel Holz, the two leading provincial officers and the two leaders of the property scouts, were fast movers. When McIntyre began in Buffalo in 1898, the Army in his province owned only national headquarters, worth $400,000, and a small frame shop used as a hall in Addison, New York; in 1920 property in the province was valued at three million dollars. In the Ohio, Pittsburgh, and Southern Province Holz purchased thirty-two properties during his command, from 1899 to 1908: when he came the Army owned nothing; book value of its holdings at his departure was $536,000. Everywhere the Army was moving into splendid new barracks of brick and masonry, like the new citadels in Oakland (1902) and Flint (1911).[61]

The old-time "flying columns" were not only becoming tied down to fixed locations, they were becoming entangled in increasing confusion over money and the purposes for which it was collected. The Salvation Army never ceased to be an evangelistic crusade, the redemption of the unchurched urban masses its sole function. Yet the means to this glorious end had proliferated, and prospered in their own right. At first spontaneous, haphazard, and immediate, the social programs had become organized on a massive scale, requiring a constant inflow of money and donations in kind. Officers and friends of the Army were anxious that the demands of administering these good works would absorb energies badly needed for the evangelistic crusade. Colonel Holz spoke officially: "Unless care is taken, there is danger that our Field Officers will become fully absorbed in the Charity and Relief work, to the exclusion of the Spiritual side of things."[62]

But there was another problem. Not all of the money collected for relief work was used solely for that purpose: some donations went into general operating funds and were later used to finance the Army's denominational activities, indoors and out. Critics pointed to this awkward feature of Army business. The first full-scale scholarly analysis of the Army, which appeared in 1909, stated specifically that The Salvation Army "collected funds, on the strength of its social work, and appli[ed] these funds to religious propaganda." The author, Edwin Gifford Lamb, a doctoral student in political science at Columbia, called for "greater definiteness and accuracy" in the Army's financial reports to the public. Professor C.C. Carstens, an important official in Massachusetts charity, was even more explicit. Writing in 1907, Carstens declared that the Army had "obtained large funds, part of which are used in the furtherance of its religious plans with which, however, many of the largest donors have little or no sympathy." In 1906, Mr Edward Solenberger, General Manager of Associated Charities for Minneapolis publicly condemned the Army's charity work as inefficient and poorly administered. Three years later in Boston the Overseers of the Poor, who regulated public collection of money for social welfare, placed heavy restrictions on the Army just before officers were to begin collecting for holiday relief operations. A sympathetic newspaper, the *Journal,* saved the day by offering to accept donations sent to it for the Army. Critics also declared that the Army was rich, "an up-to-date business enterprise," a corporation that made a handsome profit on its industrial home and salvage operations. These revelations reflected unfairly on the great bulk of the evangelical work, which was in fact painfully self-supporting, mostly by pennies and nickels; yet such recurring charges were hardly calculated to encourage Salvationists who read them.[63]

The death of the General on August 20, 1912, was another blow.

Eighty-three, blind, and dying, William Booth had spent most of his last months on earth preaching the gospel of redemptive love with all his old power. His heart seemed to flame up once more before its fire went out forever: his last public address, which is still cherished by Salvationists, was heard in May by seven thousand people, Evangeline among them, at the Royal Albert Hall in London. It was the triumph of the spirit that built The Salvation Army: "When women weep, as they do now, I'll fight; while little children go hungry, as they do now, I'll fight; while men go to prison, in and out, in and out, as they do now, I'll fight; while there is a poor lost girl upon the streets, while there remains one dark soul without the light of God, I'll fight—I'll fight to the very end!" His death was a shattering blow, not so much because it was totally unexpected as because it left an absolute void: no one had ever known another General; the Army, in one form or the other, had existed for forty-seven years under the sole leadership of William Booth, who had long since been recognized as one of the great men of his times. American Salvationists, of necessity less captivated than their English comrades by the General's constant physical presence, were nonetheless saddened by the loss of the great human fixture that had for so many years symbolized the Movement. Memorial services were held from coast to coast. In Los Angeles Vachel Lindsay, a struggling poet who had sheltered with the Army in his travels, wrote what became his most famous poem as a tribute to the old General; "General William Booth Enters into Heaven" was soon published, in *Poetry* magazine, and gained wide notice. *The War Cry,* bordered in mournful black, carried more conventional tributes. Photographs were circulated showing the General lying in state, his hands folded over Evangeline's last cable to him: "Kiss him for me."[64]

The next General was Bramwell, chosen by the Founder for that honor in 1890 according to the legal procedures designed by himself in 1878, which made the selection of a successor the privilege of the reigning General. The new General was unknown to Americans; even his name was obscure except to staff officers. He was a man of exceptional administrative ability, whose careful and painstaking organizational work had enabled his crusading, eloquent, and perambulating father to gather in the masses on a worldwide basis. Bramwell was loyal to his father—whom he never ceased to refer to as "the General" even after he had become General himself—and to what he conceived his father's wishes to have been on certain matters of Army policy. Bram-well was intelligent, a man of conviction and high principle, and he had a fine prose style; his printed messages and devotional writings were widely read and much beloved. Nevertheless, many Americans were uncertain about the character and ability of the new international leader, and his attitude toward the Army in general and their branch of it in particular, an uncertainty that was transformed into anxiety by his first exposure to them. The new General's visit to the United States in 1913 was a disappointment. Bramwell lacked presence on the platform. It is only fair to admit that the Founder was a hard act for Bramwell to follow; the contrast between the old man's impassioned eloquence and his son's lackluster delivery was striking. Bramwell was deaf and wore a wobbly pair of pince-nez, which made him appear fussy and uncertain. His views on Army administration were even more unsettling than his presence. However pure his motives may have been, Bramwell Booth was a thoroughgoing bureaucrat—Ballington had called him a "systems man." The new General had a narrow and inflexible concep-tion of the Army's hierarchical structure, fatally combined with the mystical notion that he had inherited from the now glorified Founder a sacred trust to preserve the powers of the General, indivisible and inviolate.

Seven hundred American Salvationists went to London in June 1914, for a great International Congress. Led by the Commander on horseback, the American delegation (in cowboy hats) included the two staff bands and the Flint Citadel Band, and a small group of elderly black Salvationists assembled and trained by Colonel Gifford, the Boston provincial commander. The joy that was shared by the fifty-eight national delegations was genuine, and no group enjoyed the Congress more than the Americans, who cheerfully regarded it as an honor that their place in the parade was as the last national unit (just ahead of the employees of the Salvation Army Assurance Society and staff clerks, who were the very end of the parade): natu-rally, the General wanted a grand finale—and what could be more grand than Eva on a horse, three brass bands, seven hundred waving cowboy hats, and the black soldiers, who appeared for the occasion in special star-spangled costumes. What indeed could be more grand! Patriotism itself was grand, a harmless display of camaraderie in the engaging context of a world evangelical crusade. Patriotism appeared less harmless, however, in Sarajevo, where on June 28, 1914, a Serbian nationalist shot the visiting heir to the Austrian throne along with his wife. The fifty-eight delegations to the Salvation Army International Congress paid this event no mind and departed from the Crystal Palace still in a euphoric mood, unaware that the beginning of a great world war was at hand.[65]

CHAPTER IV

1914-1929

"Fresh converts still we gain."

When the Great War began in Europe in August 1914, the
United States remained neutral and The Salvation Army in this country
was at first little affected by the hostilities. The regular spiritual and
social activities went forward, and were supplemented by new programs.
The open-air ministry continued to characterize the Army: "Born in the
street," the Army continued to thrive "in the place of its nativity, and
its power to prevent evil and encourage purity by this means" was,
according to a modest official statement, "beyond computation." Corps
activities, augmented now by the new Home League, filled every night
of the week. Youth work in the corps was expanded by the addition of
two British transplants—the Life-Saving Scouts for boys in 1915 and the
Life-Saving Guards for girls in 1916—only one of which, the Guards,
survived to flourish on these shores.[1]

The penny ice and cheap coal benefactions spread rapidly and far. By
1915 these good works were no longer confined to the larger cities:
individual corps officers in cities large and small were plying the poor
sections in hired wagons, dispensing this seasonal boon. The Army's
prison ministry so tenderly nurtured by Maud Booth grew steadily under
her successors, especially Commander Evangeline, who took a great
personal interest in its development. A converted former convict, Ensign Thomas Anderson, formed the Brighter Day League in 1904 to
offer spiritual services to prisoners and to help them prepare for that
"brighter day" when they would be free. In 1916 Anderson began the
"Lifer's Club," to convert and comfort the hopeless. Its first President,
Jesse Harding Pomeroy, spent his life in the Massachusetts State Peni-

tentiary for a murder he committed at the age of fifteen. Prison visitation became part of the duties of every nearby corps: the annual Prison
Sunday saw scores of prisons receiving this blessing. In February 1917,
Evangeline took the whole National Staff Band with her to play before
she preached at Sing Sing.[2]

The years of American neutrality, which ended in 1917, seemed
propitious for the Army. It is true, as the Army itself admitted, that the
public accorded it only "passive acceptance" so far as its evangelical
crusade was concerned, and that much of its spiritual work had lapsed
"into comparative obscurity, from which there seemed to be no escape.
Few knew the Army for what it was, and few cared." Yet the social
programs drew public praise and financial support in reliable amounts,
so that the Commander was inspired to act upon an idea with which
she, and her lamented father before her, had toyed for years: the "University of Humanity" to train officers on a national scale. The old
General put the idea forward regularly, starting in the Consul's day, but
he insisted—oddly enough—that the proposed new college be in London, which ruined the prospects, so carefully cultivated by the Booth-
Tuckers, of sufficient American funding, without which no such project
was possible. Mrs Leland Stanford, the California philanthropist, withdrew her offer to finance the "university" on this ground. Commander
Eva made no such mistake; once the Founder had passed from the
scene, the University of Humanity reappeared in a more congenial and
familiar form: a national training college for American officers, combined with an old people's home and two social institutions, to be
located in downtown New York. The Army planned to launch a national
fund-raising campaign in 1914, but postponed it at the request of the
YMCA, which had long planned a national campaign of its own for a
somewhat similar project. In 1916, when the Army began its own campaign to raise $500,000 for the "University of Humanity," the YMCA
offered its full support, as did a wide segment of the public, including
former President Theodore Roosevelt, still as warm as ever toward the
Army.[3]

If imitation is the sincerest form of flattery, then The Salvation Army
had reason to congratulate itself during these years. The problem of
imitation "armies" had troubled the Army since the Moore era. In
August 1892, an organization called the "Industrial Christian Alliance
. . . meeting somewhat on S.A. lines," solicited funds in the Ocean
Grove Auditorium: the vacationing Colonel Holz, in the audience by

chance, glumly gave a nickel. The phenomenon continued to plague officers into the 1920s, especially in Chicago. Yet these imitation armies seemed to come in cycles, and reached their peak in the years between 1913 and 1917, during which the number of these "spurious concerns" grew to alarming proportions. In December 1913, Brigadier A.E. Kimball, provincial commander for Michigan and Indiana, wrote in despair to the national chief secretary, pleading for "some way out of the present difficulty we have in connection with so many Armies." There was the Afro-American Army in Philadelphia (an especially disreputable swindle), the Good Samaritan Army in Detroit, and the Christian Army in Nashville and Louisville. In Baltimore there were the American Rescue Workers and the Volunteers of America both of which were legitimate concerns, descendant from the Army schisms of 1884 and 1896 —the Samaritan Army, the American Gospel Band, and the Salvation Army Church (not connected with The Salvation Army), all operating in the year 1915. Davenport Iowa had a Calvary Army, while Chicago produced the Redeemer's Army, the Christian Army, and the Samaritan, Saved, and Volunteer Rescue Armies. These agencies, which used uniforms, flags, and brass bands wherever they could muster them, caused great confusion to the public, who naturally mistook them for The Salvation Army, whose social programs many wished to support. Most of these tiny "armies" were simple frauds, or were conducted by deluded incompetents, however sincere, who could not provide the charitable services for which they collected money. The Army's legal secretary, Brigadier Madison J.H. Ferris, secured assistance from the courts in banishing the most flagrant examples from the streets.[4]

Meanwhile the war raged on in Europe, a disaster of appalling magnitude. There were few who imagined—or desired—that the United States would become belligerent, but the country was nevertheless drawn increasingly into the conflict. The United States was the leading supplier of war materials to the Allies, and to a certain extent, American prosperity became tied to an Allied victory. At the same time, many Americans were moved by lengthening accounts of atrocities and casualties that filled the newspapers. These developments caused great excitement and alarm among the millions of Americans whose ethnic loyalties were still strong. Although The Salvation Army in the United States was not heavily involved in war relief work before the country entered the war in 1917, American Salvationists were never indifferent to the suffering, physical and mental, caused by the war. Salvationists were urged to pray for peace, to "affect the battlefields of Europe by way of the Throne of Heaven." The American branch of the Army was of course absolutely neutral: soldiers were warned not to pray for any "particular side, but . . . in the interests of our great humanity." American Salvationists were saddened to learn that the Army work of their European comrades was "quite prostrate" as a result of the war, which affected the working people—the mainstay of the Army—more than other classes.[5]

In November 1914, the Commander announced the "Old Linen Campaign" to aid victims of the war. Corps people were asked to collect and clean old linen, fold it into bandages and surgical pads, and send these items to divisional headquarters. National headquarters would mark each package in English, French, and German, and ship them to Europe for use as needed. Funds and old clothing for Belgian refugees were collected as well, starting in 1915. In October of that year the Army's international headquarters requested that an American officer— a citizen of a neutral state—be dispatched to conduct the Army's relief work in Belgium. That country was occupied by the Germans, who were willing that the relief work be continued, but refused to accept an officer from any Allied country to run it. The Commander sent Major Wallace Winchell, an energetic, industrial home officer, the colorful Chicago pioneer who, twenty years earlier subpoenaed the devil and operated the Army's food relief program during the Pullman Strike.[6]

Major Winchell found some Army centers at work, and opened others; he began a wide range of practical charities, financed by subscriptions at home and funds from London. Clothing and money grants were given to destitute families, soup kitchens opened for school children, and milk was given to babies. The Major, always a fan of Booth-Tucker's agricultural panaceas, secured lots upon which unemployed Belgians could grow potatoes. Winchell took no sides in the war, which he diplomatically attributed to original sin. He found the Germans efficient and cooperative, and discounted Allied propaganda about German atrocities. Some of Winchell's religious activities were unfamiliar to the Belgians: he was attacked while holding an open-air meeting in Brussels by a wounded Belgian who mistook him for a German. The excitement of his war work caused Winchell to lapse into periods of hallelujah whimsy, during which he planned to borrow military trucks to take the poor children of Brussels into the war-ravaged countryside as a novelty, or to bombard the Allied lines with bouquets of flowers flung over from the German side, as the first stage in a massive peace plan of his own devising. Despite these lapses, Winchell accomplished much in the way of practical good work, and departed before his privileged status as a citizen of a neutral power had evaporated.[7]

The United States declared war against the German Empire on April 6, 1917. There were several reasons for this action, for which diplomatic and military developments during March had only partially prepared the public. Essentially the United States entered the war to defend its neutral right to use the sealanes of the world, which the Germans, driven to desperation by the endless attrition of the war and the privations caused at home by a British blockade, were determined to interrupt by the use of unrestricted submarine warfare.

The Salvation Army was caught off guard at first. American Salvationists had been officially instructed for years to value the Army's international status, which had sustained it through two domestic schisms. Initially it was difficult for Americans to write off their German comrades, whom Railton had gathered so lovingly together when he had left his pioneering labors in America, as bloodthirsty militarists determined to conquer the world. The Commander's statement of April 21 was equivocal: the Army was "international," and could glory only in the struggle against "sin and strife." Still, The Salvation Army was ready to stand by the President, and she offered the services of her "disciplined army" of thirty thousand Salvationists for Red Cross work.[8]

The government was hesitant at first to accept the Army's offer. Congress authorized and the high command issued a general order that the American Red Cross should provide all "relief work" for the US Army—that is, services for the sick and injured—while the YMCA was given by the same means an official monopoly on "welfare work," which included social, recreational, educational, and religious activities for the able-bodied troops. These grants of authority were not intended to be absolute, however: when other, smaller agencies offered their services they were not automatically rebuffed, so long as they were willing to coordinate their efforts with those of the two officially-chartered agencies. Civilian war work was divided into two areas: training camps at home, and services to the American Expeditionary Force in France. The Salvation Army was eventually included in both, but only after a period of negotiation and uncertainty. Most government officials knew little of the Army, looking upon it as vaguely beneficial, with little capacity for efficient war service. The same feeling was common among military officers in France. No one, in The Salvation Army or out of it, anticipated the impact that its war service in France was to have—not only on American servicemen but on the reputation and prospects of the movement itself. Considering the languid official response to the Army's first offers of service, it is ironic that in 1951 Professor Herbert Wisbey, preparing a doctoral dissertation on the history of the Army, concluded that World War I "probably" marked "the climax of Salvation Army history in the United States."[9]

On the home front the Army was designated as one of several "other auxiliary welfare agencies," to operate canteens and "huts" at military training camps allotted to it by the YMCA. Activities at these stations varied from those of a sort of enlisted men's club with lounge, reading room, singing, and baked treats, to full-scale soldier's hostels with dining rooms and clean overnight lodging. There were evangelical services on Sunday in all the Army facilities, and in all of them the officers maintained the cheerful, domestic atmosphere for which the rescue homes had long been famous (at least to their beneficiaries). Ninety-one such clubs operated at one time or another by the time the last of them was closed in 1919, after the Armistice. Many of these clubs were small, part-time affairs; in fact, the Army lacked officer personnel for large scale war work in camp, and its contribution to the home front war service was not great. Although The Salvation Army was officially recognized as one of seven agencies—the "Seven Sisters"—that made up the Commission on Training Camp Activities, its share of the national budget was only 2.05 percent, the same as that of the Jewish Welfare Board and the American Library Association.[10]

The Army's record of cooperation with other agencies was a credit to officers, who refrained from both the sectarian competitiveness and the heavy-handed evangelism that marred the work of some other organizations and offended many enlisted men. The Army tried to place its own small operations at a distance from those of other agencies, loaned its kettles and tripods to the Red Cross for fund-raising, and distributed to the needy the suits of civilian clothes left by the thousands at the Y huts by arriving military trainees. Nor was the Army's home front service confined to such cooperative camp work. The Army revived Booth-Tucker's vacant lot farm scheme as a patriotic gesture: Salvationists were to plant vegetable gardens on unused city lots. This would generate two benefits at once (to say nothing of the healthful effects on the happy toilers): the lots would produce extra food for the war effort, at the same time thoughtfully freeing farm laborers—made redundant by the scheme—to join the AEF. This "patriotic, useful and humanitarian" project was popular among Salvationists eager to do their bit: in 1917 a total of 126 acres east of Chicago were cultivated by the Army. Yet the Army's training camp and farm-lot ministry, however patriotic and useful they might have been, were hardly spectacular enough to constitute the "climax" of Army history.[11]

That climax—or at least turning point—came in France. The Army's war work there in 1917 and 1918 showed the movement at its old-time best—joyful, fearless, practical, and immediate: the spirit of the Great Salvation War was again brought before a sizeable portion of a people who had forgotten, if they had ever known, the capacity for self-sacrifice of the Army pioneers. The Commander appointed Lt.-Colonel William S. Barker, the property secretary at national headquarters, to be the "pioneer to blaze the way for the work in France." The Commander's plan was typically simple: find the troops and "mother" them as resources permitted; details were left to the officers on the spot. Barker proved a remarkable choice. His headquarters position, while involving important responsibilities for the selection and purchase of properties, had been routine: he warmed to his exciting new assignment, and set off to France in August in high spirits.[12]

Barker presented his credentials, which consisted mostly of a general letter of introduction secured by Evangeline from President Wilson's private secretary, to any official who would receive him in France. The American Ambassador to France and the several other military and civilian officials whom he met were cordial, but offered little encouragement: the government had granted a monopoly on welfare work to the YMCA, and while this grant was admittedly not absolute, nobody in authority could see anything special for The Salvation Army to do in France. General Pershing, the commander of the AEF, was more helpful. He, too, understood that the Y was to be responsible for all of the kind of work the Army might do. But unlike other officials in France, Pershing had a warm personal recollection of The Salvation Army. In 1915 his home at the Presidio in San Francisco had burned, killing his wife and family. The Army's provincial officer, Colonel Henry Lee, had shown great personal interest and sympathy, as had many Salvationists, while the respectable Bay Area churches had somehow ignored the incident, failing to offer even perfunctory condolences to one who was essentially a stranger. Pershing never forgot the Army's kindness, which touched him deeply. He decided after meeting Barker in August to allow

The Salvation Army to open its own huts and offer whatever ministry it had in mind in the military district of the First Division.[13]

Evangeline borrowed $25,000—and later, another $100,000—to finance the Army's war work, for which no other source of funds was at first available: certainly no corps or headquarters budget contained large extra sums for that—or any—purpose. A small contingent of eleven officers, seven men and four women, sailed on August 12, 1917, to join Barker in France. Each was equipped with a special commission signed by Eva for "Service with the American Expeditionary Forces in France", and with an enthusiasm for service that was as yet undiluted by knowledge of the dangers of the front. Pershing ordered the Salvationists into regulation khaki-colored private's uniforms, with the red Salvation Army shield on caps and epaulettes, while Barker spent the borrowed $25,000 on a large tent and a touring car. A quick tour of the district had already convinced the Colonel that women were needed to carry on proper "mothering." The troops were already bored with the "slangy," compromised Christianity of the Y workers, who were men, and yearned for respectable and sympathetic female companionship. Barker quickly wired home for more women officers.[14]

The Commander, at first surprised by this request, quickly perceived the wisdom behind it. The Army's officer ranks were promptly sifted for corps assistants, all single women officers in their twenties, and this number was augmented by soldier volunteers. These indefatigable, warm-hearted, and adaptable women showed courage even in going to France. Few had ever been on the ocean before, and the terrible novelty of a first voyage was made more frightening by the knowledge that the dark, cold sea was infested with German submarines. Officers bound for France sent off lugubrious farewell telegrams to their families and boarded the troopships filled with dread. Their arrival in Bordeaux was thus doubly providential. There were never very many soldiers abroad during the war; Professor Wisbey concluded that the popularity of the Army's work in France was "greatly out of proportion to its quantity." There were perhaps a total of 250 Salvationists in war service in France, compared to over ten thousand YMCA workers. Yet the women transformed the Army's ministry, which at first was little different from that of the YMCA, into the uniquely welcome and long-remembered service that won The Salvation Army a special place in American life after the war.[15]

The Army carefully placed its huts in places where the YMCA had no work, so as to avoid duplication in France as it had in American camps at home. The first Army hut was at Demange. When women arrived, Army work became more popular with American troops. Of course there were several other reasons for this improvement in the Army's status, although the women were the major part of the explanation. Even before they began to arrive in significant numbers the Army huts had started to gain a loyal following on their own. The government provided the troops nothing in the way of toilet articles, sweets, or writing materials. This service was regarded as part of the "welfare" for which civilian agencies were responsible. The Salvation Army charged either nothing for the kit items it offered to the men, or prices far lower than those at Y counters. Then, too, the Salvation Army freely offered credit, not only to individual men who were short of funds, but to entire companies whose pay was delayed for one reason or another. The terms for this credit were hardly rigorous: pay when you have it, no notes to sign, no interest added on; if your unit is moved up before you get the money, give what you owe to any Salvationist anywhere. The Army gained by these policies a reputation for open-handedness that spread rapidly. It hardly mattered to the AEF that the YMCA was chartered by the government and was expected to keep careful accounts of its finances, while The Salvation Army dispensed the bounty of its own loans, appeals, and street-corner collections; what mattered was that the Army gave the stuff away, or charged very little, while the Y seemed to be making a profit from its canteen sales.[16]

Nor was this all that mattered to the troops. The Salvation Army's variety of Christianity had wide appeal, too. The women officers and soldiers only enhanced this ministry; they did not create it. The Army was the Army, even in France. It remained stoutly evangelical. Attendance at Salvation Army religious services was in no way required of the men who availed themselves of the services of its huts, but those who chose to attend were presented the gospel unvarnished: in Christ alone is life and hope. The music at these services was the same as one might hear at an Army corps on a Sunday evening back home: the taste of the doughboys ran to lively numbers such as those the Army had made famous on street corners across America; soldier favorites were "Brighten the Corner Where You Are," "When the Roll is Called Up Yonder," and "The Battle Hymn of the Republic," accompanied by a piano and often a cornet. Fred Stillwell, son of the California pioneer, drove an Army canteen truck and played cornet in France. Occasionally a regimental band would play hymn tunes for a Salvation Army meeting. The troops appreciated the Army's straightfoward approach to the Christian religion, and the fact that Salvationists—men and women— did not drink, smoke, or use profanity, and would not sell liquor or tobacco (although the Army did distribute gift packages of cigarettes to wounded men who asked for them). Many Americans soldiers were confused by the religious posture of the Y workers, whose religion the men considered flawed by its irreverent tone and the commercial prac- tices of the Y huts. The leaders of the YMCA were aware of the widespread failure of the religious part of their service, but were unable to recruit a sufficient number of committed Christians to offset it; faced with the need to find thousands of workers in a few months, the Y often settled for persons of merely "Christian character" who had had no formal church affiliation before coming to France.[17]

For all the genuine good it was doing, however, the Army would have remained merely one of several welfare agencies serving the troops in France, however well thought of it was, had it not been for the "lassies," who "mothered" the troops by the thousands to their delight. The women received no formal instructions in what was expected of them in France; they simply served as the slum sisters had served before them: by doing every useful, kindly thing that came to hand. They darned socks, sewed on buttons, wrote letters, kept money for the men, and sent it home for them via the hometown corps officer. Regimental officers asked Salvation Army women, instead of the regular chaplains, to break bad news to the younger men; one of the hardest jobs Helen Purviance had to do in France was to tell a seventeen-year old soldier that his mother had died back home. The women sang at all the Army religious services—one doughboy's haunting memory of the war was of a young Army woman singing "a hymn" in a bombed-out church at the front on Good Friday, 1918. The Army women tidied up the hasty wartime graves and decorated them with wild flowers. And they baked. Above all, they baked.[18]

The role of the doughnut in the history of Salvation Army work in the First World War was of such importance that it is remembered even today. What Commander Evangeline liked to describe as "the winsome, attractive coquetries of the round, brown doughnut" practically eclipsed the rest of the Army's welfare service, and that of other agencies as well. Colonel Barker and four newly-arrived lassies set out in the touring car in September 1917, looking for some boys to "mother." Their plans

were necessarily vague; no officer, including the Colonel, had any training for war relief, and no instructions other than to make themselves
"available and helpful." At Montiers they came upon the camp of the
1st Ammunition Train, 1st Division. The women piled out, set up a
Victrola, and held a little service and sing-along. The men, young and
homesick, were reluctant to let the girls depart again. One of the officers,
Ensign Margaret Sheldon, suggested that the girls would bake something "American" for the boys if they would let them go. This jolly offer
was taken up with enthusiasm, but there were difficulties in the face of
the original project, which was to make pies: no stoves, no proper pans,
only a bit of flour, grease, baking powder and sugar. The resourceful
Sheldon, a former slum sister and ready for anything, suggested that they
make doughnuts. The noble work was performed by Adjutant Helen
Purviance, who cut the dough into circles with the top of the baking-
powder can and popped out the holes "with a camphor ice tube."
Success! With a stroke, the Army's reputation was made. The doughnut
proved ideally suited both to the insatiable craving of the troops for hot,
fresh homemade treats and to field conditions in France, where the
chronic shortage of field stoves, pans, and supplies made it difficult to
produce more elaborate baked goods like pies and cakes. Doughnuts
could be produced in large numbers in lard melted in any sort of pot
or bucket, placed over a fire built in a hole dug in the ground, while hot
chocolate and coffee to go along could be made in galvanized trash cans
heated over the same fire source.[19]

The doughnut ministry also included delivery. Here, practicality combined with courage. When the AEF was ordered up to the front lines
from its base camps, The Salvation Army volunteered to follow them.
The Army placed its new huts and field kitchens as near to the fighting
as military authority allowed: often Salvationists baked and sewed in the
secondary trenches that connected the front to staging areas. Salvationists were often under fire, literally dodging and ducking—and occasionally diving—to avoid shot and shell as they carried hot food to the men
in combat. Several times Salvation Army canteen trucks were caught by
German artillery and abandoned in the road—although daring sorties by
hungry doughboys rescued the contents before all was lost. Several
Salvationists were gassed, and most suffered extreme fatigue, dirt, para-
sites, and nervous prostration, but only one died in service—Major
Barnes, of pneumonia in 1918. Not only did most women not allow the
difficult conditions at the front to deter them, a few failed altogether

to grasp the seriousness of the situation. Helen Purviance and some of her friends ran out of their dugout one day to see a German airplane, and in a moment of laughing high spirits shot at it with a borrowed rifle, thus exposing the whole position to unpleasant artillery fire. Most Salvationists, however, were aware that they were working in perpetual mortal danger, and had to smile through constant terror. Commandant Joseph Hughes, almost paralyzed with fear, unable to think, filled a Ford car with goodies and drove it, eyes closed, hands clenched on the wheel, straight up to the front lines and into a surprised and delighted artillery company that cheered him as they continued firing away at the enemy.[20]

If all of this were not enough to endear The Salvation Army to the men in the ranks, the Army's policy toward military officers completed the process. The Army still regarded itself as the church of the working class and the poor; few financially successful or educated people had been drawn to it, except as an object of their charity. In France the Army aligned itself officially with the enlisted men, much to their satisfaction. Officers were welcome, but were not given precedence—an unusual policy in the conscript army of 1917. "Officers and soldiers take their places in the line," wrote a Salvationist in France, "as our work is particularly for the enlisted men." Evangeline regarded it as one of three "cardinal principles which were deemed necessary to success in this work" that Salvation Army personnel should share hardships with the enlisted men, eat with them in their messes, and associate with them rather than with the officers; the other two principles were "consistency" in religion, and taking the Army's work into the actual fighting zone. She recounted with pride stories of Army officers who, in order to "stay with the boys," turned down invitations from regimental commanders to lunch at chateaux. The American troops, for most of whom the military caste system was a degrading and unpleasant novelty, relished the democratic policy of The Salvation Army.[21]

The Salvation Army had secured an enviable place for itself in American military life. On September 12, 1917, the Judge Advocate General declared officially—the first such legal recognition in the Army's history in America—that The Salvation Army was a denomination of the Christian Church, with its own "distinct legal existence," creed, form of worship, "ecclesiastical government," doctrines, discipline, ministers, and members. Salvation Army officers were thereby exempt from the draft; far more importantly, they could now be enlisted as chaplains with formal military commissions. Five officers served as chaplains during World War I. The first was Ensign Harry Kline of the Omaha Industrial Home, who was appointed chaplain to a Nebraska National Guard regiment. Kline was the first Salvation Army officer to become an official military chaplain; rather ironically, he had been one of Major Milsaps' faithful eight followers in Manila in 1898. The other Army chaplains were John Allan, Ernest R. Holz (son of the famous Colonel, and father of the present national commander), Norman Marshall (who would later become a national commander), and J.A. Ryan. There was also one "unofficial chaplain": Major John E. Atkins. Sent to France as a hut worker, Atkins set up shop in the camp of the 26th Infantry, commanded by Major Theodore Roosevelt, son of the former President. When the unit was ordered into the trenches, the courageous little Atkins closed his kitchen and followed them offering spiritual counsel, caring for the wounded, bringing treats, and running errands behind the lines for men who could not leave their posts. He was enormously popular.[22]

In fact, the whole Salvation Army was enormously popular. Company officers, who had to censor all homeward-bound mail from the men in their units, noticed that praises for The Salvation Army appeared more and more frequently. Soldiers wrote to their families and friends back home extolling the Army for its doughnuts, its compassion, its religion pure and undefiled, and its front line service. "It is always in the places where the boys need help and the closest hut to the lines you'll find is The Salvation Army." By 1918 the current of tributes had become a flood, which a surprised military general brought to the attention of the *New York Times* in October. Salvationists in the United States were at first modestly surprised at the spreading news about the success of their comrades' work in France: had the Army not always "reduced the theory of Christianity to action?" Had it not always waged its own salvation war in the front lines of sin? Modest surprise turned to delight as the homefront public's approbation speedily took on a practical form: the grudging trickle of pennies and nickels upon which the Army had eked out its beneficial existence now became a golden stream. The Army's begging and borrowing days were over. Fund-raising drives were oversubscribed by large amounts: in the spring of 1918 The Salvation Army asked the country for the then-unheard of sum of one million dollars for its war work—$2,370,000 was donated! A later campaign, conducted jointly with other war relief agencies, was interrupted by the armistice in November. The Commander was elated, declaring that the Army now had excellent references for its mammoth fund-raising projects: "The average man in the trenches—the military authorities at headquarters"—even the President and the Secretary of War!.[23]

The Army's prospects on the home front were clearly improving. It is true that the Commander had been forced to brave certain difficulties in connection with the Army's war work. She was convinced at one point that German spies, thinly disguised as "women," had tried to penetrate national headquarters late one night as she sat at her desk, planning the Army's war relief strategy. A fire later at the training college was attributed to saboteurs: national headquarters was certainly their next target. Thus alerted, Evangeline had cleverly avoided giving a direct answer to a hotel porter's question about Salvationist work in France: another spy! Still, these dangers proved fleeting, and the excitement bubbled away, to be replaced by the greater and more lasting thrill of triumph that seemed to presage a new day—a new era—for The Salvation Army in America. The newspapers were full of war news, mail homeward from the front glittered with praise for the Army, and support for the movement from the American public, based now on sentiments both grateful and patriotic, grew daily warmer and more widespread. Old friends like John Wanamaker, who as a director of the War Welfare Council had a "particularity for the Salvation Army which he did not conceal," were joined by many new ones. The war occupied an increasing portion of the Commander's attention: the public seemed to expect so much, and there was so much to do.[24]

In addition to its operations in France and at military training camps in the United States, The Salvation Army administered a burgeoning military welfare program throughout the country. The Army gave away thousands of "camp kits" filled with toilet articles which the government did not provide. The *War Service Herald*, an Army newsletter, had to be produced and distributed in the camps. In June 1916, Evangeline launched the "War Service League" to enlist corps Salvationists and outside volunteers to contribute fifty cents toward Army war work and to serve as home-front auxiliaries, visiting the wounded veterans in hospitals, bringing good or bad news to families, and knitting warm clothing. Eventually thirty-one thousand people joined the War Service League, all busily knitting socks, helmet liners, and scarves. Such a mountain of woolies was produced that the Army had to donate twelve Ford ambulances to the military in France to facilitate delivery of the warm things to the men at the front. And if providing these practical blessings was not enough to keep the Army busy, its leaders conducted a national publicity campaign for the prohibition of alcoholic beverages for the duration of the war. The eliminiation of distilled liquor would conserve precious grain and sugar, while beer was denounced for being hardly less German than the Kaiser's moustache; the morals, not only of the troops but of the country as a whole, would be preserved during these stressful times and the curse of drunkenness would cease at stroke. A cause the Army had advocated for years, one of a few voices in the wilderness, now became patriotic and popular—like the Army itself.[25]

Difficulties seemed to evaporate one after another. It is true of course that each of the Army's war projects cost money; each new project in turn was a successive addition to the Army's regular evangelical and social welfare programs, all of which continued as before. These, too, had to be financed. Indeed, the extra burden of the war work staggered the Army initially, and the Commander cast about desperately for a means of increasing revenue. She first borrowed large sums, asked the hard-pressed corps and divisional headquarters for impossible increased support; next she turned to the War Service League. Finally, the daring million-dollar campaign of 1918 was launched, which meant a large extra workload for many officers. Then the golden tide began to flow. Evangeline had been confident from the beginning, when some of her staff had urged against the first loan, that the American public would support The Salvation Army's war work once it was under way, and believed the people understood that the Salvationists in France counted life less than duty and would make any sacrifice for the AEF. She was right. The million-dollar campaign was oversubscribed by more than double the amount that was asked. Sums that would have dazzled officers in 1915 were now regarded as too modest, almost a refutation of faith in God's bounty. By the time of the Armistice, November 11, 1918, The Salvation Army had seemingly passed forever from the necessity of begging in the streets and taverns to finance its war on sin. Confident in the grateful affection of tens of thousands of returning doughboys, who had promised the lassies in France that they would "always have a good word" for the Army, Evangeline opened the Army's first peacetime national appeal in May 1919. She asked for enough money to run every part of the Army's program except the corps; the money would finance the "maintainance, supervision and the extension of the work," pay off all mortgages, buy new buildings, and cover all general and headquarters expenses. Entitled the "Home Service Fund," the national campaign asked the public for thirteen million dollars, an astronomical sum in those days. The Fund was launched at a mass rally held in Madison Square Garden, at which the Vice-President of the United States, Governor Al Smith of New York, and a host of dignitaries spoke in glowing terms of the Army, and a popular new song was sung —"Salvation Lassie o' Mine." The campaign was a huge success.[26]

The Armistice did not bring an end to Salvation Army service to the American troops: Salvationists ministered in all the old ways to the thousands gathering in staging camps waiting to be shipped home, and young Army women waited with coffee and doughnuts to greet the troopships arriving on American shores. The men who disembarked from these ships had very little time at dockside before they were put on trains for demobilization camps; as a result, they could not telegraph their families with the welcome news that they were safe at home at last. The Salvation Army women provided this service thousands of times, taking the names and addresses of the men as they waited in line for the trains, then sending the telegrams in batches. The Army operated huts and "rest rooms" in the demobilization camps themselves. Nevertheless, November 1918 was the high-water mark, and The Salvation Army wound its war work down as rapidly as the federal government discharged its victorious troops. But the public's new affection for the Army did not dissipate. The era of collecting in tambourines was over: a new day had arrived, for the Army no less than for the country. *The War Cry* announced on November 30, 1918, that henceforth The Salvation Army would "apply itself in its own field for the organizing and consolidating of all the healing arts of peace": very soon the Army would announce new projects of the "utmost value to the country."[27]

The postwar decade began with Salvation Army officers in a confident mood. The signs were certainly encouraging. The "Salvation Lass" had become "a kind of doughboy's goddess," whose name, "sure of gaining the loudest applause," was enshrined already in popular song, poetry, and on the bow of at least one freighter—the SS *Salvation Lass.* The Army's "nightmare of finance" was over: "The Salvation Army will probably never again appeal in vain for popular support." Other old battles had been won, too. Wartime prohibition became permanent in January, 1919, when Congress ratified the 18th Amendment to the US Constitution. The saloon—that nest of devils and old-time provoker of police attacks—was apparently gone forever. Progress was everywhere.

The Army had a new slogan in 1919, and a new ethnic ministry. Elmore Leffingwell, the publicity director of the Home Service Fund campaign, is credited with coining the phrase "A man may be down, but he's never out" as a new slogan for the Army's social programs. (The line may have come originally from Bruce Barton, the famous publicist.) Like such cherished pioneer mottos as "the Great Salvation War," the new slogan embodied the spirit of the Army perfectly. And in California, the Army "opened fire" on the Japanese community with all the old-time blare and fervor.[28]

The Salvation Army had periodically thrown out the lifeline to California's growing Japanese population since 1896, when the "Articles of War" were hopefully translated into that language. In 1898 the Army opened a mission to reach the Japanese in the Hawaiian Islands. A Lieutenant Loxton, who spoke Japanese, was sent from San Francisco to Honolulu to start the work in August of that year; it promptly folded, to be reopened permanently in 1920. Real success in establishing a Japanese branch of the Army came in 1919, when Masasuke Kobayashi turned his admirably disciplined zeal to the task. Kobayashi was a Presbyterian minister and general secretary of the Japanese interdenominational Board of Missions in California, when he came under the powerful influence of Colonel Gunpei Yamamuro. The founder of the Salvation Army in Japan, Yamamuro had earned a well-deserved reputation as one of Japan's Christian statesmen, and was twice decorated by the Emperor. Kobayashi admired the work of the Colonel from afar for years, and in 1917 arranged a series of revival meetings for him among California's Japanese. In two weeks—all the time the Colonel, en route to London, could allow—842 Japanese were converted. Kobayashi was stunned with joy, and became convinced that The Salvation Army would win the Japanese in America for Christ. He and his wife resolved to begin the work, and abandoned all that home and career could offer to sail for the Army training college in Yokohama. The pioneers returned to California on July 24, 1919. Joined by three Japanese-American converts from the Chicago training school, they opened the first Japanese corps in the country in San Francisco in August; Los Angeles followed in September, Fresno in October, Stockton by Christmas.[29]

Ensign Kobayashi was a dedicated evangelical, whose preaching brought gratifying results. An indefatigable worker, he was gifted with the ability to win and hold the loyalty of subordinates, a quality without which no officer could succeed in command of Japanese workers. A single year saw the addition of twelve officers, eighteen noncommissioned officers (called "local officers" in the Army), one hundred fifteen soldiers, and a special rest home in San Francisco for ailing Japanese, who otherwise were likely to fall prey to the frauds and quacks who often deceived and cheated Japanese by playing on their fears of western medicine. Kobayashi's work was hard. Although regarded as something of a home-mission field—General Bramwell Booth donated an initial five thousand dollars from headquarters' funds—the Japanese corps were required to be self-supporting from the beginning, on the same basis as any other corps. Officers were frugal, however, and fund raising among the hospitable Japanese was seldom the major obstacle to progress. The real difficulty was in the nature of Japanese life itself: the Japanese did not consider themselves merely as individuals, but as members of families that stretched generations into the past. They were especially sensitive to the wishes of their parents. To sever all ties with one's family was difficult enough for occidentals: for Japanese it represented a sense of loss that was complete, final, and unendurable. Yet it was just this loss which any Japanese had to face who contemplated conversion to Christianity, a religion regarded by almost all older Japanese as illogical, weak-minded, and—above all—foreign. To become a Christian under such circumstances was bad enough. But to join The Salvation Army, to wear a Christian uniform, and parade in the streets behind a brass band was the supreme sacrifice: one's family was not only abandoned but humiliated, and one's own dignity was lost in the bargain. Every Japanese Salvationist was thus not only a Trophy of Grace, but a monument to courage.[30]

Nevertheless, the Japanese ministry prospered on the Golden Shore. Corps were opened in Sacramento in 1920, the same year that Captain and Mrs Soichi Ozaki were sent from San Francisco to commence operations (again) in the Hawaiian Islands. The Visalia corps was pioneered in 1921, and on November 6 of that year a full-fledged Japanese divisional headquarters was dedicated in San Francisco by none other than the elderly Commissioner Booth-Tucker, assisted by the new territorial commander and by various civic and Japanese dignitaries. A Japanese post was opened in Seattle in 1922, and in Oakland in 1923. Like every Army event in Oakland, the movement's premier city in the West, the opening of the new Japanese corps there was enthusiastic, and supported by "the famous Oakland No. 1 Band, who rendered most delightful service." By 1924, when San Jose was launched, the Japanese ministry boasted, in addition to the nine Japanese corps and the Home of Rest, a medical clinic, children's home, and day-care center in San Francisco, a summer camp near Seattle, and a Japanese-language version of *The War Cry* with a weekly circulation of five thousand. The success of the Japanese division seemed assured. Many West Coast officers came to share Kobayashi's prediction—once regarded as commendably overly enthusiastic—that the Army *would* save America's Japanese.[31]

By 1920 the Great Salvation War had seen many battles won. The Salvation Army was popular—and while some officers had been warning on and off since the 1890s that success brought special dangers of its own —the consequent easing of financial strain was welcomed by all. The Army had acquired millions of dollars in property, and had created in the Home Service Fund the machinery for collecting millions more on an annual basis. There had been indications before the war that the growing complexity of Salvation Army operations, spread over the vast territory of the United States (which continued to astonish European Salvationist visitors) put a strain on national headquarters, which the creation of a deputy commander in Chicago had only partially and temporarily relieved. A further division of administrative responsibility was required. The end of the war made it possible to effect the change, which the Commander welcomed—for in addition to its other benefits, the new structure would enable her to reward several faithful senior officers with commands and higher rank. General Bramwell Booth may also have contemplated transferring the Commander to another position elsewhere in the Army empire; the new administrative structure would make any transition go more smoothly.

In October 1920, three separate territorial commands were created, and the historic dominance of national headquarters came to an end. The leaders of these were still "directly responsible" to the Commander, but had large independent authority of their own. A study of The Salvation Army conducted for the Rockefeller Foundation in 1924 found that only matters of "large importance" were referred to national headquarters, which had "a very small staff of but ten and administers no activities." The new commands were the Eastern territory, under the same Commissioner Thomas Estill who since 1908 had skillfully commanded the old Department of the West; the Central territory, still headquartered in Chicago under Commissioner William Peart, who had been national chief secretary since 1905; and the new Western territory, under Lt.-Commissioner Adam Gifford, the heroic pioneer who, as a young captain, had lacked the few dollars to pay for his infant's grave. Gifford came to San Francisco, the new territorial headquarters, from Boston, where he had served since 1908 as provincial commander. All three men were officers of exceptional experience and ability. The apportionment of states within the new territories was mostly based on geographical proximity, and had little historic significance: the East comprised the Union east of Indiana, from Kentucky to the Gulf coast; the Central ran from Indiana to the Dakotas, including Texas, Oklahoma, Arkansas, and Louisiana; the West included Montana, Idaho, and the nine western states.[32]

The War Cry had grown more sedate by 1920. Still the repository of a militant form of reporting about the salvation war, the "jubilee boomlets" and "small-shot" of pioneer days were seen no more in its pages. The change did not stand in the way, however, of the great increase in circulation stimulated by the Army's war work and by publicity for the Home Service Fund: weekly circulation almost tripled from seventy thousand 1918 to two hundred thousand 1920. Corps officers were still expected to boost *The War Cry;* circulation contests were part of a "Drive that never ends," and this despite the announcement in October, 1920, that the price of the magazine had to be increased—doubled, in fact, to a dime—to compensate for higher production costs. The new territorial commands required *War Cry* editions of their own: the Western territory had sponsored a Pacific coast version since 1883, while national headquarters had published the American *War Cry* since January 15, 1881. The Pacific coast edition now became *The War Cry,* Western Territorial Edition—that new "white winged messenger of the West"—on January 1, 1921. The new Eastern and Central territorial editions appeared on the same date.[33]

Although staff officers knew that behind all of these gratifying developments, certain difficulties were developing between New York and London headquarters, it had little effect on the work and was unknown to the rank and file Salvationists. Commander Evangeline's public references to her brother, General Bramwell Booth, were infrequent, quite unexceptional. Privately, the Commander regarded her relationship to her brother as anything but encouraging. She and Bramwell had shared an abiding affection for the now-glorified Founder; of the Booth children, these two had been closest to the old General. Beyond that and a thoroughgoing commitment to the evangelical purposes of the Army, they had little in common and were, in fact, suspicious of one another.

Bramwell must have felt that once the war was over he could safely transfer the Commander; the triple-territorial reform may have been part of that overall plan. By 1920, after all, Evangeline had been national commander in the United States—the Army's premier appointment—for sixteen years. The difficulty was, of course, that she did not wish to be transferred and did not care to be ordered about by Bramwell, any more than Ballington had; but unlike Ballington, Evangeline was absolutely loyal to The Salvation Army, which her father had created. She was in a strong position. She did not have to threaten resignation or schism: the war work and the Home Service Fund—and after 1920 the territorial fund drives that replaced it—made the American branch of the Army the richest and most powerful in the world, and Evangeline Booth—patriotic, winsome, and fiercely evangelical—was its living symbol. Rumors that her transfer was being considered produced cyclones of protest from the American public. One such flurry occurred in 1922, when the national convention of Elks cabled Bramwell that Eva had become the "angelic personification" of all the Army stood for in America.[34]

The General could, however, insist on small concessions: when he reappointed the Commander in 1924 to another three years in America, he took from her the right to approve any promotions beyond the rank of staff-captain, or to approve medium level territorial headquarters appointments (which she resented and ignored). But he could not, without wrecking the Army in America, transfer her if she insisted in public on staying. Bramwell Booth could not have been certain that his sister would not refuse to obey an outright order, a refusal that now seems to have been extremely unlikely. Rather, she might have succumbed to "nervous prostration" under the strain of what she interpreted as her brother's enmity and jealousy; or the issue might have been raised again of London's attempts to "Anglicize" the American branch of the Army; or the whole matter of the General's "autocratic" powers, or his "dynastic" susceptibilities—the suspicion (which has never been substantiated) that he planned to name his daughter, Commissioner Catherine Bramwell Booth, to be his successor—might be broadcast through the American newspapers. The results of such publicity would have been disastrous.[35]

Territorial-level staff officers knew of the unfortunate state of affairs between the General and the Commander—her letters to the territorial commanders were remarkably frank; she even devised a code name for

Bramwell ("Brown") and herself ("Cory")—and a few lower-level officers guessed. Most officers and soldiers knew nothing of these matters, so that when the breach between New York and London began to widen and occasionally became public the rank and file were either stunned, or had the opposite reaction and refused to believe that anything seriously could be the matter between two such trusted leaders.[36]

In March 1925, the first of several "manifestos" appeared (by an odd coincidence, they arrived simultaneously at many Army headquarters in Britain and America) signed by "W.L. Atwood," supposedly a soldier at the Wichita Falls, Texas, corps, but apparently written by another hand. These statements denounced the General as an autocrat and a dynast, demanded that he relinquish the privilege of naming his own successor, and demanded vastly increased independent powers for Commander Evangeline Booth and the American branch of The Salvation Army. Once the danger was past that the Commander would be transferred any time soon, the chief grievance of those who publicly upbraided the General was his undoubted legal right to name the next General, as he had himself been named by the Founder. This was a grievance, however, which affected only the Commander and those in her circle whom loyalty or interest prompted to support her. The rank and file continued to celebrate the General's birthday as an Army holiday, and in 1923 E. Irena Arnold, something of an official Army poet, composed a birthday poem to the General entitled "Oh, America Is Loyal." The work of the Army, which as always was carried on by the faithful field and social officers and their soldiers, progressed at an encouraging rate as the roaring twenties unfolded.[37]

The decade opened auspiciously enough in 1920, when The Salvation Army was asked to contribute a brass band to the annual Rose Bowl Parade in Pasadena. The Army was in a great many parades in the 1920s —particularly those held to commemorate Memorial Day, the Fourth of July, or Armistice Day. The theme of the Army float or entry was almost always the same: a sign on the Army's truck-bed display in a 1923 Nashville parade declared that "Some say it was the doughnut, But the Boys know that it was the Spirit Behind It." In Hattiesburg, Mississippi, the Army's entry in the 1927 Armistice Day parade was an enormous coffee cup on a Model-T Ford flatbed, while in 1925 in Shreveport The Salvation Army distributed doughnuts along the parade route from a float helpfully marked with a sign that read, "Salvation Army. Just a Reminder." The doughnut was rapidly becoming the new symbol of the

Army. When Colonel Edward Parker asked a professional artist for a proposal for a Salvation Army exhibit for the 1926 Philadelphia Sesquicentennial Exposition, he was presented with a sketch of a huge lassie holding high a doughnut: Parker was horrified to discover that the artist assumed that The Salvation Army had begun in France as a doughnutmaking crusade![38]

The Army remained highly popular among veterans' groups. The Commander, who had been decorated with the Distinguished Service Medal in 1919 for the Army's contribution to the war effort, quite correctly told a huge ten-year convocation of the American Legion in 1927 that The Salvation Army's "substantially bettered financial condition, and the unqualified blessings of the people we enjoy today under the Stars and Stripes" were largely due to the support of veterans. The boosters, too—those civic and fraternal organizations that drew upon so much of the loyalty and energy of middle class American men in the twenties—took up the cause of The Salvation Army with lively enthusiasm. Many of the members of these clubs were grateful veterans; in addition, the Army's practical and efficient community services, combined with the familiar trappings of homespun Protestant religion, appealed to the booster ethic of the time. The Elks, Eagles, Rotarians, and members of the Lions, Kiwanis, and the Civitan Club, in towns from Passaic, New Jersey, to Santa Monica, California, put their energetic hands to the Army's wheel, producing new buildings, donating Ford touring cars, and providing legions of bellringers for annual Christmas kettle campaigns. Across the country the Army basked in the golden glow of public approval. Older officers who could still remember the hailstorm of abuse that greeted the Army in the 1880s reflected wonderingly on "the great change" that had come about, as officers hastened for the first time to join civic clubs, and territorial and divisional budgets began to include officers' club dues as a regular item.[39]

Field officers and soldiers were gratified by the popularity of the doughnut, especially when they needed to raise money, but they did not allow themselves to be deflected from their zeal for souls. Evangelism remained the Army's chief purpose and the Great Salvation War raged on. A new edition of *Orders and Regulations for Officers* declared that the "ingenuity of the all-alive officer, inspired by the Holy Spirit" was expected to constantly devise "attractions [to draw] fresh people—at first out of curiosity." Open-air meetings remained the Army's most reliable "attraction": many corps continued to have six such meetings each week; the standard corps schedule called for an open-air on Saturday night, when tens of thousands strolled the streets and window shopped, and three on Sunday. The weekend open-air meetings were preceded by a lively street parade, with all the soldiers marching behind the band, patting and jingling tambourines, and firing volleys. In 1921 and 1922 Captain Rheba Crawford conducted open-air meetings from the side steps of the Gaiety Theatre on Forty-Sixth Street in New York City. The Captain was a strikingly beautiful woman whose presentations drew large—at times, enormous—crowds. Although her dress and theology were a trifle unorthodox (so much so that the Army was soon forced to order her on a "rest furlough"), her unique ministry lasted long enough to win the heart of the young reporter Walter Winchell, and through his good offices to win for Captain Rheba Crawford a kind of immortality as the "doll" from the "Save-a-Soul Mission" in Damon Runyon's classic short story, "The Idyll of Miss Sarah Browne." It was this story, which when combined with another Runyon sketch, "Pick the Winner," gave Frank Loesser the inspiration for the ingenious and popular musical comedy *Guys and Dolls.* [40]

Other old methods besides the open-air ministry survived, or were revived in a new guise: out West the beloved Charioteers appeared again in 1922 and 1923, this time in a motorbus. The six officers, all in special trooper uniforms, displayed the old-time, horse-drawn zeal as their gypsy mission traversed California. On a smaller scale, Captain Fred Brewer of East St. Louis carried the gospel to mining camps in a Model-T Ford truck covered with such inspiring slogans as "Where Will You Spend Eternity?" The campaign saved 120 souls, and the Captain earned special commendation in *The War Cry* for "this wide-awake method."[41]

Nor was Brewer alone in inventiveness. In November 1922, Commissioner Gifford, in goggles and scarf, flew from San Francisco to Sacramento in a DeHaviland US Army observation plane, the first Salvation Army officer to take a plane on official business. Other leaders eyed Gifford's daring with misgivings: "Don't risk too much," warned the Commander on the eve of the big flight. But Gifford enjoyed the experience hugely, and vainly urged his nervous colleagues to indulge in air travel. Innovation was in the air. The automobile did not immediately replace the horse in Army work, of course—indeed, the ice and coal ministry depended on horses throughout the decade, and the industrial homes used wagons well into the 1930s. Enough officers acquired cars, however, that the Army had to issue a special memorandum: cars must be modest, black, and cheap to operate. Radio, the popular wonder of the decade, was also pressed into service in the salvation war. In 1922 the Chicago Staff Band began playing over station WDAP, atop the Drake Hotel.[42]

The Army was advancing socially as well as technologically. For the first time, the saved drunkards and rescued roughnecks were being joined in the ranks of the Army by sizable numbers of literate, conventionally respectable persons. Many second-generation Salvationists now attended high school. Ensign Wesley Bouterse assured this new class of soldiers that the Army understood that the temptations that faced them were as real as those that faced the saved miners and millhands of former days. There were even a few Salvationists who ventured beyond high school, into the rarified atmosphere of college. At this development, so completely unforeseen by the pioneers, some veteran officers took positive alarm and feared the worst: how could the zealous, but guileless faith of the Army withstand the disdain of higher culture, the criticism of sophisticated academics? Desertion of the disillusioned young person would be the inevitable result. If teenaged soldiers in their charge still insisted on higher education, officers urged them to reflect on the benefits of small, rural, Christian colleges, in which faith and holiness would be part of the course of instruction. Especially favored in this regard was tiny Asbury College in Wilmore, Kentucky, a hospitable little institution near Lexington. Its doctrinal foundation in Wesleyan holiness made it especially congenial to The Salvation Army. The saintly Brengle, still the National Spiritual Special, spoke several times in the college auditorium.[43]

The fear that educated officers and soldiers would shrink from the ardors of warfare fortunately proved groundless; yet such fears were not unnatural. The life demanded of a Salvationist remained hard, with few tangible rewards. The career of a social officer required years of relentless work and penury; at the same time the constantly increasing welfare programs administered by the corps frequently threw the newly respectable soldiers into the company of the sots and bumpkins from which the first generation of Salvationists had been drawn. Despite these problems, the Army's social programs grew and became more diversified in the 1920s.

Alongside the services provided by the Army's regular social institutions, a large number of corps offered social welfare of one sort or another. This covered a wide range of human need and was typically immediate and practical: a day-work employment service to connect needy men with local odd jobs; the loan or gift of small sums to purchase kerosene, coal, or food; a warm cup of coffee, soup, and a place to sleep; simple, kindly family counseling; sheltering (and helping to trace) runaways; and directing especially desperate persons to Salvation Army institutions better equipped to provide long-term attention. Nor was this beneficence dispensed only at the corps: the League of Mercy, founded in Chicago in 1905, flourished after the war. Its members were corps people who brought many forms of kindness—baked goods, reading materials, flowers, kind words—to the inmates of prisons, old people's homes, and asylums. In 1928 these short-term welfare services were extended to areas in which there were no Army corps, by the creation of Rural Service Units, the first of which was in Bennington, Vermont. A group of local volunteers would collect and distribute such bounty as resources allowed and need required, or an employee from divisional headquarters would oversee the operation of one or several service units.[44]

The heart of the Army's social welfare program lay, however, not in short-term, small-scale boons on the local level, however practical and welcome these might be to the recipient. The regular social institutions of The Salvation Army offered both social and spiritual redemption as well as assistance; their programs were not only ameliorative, but provided rehabilitation designed to lead the beneficiary to a permanent change. Social officers met together on a regular basis to discuss problems common to their branch of the Army. The necessity of centering every welfare program on Christ was emphasized at these large meetings, at the same time that new techniques—new means to the traditional redemptive end—were freely discussed. The Salvation Army social program prospered in the 1920s; old programs were strengthened, new institutions were built. It is not possible, in retrospect, to arrive at any clear idea of the magnitude of the Army's social program in the 1920s; the Rockefeller study of 1924 found that the Army's published statistical tables of beds, meals, pounds, and hours given away had "little significance." It is nevertheless certain that tens of thousands of different individual people were helped, and hundreds of these—like the drunken poet Charles Taggart—were rescued permanently and became fervent Christians.[45]

The most effective welfare activity in the Army during these years continued to be the Rescue Home, which as of 1920 was officially restyled as "The Salvation Army Home and Hospital." What had originally been a refuge for all kinds of desperate women had become a ministry exclusively for unwed mothers. These homes offered modern medical care, prenatal, delivery, and recovery care, infant care, and a discreet adoption service. The emphasis, beyond medicine, was in discipline, religion and the traditional homey atmosphere, complete with the obligatory Victrola in the front parlor. Officers detected a change in the nature of their charges: they were getting younger. At the turn of the century, most of the clients in any given rescue home had been "mature"; by 1926, forty-two percent were schoolgirls and the average age of a client was only sixteen. The head of the Women's Social Service Department, which administered this branch of Army welfare, blamed the automobile: these unwanted pregnancies were the result of "automobile flirtations," rather than the poverty and prostitution of the old days. Whatever the cause, the twenty-six Salvation Army Homes and Hospitals provided most of its beneficiaries with the cure. The Army claimed that eighty-five percent of the girls who passed through its maternity homes went on to live "wholesome lives." Objective outsiders agreed: the Women's Social Services were the least criticized of all Salvation Army social activities. The Rockefeller study of 1924 concluded that "these Homes collectively [were] without question the Army's most successful contribution to the social field."[46]

The Army continued to rescue alcoholic and homeless men. The Industrial Homes offered residents a wholesome living environment and practical work therapy. Although the social secretary, Colonel Parker, acquired a car—a Kohler—the Army wagons were still mostly horse drawn. The cleaned and patched used clothes and repaired furniture were still a welcome boon to the needy but proud householders who acquired these things for a pittance at the Army's salvage stores. The Army still drew welcome revenue from the sale of its thirteen grades of waste paper. The difficulty in the industrial home program was not in sales, but in production. Prohibition had practically ended public drunkenness, at least in the first flush of popular enthusiasm that accompanied the enactment of the Volstead Act to enforce the 18th Amendment. The Salvation Army's ministry to drunkards literally evaporated after 1919: before that year, seventy-five percent of the nineteen thousand men in the Industrial Home shops had been habitual drunkards; after the Act took effect, the Army could not "corral a handful" for Boozers'

Day, and "dead calm" reigned in deserted Industrial Home dormitories and workrooms. The Army fell back on hired labor to keep its industrial operations afloat.[47]

Yet many rootless men were still at large, and the Army opened its doors to them. The cheap "workingman's hotels," like Boston's Peoples' Palace and the Workingman's Palace in Chicago (one of three hostelries operated by the Army there) provided a badly needed service, especially in the brief, sharp recession that came in 1920 on the heels of peace. There were still migrant workers, homeless transients, beggars, rootless, desperate men in America, and The Salvation Army may have cared, on and off, for as many as half of them. Nor did alcohol disappear completely: Canadian and Scotch whiskey, the cocktail party, and the speakeasy proliferated; but these affected persons of a class over which the Army had never exercised much influence. The saloon and its most popular lines of merchandise, beer and cheap watered liquor, were gone, and gone with them was the working-class drunk who had been the main object of the Army's street-corner appeal.

The Army hardly regretted the end of that part of its ministry. Officers from the Commander down were loud in their determination that Prohibition should remain the law of the land. Evangeline endorsed the 18th Amendment "without hesitation." This remained the Army's official position, fully supported by General Bramwell Booth and international headquarters, until Repeal came in 1933. The Salvation Army believed so completely in "the beneficent influence of prohibition" on the United States that it abandoned, for the only time in its history in this country, its non-partisan stance. In the Presidential election of 1928, the Army endorsed the candidacy of the Republican nominee, Herbert Hoover. In 1931 Evangeline publicly praised Hoover for his "magnificent conflict with the forces of organized and defiant disorder" who were working for repeal of the 18th Amendment. Officers were urged to combat "reactionary forces" that sought to ignore or annul the prohibition laws. Evangeline herself was a tireless speaker on behalf of legislation for which the Army had yearned for years. Lower ranking officers spoke to local rallies, and paid for advertisements on radio and in the press. E. Irena Arnold, the gentle officer-poet of renown in the Southern states, produced a short poem with the opening line: "We thank God for Prohibition in America today." Out in Honolulu, in an outburst of reciprocal solidarity, the Hawaiian Anti-Saloon League elected as its president Brigadier C.W. Bourne, the new divisional commander.[48]

This is not to say, of course, that The Salvation Army was preoccupied with Prohibition. The readers of the Central *War Cry* were assured that even with Prohibition on the books, the Army was still eager to help the down-and-outer: it was "the same old Army," and some of its programs were unaffected by Prohibition. The first social welfare had been in the Hartford Jail in 1885: work among prisoners continued to expand and flourish after the First World War. The Army's prison ministry was probably next only to the Women's Social Services in the number of souls it rescued and in the approval it gained from professional observers. The Lifers' Club, formed in 1916, was rejuvenated in May 1920, still under its first and most famous president Jesse Pomeroy. There were several branches, the largest of which, in the New Jersey State Prison in Trenton, had 142 members in 1929.[49]

Entire corps, with sergeants, flags, and brass bands sprang up spontaneously in several prisons, nurtured after the first burst of enthusiasm by regular visits from nearby corps officers and from representatives of the Salvation Army Prison Department at territorial headquarters. The first of these corps was at San Quentin, established in Maud Booth's day, the next was at the Michigan State Prison in Marquette. In 1920 a Salvation Army open air meeting was held in the yard of the Indiana State Boys' Reformatory at Jeffersonville, which touched off a religious revival among the youthful inmates. Many came forward to offer themselves to be rescued from sin. The prison chaplain, Lucien V. Rule, and the Army officers were naturally overjoyed; the former "worked like a Trojan" to prepare the six hundred boys who wished to join the Army's Brighter Day League. Sixty-five of these wanted to become full-fledged soldiers in the Army. A corps was promptly started, supervised by Adjutant Ladlow of Louisville No.1. By 1921, when Commissioner Booth-Tucker came to conduct the ceremonial enrollment of the new soldiers, their number had swelled to ninety. The corps movement spread to other prisons, and soon there was a corps in the Oklahoma State Prison at McAlester. The seventy soldiers of "McAlester No.2" corps marched through the prison yard with flag, drums, and a guitar band, and secured over seven hundred converts. In 1924 these soldiers fitted out a Ford truck with a van body, suitably covered with evangelical appeals, and proudly presented it to their comrades at McAlester No.1 as the "Salvation Army Gospel Truck." The corps officer used it for years to conduct meetings in outlying districts. Corps were added at Folsom Prison in California, and in the state prisons at Trenton, New Jersey and Hutchinson, Kansas, bringing the total of these prison corps to seven. This is touching and remarkable evidence of the Army's appeal to the cast-offs and lost souls of life; soldiers in these corps valiantly held their services in the prison yard, amidst the kind of abuse and skepticism that greeted the salvation war everywhere in the 1880s.[50]

Nor did The Salvation Army coddle these warriors: they were told outright that prison was not the "cause of the prisoner's calamity" but the "consequence of his crime." Individual officers did what they could to alleviate especially brutal conditions, but the Army had little to say about basic prison reform: its "real work" was to bring the sinner to Christ, and thereby to "change the inner mind of the criminal." Men who joined prison corps or the Brighter Day League were expected to witness to their new faith in Christ, to abandon drink, drugs, and gambling, and to obey prison officials. The latter, naturally pleased at these requirements, beamed approval on Army work within their walls. The approbation of the guards sometimes made things difficult for the prisoner-converts; the other inmates accused the converts of feigning religion to ingratiate themselves with the authorities, and harassed them. Many of these convict-soldiers nevertheless remained doggedly faithful to their new Lord and continued to live within the law when they left prison—some of them forever.[51]

Many released men passed again into the hands of The Salvation Army. The decade of the 1920s saw "an increasing reciprocity between the Bench and The Salvation Army." The Army developed parole programs in New York, California and Massachusetts. Almost half the men released to the Army had been convicted of violent crimes. Officers made much of this fact, convinced that it reflected the Army's reputation "of being a sort of sociological sieve for getting the best out of the worst." Formal parole programs were widely supplemented by officers who acted as unofficial probation officers for youth in legal difficulties, especially for first offenders and those driven to crime by poverty. Army prison work gained full judicial recognition when officers were appointed as chaplains in the Federal prison at Atlanta and at McNeill Island near Tacoma, Washington. The McNeill chaplain, Ensign C.W. Burr, conducted himself like a Salvationist in his new appointment. He counseled the seven hundred men with the Army's lively, practical version of Christianity, and conducted the prison band using a full set of *The*

Salvation Army Band Journal that had been given by Commander Evangeline, who had a great interest in prison work.[52]

It was the "same old Army" in other ways, too, as the twenties roared along. The Great Salvation War, whether fought in corps, street, social institution, or prison, was bouyed up as always by the Army's own brand of music. The decade saw widespread improvement in that bane of the devil, the Salvation Army band. After 1921 all three territories had headquarters' staff bands—the Western Territorial Staff Band, the Chicago Staff Band, and the New York Staff Band (actually the long famous National Staff Band in new uniforms). There were new regional ensembles as well, such as the New England Divisional Staff Band, which played in Boston under its gifted young leader, a Swedish immigrant named Erik Leidzen. And in 1921 the Army opened its first music camp, at Long Branch, New Jersey. The camp leader was Captain John Allan, safely returned from his chaplain's duties in the war. Many corps mustered large bands of considerable proficiency, able to perform concerts and put on handsome parades in addition to their street corner and congregational accompaniment duties. Some of these bands had been long established, like those of Oakland No. 1; Flint, Michigan; East Liverpool, Ohio; South Manchester, Connecticut; and a dozen Chicago corps; others, such as Los Angeles No. 1, Boston Palace, and the Honolulu Girls' Home Band, developed fully only after the war. Gradually the colorful variety of instruments—the keyed bugles, valve trombones, and fifes of pioneer days—disappeared from the scene, as a regulation brass instrumentation was ever more widely adopted. Clarinets and saxophones held on longer—in a few places into the 1930s— but only doubling parts written for brass. (Woodwinds ceased to have an *official* place in Army bands in 1902, when the Army published for the last time a part for the "clarionet" to play.)[53]

The Salvation Army's willingness to steal tunes from the devil continued into the 1920s, although on a reduced scale. But it was difficult to acquire material in sufficient quantity at reasonable prices that met the Army's requirements for its music: it must be religious; every arrangement and selection must contain a recognizable strain of Christian hymnody; and the music must be written entirely in the treble clef, even the bass parts. This was a British custom for all brass bands, Army or not, but the Army adopted it eagerly for the practical benefits—in a pinch (which often occurred), a player could be switched to any instrument without learning new fingerings for the valves. It was also much easier to start a band from scratch if there were only one set of fingerings to explain to everyone. Army bands were all brass, another British device The Salvation Army in America gladly adopted—it was easier for a beginner to squeeze at least *some* kind of sound out of a brass horn than from a woodwind, and brass instruments held up much better to the rigors of street warfare. Unfortunately, however, music arranged for all-brass bands was not easily obtained in the United States.

So the Army published its own band music. At first this consisted merely of familiar hymn tunes arranged to accompany singing indoors and out. Gradually selections, marches, and "meditations" were added. By 1920 the Army was publishing three series of band journals: the "Festival" series, intricate pieces requiring a full band; "Ordinary" (later "General") series, still difficult but playable by a smaller, slightly less proficient band; and a still-easier "Second," later "Triumph," series. The familiar set of straightforward hymn tune arrangements, playable by four or five bandsmen of indifferent skill, were published periodically in sheets as part of the "Ordinary" series; these sheets were later collected together, supplemented by other tunes and published as *Band Tune Books,* the first of which appeared in 1900. But the increasing number and ability of Army bands did not allow the music publishing branch, which was in London, to rest on past accomplishments. The director of that branch, Colonel Frederick Hawkes, an amiable soul with an interest in the small band, resolved to produce a new improved version of the *Tune Book.* He sent melody lines in bunches to his many bandmaster friends throughout Britain, asking them to supply band arrangements, while he produced the remainder at his desk at headquarters. The results were published in 1928 as The Salvation Army *Band Tune Book* of 541 hymn tunes. Bound in a complete set in red-varnished cardboard covers, it is a remarkable collection, with many curiously beautiful little pieces, some somber and sonorous, others sprightly and full of hope. The *Band Tune Book,* which is still in use, may well contain the most often heard band music on earth. In the more than fifty years that it has been in use there have been thousands of converts who have attested to the convicting Grace of God that came upon their souls when they heard an Army band playing a familiar old hymn.[54]

Although quite content to use the lovely *Band Tune Book* for hymn tune playing—which was all that many small bands played—serious Army musicians in the United States wanted a band journal of their own in which to publish meditations and selections of their own composition.

The Commander, who was by now so thoroughly American in her sentiments that no one but Bramwell remembered that she had ever been English, easily secured the approval of the territorial commanders for an *American Band Journal* in 1928. American bands would, of course, continue playing the material published by London as well. Thus supplied with an endless stream of music from England and America, the Army's bands multiplied. Every corps capable of mustering a band did so. The bands of older, established corps were staffed no longer by zealous bumpkins newly rescued and handed a horn, but by second-generation skillful Salvationist instrumentalists. But no matter the size of the band or its musical ability, it was expected to play in the street five times per week, while experienced bands held endless concerts and special musical weekends. The quantity, variety, and charm of Salvation Army music came to the favorable attention not only of the public but of professional musicians and critics. By the mid 1920s, the Army's street-corner bands had become among the most common sights in the United States: "One of the most familiar sights in America is a little knot of Salvation Army preachers at a street corner blaring fundamentalist hymns on brassy horns. . . ." Their zeal and ability won the affectionate respect of America's finest musicians. "The next time you hear a Salvation Army Band, no matter how humble," declared John Philip Sousa in 1930, "take off your hat."⁵⁵

The Army's place in public esteem seemed assured. Yet this happy state of affairs failed to penetrate entirely to the corps. The social institutions, camps, territorial, and national projects were able to draw on the benefits of the two Home Service Funds and their territorial successors. The corps, it will be recalled, were excluded from these schemes; as denominational congregational units, they were expected to be self-supporting, as were all other churches. This did not occur as widely in the Army as leading officers had hoped—and predicted. Instead, many corps participated in annual unified fund-raising campaigns, in which the community was solicited once for enough money to finance all the major charities and good causes in the area. The most common of these was the annual Community Chest, which began on a limited basis, here and there, after the war. Its convenience and practicality, combined with its appeal to bumptious community loyalty and the boosterism of the decade, caused the Community Chest to spread rapidly.⁵⁶

For many corps the Chest was a welcome boon. As the Home Service

Fund was to the rest of the Army, the annual community appeal of the "Red Feather" (symbol of the Community Chest) was to the corps. Before the arrival of the Chest, officers in small corps had been hard-pressed to meet expenses. Young Bertha Shadick, sent to Saratoga Springs, New York, found the corps—and herself—penniless. When an elderly soldier died, the fledgling lieutenant had to find an undertaker who would bury the departed comrade for the few dollars her pathetic possessions had brought. Mr Otis S. Carr agreed; he was a kindly sort of man who was touched by Shadick's courage and resolved to help her by arranging all on his own a kind of community appeal on behalf of the Army. Many officers in small corps sustained themselves in the early Twenties as the pioneers had, on stale bakery goods, and walked long distances in all weather to save a nickel carfare.[57]

The "Red Feather" changed all that. Because of the welfare services offered there, the local corps qualified as a public charity, and the Army was entitled to a share of what the Chest raised. This made it possible for many corps to survive, by providing funds the soldiers had not contributed for the corps' varied programs. Salvationists were notoriously poor at providing financial support for the corps. This was partly due to poverty; by the mid-1920s it was also partly due to the ready availability of "outside" funding. The result was that the amount given in the individual soldier's cartridge packet was often "ridiculously low." Despite official Army policy, which required that corps be self-supporting, the Rockefeller investigation in 1924 found only one such corps in the entire Eastern territory. Yet the same study estimated that any corps with one hundred soldiers could be self-supporting on much less than ten percent of their combined salaries. (Like other evangelical denominations, the Army accepted ten percent—the Biblical tithe—as a reasonable donation from its members.) The fact that almost no soldier returned more than a pittance to the salvation war was attributed by officers to the availability of community appeal funds.[58]

Still, it was difficult for officers to become overly depressed over the meagerness of the weekly cartridge collection, when the Home Service Fund or the Community Chest made up all deficiencies and more. In fact, the prospects before the Army in the 1920s were bright. Prohibition had eliminated the saloon and most public drunkenness. The Army's standard for membership was the highest of any evangelical sect. The ranks continued to increase, albeit much more slowly than in the past, and with a much larger percentage of new soldiers coming from the second and third generation of converts rather than from an influx of freshly rescued sinners. The lack of money was no longer troublesome. The Army's social programs, evangelical activities, bands, and summer camps all flourished. The American public clearly loved The Salvation Army. One writer declared in 1926 that the Army had experienced "a rapidity of March [which was] in many aspects . . . little short of phenomenal." The first half of the decade recorded dramatic statistical increases, in net assets, buildings, total seating capacity, and "senior soldiers" (adult members). Sometimes conversions occurred at an extraordinary rate. In the fall of 1924 the "entire population of 159 men and women [of Samptown, New Jersey] knelt at the drumhead and in the words of the Army, claimed salvation." This encouraging development followed the labors of a team of officers from nearby corps who held a revival in Samptown at the request of the owner of the town's steel mill.[59]

Caught up in the spirit of advance, which her own flamboyant and popular personality helped to reinforce, the Commander decided in 1926 to open a new territorial headquarters for the South. This move would serve several happy purposes at once: it would capitalize on the regional pride of the old Confederacy by giving the Army there its own headquarters, *War Cry*, and war college; it would eliminate the very long distances staff officers now traveled on visits and inspections in the South; it would create a group of leaders who could devote their entire energies to developing The Salvation Army in the South, a region in which progress had been languid; and—best of all—it would be dramatically symbolic of growth and progress.

The new territory was made up of the southern parts of the Eastern and Central territories; it consisted of all of the Southern states: Maryland, Kentucky (except for an enclave south of Cincinnati, which was left in the East to provide regional financial support for the small general hospital in Covington, a suburb of Cincinnati), Oklahoma, Arkansas, and Texas (except El Paso on the New Mexico border, which was left in the Western territory). Atlanta was selected as territorial headquarters after Major Bertram Rodda, the Georgia-South Carolina divisional commander, aided by Atlanta's Rotary Club and various local boosters, had neatly disposed of the claims of Birmingham, Memphis, and Washington. Rodda, whose divisional headquarters was in Atlanta, had been appointed to arrange the legal and business aspects of the transition. A cheerful, expansive officer with unlimited energy, Rodda scurried about like a worker ant, creating a headquarters out of whole cloth. He secured the Elks' Temple on Ellis Street for the new headquarters building and arranged with a local printer for an inaugural issue of a Southern version of the *War Cry* even before the new editor arrived.[60]

To serve as territorial commander, Evangeline selected William McIntyre and promoted him to Lt.–Commissioner—an inspired choice. Evangeline Booth had, in fact, a special gift in finding and utilizing men of exceptional talent: the territorial and divisional officers who served under her were some of the Army's most effective and dedicated leaders. McIntyre, a provincial commander, was overjoyed at this challenging promotion in rank and responsibility. An amiable eccentric, a colorful speaker, plain, almost rough in manner, McIntyre was an innovative and courageous leader, a zealous evangelist, and wholly unorthodox in this methods. He occasionally promoted officers on the spot for a good suggestion—he called good suggestions "hat-stretchers"—and drove serenely about the territory in a stately green Graham-Paige sedan (in bland defiance of the Army's regulation requiring officers to use cheap, four-cylinder black cars), because he had secured the luxurious old car at such a bargain that it would have been a shameful waste of the Lord's money to let it escape. The Commissioner loved buildings as much as he had when he and Colonel Holz (who had replaced the noble Estill, who "died in harness," as territorial commander of the East) had been the leading advocates of the purchase of property for the Army before the war. He was devoted above all to the welfare of the corps officer, and was determined that each one would have a decent corps, a decent quarters, and a regular salary. There have been few territorial commanders more loved by his officers than William McIntyre.[61]

The new Commissioner faced a large task, and wasted no time. There was much to arrange in any case, but the fact that both the Central and Eastern territorial leaders were forced to relinquish vast areas and hundreds of officers from their control, and the fact that many officers from the Northeast and the Midwest now faced the prospect of being marooned in a distant and unfamiliar region for the rest of their careers, required prodigies of tact and patience, which McIntyre produced. He and Rodda smoothed over objections from Chicago and New York to the proposal that cadets destined for Southern appointments be taken at once to form a new Southern war college; it was agreed as a compromise that these cadets would remain in their current training colleges, joining the new Southern training branch only for their last month of preparation. McIntyre knew that the advance of the Great Salvation War would be delayed in the South only as long as the feeling persisted among officers of being stranded like gypsies in a strange land. The Southern Territory, officially inaugurated in 1927, was actually born in 1928, when the first big Congress in Atlanta brought Salvationists from the former Eastern and Central parts of the new territory together for the first time.[62]

McIntyre set incredible goals for the first five years of the new territory, and inspired the rank and file to reach them. His "Salvation Offensive" captured the old-time war spirit: he called for ten thousand new soldiers and 150 new corps buildings. It is a monument to the ceaseless toil, sacrifice, and prayer of hundreds of officers that so much of the "Salvation Offensive" was achieved before McIntyre departed for the Chicago command in 1930: nine thousand new soldiers and 163 new Army halls. The first issue of the Southern territorial *War Cry* appeared on March 26, 1927, full of hope—and predicting that the people of the South would soon be disabused of the notion, which seemed to be held nationwide, that The Salvation Army consisted only of street-corner bands and warm memories of the services rendered on the battlefields of France.[63]

A Southern Staff Band was organized, and departed almost at once in June on its first tour in a "comfortable touring bus." Brass banding, however, did not flourish in the new territory, despite the gentle climate and the religious disposition of many of the people, which should have encouraged the Army's open air and march ministry. The corps were small—the average Southern corps had but six soldiers in 1929—and poor. There was no tradition of brass music in the Southern branch of the Army, and little interest in it outside of the Army. There was little immigration into the South from Britain or Canada, whence many Army bandsmen had come to more northerly corps. Only a few large corps in the South had bands, none of them experienced enough to play the more difficult and challenging pieces. When national headquarters optimistically sent one hundred full sets of *Festival Series* music and five hundred sets of the new *American Band Journal* to the new Southern territorial trade department, McIntyre sent it all back: the South had no bands, except the Staff Band, that were "able to handle this class of music." Still, progress was made even in banding. In a year McIntyre reported there were forty-two regular and young people's bands in the territory, although these aggregations were mostly very small and unskilled. In other areas success was remarkable—within the first year in the South, the Army added one hundred new soldiers per month.[64]

The Salvation Army's interest in extending its ministry to blacks had never abated and was freshly stimulated by the official opening of the Southern territory, where almost ninety percent of American blacks still lived in 1927. Two black corps, in Washington, D.C., and Charleston, South Carolina, had been opened on the eve of the First World War. Fredericksburg, Virginia, was reopened in the summer of 1920, a relic of the Army's Victorian "Colored Campaign" reborn in what was hoped were better times. All indoor religious services in the South were segregated on the basis of race, the Army's included, but open-air services attracted large mixed crowds that were often more than half black. This encouraged Salvationists: when it proved impossible in 1920 to buy or rent a hall in Norfolk to open a new black corps, the officers decided to hold open-air and cottage meetings indefinitely, or until a suitable hall was found. The Army nurtured other little cracks in the "color barrier" as well. Spiritual retreats for the officers of a division—called "officers' councils"—and large public youth rallies were integrated in the 1920s, although travel, hotel, and restaurant facilities were not, which embarrassed officers of both races. In fact, few blacks were won to Christ through the ministry of The Salvation Army in the 1920s. The shortage of black officers was cited at the time as the major obstacle to progress in the South.[65]

Elsewhere blacks were successfully integrated into Army programs, but in small numbers. There was a sprinkling of dedicated black Salvationists throughout the country. Several New York corps had active black sergeants; the band at the Brooklyn No. 1 corps—one of the best in the country—had four black players in 1922. Yet there were several segregated facilities outside the South as well: New York No. 8 was listed as a "colored corps" in 1920, and in 1921 the Army turned the old Chicago No. 2 corps on South Division Street into a black corps, announcing it as the first corps for that race in Chicago. In 1925 a maternity hospital for black women was opened in Cleveland; in 1930 it was relocated in the city and named the Mary B. Talbert Home and Hospital. In the north as well as the South, the Army's authentically good intentions, the courage of black Salvationists, the love that is properly the mark of Christian work produced some touching and remarkable results in improving relations between the races, but the overall result of the Army's intermittent efforts to extend its work among black Americans was slight.[66]

The advance of the salvation war was clearly not uniform in the 1920s, but overall The Salvation Army had made encouraging progress as the decade drew to its end. A second, and in some cases, third, generation had taken its place in the ranks of the "dear old Army," while the traditional street and welfare ministries had yielded up many remarkable conversions. While most denominations lost members and the status of organized religion seemed to sink, the Army joyfully expanded. The Commander continued to embody, so far as the public and the Army rank and file were concerned, the zealous evangelical spirit of the Army and the booster patriotism of the Republic. Her "World's Greatest Romance" supplemented by that old classic "The Commander in Rags," her motorcades, lectures, and mass rallies, earned Evangeline Booth, and the Army she so consciously represented, a lasting place in the affection, the respect and bounty of the public. It was inevitable that she would require a new headquarters building, a "Salvation Skyscraper" in the latest style, to replace the Victorian Gothic fortress that had once been Ballington Booth's pride and joy. As the new structure went up over the old address on Fourteenth Street in New York City now joined by a new residence for working women—the Evangeline Residence donated by John Markle, whom the charming Commander had encouraged to donate a half-million dollars—the prestige and pride of The Salvation Army seemed to rise with it. The new year 1929 dawned full of hope, for Army and country alike.[67]

CHAPTER V

1929-1950

"How the anxious shout it . . ."

The bouyant spirit that animated the Army throughout the 1920s ought to have been chilled by the events of 1929, when two crises in succession overtook the movement: the deposition of General Bramwell Booth in January and February, and in October the beginning of the Depression. The fact that the evangelical and charitable zeal of the average officer and soldier did not falter during these troubling events—and during the prolonged years of depression and war that followed—is one more of many monuments to the sense of loyalty to Christ and the soul-saving mission of the Army that inspired the lives of most Salvationists.

The administrative crisis that overtook the leadership of The Salvation Army in early 1929 had been developing for several years. Printed statements on the issues at stake had been distributed among selected staff officers in the United States as early as March 1925. The discussion concentrated on two points: the powers of General Bramwell Booth, who had succeeded his father the Founder in 1912; and the procedure by which his successor in turn was to be chosen. The Founder had fixed the conditions of the Generalship in the Deed Poll of 1878, an act of Parliament that served The Salvation Army as its legal charter. This act placed in the hands of the General all executive power over the Army, including the rights of a legal trustee in whose personal hands all properties were held (except in the United States, where since 1899 the Army had been separately incorporated), and the right to name his successor. His authority was absolute and final: there were no councils, conferences, or committees that he had to consult, or even to inform as to his actions. The appointment was for life; there was no provision for a General to retire.[1]

There was, however, a means for removing one. In 1904 William Booth had accepted the advice of legal counsel and added a Supplementary Deed to the 1878 Deed Poll. It did nothing to diminish his autocratic powers, but it did provide for the removal of an insane, morally corrupt, or bankrupt General, or one whom three-quarters of all active commissioners and territorial commanders, meeting together as a High Council for that purpose, declared to be "unfit for office." This High Council could be summoned by the "joint requisition" of the Chief of the Staff and any four other commissioners, or by *any* seven commissioners. The Council could elect by a two-thirds majority a successor to a General deposed in such a manner; all powers of the one overturned ceased at once, including the right to name a successor. Thus far had the Founder tempered the absolutism of his office, and no farther. The monarchy remained autocratic, and almost certainly hereditary. The contingencies under which a High Council could be summoned were regarded by the Founder and later by his chosen successor Bramwell as fantastically remote.[2]

Others, alas, did not take such a relaxed view. To them, the prospect of summoning a High Council and deposing the General seemed increasingly more practical and appealing. The problem in their eyes was, in general, Bramwell, and in particular, the widespread belief among senior officers that he had named a member of his immediate family to succeed him; at first speculation centered on his wife, Florence Soper Booth, later on his eldest daughter, Commissioner Catherine Bramwell-Booth. No one could deny that the General was a man of extraordinary administrative skill: much of the structure of The Salvation Army, which has survived remarkably intact until the present day, was the work of Bramwell Booth. He was a wholehearted evangelical, master of a handsome prose style, and a kindly, well-spoken man, and his immediate subordinates as well as the rank-and-file held him in great personal affection. Bramwell had a high—indeed a mystical—conception of his office, which he viewed, perhaps naturally, as a sacred and inviolable trust placed in his hands by the glorified Founder.

That he had defects, however, was undeniable. While less marked than his virtues, they led him and the Army into the tragic affairs of 1929. Some of his faults were mere foibles. Those who were around the General knew him to be fussy, rigid in his habits, and old-fashioned in some ways to the point of eccentricity: he signed his name with a quill, for instance, and blotted the ink with sand. There were more serious disabilities. Many high-ranking officers who loved Bramwell as a man believed him to be an absolute autocrat, inviting no advice or argument and brooking none, except from members of his own family. These officers feared, rightly or wrongly, that criticism of the General would bring swift transfer to some less prestigious position, far from the center of power. The case of Colonel George Carpenter, the international literary secretary, was widely regarded as proof of these suspicions. In January 1927, that officer was transferred to the editorship of *The War Cry* in Sydney, Australia, after a period of chilled relations between him and the General. These officers were also alarmed by what they regarded as the General's unfortunate predilection for members of his own family, whom he was suspected of consulting on Army matters great and small, and favoring with appointments beyond their abilities. These critics did not suggest that the General's children—especially Catherine, Bernard, and Wycliffe—were not dedicated and talented officers: rather, other officers took exception to the Booths' deportment, which seemed breezy and presumptuous, their easy assumption of being destined for great things, and their access to the ears of power when other, more senior officers were consulted on nothing.[3]

The feeling that the Army's system of government should be changed was widespread among leading officers. It did not all center on the personality traits of Bramwell and his children: many officers acted on principle, convinced that the autocratic military system developed by William Booth in the days of rapid advance and terrible warfare was no longer entirely practical in the enlightened 1920s, and certainly could not be allowed to pass intact into the hands of Commissioner Catherine (who was only forty-five in 1928) for what might be a very long reign. Officers who felt this way made up the majority of commissioners; highly principled men in every regard, sincere in their devotion to God and the Army, they had no consciously selfish motive for advocating change. Others had motives that were less noble. Some had, or imagined they had, personal grievances against the General or one of his children. Frederick Booth-Tucker, the General's brother-in-law, had been retired in 1926 at age seventy-three, very much against his will, according to a policy newly introduced by Bramwell that set age limits, according to rank, for active service. Booth-Tucker still had a warrior's heart, and felt cast aside and useless. His resentment against Bramwell and the system was great. Still other officers sought the General's office for themselves, or for some candidate other than the supposedly-predestined Commissioner Catherine.[4]

National feelings were involved as well. Evangeline Booth and the four American territorial commanders made it clear to the General and to the Chief of the Staff Commissioner Edward J. Higgins, who knew America and loved it, that they felt that the American command of the Army—which they considered to be the richest and most powerful segment of the movement—should be given considerably more autonomy in administrative matters. There is abundant evidence to demonstrate that Commander Evangeline felt uncharitably toward Bramwell as a person, and resented on principle his authority over her and the American Army. There is evidence as well that strongly suggests that she craved the office of General for herself, which would of course have been impossible had Bramwell been allowed either to remain in office indefinitely—she was sixty-three herself in 1928—or to name his own successor, who most likely would not be Evangeline.[5]

The events that led to the first meeting of the High Council of The Salvation Army on January 8, 1929, can be traced with accuracy in a chronological line. It is far more difficult to trace the motives of the principal actors in those events, and more difficult still to describe or explain the sadness and confusion that linger around this story in Army circles today after more than half a century. Two things are certain: although Bramwell Booth's ill-health was a major factor in the crisis of 1929, the issues of his autocracy and the succession also figured largely in the calling of the High Council. Agitation on these subjects began long before the General fell seriously ill. The second is that, from the beginning, the movement to reform the Army in both of these particulars was organized by American officers, including Evangeline Booth, who rapidly came to dominate it.[6]

Bulletins, manifestos and "blasts of a trumpet" appeared regularly from 1925 to 1928 from the pen—more accurately, the mimeograph—of the mysterious Atwood, supposedly a local officer in Wichita Falls, Texas. Commissioner Brengle was horrified at these bulletins, which denounced the General as a tyrant whose pretensions were practically criminal and whose nepotism was laughable, and he labeled them "absolutely ridiculous." One of the bulletins called for its readers to "fight" for the "interests" of the Commander, and urged that all of the General's authority over the American branch be vested in her. Brengle exchanged letters with Booth-Tucker over the subject matter of the Atwood bulletins in June 1927. The latter's reply, defending Atwood and adding more charges of his own to the indictment, was printed and widely circulated; it convinced Brengle (and the Booths) that Booth-Tucker and Atwood were at least in correspondence, if not more closely associated.[7]

The opposition to the General, however, did not make use of subterfuge for long. In October 1927, the Commander called upon the General in London. Fresh from the triumph of an important address in Paris delivered before the Ten-Year Convocation of the American Legion, she now delivered a sort of manifesto of her own. This was in the form of typewritten "Notes for Interview with the General, October 11, 1927," which were likewise widely and judiciously circulated in mimeographed form. There were fifteen points in this important document, which can be distilled to the familiar two: the General had "absolute power," which was no longer acceptable to leading officers; and he must not attempt to appoint his own successor, who should be elected instead by the "High Council or some such body within the Army." "The conviction is growing everywhere that the time has arrived when some change must take place in the Constitution of the Army," she declared, "particularly with respect to the appointment of its General."[8]

The General replied on November 24 in a typed, seven-page letter (which Evangeline also distributed among the staff), in which he rejected all of the Commander's arguments and announced that he was now convinced that British law did not allow a trustee (such as himself) to alter the Deed Poll under which his trust was held: the system created by the Founder in 1878 and bequeathed to Bramwell was eternal and inviolate; the Supplementary Deed of 1904 had not altered, but strengthened the 1878 trust. Bramwell also touched on a fact that must be kept in mind when reading about this unhappy quarrel: he noted that he might take his critics more seriously if the great work of preaching the gospel were "really suffering" under the present system. He was quite right: the extent of the General's authority and the question of the succession to it mattered not at all to the great majority of Salvationists, who made their daily contributions to the salvation war all unaware of a war of a different, less creditable nature, slowly brewing above them.[9]

The Commander responded to her brother with a twenty-one page letter, which inevitably followed the others into print and distribution among staff officers. Her remarks were to the point: the General's belief in the inviolability of the 1878 Deed was "utterly repugnant" (a word she used twice in the letter); there were "widespread questionings consequent upon the nepotism existing." There were dark hints in the letter: the "present conditions" were "filled with those very things that threaten, ultimately if not speedily, to break out in internecine war," to which ominous remark she added the even more pointed observation that the sacred Deed Poll of 1878 was in any case a piece of British law: it was "alien" and had "little or no standing" in the United States! Finally, on page eighteen, she stated her position openly to the General: if the "claimed provision" in the Trust Deed that allowed the General to name his successor were not removed, "then disturbance or rupture seems inevitable." These remarks were circulated by the Commander herself among the American territorial commanders. It was hardly surprising that the General and his family regarded Evangeline as actively disloyal and ambitious for the Generalcy herself. What the General did not realize was how widespread was the dissatisfaction with him among high-ranking officers.[10]

In April 1928, the seventy-two year old General Bramwell Booth fell ill, with what he supposed to be a mild case of influenza. In May, he was well enough to lay the foundation stone for the new International Training College at Denmark Hill in south London, but it was his last public appearance. Always nervous by nature, now burdened by age and the conviction that the American branch was a nest of enemies, the General grew weaker. He availed himself, like his father before him, of the water cure at Matlock, likewise in vain. In October he was ordered to bed by his doctor. The daily administration of Army business passed into the hands of the General's wife and the Chief of the Staff. The General's illness gave the officers who wished to alter his powers their opportunity, but it also placed them in a quandary. They did not wish to appear to be taking advantage of a sick man by acting against him in his absence; on the other hand, they did not know the extent of his illness: if he should die before they could act, all would be lost: his chosen successor would rise to power automatically, healthy and alert, and there would be no excuse for calling the High Council. The chance to make the Army government more democratic, and the Generalcy elective, would be lost for years. On November 14, 1928, after several meetings together and considerable soul-searching, seven commissioners made a formal request to Commissioner Higgins that he summon the High Council to adjudicate William Bramwell Booth unfit for the office of

General of The Salvation Army and to elect a successor to him.

The events of the next few months were marked by confusion, rancor, and heartfelt anguish. The dispute now became public knowledge. *The War Cry* began to carry noncommital news briefs about the General's health and the calling of the Council. Salvationists were horrified. So was the General, who had recovered enough to receive the bad news that the Council had been summoned; it was only then that he learned for the first time that dissatisfaction was not confined to the Americans and Booth-Tucker, but was widespread among senior officers.[11]

Worse news was to come. A letter, signed by all but seven of the commissioners assembled for the Council, and later a small delegation (which included two of the Army's saints, Yamamuro of Japan and Brengle of the United States), urged Bramwell to resign with dignity and allow the High Council to choose a new General. He refused through Commissioner Catherine, who was a member of the Council and allowed to speak for her father at their deliberations. On January 16, 1929, Bramwell Booth was declared to be unfit for his office by the three-quarters majority required by the Supplementary Deed, and deposed from his position as General.

Stunned, confused, desperate, and still convinced that he must preserve the Founder's system at all costs, the falling leader sought the intervention of the British law courts. His case was in part, a good one: his legal counsel had not been permitted to address the High Council on his behalf. The commissioners had wished to spare the General and themselves unnecessary humiliation, but the British court regarded this refusal as a violation of natural justice. On the strength of that charge, an injunction was granted that prevented the commissioners from meeting again to elect a successor until they had been addressed by the General's attorney. The General also requested the court to invalidate the Supplementary Deed Poll of 1904—which created the High Council—on the grounds that a trustee (even the Founder!) cannot alter the terms of his trust.

The commissioners were shocked and dismayed by the General's action. So far as they were concerned, the legal merits of his case mattered nothing compared to the fact that he had brought a case at all. Like other literal-minded Christians, the commissioners regarded any attempt by one Christian to bring the secular arm of the law to bear on fellow believers as a clear violation of the teachings of St. Paul, who in I Corinthians 6:1-8 instructed his followers to allow themselves to be defrauded rather than "go to law one with another." His lawsuit damned the General in the eyes not only of the Council, but of almost all Salvationists, who read of it in *The War Cry*. American staff officers, led by the national chief secretary Colonel Walter Jenkins, cabled a protest from the United States denouncing the lawsuit as "disastrous combat," calling the General a "recreant," and pledging full support to the "constitutional" High Council. On the Council itself the handful still loyal to the General shrank to the four members of his family and one other. The General's lawyer was courteously heard on February 13, after which a second vote confirmed the first: the General was deposed.[12]

Later that day Commissioner Higgins was elected as the third General of The Salvation Army. Commander Evangeline had taken little part in the proceeding that she had helped to precipitate, apparently certain that her elevation as her brother's replacement was assured. If Bramwell had underestimated the opposition to him, so too had Evangeline. The American commissioners (except Brengle, too heartsick to take much interest in electioneering) and a few international supporters, like Commissioner Henry W. Mapp, had made her confident of election without knowing the hearts of the majority. The prize eluded her, but she was soon consoled: the precedent of election was established and would inevitably become a principle. Many commissioners favored a mandatory age limit, even for the General. Higgins might not serve for life. There was hope. What mattered far more to Salvationists around the world was that the Army's greatest crisis had passed. The Salvation soldiers, alarmed and confused by the many press and *War Cry* reports about the High Council, lawsuits, and electioneering, now gratefully turned their hearts' energies back to the street corners and penitent forms where The Salvation Army still lived and had its being.[13]

On June 16, 1929, Bramwell Booth was promoted to Glory, at the age of seventy-three. He had served in The Salvation Army for fifty-one years.

Back in the United States, Evangeline was hailed as a heroine by the American staff. "The leader of the Reform Cause," announced the Eastern *War Cry* in March, "was our Commander Evangeline Booth, whose return as the leader of a cause that triumphed is hailed from shore to shore. God bless the Commander." Commissioner Holz introduced her to a huge welcome rally in New York as "the Joan of Arc in this Reform Movement." The press offered overwhelming endorsement of the victory of the "democratic" side in the recent conflict. "Admiration for the work of the Salvation Army" ran through "all the American comment" on the High Council. Yet many sympathetic observers were troubled, and expressed the hope that the conflict would leave no permanent damage. Writers declared their fears that "a mighty Victorian impulse [had,] perhaps, spent itself," that deposing the old General would cost the Army its old-time "crusading air," the "wholly unworldly martiality" of its pioneer days.[14]

The Army's friends need not have feared for its future. The great strength of the movement lay as always in the thousands of soldiers and officers who fought on for Christ after only a brief, confused pause to contemplate in wonder the activities of the High Council, whose deliberations might as well have taken place on Mars for all they affected the life of the corps and rescue work in the United States. The American commissioners were glad to return to what was, for them as well as for their troops, the end and purpose of their calling as Salvationists: the redemption of the world through the Blood of Christ—or at least as much of the world as could be drawn to the Saviour by the Army's unique combination of evangelism and practical charity. It is well that the Army did not lose sight of its mission in 1929; it was soon to face a long and severe test of that mission. In late October the values on the New York Stock Exchange collapsed.

The severity of the crisis was not immediately recognized, however, and the worst was still in the future when The Salvation Army celebrated a grand and glorious event in March 1930: the Golden Jubilee of Salvation Army work in the United States, celebrating the fiftieth anniversary of the arrival of George Scott Railton and the "Hallelujah Seven" on March 10, 1880. Commissioner Holz held a mammoth open-air meeting on March 10, 1930, at the very spot on Battery Park upon which Railton had stepped from the *Australia* on that memorable day. The last surviving member of the pioneer party, Field Major Emma Westbrook, overwhelmed by the cheering and the multitudes of Salvationists all around exclaimed in wonder, "What hath God wrought?" In May a National Congress was held, with mass rallies and an enormous parade up Broadway by four thousand soldiers and twenty brass bands. With Evangeline in her open car rode the beaming Major Westbrook, alongside still another who had reason to feel humbled by what the Army saw as the faithfulness of God: retired Commandant Eliza Shirley Symmonds. Prizes were offered for commemorative songster and band music, and two gems took the honors: "My Keeper" a choral piece by

William Bearchell, and the march "Army of God" by Emil Söderstrom, a Danish-American Salvationist. The new Salvation skyscraper on Fourteenth Street, housing national and territorial headquarters, was opened officially, and jubilant Salvationists swarmed into the new Memorial Temple to sing and cheer (which doubtlessly produced a pleasantly deafening effect in a hall acoustically designed by the Commander so that a pin dropped on the platform could be heard anywhere in the auditorium.)[15]

The Army would shortly need all the encouragement it could find. The economic slide begun in October 1929 became a general collapse. By March 1933, fifteen million people were unemployed, nine million bank accounts had vanished, and national income had fallen to less than half of its level in 1929. The Great Depression settled over the country, and The Salvation Army passed into a time of desperate and prolonged struggle, as taxing and heartrending in its way as the salvation warfare of pioneer days.

The Army's traditional mainstay for contributions required to sustain the social and evangelical programs was the working class—the very people upon whom the Depression bore most heavily. The Army's membership gained during the 1930s, but contributions were reduced sharply. Yet from 1929 to 1932 Salvation Army emergency relief expense, taking social institutions and corps together, increased by seven hundred percent. It was not surprising that *The War Cry* reported in 1931 that the Army was "strained to the utmost to successfully cope with the tremendous emergency relief load suddenly placed on it in addition to its normal work of social salvage." Indeed a considerable part of the "normal work of social salvage" ground almost to a halt. The Industrial Homes (renamed Men's Social Service Centers in 1936) had begun to show a small profit in the 1920s, as had the workingmen's hotels. Now both kinds of institutions were swamped with the homeless, penniless, and desperate. Many facilities were converted into soup kitchens and free sleeping shelters; regular rehabilitation programs were temporarily laid aside. In any case there was little that could be fixed or resold being given to the Army after 1930, and almost no market among the poor for the few cleaned and repaired articles that were processed. The financial circumstances of the industrial homes grew daily more desperate, as funds from every source evaporated and expenses multiplied. Social officers regarded it as a "nightmare"; there were days in which there was no food of any sort to offer the desperate men, and no money to pay them even the twenty-five cents a week over their board that they had been promised for their labor.[16]

The Women's Social Service Department fared better. The maternity homes were not besieged by homeless, jobless women, but it was nonetheless impossible to raise enough in traditional ways to finance the Army's maternity program. Women officers were reduced to begging food for their hospitals. Young Magna Sorenson traveled around a circuit of farms near Boise, Idaho, in a borrowed truck in the 1930s, collecting free vegetables for her pregnant charges in the city. In New York City, Emma Ellegard was forced to make a long weekly trip by streetcar to a fish market to get a basketful of donated fish for the girls. All officers in the Women's Social Service Department accepted large reductions in their meager salaries, and many served for nothing more than board and lodging. Unlike the hard-pressed men's social programs, however, there was no curtailment of services in the maternity hospitals during the Depression—a fact of which veteran officers are still proud —although the small general hospital in Covington, Kentucky was forced to close from 1932 to 1937.[17]

Financial problems pressed heavily on the Commander and the commissioners. General Higgins wrote from London in June 1931, gamely assuring the territorial commanders that the Army hoped to avoid "lowering the Flag" anywhere because of the Depression, which was now worldwide, but instructing them to curtail all expenses to those that were "absolutely essential." By 1931 the commissioners may well have wondered what was *left* to curtail. Buildings had been mortgaged, and in some cases—like that of the seven-story hotel in Norfolk "snapped up" by Commissioner McIntyre in happier times—the Army could not even pay the interest. Officers who had comforted evicted families might soon join them on the curb, surrounded perhaps by office furniture and one of the ubiquitous framed portraits of the Commander. Staff officers had their salaries reduced several times. Divisional officers lost even the small bonuses that they were used to receiving for maintaining *The War Cry* circulation in their districts: that journal recorded a "gradual decrease in circulation" throughout the Depression. The territorial commander of the West pared the headquarters budget so close to the bone that the territorial staff band was forced to disband, and officers wrote new memos on the back of old ones to save paper. In Chicago, Commissioner McIntyre had to take out a loan on his beloved Graham-Paige in order to pay the headquarters staff part of their (reduced) salaries. The Depression blighted even some programs that were still capable of producing revenue. When a new Evangeline residence for working girls was opened in Detroit—a project begun before the hard times—the entire operating budget disappeared the next day when the city's banks failed.[18]

It was on the corps, however, that the Depression bore with the most severity. Never a part of the national and territorial fund campaigns that followed the First World War, the corps had been dependent in the prosperous twenties on the Community Chest and the soldiers' usually meager cartridge contributions. These sources were everywhere sharply reduced after 1930, and in many cases dried up altogether, so that even without the extra demands caused by the hard times many corps would have been faced with debt just to maintain their regular activities. As it was, of course, concern with financing their regular activities was the least of the officer's problems: homeless, jobless men, worried families, tens of thousands of anxious, penniless transients, joined by more thousands of neighborhood unemployed and hungry people poured in on the corps, drawn in their desperation by the promise held out to them by the name of the organization.

Corps officers distributed to the jobless all manner of things that they had collected from kindhearted local merchants and farmers—coal, firewood, flour, milk, day-old bakery products, vegetables, and the leftover unsold food from restaurants. Many corps halls were used at night to house homeless men, who slept on the seats or on the hardwood floors under newspapers. In Roanoke, Virginia, where the Army hall was one block from the yards of the Norfolk and Western Railroad, a hundred men a day swamped the little corps. Young Captain Ed Laity housed them all in an empty dance hall upstairs over the chapel and begged enough scraps from restaurants and a local vegetable market every day to make soup or stew for the men. In the worst months of the Depression the officer and his family had nothing for themselves but this soup, and had to sleep with the transients when they could no longer pay the rent on their living quarters. On one of his tours, Commissioner McIntyre found that the two young women officers in International Falls, Minnesota, had lost their house and were forced to live in the Army hall, reduced to using a nearby filling-station restroom, and drawing their water from its sink. Even officers in better circumstances lost all or most of their salaries during part of the Depression years, and some officers received no salary through the entire period. Corps, like headquarters, fell into prolonged debt; a national survey in 1936 revealed that only thirty-two percent of the corps in the United States were not in debt.[19]

The Army's difficulties in the Depression were not all financial. Because of the volume of relief work administered by Salvationists, they were often frustrated in their efforts to provide spiritual and personal counseling to the recipients. As a result, in the minds of many of those who availed themselves of its philanthropy in the 1930s, The Salvation Army did not appear to be a religious mission, but a mere charity, little different from other agencies doing similar work in the hard times. This is the more unfortunate since the Army launched several national evangelical campaigns in the 1930s, centered on the theme "Try Religion —All Else has Failed!"

The fact remained that the attitude of a portion of the public toward The Salvation Army had changed. Those who received assistance at the Army's hands during the Depression differed from those who had received help before 1930. Most of those who came forward for relief now had been working- and middle-class people, decent and respectable in their own eyes, whom, innocent and unprepared, economic disaster had overtaken. These people were unaccustomed to charity, and to the proverty that preceded it, and found the experience of requesting it humiliating. Many were discouraged and bitter, and transferred their natural resentment onto the agency to which they were forced to go for relief. This was especially true when some delay or inconvenience was encountered. John Steinbeck's powerful novel of the Depression, *The Grapes of Wrath*, expresses the confusion and hostility of these newly-poor in graphic terms.

> "If a body's ever took charity, it makes a burn that don't come out. . . . Las' winter; an' we was a starvin'—me an' Pa an' the little fellas. An' it was a-rainin'. Fella tol' us to go to the Salvation Army." Her eyes grew fierce. "We was hungry—they made us crawl for our dinner. They took our dignity. They —I hate 'em!" . . . Her voice was fierce and hoarse. "I hate 'em," she said. "I ain't never seen my man beat before, but them—them Salvation Army done it to 'im."[20]

To these people, the Army seemed to have lost its way, to have drifted far from the bright and touching sacrifices of happier days when Salvationists gave up their lives to Christ and the Great Salvation War without a thought for costs and procedures. In fact, the salvation war-spirit continued to be the main driving force of the Army in the 1930s. The fact that some Americans had come to regard the Army as merely a welfare agency was a price that both the successful fund campaigns of the 1920s and the Depression relief work exacted. It was a price far dearer than money, and far dearer than most Salvationists—whose zeal for souls remained undimmed—would have paid, if at any point they had been certain of what was happening to the reputation of their crusade.

Criticism of the Army's charity did not gainsay that the organization produced prodigious relief work on behalf of the Depression-poor, most of it practical and timely, and given out with tact and kindness, even if the old-time personal counseling was set aside in the press of applicants. Huge shelters for homeless men were opened in major cities, whither many drifted in a vain search for work. An old river steamer, the "Broadway," was loaned to the Army in 1930 by its owners, and opened at a Brooklyn pier as a hostel for stranded unemployed merchant seamen. In Chicago the Army launched Wrigley Lodge on Union Street in 1930. Operated by the veteran Brigadier Sam Wood (once a California Charioteer), it was an enormous building, in which workers could feed 8,000 men a day. In New York the "Gold Dust Lodge" (named for a brand of flour) opened its doors in 1932 on the corner of Corlears and Cherry Streets in a factory donated by the Hecker Flour Company. The Lodge was presided over by Major and Mrs Andrew Laurie and another graduate of zany pioneer adventures, Lt.–Colonel Wallace Winchell. These huge facilities were donated, and partly supported, by sympathetic wealthy men in the desperate days before the federal government began its own massive and varied attempts to relieve the unemployed. The Hutton Food Station at Thirty-sixth and Tenth Avenues was another such facility, operated by the Army to provide breakfast and supper to two hundred needy school children every day. These programs and scores of smaller ones operated throughout the country in institutions and corps were intended by the Army to serve as an expression of Christianity in practical form. They provided food and shelter at a time when no large-scale government welfare existed.[21]

The Army was aware that those who came to its doors now were not accustomed to charity, and efforts were made to ease their humiliation. The cover of the Eastern *War Cry* proclaimed in October, 1931: "Mr Citizen, Temporarily Embarrassed, The Salvation Army Understands— and is Your Friend. Every Salvationist is pledged to extend to you, during these anxious times, as always, the right hand of aid and fellowship." To spare the feelings of such persons, the Army set up a Confidential Counselor's Bureau in New York to offer advice: in two days there were one thousand applicants.[22]

The Army, in fact, was full of advice during the Depression, most of it cheerful and filled with hope. Officers regarded the Depression as due in the first place to a loss of confidence, which their own brand of spiritual joy and practical, short-term relief would speedily restore. Large-scale political and economic solutions no longer interested the Army. Prohibition had clearly failed, and was doomed; the Republican Party which supported it was falling from power. It was time for the Army to take up again its traditional position that political solutions did not touch the central need of the heart. Evangeline, whose officers had endorsed Hoover in 1928, gladly accepted an invitation to open the Democratic National Convention in prayer in 1932, a fact which she gamely announced in Chicago while addressing a Prohibition rally. It was certain that the Democratic platform would demand the repeal of the prohibition amendment; it was almost equally certain that whoever the Democrats nominated would win the election. "The Salvation Army knows nothing of parties or politics," she declared. "Tomorrow I shall enjoy the memorable privilege of opening the Democratic Convention in prayer."[23]

Just as The Salvation Army brought two quarreling rival football teams—Army and Navy—together again to play for the benefit of the Army's Depression relief, so the Army's leaders were convinced that religion, hearty good cheer, and a cooperative spirit would soon eliminate the Depression itself. Commissioner McIntyre conducted a "Good Cheer Council" for the officers of the Wisconsin-Upper Michigan Division who had allowed themselves to feel uneasy because their division was slowly going bankrupt. A writer for the Central *War Cry* declared in 1932 that there was a "glory" in adversity: overcoming it brought a sense of satisfaction, a willingness to help others, and more complete reliance on God. Adjutant Vincent Cunningham, the talented editor of the Southern edition, offered even more direct instructions on overcoming the unwelcome effects of hard times: "Stop Talking Depression!" Politics and social theories were clearly not the answer; even a cheerful heart and a willing hand went only so far. The final solution to the Depression was individual salvation in Christ, multiplied many times: "What this country needs," declared Commissioner Brengle in 1932, "is a Revival!"[24]

However it may have appeared to some of its transient beneficiaries,

The Salvation Army was not merely—or even primarily—a charity after all. It was an evangelical crusade, and its soul-saving activities continued without interruption through the Depression years. Salvation Army street parades and open-air meetings still attracted crowds. Large corps like Oakland, Flint, and Brooklyn Citadels divided their musical forces into sections and held several open-air meetings at once, reforming into a long parade for the march back to the hall. Even medium-sized corps held sway on the streets: in Sioux City, Iowa, in 1933, crowds following the Army band became so large that police had to be called to control traffic. Bands with too few players for an effective march still went forth several times per week to play on the street corner. In New York City young Richard Holz (grandson of the famous pioneer) led the tiny band at New York No. 3 out to Times Square four times per week in 1936 and 1937. The corps was commanded by Adjutant Lyell Rader, a zealot for souls of the old-time variety, and became known as the "Glory Shop." A writer for *Newsweek* at the end of the decade estimated that there were perhaps a thousand corps bands in the United States, the majority of them between eight and fourteen pieces. In the hundreds of corps where there were only two or three players, or none at all, officers and soldiers were expected to sing and pray on the street corners. Carl Blied and his wife bravely sallied forth several times a week for five years in Bridgeton, New Jersey, with only a French horn and a drum.[35]

The Army's indoor activities flourished as well during the Depression. Christian people turn naturally to their religion in adversity, and many working-class Salvationists were unemployed. The Army offered its soldiers, who had time on their hands, a considerable amount of plain fun and good company at no cost. Many who were drawn to the Army for relief became interested in the organization itself, and curiosity turned to conviction when they learned of Christ and His claims. If membership grew in the 1930s, attendance soared. Total attendance at Army activities in the Eastern Territory, for instance, was higher in 1932 than in any other year from 1927 to 1975. Programs for young people were particularly successful: band instrument classes, Scouts, camps, after-school sports, the Girl Guards—and a charming addition for smaller girls, imported from England in 1925, the Sunbeams, which grew rapidly in the 1930s. The Scandinavian work, which celebrated its own Golden Jubilee in 1937, was at the height of its success and provided material relief and spiritual comfort to thousands "who, handicapped by a lack of knowledge of the language, or by a natural reticence and pride, would never have made their physical or spiritual needs known." There were Scandinavian Departments in every territory except the South, led during the Depression by men of exceptional piety and zeal—Lt.–Colonel Axel Beckman (East), Colonel Tom Gabrielsen (Central), and Brigadier Hal Madsen (West). Along with the retired Commissioner Brengle in the American corps, these men traveled widely, holding highly successful evangelical services. Many Salvation Army corps, in fact, experienced genuinely spontaneous revivals in the Holy Spirit during the Depression, and in their joy forgot the very fact of hard times.[26]

The Commander was at her best during these years. Although nearing seventy, Evangeline had lost none of her flair nor the graciousness that made her, year after year, the personal darling of her troops. Her public addresses continued to draw packed halls. The "Commander in Rags" —sad to say—had been put aside forever as a trifle inappropriate for a woman well past middle age, but the "World's Greatest Romance," practiced and refined to a degree near perfection, remained a popular favorite. Nor was Evangeline dependent on a few set pieces: in 1931 she traveled with the New York Staff Band in a motor tour of New York and Pennsylvania. She spoke forty-seven times and never repeated herself. The tour was a success for many reasons, not the least of which was a revival of old-time hallelujah clowning. The Staff Band, for instance, paraded into Butler, Pennsylvania, in tiny Austin cars—one car to each bandsman! Evangeline herself had a zany side: she liked to do her personal shopping in what she imagined to be a foolproof disguise, which consisted of dressing in civilian clothes and calling herself "Miss Cory." Once she went incognito to purchase flagstone for a walkway at her cabin at Lake George, New York, only to be spotted by the quarryman at once—by her nose![27]

Several aspects of the Commander's personality could be seen in the development of a series of special weekly Friday evening meetings she arranged for the new Centennial Memorial Temple at national headquarters on West Fourteenth Street. The programs were ably planned by the territorial commander, Commissioner John McMillan, assisted by Brigadier W. Alex Ebbs, and their quality was superb. The Army's best musicians sang and played, and there were special compositions for many of the services. The Commander, at her polished and eloquent best, spoke often. A special brass ensemble under the direction of Erik Leidzen, the gifted Swedish-American composer and conductor who now served as divisional bandmaster, was brought together in 1930 to play for these meetings.[28]

Leidzen was a man of rare ability, a zealous Christian whose standards of personal piety and musical performance exerted a profound and long lasting influence on the lives of many young Army musicians. He did not suffer fools gladly, however; like the Commander, whom he once described as "the Lord's handmaiden," Erik Leidzen could be cranky and was sensitive to the point of fragility. These two Salvationists struck sparks off one another at the end of the last of the Friday meetings at the Temple, in an incident that is too well-known in Army circles to ignore here.

The last of these special meetings was held on May 26, 1933. An especially prestigious and enjoyable program was offered to the jammed hall: a new march, "Brooklyn Citadel" by Adjutant Bearchell, who led the band at that famous corps; a new composition by Evangeline called "Streams in the Desert"; and a galaxy of songs, duets, and solos. The Commander spoke, but the guest of honor was Edwin Franko Goldman, a band conductor second only to Sousa in accomplishment and fame. Leidzen had written a special march for the guest, "E-F-G," based on Goldman's initials. The great man was dazzled by this array of Army music, and especially by Leidzen's flattering march: he promptly declared Leidzen to be a "genius," and praised all that he had heard to the skies. A thrill of pride swept the delighted crowd, most of whom were Salvationists and musicians themselves.

Evangeline was caught up in the excitement and felt inspired to end the carefully planned program in a burst of hallelujah enthusiasm with an old-time chorus called "The Salvation Army Doxology." Such alterations are commonplace in Army meetings, but Leidzen, always stiffly formal about such things, and with Goldman's praises still tickling his ears, cooly informed the Commander that the band had no music for that piece and would not play it. The song was known to everybody— could they not play along without music? They could not—not after a superb, well-rehearsed, and brilliant evening: it would be a ruinous anticlimax. Perplexed, Evangeline turned to the band and asked them to play the song. Leidzen, now thoroughly irritated, intervened by laying his baton down on his music stand, and the band followed his lead, putting down their instruments. The audience saw none of this, and happily sang the chorus with a single cornet. The following Monday morning Leidzen refused a summons to the Commander's office, and she reluctantly dismissed him from his employment with the Army. He became the arranger for the Goldman Band almost at once and nursed wounded feelings for years, until patience and tact drew his great talents back into Army service. The incident, trivial in itself, caused confusion and resentment at the time among Salvationist musicians, who naturally admired Leidzen for his gifts. It illustrated the dangers to which leaders and Army musicians alike had become prey in the new era of professionalism, when personalities and protocol seemed to replace service and zeal as the forces driving them to action.[29]

The Salvation Army continued to make musical progress, however, despite these little setbacks. In 1934 the Central Music Institute (CMI) opened for the first time at Camp Lake, Wisconsin, north of Chicago. The Eastern Territory launched its own annual camp the next year, at Star Lake, New Jersey, under Lt.–Colonel John Allan, who had pioneered the Army's first band camp in 1920. These camps offered sectional rehearsals and several bands, graded according to the players' abilities. CMI and Star Lake each developed its own traditions and proud alumni, and both have proved lasting successes, annual beacons for aspiring young Salvationist musicians. The great distances in the West and the poverty of brass music in the South were insuperable obstacles in the path of effective territorial band camps in those regions. London offered correspondence courses in brass band conducting to adult leaders, but by the end of the decade only one American, Bandmaster Samuel E. Collins of San Francisco Citadel, had completed both the intermediate and advanced courses.[30]

There were other renovations besides music—the *War Cry* editions appeared in a smaller, more modern format in 1939—but the Army also opened its evangelical work in new fields. In 1937 Captain Cecil Brown laid the cornerstone of the Maple Springs Citadel in the mountains of North Carolina. It was the first of a string of log cabin and trailer chapels set up to serve the mountain people. Captain Brown, like one of the Outriders of old, traveled alone on horseback over the circuit between the rustic little outposts and declared in word and in many good deeds a simple gospel of love. In that same year The Salvation Army opened fire on the Republic of Mexico, which was promptly annexed, in a spiritual sense, to the Southern Territory. The heroic pioneer was a struggling Mexican evangelist named Alejandro Guzman, who had traveled to Dallas from the Mexican capital to offer his tiny band of coworkers to The Salvation Army, of which he had heard only recently. This

"Salvation Patrol" was invited to Atlanta to meet the General, who was in the city to celebrate the tenth anniversary of the opening of the territory. The Mexican valiants were enrolled in the Army and sent off with great enthusiasm to make war on their countrymen. The Mexican branch of the Army, although almost entirely financed from American funds, was not considered a foreign mission but a regular division of the Southern Territory. The work remained under the noble Guzman, who struggled on for years with only a handful of soldiers against the opposition of Church and government and the indifference of the people—proving, like Captain Brown and thousands of street-corner warriors, that the old-time crusading spirit continued to flourish.[31]

Still, the old Army was changing in the 1930s. A quartet of venerable officers' ranks were dropped in 1931—Staff-Captain, Field-Major, Commandant, and Ensign. In 1935 the traditional system of numbering Army corps was at last abandoned, in favor of giving each corps an individual name. A relic of the glorious days when the Army was expanding so capriciously that it was difficult to keep track of all the new corps, the number system was too familiar to most old soldiers for them to part with it. The new names had a certain dignity, however, and soon offered competition to the old numbers in younger hearts. New York No. 3 became Times Square Corps, Minneapolis No. 4 became Central Avenue Corps, Washington, D.C. No. 2 became Central Corps, and Los Angeles No. 1 became Los Angeles Congress Hall. Some corps, like Oakland, Brooklyn No. 1, and Flint, had been known as "Citadel" for years before the change became official. Inevitably, there were other changes: pioneers and heros began to be promoted to Glory, and disappeared one by one from scenes they had enlivened and graced. Booth-Tucker died soon after Bramwell in 1929, Major Milsaps and Eliza Shirley in 1932, Emma Westbrook in 1933, the sweet-spirited Brengle in 1936, and Joe the Turk, the "Sanctified Salvationist Showman," in 1937.[32]

There was another change as well: the Commander was gone from the American scene. The "Joan of Arc" of the reformers was elected General at last, on September 3, 1934. Her rise to that eminence was long and uneven, but she made it at age sixty-nine on the fifth ballot, with not a single vote to spare. Evangeline had disagreed—but blessedly, mostly in private—with her predecessor, Edward Higgins, over certain details in The Salvation Army Act of 1931. Higgins and other Army leaders had prepared the bill for Parliament in order to regularize the election of the General, to set a retirement age (seventy-three), and to create a corporation to take up legal title to Army property (which was still held in the General's personal name). Her objections were that the new bill did not provide sufficient protection for the financial independence of the American branch, and that the new structure was not democratic enough. Evangeline's correspondence with Higgins took an alarming turn; enough of the story leaked so that a few officers became unreasonably frightened, and the territorial commanders had to reassure them. The bill, adjusted slightly to suit the Commander, passed. Higgins was a generous-spirited and honorable officer, and voluntarily retired at the age he had originally proposed as the limit (seventy), even though the new law did not apply to the incumbent. His graceful departure left the way open for Evangeline.[33]

The Commander's election marked the end of an era. To millions of Americans, she was the symbol and embodiment of The Salvation Army, while the great majority of American Salvationists had never known a different leader. Evangeline had ruled the Army from 120 West Fourteenth Street for thirty years. Her triumphant return to America as General, and her farewell parades and congress in New York in November, were gala events, marked not only by an avalanche of tributes, from President Roosevelt downwards, but by an outpouring of genuine affection that touched the elderly new General to the heart. She departed these shores in a cloud of ticker-tape, fireboat sprays, tugboat whistles, hallelujahs, and tearful farewells ringing in her ears.

When the excitement died down, staff officers had time to reflect on the administrative changes the new General had made: her successor, Lt.–Commissioner Edward J. Parker, would serve not as "Commander"— the title disappeared—but as "National Secretary," with reduced powers. The territorial commanders were to gain responsibility at the expense of the now-truncated national headquarters; the commissioners were to answer directly to the General, with copies of all correspondence to the National Secretary. The latter was authorized to serve as legal head of the Army corporation, and to communicate on behalf of the Army with the federal government in "any great national crisis or in connection with National Efforts on great moral questions and the like." Parker's powers were so shrunken and conscribed that the *Literary Digest* assumed that Evangeline as General had "retained her . . . Commandership of the United States Salvation Army." She certainly retained her command of the worldwide Army: no more was heard from Evangeline about democratic reforms.[34]

For all that, American Salvationists loved her still—the more so, perhaps, when rumors began to circulate that her flair for the dramatic was not having a good effect on the British. Americans knew Evangeline was an American citizen, loud in her praises for this country and for the Army here. She announced early in her period of command in London that she intended to return to her adopted country in retirement. Her one official visit to the United States in 1937 gave American Salvationists a last opportunity to acclaim their old Commander. The highlight of the tour was the ten-year jubilee celebration held in Atlanta in September. Many staff officers grieved for Evangeline when Lt.-Commissioner Richard Griffith died suddenly in London in October, 1938. He had been her private secretary and trusted aide for thirty-five years, loyal and discreet. Officers who had been in the Commander's inner circle cherished their memories of Griffith playing his cello while she played her harp, during long evenings before the fire at Arcadia, her home in Hartsdale, New York.[35]

The Army began to improve its operating facilities as the Depression eased. Eva's Atlanta meetings caught the attention of a local businessman, who offered the Army the entire campus of the Atlanta Theological Seminary on Stewart Avenue for a "remarkably low figure"—too low to resist for the spacious old campus, which was ideally suited for a new training college. The Southern Territorial Training College was officially opened there on June 5, 1938, dedicated by the retired General Higgins, who had settled in the United States.[36]

In San Francisco, the indefatigable Major Kobayashi presided over the opening on February 28, 1937, of a new headquarters building for the Japanese Division. The structure at 1450 Laguna Street represented the culmination of the Major's lifework: he had raised "by far the major portion" of the money for it himself, during a heroic five-year campaign among Japanese in California and Japan. The Emperor of Japan himself donated five thousand yen in 1931, and a framed decree to that effect hung in the new chapel. The building housed the social service head quarters and a corps, and was opened with great ceremony by Commissioner Benjamin Orames, the territorial commander, and the Consul-General of Japan, who raised the Japanese flag alongside the American and Salvation Army flags. The training college band played American and Japanese patriotic music for the two thousand persons who attended the festivities. It was the greatest day in the history of the division.[37]

The Second World War began in Europe in September, 1939. Evangeline Booth retired as General with little ceremony, and returned home to Hartsdale. She had reached the age of seventy-three on Christmas Day, 1938, but remained in office another year in the vain hope that the world situation would become less troubled, allowing the international commissioners to collect for another High Council. She finally departed London the day after the war began in Poland. Her successor was George L. Carpenter, whose name had figured so prominently in the Bramwell crisis ten years before. Britain's role in the war and the fact that he had no close associations with the American branch of the Army caused the new General to focus the attention of the beleaguered international headquarters on the Army's other branches. Territorial officers in the United States were given wide latitude. In 1943 the title of National Commander was revived and bestowed on the deserving Commissioner Parker shortly before his retirement.

In America the war in Europe at first meant an end to the unemployment still lingering from the Depression: munitions and war-supply orders from the Allies caused a business boom, and the Selective Service Act of September, 1940, took up hundreds of thousands of men. For The Salvation Army, change came rapidly. The Men's Social Centers, so recently swamped with applicants, gradually became almost deserted. An attempt to broaden systematic alcoholic rehabilitation, begun in Detroit in 1939 when the divisional commander, Lt.–Colonel James Murphy opened the first Harbor Light corps, had to be postponed (although the Detroit corps continued to function, and soon rescued a notable convert, Tom Crocker). Services had to be arranged quickly for the rapidly swelling armed forces—perhaps, suggested *Newsweek* helpfully, the Army might bring back "the coffee and doughnuts that American veterans remember so well."[38]

The Army remembered the First World War, too. Commissioner Parker and Lt.–Colonel John Allan, who had served as a chaplain in 1917 and 1918, were determined to revive the cooperative spirit of those years in advance of the actual need, while praying all the while that the United States would not be drawn into the actual fighting. Except for the Red Cross (which provided no social or welfare services and declined to join), the other agencies responded in a spirit of patriotic camaraderie. The leaders of the Catholic Community Services, the Jewish Welfare Board, the YMCA, the YWCA, The Salvation Army, and the Travelers'

A Salvation Army officer serves soup to a line of hungry men during the Depression. (Source: The Salvation Army National Information Service.)

Commander Evangeline Booth, and two children receiving packages from The Salvation Army during the Depression. (Photo: Paul Parker; source: The Salvation Army National Information Service.)

Chinatown Corps in San Francisco, California, in the 1920s. (Source: Property Department, Territorial Headquarters, Western Territory.)

The fashionable Waioli Tea Room in Honolulu, Hawaii, was a popular tourist attraction in the mid-1920s. (Source: Property Department, Territorial Headquarters, Western Territory.)

Evangeline Booth, National Commander, seated at her office desk. Standing are, left to right, Commissioners Edward J. Parker, Richard E. Holz, and William Arnold (1929). (Source: Commissioner Ernest W. Holz.)

Commissioner Samuel Logan Brengle, preacher, teacher, and author of books on the subject of holiness, in the 1930s. (Source: The Salvation Army Archives and Research Center.)

Commissioner Adam Gifford and Major Emma Westbrook, one of the seven lassies who accompanied Commissioner George Scott Railton to America (c. 1930). (Source: The Salvation Army Archives and Research Center.)

National and territorial headquarters building in New York City, which replaced an earlier building. In use by the 1930s, the complex consists of a large auditorium (left), the headquarters building (right), and a residence (rear). (Source: The Salvation Army Archives and Research Center.)

Major John Milsaps and a co-worker, Manuel Valencia, at the Western Territorial Congress held in San Francisco, May, 1931. (Photo: B.W. Hellings Photography, San Francisco; source: The Salvation Army Archives and Research Center.)

Group of children and youth associated with Girl Guards, Sunbeams, Boy Scouts, and Cub Scouts from Washington D.C. about 1936. (Photo: Joe Tenschert, Washington D.C.; source: Captain Allan Wiltshire.)

"The Glory Shop" open-air wagon of New York's Times Square Corps in 1937. Adjutant Lyell Rader is behind the two little girls. (Source: The Salvation Army National Information Service, New York.)

Children pictured with their counselor at a Salvation Army camp in Long Branch, New Jersey, 1938. (Source: The Salvation Army Archives and Research Center.)

New York City's Mayor Fiorello LaGuardia helps to kick off a Christmas appeal during the early years of World War II. Commissioner Alexander Damon is standing beside the mayor. (Source: The Salvation Army National Information Service.)

Home League ladies from Atlantic City, New Jersey, preparing soldiers' kits in 1942. (Photo: Frank Hess and Son, Atlantic City; source: Mrs. Brigadier James Henderson, Brigantine, New Jersey.)

Citadel Boys' Band of Cincinnati, Ohio, 1944. (Source: Lt.-Colonel David Moulton, Wilmore, Kentucky.)

Corps band of Chelsea, Massachusetts, marches back to the hall from an open-air meeting in 1946. (Source: Lt.–Colonel David Moulton, Wilmore, Kentucky.)

The Army launching the work among blacks in Atlanta, Georgia, at a 1948 open-air meeting. (Source: Publications Bureau, Territorial Headquarters, Southern Territory.)

Erik Leidzen, musician and composer, at the keyboard in the 1960s (Source: **This Man Leidzen,** in the Salvation Army Archives and Research Center, New York.)

Small-town open-air meeting conducted by Asbury College students in 1979. (Source: Salvation Army Student Fellowship Band.)

General Arnold Brown (center) installs Commissioner Ernest W. Holz (right) as National Commander of the United States of America on March 23, 1979. Mrs Holz was installed as National President of Women's Organizations for the Army. (Photo: Irving Newman; source: The Salvation Army National Information Service.)

Aid Society all agreed on January 31, 1941, to form the United Welare
Committee. This was incorporated on February 4 as the United Service
Organization (USO). The Salvation Army, having launched the USO
as a cooperative venture, opened a number of war emergency service
centers of its own called "Red Shield Clubs," which offered showers and
emergency sleeping accommodations.[39]

Then, too, the swelling ranks of servicemen required spiritual guid-
ance. The Army's offer to provide at least part of its quota of military
chaplains was accepted at once; in November 1940, Colonel John Allan
was asked by the Secretary of War to join the five-man staff of the Chief
of Chaplains in Washington and, with the Army's official permission,
he gladly accepted. By the end of the war, thirty-two Salvation Army
officers had served as military chaplains. All of them were in the US
Army and the Army Air Corps: the Navy would not waive its requirement that its chaplain officers have a college degree and three years of
seminary, a requirement that no Salvation Army officer could have met
in 1941.[40]

On Saturday, December 6, 1941, the Western *War Cry* announced
a three-day conference of Salvation Army leaders in New York to arrange broader Army participation in the USO; there were already seventy-five posts and close to a hundred officers dedicated to the work. Still,
America was not yet in the war, and Salvationists were to pray for peace.
These issues of *The War Cry* went on sale in the lobbies of West Coast
corps on Sunday, December 7.[41]

The Salvation Army suffered two casualties at once. One was Aviation
Ordnanceman 3rd Class John D. Buckley, a Salvationist from Provi-
dence and a member of the Future Officers' Fellowship who joined the
Navy in November 1940, and died manning a machine gun at Pearl
Harbor on December 7. The other immediate casualty was the entire
Japanese division of The Salvation Army on the West Coast.[42]

The division was officially terminated when the valiant Major Kobayashi died suddenly of heart failure on October 15, 1940. Venerated by
his troops, respected by the Japanese community, Kobayashi was irre-
placeable as divisional commander: no other Japanese officer would
accept the responsibility. And, truth to tell, the Japanese Division was
too small—eight corps and the two social institutions on Laguna Street
—to warrant the expense of a separate divisional structure. Kobayashi's
funeral was a full-dress Army affair, conducted by the territorial commander, Commissioner Donald McMillan, and the training college

band. Kobayashi had suffered from a bad heart for years, and sensed that overwork might kill him; yet he refused to slacken his pace lest the Army work suffer. The Major's funeral was quite correctly a hero's send-off.[43]

The case was, unfortunately, quite different for the remaining Japanese officers. For the first months after Pearl Harbor these officers attempted to carry on their normal activities in the face of widespread and open hostility directed not against their religion, but their nationality. Even some American Salvationists were caught up in the wartime hysteria: officers now regarded Kobayashi's death, so near in time to Pearl Harbor, as "mysterious." The Emperor's innocent gift to the Japanese building fund, the decree in the chapel, the imperial portrait in Kobayashi's office, his "frequent" trips to Japan—all these things now appeared in an ominous light. The fact that the Japanese officers were sometimes shy and reticent around their American comrades was taken as more proof of oriental perfidy. Dismayed and confused, several Japanese officers resigned or accepted leaves of absence from active duty. The Japanese children's home on Laguna Street was placed under American officers from the Women's Social Department. In March 1942 all Japanese on the West Coast, Salvation Army officers included, were transported to relocation camps in the interior, and the Japanese work of The Salvation Army in the Continental United States virtually ceased to exist.[44]

A few Japanese officers, however, who once before gave up everything for God and the Army, remained loyal through the ordeal of arrest, deportation, and the long years in the camps. Major Masahide Imai was in command of the Japanese corps at Fresno (one of only two in the division with a brass band) when the war began. In March 1942, he and his family were taken to a camp near Little Rock, Arkansas. He resolved to wear his uniform, to minister to any other Salvationists in the camp, and to take his turn to preach "the Salvation Army way" at the united Protestant services held weekly in the camp. Word that an officer was in the camp reached the nearby Army headquarters in Little Rock: the divisional secretary and corps officer came at once, greeted the Imai's like lost lambs, sang and prayed with them, and offered to take them out of the camp every Sunday so that they might speak in various corps around the division, enjoy Sunday dinner with comrades, and go sightseeing. The camp commander made it clear from the outset that he admired The Salvation Army, and had been sorry to see Imai put in the camp in the first place: the Major was free to go whenever he liked, on trust. Imai's faith in the Army was thus rewarded, and he was "so happy, so encouraged." He later attended five conferences in five major cities as a representative of Japanese ministerial groups in the camps, to plan for the future of Christian work among Japanese-Americans after the war.[45]

The war bore heavily on The Salvation Army in the United States. Providing officer personnel for 210 Red Shield clubs and 201 USO clubs, and thirty-two chaplains placed an enormous strain on human resources. Selective Service and the patriotic impulse combined to draw many young Salvationists of officer caliber into the service. A study of the Southern Training College for the years 1942 through 1945 reveals a steady shortage of male cadets. In 1942 there were four men out of twenty cadets; in 1945 three single and four married men out of thirty-one. The case with the other territories differed only in detail. At the same time corps officers were asked to take on extra duties for the duration of the war, especially if their corps were near a military base, port of embarkation, or prisoner-of-war camp. The demands of war service, combined with a shortage of officer and recruits, threw a terrible weight on remaining corps and social officers alike. Men's social centers, training colleges and territorial purchasing and supply departments lost clientele and suffered officer staff reductions steadily throughout the war. In 1942 the Eastern Training College principal also took on the duties of New York divisional commander, and had to plan the budgets of twenty corps into the bargain. Commissioner Ernest I. Pugmire served as both national commander and Eastern territorial commander after 1944.[46]

The war hit the Men's Social Service Department with special force. The ease with which men could secure profitable employment, and the repeated siftings of the male population by local Selective Service boards, meant that only elderly men and habitual drunkards were left in Army centers. All institutions suffered a loss of clients; most could barely operate even a reduced program. Social officers were forced to reappraise their entire mission. A series of important conferences were held; these culminated in the Eastern Territory in "Institutes" held in 1944 for all Men's Social Service officers. From a "deliberate and organized reemphasis of the original aims and purposes of our social work with men" there emerged the conviction that the Army must greet the post-war era with a new program for men—one designed to bring together professional counseling, Alcoholics Anonymous, medical advice, and Christian evangelism to focus on the men's problems, most of which were caused by alcoholism. In 1944 not a single center had a program specifically designed for alcoholics. This had to change. Above all, the Army had to abandon the idea that the social institutions were a "business," to employ men merely to raise revenue for the work; the purpose of the Men's Social Service Department to make "better men" must be reaffirmed. Out of the ruins of the "industrial home" concept, which World War II destroyed, there emerged the "Service-to-Man" program, which transformed the Men's Social Service Department after the war.[47]

The Women's Social Service Department, on the other hand, enjoyed something of a boom during the war. The maternity program was already a proven and acknowledged success; wartime romance provided an increased volume of clients. The war did bring its exigencies, of course—two young women in the Oakland home went into labor during the first air-raid practice—but war brought no lasting changes to the department. Individual officers found an opportunity for an occasional innovation, all on their own. Brigadier Marian Kimball had opened the Catherine Booth Hospital in Cincinnati to black physicians before the war, the first nonsegregated medical facility in the city to officially recognize their professional capabilities. This policy was courageously continued during the war years, despite the fact that the beginnings of black migration from the South into Ohio in search of war-related employment caused racial antagonism to develop in Cincinnati.[48]

The Salvation Army was placed on a "war footing" everywhere on the home front. In the frightened days of January 1942, Western territorial headquarters offered the facilities of all three hundred six of its institutions and corps to civil defense authorities to serve as bomb shelters. Officers were prepared to assist in the mass evacuation of the West Coast, and the national commander gamely offered the Army's entire fleet of 1,125 salvage trucks to help in the operation. In Pittsburgh the divisional commander, Brigadier William Harris, ordered a mobile canteen—a panel truck equipped to prepare and serve hot meals, drinks and sandwiches—to accompany units of the Pennsylvania Home Guard as they defended "strategic points" around the city. Another mobile canteen served the men on the first blackout watch in Tacoma, Washington. A corps officer, Adjutant Henry Dries, convinced pharmaceutical magnate General Robert Wood Johnson to finance the rebuilding of the corps at New Brunswick, New Jersey, into a "model" bomb shelter.[49]

The Salvation Army adopted a positively belligerent tone, even in its spiritual ministry. The Western territory's revival campaign for 1942 was entitled "Enlistment for Christ," and was heralded by mottos like "CalVary for Victory!" The departed Brengle was quoted reassuringly that killing in battle is not the same as murder. The Army's home-front service lost none of its militancy for the fact that it was largely administered by women. Encouraged by officers and filled with the same patriotic sentiments that filled their husbands, brothers, and boyfriends in the service, the women of the Home League threw themselves into the Army's war work. The service they gave or directed others in giving was varied, but it was all typical of the Army: immediate, practical, and free.[50]

In Alaska a "sewing brigade" mended jeeps-full of uniforms, as hordes of arriving troops swamped the few civilian tailors. The women of the Freeport, Long Island corps tended the severely wounded arriving at Mitchell Field, showering them with cakes, cookies, cigarettes, and writing their letters, while another group of volunteers knit scarves and helmet liners for the men overseas. The women volunteers of the Asbury Park, New Jersey, corps supplied goodies and all manner of kindly attentions to the patrols of the Coast Artillery guarding the North Jersey beaches; the grateful young men voted one of the women, Marion Kuster, their favorite pin up. All over the country the members of Home League and non-Salvationist volunteers of the Women's Auxiliaries served throughout the war; the refreshments, letters, knitted garmets (there was even a national "Home League of the Air," with the motto: "Remember Pearl Harbor—Purl Harder!"), utility kits, layettes for service wives, fracture pillows, and afghans produced by these women "reached astronomical proportions." This mountain of good works was the more remarkable when one remembers that Salvation Army women were also called upon to take up many regular corps duties vacated by men absent in the service. In Oakland Citadel, for the first and only time in the corps' history, women were allowed to play in the band. Every Home League kept a "Book of Remembrance" that listed the name of every serviceman in the town, so that the ladies could pray weekly for each man individually.[51]

In Hawaii and Alaska the Army's USO and Home League service were especially arduous; conditions sometimes approximated the front-line ministry of the First World War. Only Salvationist chaplains were closer to actual combat. Major and Mrs Alva Holbrook, USO officers at

Schofield Barracks at Pearl Harbor, were under fire on December 7, and responded by making four thousand doughnuts for hungry defenders. Throughout the war the Army visited hospitals, made bandages, and ran child-care centers for working mothers. Major Jeanetta Hodgen comforted her frightened young charges in Honolulu's Damon Tract during air-raid alarms, while the classy little Waioli Tea Room, an auxiliary to the Army's girls' home in Honolulu, made thousands of doughnuts before it was taken over by a government concessionary in 1943 to make fruitcake for the US Army. Officers were dispatched to the islands from the mainland to help in the increased war work. Major Leah Schmuck, for instance, came from the Central territory, and Captains Olive McKeown and Luella Larder from the East. The latter two officers operated a Salvation Army mobile canteen on fifteen runs per week around Honolulu, visiting the men in lonely and isolated guardposts near the city. The girls also developed a unique ministry among the men working in the US Army mortuary in Honolulu. These men were all sergeants in their thirties, all of them undertakers in civilian life, and they were understandably liable to periods of depression and loneliness, from which the Salvationist womens' patience and kindness regularly lifted them.[52]

The Salvation Army had arrived in Alaska in 1898 under the auspices of the Canadian branch of the movement. After an initial flurry of heroic evangelism in the Klondike in 1898 and 1899, the work had not flourished among the small white population of the territory. Quite different was the case among the Tlinget Indians, a fishing people who lived in small villages along the southeastern coast. A courageous Tlinget Salvationist, Charles Newton, designated by the special Army rank of "Field-Captain," had carried the gospel and the Army's carefree style of worship everywhere among the friendly and receptive Tlinget before he settled down to command the thriving corps at Kake. By the Second World War there were fifteen corps in Alaska, all of them except Anchorage "principally of native identity." These goodhearted soldiers were as patriotic as they were religious, and were overjoyed when the twin facts of a massive American military presence in Alaska and the difficulties of wartime communication and finance from Toronto caused the transfer of the Alaskan corps from Canada to the Western territory of the United States on June 1, 1944. The first American divisional commander was a genial veteran, Brigadier Chester Taylor, who assumed command not only of the cheerful Tlinget but of a varied program of USO and military relief activity in what was still considered an active theater of war.[53]

Salvationist chaplains, on the other hand, found themselves in actual theaters of war. Their duties were varied: the religious life and morale of the troops, such cultural life as could be provided by records, movies, and portable paperback libraries, regular daily visits to field hospitals and guardhouses, and three to five services on Sunday. Dignified and respectful funerals were an essential part of a chaplain's duties. Salvationists found that their Army background fortified them for the demands of their new duties: comforting the sick and dying, patiently counseling with drunken soldiers, holding the attention of crowds of men who were indifferent or hostile to religion, and conducting decent burials with a minimum of funeral furnishings were all part of a Salvation Army officer's experiences in civilian life.[54]

The Army's reliance on music was also a boon to officer-chaplains. Chaplain Richard E. Holz of the 882nd Airborne Engineers found his cornet an invaluable tool. He used music extensively in his ministry, organizing a special chorus on his own in 1944 to accompany a Christmas Eve program on Leyte. When a surprise air raid spoiled the meeting, Holz took the chorus around to sing carols to the freshly wounded men, to their delight. Holz was well-regarded by the men around him, but other officer-chaplains had to face a kind of mild prejudice when they first arrived at their new commands. Many military officers were unaware that The Salvation Army was a recognized Christian denomination: when Giles Barrett reported for duty as a chaplain at 2nd Army Headquarters, he was asked, "Where's your drum?" This condescension did not last, however, and military officials repeatedly urged The Salvation Army to fill its quota of chaplaincies, which, sad to say, the wartime shortage of officer personnel made impossible.[55]

The war ended in Europe in May 1945, and in Japan in August. The Christmas *War Cry* was eloquent: "Home Again to Sing the Songs of Peace." The USO operated on a much-reduced scale for another two years, but for the most part, The Salvation Army looked home again, too. American commissioners looked over a scene bright with promise: a rich and powerful country supremely confident in victory, a country in which the evangelical and humanitarian activities of The Salvation Army during the long years of Depression and war had confirmed a place beyond all challenge. Even the new General, Albert Orsborn, who visited here shortly after his election in 1946, was dazzled by the Army's prospects in the United States. A poet of ability and a zealous Christian, Orsborn selected Commissioner John Allan to be his Chief of the Staff, the first American-born officer to rise so high.[56]

There was still much to do. One old ministry was gone: the Japanese Division was not restored after the war, nor were the few Japanese officers who had remained loyal sent back to California; the valiant Imai was sent to command a Japanese corps in Hawaii. An old familiar rank —Adjutant—was dropped in 1948 (although two new ones were added, Senior-Captain and Senior-Major, to confuse the public for another ten years). The Army's traditional emphases had not suffered irreparable damage during the war, however, and some, like the Men's Social Service Department, had been galvanized into producing an entirely new rehabilitation scheme, the "Service-to-Man" program. When a number of homeless, unattached men began to circulate again in the first year after the war, the Army's centers were ready with a program that included all "that The Salvation Army stood for," applied "in a thoroughly thoughtful, organized and constructive manner, focused on the individual man, according to his individual needs," aimed at his "permanent rehabilitation" through a "definite Christian experience."[57]

Salvation Army music flourished after the war. The two remaining Staff Bands and many large corps bands welcomed home their returning servicemen and carried on as before the war, to the chagrin of the now-redundant women players. Smaller bands grew and developed as teenaged Salvationists grew old enough to take their places in the ranks, in the sunshine of peace and public approval. The number and proficiency of corps bands reached a kind of peak in the late 1940s. "These organizations [were] the most numerous of their kind in the world," observed a writer in 1949. "Nowhere, other than in the school music program of the United States," could there be found "such a large number of excellent bands as at this level of Salvation Army participation." There were "literally hundreds of these bands." Band camps were thronged, not only the popular Star Lake and CMI, but divisional and even corps music camps, drew large crowds—five thousand in the summer of 1947 alone. Seventy-eight rpm records of Army brass music on the Regal label appeared, radio broadcasts became routine, and—the final innovation—in June 1946, the Los Angeles Citadel Band chartered a DC-3 to fly themselves to Phoenix to play for a fund-raising drive— the first time a Salvation Army band flew to an engagement.[58]

A large step in the development of Salvation Army music came in 1946. The national commander, Commissioner Ernest Pugmire, had replaced Commissioner Parker, who retired in 1943, the last of the pioneers to remain in active service. A man of rich dignity, Pugmire knew the value of music in winning the hearts of men. He asked Captain Richard Holz, returned from the war, to form a special music department in New York under the auspices of the Eastern territory (which Pugmire conveniently commanded as well, and which possessed the necessary funds for the new project). Holz acquired an able assistant in Alfred V. Swenarton, an alto horn soloist with the Staff Band; together these two coaxed Erik Leidzen back into the Army fold, and the department was launched. They must have been a busy trio: Holz was solo cornet with the Staff Band, worked closely with its leader Brigadier Bearchell, and led the Male Chorus; Swenarton was in the midst of the Herculean task of organizing the musical forces at the Asbury Park corps; and Leidzen, whose enthusiasm for the musical ministry of the Army had returned with a rush, was active in Army band weekends and as the yearly honored guest at Star Lake camp. Yet the department managed to produce a variety of important new brass compositions for the medium-sized band.[59]

Nor was its reliance on music the only thing the Army reconfirmed in these years: the traditional doctrine of holiness was the focus of attention in Chicago in August 1947, when the first Brengle Memorial Institute was opened. The three-week session was the brainchild of the national commander, Commissioner Ernest Pugmire. Its first chairman was the kindly Brigadier Albert G. Pepper, the principal of the Central training college who was himself considered a living exemplar of the doctrine of the perfectability of the human heart in love. Officers were to be invited from all over the country on a rotated schedule, so that eventually every American officer would be exposed both to an explanation of the doctrine and an experience of it. The first staff included Commissioner Norman Marshall, the territorial commander, the fiesty old McIntyre, Brigadier Edward Laity, (whose specialty was a lengthy demonstration of how the Old Testament Tabernacle offered examples of New Testament Christianity), and Major Mina Russell. The Institute was a huge—and lasting—success.[60]

The Army did not entirely forget its commitment to blacks after the war. Salvation Army USO activities were segregated during the war—as was the US Army itself. There were separate Salvation Army USO clubs for black troops throughout the south, in Washington, D.C., in Harlem, in Junction City, Kansas, in Mt. Clemens, Michigan, and in Ipava, Illinois. The Army's indoor evangelical activities likewise remained segregated in the South in the late 1940s. The black corps were often full of lively spirits, and many lasting conversions were recorded in them. One of the most effective corps ministries in the South was housed in the "Washington No. 2 (Colored) Corps" on Seventh and P Streets, commanded for thirty-eight fruitful years by Brigadier and Mrs James Roberts, and from 1941 to 1950 by Major and Mrs Lambert Bailey. There was even one step toward integration in Washington: in 1941 the National Capital Divisional Band abandoned the color bar when a black tuba player was asked to join. After the war, several white officers made determined efforts to broaden the Army's appeal to blacks, and if possible to provide activities that would not be narrowly racial in participation.[61]

The best solution, which utilized another traditional Army ministry that was re-emphasized during these very years, was the open-air meeting. Adjutant Vincent Cunningham, editor of the Southern *War Cry*, was the driving force behind a campaign to launch open-air meetings, first in the black districts of Atlanta, then—on the heels of the success that he felt was certain—all over the South. Encouraged by Commissioner William C. Arnold and his successor as Southern territorial commander, Lt.–Commissioner Albert Chesham—both solidly evangelical in their priorities—Cunningham laid his plans. On April 3, 1948, the entire territorial staff and cadets held an open-air meeting on the corner of Auburn and Bell Streets in the heart of the "colored part" of Atlanta. Four blacks were converted. Cunningham, overjoyed at these conversions, which he was certain were a sign of Divine approval, gave this auspicious beginning the fullest coverage: "The Salvation Army Launches a Program for The Southern Negro." Vaguely congratulatory letters from five Southern governors, the Mayor of Atlanta, and Senator J. Strom Thurmond of South Carolina (who added gratuitously that he regarded "segregation" as "essential to be maintained in the South") were conspicuously published in *The War Cry*. Thus stimulated, other officers launched smaller efforts of their own: soon the happy editor was able to publish cheerful accounts of open-air meetings and other outreach programs aimed at blacks in Gastonia, North Carolina; Alexandria, Louisiana; Birmingham and Tuscaloosa, Alabama; Lawton, Oklahoma; and Little Rock, Arkansas.[62]

The end of the decade brought an end, at last, to the career of one who had been, in her day, the very symbol of The Salvation Army. After her return to the United States in 1939, Evangeline had lived in Hartsdale, a dowager queen. Invitations to visit her at home were still considered an honor, even if the cause were some trivial piece of business. She regularly arrived late for the Sunday morning service at the White Plains corps, knowing the respectful officer would begin the program all over for her. As Evangeline grew older, however, she began to feel abandoned, isolated not only from the reality of power for herself but even from those who held it after her—even from the very presence of power.[63]

Yet American Salvationists still revered Evangeline. The hearts of her old associates enveloped her in her aged and helpless isolation. Brigadier William Maltby, the commander of the New York City Metropolitan Division, had often sung for her on her campaigns in the 1920s. Together Maltby, Brigadier William Bearchell of the Staff Band, and Captain Holz planned a gala evening to honor her: a whole program for a "Friday Evening at the Temple," featuring the compositions of Evangeline Booth. On Friday, November 19, 1948, they pulled it off, a grand, full-dress affair before a packed house.[64]

Only July 7, 1950, Evangeline Cory Booth was promoted to Glory at the age of eighty-four. She had done all that a leader could do to make The Salvation Army strong and popular in the United States. She had been proud of Christ, proud of the Army, proud of the uniform, and proud of the poor and lonely people that mostly filled the ranks behind her; they sensed that pride, and returned it with love. The Commander left behind her a legacy of high courage, of zeal, of kindness, of caprice, and a sense of the dramatic that lurks in the heart of every Salvationist: she could make a stirring little production out of walking from her car across the sidewalk on Fourteenth Street to the front door of headquarters. She filled the Army with excitement, and gave it a sense of high purpose. She loved people for loving her, and for their souls' sakes. To Americans, her Generalcy was anticlimactic: to them she was the woman who had commanded The Salvation Army in the United States for thirty years, the Commander, a presence that was returned to them when she came back to America in retirement, and which was taken only when she died.[65]

CHAPTER VI

1950-1980

"Sing it as our comrades sang it
Many a thousand strong,
As they were marching to Glory."

The Christmas issue of *Time* in 1949 displayed the national commander of The Salvation Army on its cover, surrounded by a wreath of the little hand-rung bells that had become symbolic of the Army's annual Christmas appeal. When Evangeline Booth died seven months later, the leading magazines and every major newspaper in the country lavished praise upon her memory and upon the work of the Army. The Salvation Army had become more than respectable, more even than popular: it had become venerable. Certain parts of the Army's mission had especially endeared themselves to the heart of the public over seventy years, and had come to represent, in a reassuringly visible way, the wide strain of generous and practical philanthropy that was characteristic of modern American life. The particular scenes in this pageant that were selected as favorites varied with the observer, but included on every list were the doughnut girls in the First World War, the Army's long and valiant struggle to lift up the down-and-out (which had included nearly everyone during the Depression), the maternity homes, and best known and perhaps most cherished of all scenes, the little brass bands thumping away on the street corners of the country. No religious organization has ever become more certainly identified with one part of its ministry (albeit the most important part) than has The Salvation Army with its street-corner bands. Their genial and brassy evangelism had long since become a part of the national life.[1]

Not even officers were surprised to see it portrayed in good-natured (and often very funny) cartoons in the best repositories of that art form, *The Saturday Evening Post* and the *New Yorker*. An even more lyrical expression of the public's bemused but genuine affection for the Army's open-air rescue work was the musical *Guys and Dolls*, which opened to rave reviews on November 24, 1950, at the Forty-Sixth Street Theatre in New York. The still-charming story is built on the encounters of Sergeant Sarah Brown of the Save-A-Soul Mission with a collection of Damon Runyon's choicest Broadway characters. Nor could officers object: had not the Army pioneers conceded a half-century before that it was better to be laughed at than ignored? And who could deny that the cartoons, plays, and movie scripts were not mere ridicule, but a kind of left-handed tribute, nonetheless real for being a trifle indirect [2]

No, indeed the Army could not object. It took justifiable pride in its unwavering dedication to outdoor evangelism. "Except for the blaring auto horn and the roaring motorcycle," Senior-Captain Don Pitt observed in 1950 in an official booklet, "the setting in which the officer seeks to win men and women to Christ has changed little" since the Army's early years. "The open-air ministry still goes on." In fact, the Army conducted 98,417 open-air meetings during that year. And the Army maintained not only its street evangelism, but a full schedule of weekday evening meetings and Sunday marches, and a complete range of traditional corps and social programs through the 1950s, often with gratifying results.[3]

The Salvation Army's efforts to restore alcoholic men to grace and useful lives took place in both specialized corps, called Harbor Light corps, and in the Men's Social Service Centers. The Army's Harbor Light corps reached out directly to skid row drunkards with spiritual and material solace. These corps were new, and uniquely American: General Orsborn had never seen an Army ministry for alcoholics before he visited the Detroit Harbor Light in 1946. Captain Tom Crocker, who commanded the Detroit mission for four years before he was transferred to another on Chicago's skid row in 1948, was especially effective in this type of warfare. In New York Captains McKeown and Larder, the Honolulu "doughnut girls," found themselves after the Armistice in a less dramatic (but no less exciting) form of combat when they were sent to command the Army's Bowery mission in New York. When McKeown explained the nature of their work to a fashionable congregation in 1951, Metropolitan Opera star Jerome Hines was touched and kindly offered to "sing for the men." His musical ministry to the down-but-never-out at the Bowery corps was no transient whim: Hines and his wife Lucia sang at Army services there regularly for years, laying their musical talents alongside those of Robert Merrill and thousands of less conspicuous volunteers in the service of the Salvation War.[4]

The Men's Social Service Department had been revitalized after 1944 by the Service-to-Man program, fully implemented in the 1950s by progressive social officers who had been in the forefront of reform in the decade before. Through correspondence and frequent meetings, energetic officers like A.E. Agnew, Edward Baggs, Peter Hofman, and George Duplain kept one another informed of innovations each had introduced in his own center. Hofman and Baggs were early advocates of the program of Alcoholics Anonymous, which stressed self-help, courage, honesty, and group support, to which the Army added its own straightforward religious appeal. AA "Anniversaries"—one year without a drink—reached a peak of one hundred fourteen in Hofman's Cleveland center in 1956.[5]

The Army needed every human resource—and help from above—in the work of the Men's Social Service Department. Not only were as many as eighty percent of its beneficiaries habitual drunkards, but most of the men also had difficult personalities. A painstaking professional survey of the men in the Men's Social Service Center in Minneapolis in 1958 revealed a personality composite very similar to that of prison inmates: socially maladjusted, subject to depression and self-pity, dependent, dishonest, and often pathological. The Men's Social Service remained a missionary endeavor as taxing to the heart and faith of its officers as any field on earth, so that frequent reports of "conversions of old-time trophy caliber" were powerful testimony to loving patience and faith in God's Grace together.[6]

The business side of the social centers was also refurbished in the 1950s. Bins of junk and piles of old clothes were replaced by clothes racks and shelves of goods; the Army's retail stores lost the rummage-sale appearance that hard times and war shortages had forced upon them, and regained the air of respectability they had not enjoyed since the days of Colonel Edward Parker, fifty years before. Knowledgeable officers even squirreled away antiques and art objects for sale to collectors and dealers, who began to frequent the Army's stores for just this purpose. Placing these objects in the hands of those who would appreciate them was a useful service and brought welcome income to the Army. Retail sales—and ledger profits—climbed through the decade, surpassing by far the Army's income from waste paper and rags.[7]

This happy development, however, brought problems of its own. Comfortable income was a source of funds for the Army's rehabilitation schemes, but even apparent profit margins—social department accounting procedures did not always allow for depreciation as a charge against income, so that profits often appeared larger than they actually were—meant that officers would have to distinguish carefully between "employees" and "beneficiaries." The Army had recognized this need since the 1940s. A national conference of Men's Social Service Department officers was called in October 1956, at which a series of regulations were drafted to draw such careful distinctions. Beneficiaries (who were not covered by the labor laws) were defined by the Army as men with "primary handicaps"—temporary disabilities the Army center's program was designed to "overcome or alleviate," such as alcoholism, drug addiction, or antisocial attitudes—who voluntarily entered the Army centers as the subjects of religious and social rehabilitation. Employees were those who worked for the Army solely for financial reward. To maintain this distinction the Army set an official, nationwide ratio of beneficiaries to employees at two to one. Officers were careful to demonstrate that nationally the Army invested more in its clients than it received for their services. Individual centers that enjoyed "surpluses" were told to add "new services and facilities for the rehabilitation of the beneficiaries," to use up the extra money in worthwhile ways. At the same time the Army acknowledged the awkward fact that financial practices varied considerably from center to center. The Men's Social Service Departments for the four territories clearly needed to adopt policies and procedures that were uniform across the country. Delegates from the four departments met in 1960 for that purpose, under the chairmanship of Lt.–Colonel Peter Hofman. They produced the monumental *Handbook of Standards, Principles and Policies,* which was approved by the five commissioners in October as the first national guide for Men's Social Service Department operations since Colonel Parker's series of *Minutes,* issued in 1910. The *Handbook,* with many revisions, remains the fundamental basis for the Army's social work among men to this day.[8]

The venerable Women's Social Service Department remained one of the Army's "most active" social programs in the 1950s, its thirty-seven maternity hospitals operating at nearly full capacity throughout the

decade: the 83.5 percent adult occupancy reported for the Buffalo facility by Senior-Major Jane Wrieden, a leading expert on the Army's
maternity care, was a typical figure in 1953. The period was nonetheless
a time of change for women's social officers. The traditional maternity
home program had provided unwed mothers with hospitality, kindness,
and evangelism; in the 1950s officers began to experiment with accred-
ited secondary educational programs, to enable women to employ the
time of their confinement in a useful manner. Craft classes, group
therapy, and professional social counseling were also introduced. The
women were gradually given more personal freedom, to leave the hospital for shopping, and to visit and receive friends. Many officers found
an RN degree necessary for an effective and professional ministry. A
national conference was appointed by the commissioners in 1955 to
evaluate the entire Department and to recommend any necessary
changes in the Army's services to unmarried mothers. The result was a
national statement in September 1955, which was reaffirmed in principle and elaborated upon in February 1960: it declared that there should
be "only one standard—good service to the whole person—physical,
mental, social and spiritual." The statement noted in passing that "unmarried mothers mirror faithfully the degree of social disapproval existing within the overall cultural setting"—a truism with disturbing implications for the Army's maternity homes, which officers at that time
ignored.[9]

Indeed, the decade of the 1950s was full of implications for the Army.
Although present-day nostalgia has cloaked this period with bland tran-
quility, there were many changes in American life after 1950 and The
Salvation Army did not escape them, although the movement was never
more popular or prosperous. The 83rd Congress of the United States
declared, and President Dwight D. Eisenhower proclaimed, the week of
November 28 to December 4, 1954, as the first "National Salvation
Army Week." Yet all during the Fifties the Army was losing its traditional base of strength in the city, as the ethnic complexion of America's
large northern cities continued to change. Juvenile delinquincy was
increasing, as was violent crime. The nation's attitudes towards racial
minorities, and toward religion, unwed mothers, and many social problems were changing, slowly, but in the end, drastically. These were
changes to which the Army, for all its popularity, was forced to adjust.

The Salvation Army's work among prisoners had been its first social
work program in the United States; yet this ministry offered only vari-

able returns over its long history. The prison work in the East had profited for many years from the leadership of Envoy J. Stanley "Red" Sheppard, who regarded the prison population as "the last virgin ground for Army evangelistic service among the type of men that the Army originally was designed to serve." Yet some of the Army's most active programs among prisoners had wound down. The prison corps had not outlived the original converts, nor did the Army have the officer personnel to provide many full-time prison chaplains. The Salvation Army was represented officially in the American Prison Association, and each territory now had a "correctional services" department to coordinate the prison visitation, Christmas welfare for prisoners' families (which often took the form of toys selected beforehand by the inmate parent and delivered to the child by the Army), and the annual Prison Day band concerts that continued. The Army increasingly interested itself in counseling and probation programs designed to prevent, rather than alleviate, detention, especially for delinquent youth.[10]

Progress was often difficult to evaluate. There were areas in which advance and retreat occurred together. Youth programs like the Corps Cadet brigades (a religious training program more advanced than Sunday school, for the interested young Salvationist), Girl Guards and Boy Scouts, the Young People's Legion (a weekly evangelistic program for those aged eleven to eighteen years), and the Young People's (or "Junior") Band still prospered, despite growing competition from television and a captivating array of after-school activities offered in many American high schools. The Army's youth activities were the envy of other denominations, whose young people drifted off in bored distraction. The Army won national recognition for its role in the White House Conferences on Children and Youth in 1950 and 1960. Yet attendance at Salvation Army Sunday schools, which officers at every level regard as the Army most's important religious activity for young people and a reliable indicator of the future vitality of the corps, began a long, gradual, and steady decline, which over the next twenty-five years would result in a thirty percent reduction in numbers.[11]

The Service Extension program spread rapidly in the 1950s; a manual issued in 1958 for nationwide use prescribed in detail a practical program of short-term welfare to be administered by local volunteers in areas where there were no regular Army corps. And although the Army was "not primarily an emergency disaster relief organization," its members were drawn "by tradition and inclination" to scenes of catastrophe, dispensing hot food from the ubiquitous white mobile canteen, offering clothing and shelter to victims, and proferring the consolation of Christ and His love. The entire lack of bureaucratic delay in these on-the-spot acts of kindness made the Army's emergency services highly welcome to disaster victims, and very popular with the public, although other agencies provided more in the way of systematic, long-term welfare. Yet at the same time that the service extension and emergency relief programs were winning friends for the Army, officers began to encounter difficulties from local Community Chest administrators, who questioned the value to the community of some the Army's religious programs.[12]

The Advisory Board program flourished in the decades after World War II. Born in the Auxiliaries of Ballington Booth's day, developed twenty-five years later by Colonel Fletcher Agnew in Chicago, Advisory Boards became a mainstay of the Army's community service. Local business and professional leaders who sympathize with the Army's total mission serve on these Boards, giving their financial support, advice, and encouragement to the officers and soldiers of the Corps. The Advisory Boards were uniquely American until the 1960s, when the Army in Canada, Britain, and elsewhere began to adopt the idea.

There were developments that affected the Army internally, of which the public took little note. Some of these were highly beneficial to Salvationists. The Salvation Army has always cared for its own. Retired officers have never been left to languish in obscure poverty, but as their numbers increased some more reliable provision had to be made for them. In August 1953, General Orsborn officially opened the Retired Officers' Residence in Asbury Park, New Jersey, within earshot of the corps band's seaside open-air stand and close to Ocean Grove, the Sabbatarian piety of which had drawn many retired Salvationists. A later divisional commander, Major David Baxendale, took special care to utilize the skills and experience of New Jersey's 250 retired officers as counselors, prayer warriors, and visitors. The Army provided subsidies and special programs for those veterans who settled elsewhere as well, in such silver-haired enclaves as Old Orchard Beach, Maine, St. Petersburg, Florida, and southern California.[13]

There was mere bureaucratic change as well: two Army ranks, Senior–Captain and Senior–Major, were dropped from active use in 1959 (although these, like previous discontinued ranks, are retained by those who retired holding them). The Army's liability to elaborate record keeping was nothing new—a writer in 1893 observed that "Every part of The Army is accurately labelled and pigeon-holed"—but this tendency became more marked with the increasing complexity of Army operations in the fifties. Officers were asked to prepare a steadily increasing number of statistical reports, which young Captain John Waldron of the Western New York division described in 1953 as "statistical measurements of a work that can't be measured, a numerical evaluation of a work beyond human values." Yet for all of its incessant collection of data, careful outside observers of the Army's administrative structure found it complicated and overlapping.[14]

The Army experienced other kinds of change, too, which no one welcomed. The movement, once so mobile that it numbered its proliferating stations to keep them in order, had long since acquired property and settled down in neighborhoods that began to change in the 1950s. The average age of the Army's neighbors, their income, their race, or their language made the new arrivals different from those among whom the corps had once flourished. This trend was not yet a strong one in many places in the decade, but already some officers were uneasy. At the same time the open air ministry began to decline, as television, public transportation, and the private automobile emptied the city's sidewalks of their crowds. Shopping centers began to draw off large numbers of shoppers, who now meandered between shops enclosed, whither the Army's brass-band evangelism could not penetrate. Yet officers in many places doggedly stood by their commitment to outdoor evangelism, which they rightly regarded as the lifeblood of the movement.[15]

One especially lamentable victim of time was the Scandinavian work, once one of the most enthusiastic and successful branches of the Salvation War. The decline was caused by the cessation of fresh Scandinavian immigration and the rise to adulthood of second and third generation Salvationists who had been raised in the United States and did not require, nor even desire, religious activities conducted entirely in a Scandinavian language. The end came first in the West, in 1950, when the fourteen corps of the Scandinavian Division were incorporated into the American divisions in which they were located. The Scandinavian work was larger in the Central and Eastern territories than in the West (although no stronger in evangelical zeal) and lasted through the decade, but with flagging confidence. In January 1961, the Scandinavian division of the Eastern territory ceased operations. The last divisional commander, Lt.–Colonel Gustav A. Johanson, was given the newly created post of Assistant Field Secretary for Scandinavian Affairs to supervise the reduced activities in those languages, which were now administered under American divisions. In the Central territory the Scandinavian division was absorbed over a two-year period, from 1963 to 1965. The last divisional commander, Brigadier Stig Franzen, and his second-in-command Major C. Milton Anderson, both good-hearted evangelicals, emerged from the transition in charge of the new Northern Illinois division. These administrative changes were accepted by the Scandinavian troops with gloomy resignation. Their spirits recovered considerably, however, when it became apparent to them that Army leaders would continue to appoint officers of Scandinavian descent to command their corps, and that every effort would be made to help them keep their festivals and special music alive in an Army that has never ceased to cherish them as comrades.[16]

The decline of the Scandinavian work was an unsettling development, and there were other developments about which officers were uneasy. The Army's very strengths seemed to work against it. The movement had become so popular and so respectable that in 1965, the centennial year of the beginning of William Booth's work in London, the Army in the United States was honored with a commemorative postage stamp. The Army's practical philanthropy had secured for it property, connections with the Community Chest, and the support of local businessmen organized into Advisory Boards. Yet the public who so generously gave its money to the Army was indifferent, even mildly antagonistic to its religious appeal. Officers who felt they had been called by God to a great crusade for souls were frustrated with their role as administrators of a charity, no matter how popular. In addition, the intricacy of the Army's philanthropic and financial affairs forced officers to hire an ever-increasing number of professional and clerical employees, whose supervision took more and more time; from 1951 to 1961 the number of lay employees of the Army doubled. Frustrations multiplied. The neighborhoods surrounding many corps not only ceased to be filled with persons who were easily accessible to the Army's traditional evangelical methods: many places were becoming actually dangerous. The late fifties witnessed a sharp increase in violent crimes against persons in urban areas, so that even the most faithful soldiers were reluctant to venture downtown to the corps hall for evening services for the people in an indifferent or hostile neighborhood.[17]

Slightly more than half of officers were the children of officers, and almost all had come up through the corps youth programs; their experience with Salvation Army life was almost entirely confined to traditional religious services. For instance, a study of officer training in the West in the early 1960s revealed that the average cadet had been in the corps for six years before coming to the training college, and three-quarters of them had been corps cadets. The public, however, persisted in believing that most officers had been rescued from debauchery, while the Army just as persistently pointed out that the best source of its officer-candidates was not the street but the corps. As active young soldiers, busy in the corps building in the evenings and on Sundays, these future officers had little contact with the Army's day-to-day welfare activities. Their first exposure to a corps welfare program often came when they were appointed to their first command.[18]

Then, too, many officers, particularly in the lower field ranks, are single women. Women have always outnumbered men in The Salvation Army, both as soldiers and as officers. At times the imbalance was high, but from the 1950s to the present the proportion of Salvationists who are women has never been less than sixty percent. The Army requires that men officers marry women officers, or women who are willing to become officers at once; even if every male officer marries, at least twenty percent of the officer corps are women who will never marry (and there are many widows). This percentage is much higher for younger officers in their first five years of officership, the very years when discouragement is most frequent, even for a married couple who have the consolation of mutual support and companionship. Wartime reduction in the number of cadets made it impossible to fully overcome the attrition due to post-war retirement. The inevitable result of these developments taken together was a decline in the number of officers after 1950. One of the most frequent reasons given for resignation was simply "dissatisfaction."[19]

Yet there was a large basis for hope; and while it may be a little harsh to condemn officers who resign out of dissatisfaction as "deserters"—as General William Booth was wont to do—still, many latter-day quitters put behind them the calling of God before all the returns were in. All was a long way from lost. The Salvation Army was the Army still, and valiantly carried on its evangelical crusade in many places, under the banner of the Cross. Many bandmasters held their musicians to the high standards of an earlier day: men like Garfield Thomas of Oakland Citadel, Ron Smart of Hollywood Tabernacle, Kenneth Luyk of New Kensington, Pennsylvania, and Al Swenarton of Asbury Park led their corps bands out on street marches and open-air crusades into the 1970s. Bands still march in the muddy streets of Alaskan villages and young musicians are still taught the rudiments of street marching at the Army's annual territorial music camps across the United States.

The Army's musical ministry continued to bring life and joy to Christian worship, and a rich production of band and choral music flowed steadily into print in the 1950s. This included the several series published in London, which also produced a *Supplement* to the beloved *Band Tune Book* in 1954. From New York came *Band Music for Evangelism* scored for a nine-piece band with four optional parts, which presented forty-eight pieces by the end of the decade, including compositions by Erik Leidzen, Richard Holz, Vernon Post, Stanley Ditmer, and Emil Soderstrom. The Eastern territorial music bureau also published a welcome little book of forty-two gospel band tunes called the *American Supplement to the Band Tune Book* in 1956, and a year later a collection of brass quartet arrangements of Christmas carols by Erik Leidzen called *Carolers' Favorites.* [20]

The Salvation War advanced on other fronts as well. The Army's honest, if sporadic, efforts to draw more Southern blacks into the circle of its ministry had not resulted in a direct official assault on racial segregation before 1950; to have done more would have inflamed local authorities and public opinion to drive the Army from the scene. Still, the Army did not entirely delay action until after the massive shift in national opinion that slowly followed upon the Supreme Court school desegregation decision of 1954. Professor Wisbey, pursuing his doctoral research in 1949 and 1950, found that segregation was "not accepted by the Army with an easy conscience." In 1950 a national commission, established along with territorial ones, to prepare for Army participation in the White House Conference on Children and Youth officially declared itself to be "concerned about continuing legal separation of race"; while the Southern territorial commission optimistically reported "an upsurge . . . of good will in a tradition-ridden area of the nation, in point of prejudice and discrimination." [21]

The Army was the first social agency in Washington, D.C., to integrate its facilities. After 1946 the Army's fresh air camp for blacks in Maryland had an integrated summer staff. In 1952 the camp itself was closed, and the entire program was transferred to the formerly all white camp in Virginia. The newly integrated and enlarged facility was called Camp Happyland, the name of the defunct black camp. The first director of the new program was a black, Sam Covington. In 1949 the Army responded to the request of a black officer, Major B. Barton McIntyre, in charge of the Cleveland, Ohio, "Colored Corps," that his command be designated the "Central Area Corps." In 1951 the adjective "colored" disappeared from Washington, D.C.'s Ninth Street Corps, which emerged as the Central Corps.[22]

By 1955 activities conducted on the divisional and territorial level, such as Young People's Councils, Girl Guard, and Home League rallies, were integrated throughout the South, although local units remained segregated. In northern cities neighborhood racial complexion combined with the preference of black Salvationists for a local center for worship and service caused some corps to remain largely or entirely all black without conscious design: examples are St. Louis Euclid Avenue, Omaha Northside corps, Cleveland Central Area, Harlem Temple, Brooklyn Bedford Temple, Pittsburgh Homewood corps, and Milwaukee West corps. Where segregation was the result of past official policy, divisional leaders were allowed, even encouraged, to eliminate the barriers; thus in 1960 the Mary B. Talbert Home and Hospital in Cleveland, the Army's only all-black maternity hospital, was merged with its white counterpart, the Booth Memorial.[23]

The decade of the 1960s brought sudden, violent, and permanent change to race relations in the United States. The Salvation Army brought a good heart and a near-military efficiency to the successive crises, and carried most of its soldiers with it onto a new level of understanding of the Brotherhood of Christ. In May 1964, the territorial commanders issued a joint statement on "racial justice," in which they declared that officership, employment, membership, and participation in The Salvation Army were open to any person regardless of race, and that "all social welfare services" would be offered on the same basis. In November the territorial commander of the South had to overrule local advisory board members in Mississippi who had refused to distribute free Thanksgiving turkeys to black families after civil rights activists had collected the dinners among supporters in the north. More difficulties followed: the riots in many northern cities threw the Army into a dilemma. The Army was traditionally non-political, wishing only to be of service to all people, yet it had long-established and warm ties to military and emergency personnel. It was natural for officers to arrive at the scene of urban rioting and burning to offer canteen refreshment to weary national guardsmen, firemen, and police. It was no less natural for radical blacks to resent it.[24]

Yet officers attempted to succor those whom the fires victimized. In Pittsburgh, during the 1963 riots, Captain Israel Gaither of the Homewood corps distributed encouragement and groceries to many black families after their local supermarkets had gone up in smoke. Colonel Paul Seiler, the territorial Men's Social Service secretary, collected all the spare trucks from eleven centers for this massive project. In the Cleveland riots of 1966 Colonel Giles Barrett, the divisional commander, mustered canteens from three cities and ordered them to distribute their boon to police and riot victims alike. There were many similar accounts. Such evenhandedness, combined with the Army's genial willingness to open its youth programs to neighborhood young people and to distribute its practical welfare with a minimum of red tape, rescued the movement from otherwise certain condemnation by blacks as just one more agency of a bigoted and hateful "establishment." As it was, several Army centers—like Milwaukee's West corps—were apparently deliberately spared during the window-breaking and arson that accompanied riots everywhere.[25]

The Salvation Army was not content to escape condemnation; it redoubled its efforts to broaden its evangelical ministry among blacks, who formed a larger percentage of the urban population with every passing year. Recognizing that "inner city" was often a synonym for black, some officers were convinced that the Army in the city would have to become what one officer called "a largely black organization" in order to survive. Certainly the Army's existing all-black corps showed no signs of abandoning their enthusiastic evangelical outreach. Harlem Temple Corps, under Brigadier B.B. McIntyre (succeeded in 1972 by Major Abraham Johnson) offered helpful programs, hot meals, remedial reading, and Spanish-language classes, arranged gymnasium facilities for the neighborhood, and capped it all with an old-time hallelujah street service with a brass band on the corner of Seventh Avenue and 125th Street. The warmhearted evangelical zeal of the soldiers of Brooklyn Bedford Temple, under Senior-Major Pearl Hurdle, Major Lebert Bernard, Captain Israel Gaither, and (after 1975) Major Lilian Yarde, remains proverbial in Army circles. There are a dozen other lively, hospitable, and flourishing corps under black leadership in Boston's Roxbury, Washington, Philadelphia, Pittsburgh, Chicago, St. Louis, Omaha, Cleveland, Richmond, Little Rock, and Atlanta.[26]

New programs were launched and new ministries devised to meet what several knowledgeable staff officers called the "felt-needs" of the ghetto. In 1964 Major Mary Nisiewicz, with the pluck and zeal of a Victorian slum sister, began a one-woman rescue crusade on East 125th Street among New York ghetto youth and drug addicts. Two years later, in the aftermath of the riots in Cleveland, the Army resolved to plunge back into the burned-over area with a new ministry—or rather, an old ministry in a new form. Colonel Barrett inspired the city with his vision of a vast new Army center, full of hopeful programs, that would rise phoenix-like from the smoking ruins of the Hough Avenue slums. Millions were contributed, and the Hough Multi-Purpose Center, a kind of religious recreation welfare shopping mall, was opened in October, 1969, by civil-rights activist James Farmer. The first director of the center was Major Henry Gariepy, a long-time advocate of a more diverse Army program in the inner-city. Gariepy quickly built an effective staff, the star of which was Madeline Manning Jackson, black Olympic runner and a fervent Christian.[27]

A retired Army missionary to India, Colonel Dr. William Noble, opened a free medical clinic for blacks in 1967 in Atlanta's slums; he ran it for five years with a volunteer staff and free samples given to him by sympathetic drug salesmen. In 1968 a new multi-purpose corps facility was opened for the Hartford, Connecticut, North End corps, named for Henry W. Jennings, a black policeman killed in action. The new center offered an innovative remedial reading program for slum youths who were functionally illiterate in traditional English, but expressive, even eloquent, in ghetto dialect. The Army command in Chicago, long a scene of many triumphs, organized an entire administrative branch for "Inner-city Services," that included several community centers, the Freedom Center complex on West Monroe Street, the Tom Seay Service Center, an old-time rescue shelter called the New Life House, and the Chicago Southside Settlement.[28]

In 1971 the commissioners' conference appointed a Task Force for each territory, to survey Army services to racial minorities. The results revealed a remarkable range of new and special programs designed to supplement the traditional Salvation Army evangelical ministry; these new programs included counseling, employment referral, day-care centers for working mothers, "probation, parole and court work," medical clinics, recreational, gymnasium, and camping opportunities, black studies, community planning sessions, vocational training, and even several attempts to organize drum and bugle corps, long a favorite with some inner-city youth. The official Task Force Report, written by Major Robert A. Watson, appeared in 1973. It admitted that the Army faced serious problems in its ghetto outreach: overworked officers; the presence in the ghetto of "militant factions" that deliberately undermined the Army's influence on youthful blacks; the transient nature of much of the ghetto population, which prevented the Army from building a stable following among them; increasing violence, vandalism, and burglary; and the fact that some inner-city corps were enclaves of middle-class blacks who had escaped to the suburbs and now had little influence in the immediate neighborhood of the corps, to which they returned once every Sunday morning. The report declared twice that the Army faced a "critical need" for more black officers. Still, there were solid grounds for encouragement: Major Watson was glad to note that there was a "significant evangelical thrust" in many of the new activities, that "traditional programs" continued to play a major role in changing lives, and that "heroic and dedicated service" was being rendered on the inner-city front.[29]

Black officers shared their comrades' concern about the the Army's ministry among black Americans, and their pride in being officers in the movement. Black Salvationists were also increasingly proud of the contribution they had made over many years, and were making still, to the Salvation War. In 1969 the black officers of the Eastern territory met together for the first time on a formal basis, during a territorial congress in New York. Arranged by Brigadier McIntyre (who had become divisional secretary—second in command—in the Metropolitan New York division) and led by Captain Gaither and Lieutenant Noel Christian, the meeting heard expressions of loyalty and commitment to the Army that were mixed with anxiety. The black community "recognized and liked" the Army for the services it provided, but few ghetto youth joined the ranks as soldiers. It was difficult to encourage young black soldiers to become officers, because black officers were appointed only to the few "black" corps and apparently were not considered for headquarters or training college positions. It was noted that many black Salvationists were immigrants from the Caribbean, and while these comrades should be actively cultivated and many others like them drawn into the Army, "instead of turning to the West Indies when Officer personnel is needed, effort should be made to acquire black American Soldiery and Officers."[30]

A number of the difficulties brought to wider notice by the black officers in 1969, like some of those in Major Watson's 1973 report, have proven nearly intractable. Of these the most critical remains the Army's failure to recruit sufficient numbers of American black officers. On the other hand, problems that were amenable to mutual good will and administrative action have in many cases ceased to trouble the movement: black officers are now considered for promotion and service on the basis of ability alone. B. Barton McIntyre, for instance, retired in 1975 with the rank of Lt.–Colonel, his last appointment having been on the territorial staff, as territorial evangelist. Captain Israel Gaither was promoted to a staff position in 1975, and in 1978 was appointed divisional secretary in the Greater New York division. In March, 1979, Captain Gaither led a "Black Heritage Night" at a Friday Evening at the Temple meeting in New York City, which was regaled by the New Found Sound —a special band made up of black players from all over the territory— and blessed by a gospel message from Dr. Martin Luther King, Sr. In June the "first all-black brigade of cadets in the history of The Salvation Army" invaded Cleveland; the six valiants conducted a series of special evangelical services at the Hough Center and the Miles Park Corps (since 1976 the name of the Central Area Corps) with happy results.[31]

The Army has made efforts to "throw out the lifeline" to Spanish-speaking immigrants as well, efforts that are no less honest and strenuous for being mostly recent. The Army had run courageous little Spanish-language missions in Laredo and El Paso, Texas, for many years; El Paso Southside (Spanish) corps began in 1907 with a street-corner meeting in the Spanish language. The Salvation Army did not launch a major Spanish ministry, however, until after the Second World War, when massive Mexican and Puerto-Rican immigration began. This large population movement turned large sections of American cities into Spanish-speaking ghettos, to which The Salvation Army had either to address its ministry or depart from still another part of its traditional downtown harvest field.[32]

The Bronx Spanish-American corps opened in 1960, with almost instantly encouraging results. Mrs. Gladys Torres was the first to enroll as a soldier there, in January 1961. She was nothing if not enthusiastic about her new religion, and while home in Puerto Rico for a visit in March, she stirred up enough local interest in the Army that work was soon started on the island. Within a decade there were Spanish-speaking corps in Los Angeles, San Diego, Phoenix, El Paso, Laredo, Chicago, the Bronx, Jersey City, and Paterson. In the Eastern territory the Army organized a Spanish Ministries Committee under Major Frank Payton to develop new forms of outreach to the more than one million Spanish-speaking people in the New York-Northern New Jersey area. The Inner-City Task Force of 1971 and 1972 was also charged with surveying Army work among " 'Hispanic' persons," and found that Spanish-language tutoring, case work interviews, counseling, and evangelization were proliferating. Inner-city coordinators were appointed for Philadelphia, Cleveland, and Chicago to coordinate and expand both black and Hispanic ministries. The "critical need" in this mission, as in work among blacks, was for qualified personnel to come forward as officers.[33]

Two traditional ethnic ministries continued to thrive. The Chinatown Corps in San Francisco, opened in 1896, had outlived the vicissitudes of 166 different officers until 1959, and had somehow survived them all as the Army's only Chinese corps in the United States. For the first twenty-nine years of its existence the Chinese ministry was sustained largely by the valiant color sergeant, Looey Gooey, who provided what continuity he could beneath a never-ceasing kaleidoscope of officers, none of whom could speak Chinese. In 1959 Captain Check Hung Yee was given the command, and the corps began to prosper. By the mid-1960s there were almost three hundred Chinese involved in one or another of the many helpful activities offered by the energetic and resourceful Yee: counseling for recent immigrants, family welfare, a small Evangeline residence for working women, a Home League, tambourine brigade, and a complete complement of musical forces all glowing in the gospel fire of the Captain's quiet, earnest evangelism. In 1978 the Chinatown Corps began to produce a fifteen-minute religious television program in two dialects of Chinese and in English, broadcast once a week on Sunday evenings and intended, like the corps' traditional open-air meetings in Chinatown itself, to fulfill the Army's fundamental mission: to carry Christ to those who do not seek Him out.[34]

Likewise, the Scandinavian heritage continues to enliven parts of The Salvation Army in the Central and Eastern territories. Despite the still-unforgiven termination of their separate administrative divisions, many Scandinavian Salvationists have doggedly kept alive their several delightful traditions (not the least of which, luckily, is cooking), and have raised their children and grandchildren to share their affection for the old festivals and songs. Five such corps exist in Illinois; three in Chicago (Mt. Greenwood, Irving Park and Andersonville); Moline and

Rockford Temple; and four in Minnesota: Minneapolis Temple and Central Avenue; St. Paul Temple and Duluth Temple. The Eastern territory has eight "Scandinavian" corps; in five of them—New York Central Citadel on East Fifty-second Street; Worcester, Massachusetts, Quinsigamond Corps; Brooklyn Bay Ridge and Jamestown Temple in New York—the Swedish language is still frequently used in services; Jamestown Temple even sponsors a Swedish-language radio program. The remaining four corps are Erie Temple, Pennsylvania; Providence, Rhode Island; Hartford Temple and New Britain, Connecticut. The Army in the Eastern territory nurtures its remaining Scandinavian forces with an annual Scandinavian Night at the New York Temple, and later in the year a Congress at Camp Ladore in Pennsylvania, all organized by the genial Lt.–Colonel Olof Lundgren, a (nominally) retired officer especially appointed in 1975 as Director of Scandinavian Activities.[35]

The Salvation Army has always found strength in adaptability. This has been due in part to its military command structure, which (theoretically at least) allowed for quick and efficient adoption of new policies, and in part to the fact that the Army has never wavered from its historic purpose, which is to win converts to Christianity among those who have fallen away from, or have never known, the Savior; any practical means to this end could be tried and then either developed or abandoned, solely on the basis of results. There have been some awkward moments, to be sure: in 1970 there was a brief flurry of adverse comment in some religious journals in this country when an officer was dismissed in London for publishing a heretical book, and in Atlanta a disgruntled ex-officer sued the Army for discriminating against her in assignments on the basis of her sex. The Army claimed that the charge was false, but won the case on the grounds that the relations between a church and its ministers are exempt from the relevant provisions of the Civil Rights Act. Still, a collection of single-minded zealots dedicated to a glorious cause, organized under military discipline and commanded by the Lord, ought to have been able to adapt quickly to the rapidly shifting conditions of American life in the twenty years after 1960. Happily, this has mostly been true.[36]

The high attrition rate among officers during the first five years of officership and the complexity of social and religious problems that all officers had to face convinced Army leaders that the program of officer preparation at the territorial training colleges was no longer sufficient. The Army had admitted for years that the traditional nine-month course was a "limited period in which to accomplish much in training future officers," but lack of funds and the incessant demands of the field for fresh officers had delayed any enlargement of the program. In 1960 the training college curriculum was lengthened to two years, and the institution was renamed The Salvation Army School for Officers' Training. The new curriculum was still largely "practical"—forty percent of the weekly class hours in required subjects went for "Field Training"—but courses were added in theology, history, literature, and psychology, and much more time was allowed to prepare officers for the bookkeeping and administrative details of their work.[37]

Nor were Army officers closed to the benefits of formal higher education for those young Salvationists who felt called to some form of service that required a baccalaureate degree, or who wished to thus prepare themselves more completely before entering the Schools for Officers' Training. Soldiers have attended colleges and universities in steadily increasing numbers since 1950. There has been a concentration of Army collegians in schools near areas in which the Army itself has well-established corps and musical activities, which are a major factor in holding young people in the ranks during the college years. Such areas are eastern Michigan, Chicago, the San Francisco Bay Area, southern California, Philadelphia, New York-northern New Jersey, and southern New England.

Other Salvationists have been drawn to small private Christian liberal-arts colleges. Of this number, the large majority have attended Asbury College, near Lexington, Kentucky. Over a hundred commissioned officers, and several times that many soldiers and Army employees, have graduated from the college since the first Salvationist enrolled there in 1924. The Salvationist students, who are formally organized as The Salvation Army Student Fellowship (SASF) of Asbury College, have a thirty-seven-piece brass band of their own, and take an active part in the activities of the campus and nearby Salvation Army corps. The relationship between the college and the Army became so congenial that in 1973 General Arnold Brown (at the time still Chief of the Staff) commented favorably upon the educational influence of Asbury upon The Salvation Army. Several recent events have placed a crown of mutual and official approval on this fruitful marriage: a Salvation Army officer (Colonel Andrew S. Miller, currently the Chief Secretary—second in command—of the Central territory) was elected to the college board of trustees in 1968; in 1975 the national commander, Commissioner William E. Chamberlain, attached the Asbury SASF directly to national headquarters—a singular honor—and appointed a retired officer, Lt. Colonel David W. Moulton, to serve as national liaison officer, and two faculty members as local officers: Professor James E. Curnow as Bandmaster, and Professor E.H. McKinley as Corps Sergeant-Major. The territorial commanders have generously provided the SASF Band with a number of new instruments, and in 1979 the commissioners' conference authorized the attendance of the Band to represent national headquarters at the Army's national centenary congress in Kansas City in June, 1980.[38]

Asbury, of course, is not the only Christian college to benefit from a warm connection with the Army. In the Central territory cadets from the School for Officers' Training are enabled to obtain academic credit by attending selected classes at Olivet Nazarene College in Kankakee, Illinois. A similar but more advanced arrangement in the Western territory allows cadets to obtain associate of arts degrees from Azusa Pacific College when they are commissioned as officers.

The Army's benevolent attitude toward higher education flowed from its century-old determination to adapt its ministry to contemporary conditions. A generation of young American Salvationist composers has arisen who share that determination and who are committed to the Gospel, to the Army's musical traditions, and to legitimate and timely professional expectations. Perhaps the best known of these outside Army circles is Professor James E. Curnow of Asbury College, who has published extensively in the literature of secondary and college-level concert and marching bands, and has written a number of pieces for Army bands. Other noteworthy young Army composers are William Himes, Bandmaster of the Chicago Staff Band and head of the territorial music bureau, Bruce Broughton, and Steve Bulla. There are several Salvationist performers with established professional reputations as well, including Philip Smith, principal trumpet with the New York Philharmonic; Charles Baker, principal trombone with the New Jersey Symphony; Peggy Paton Thomas of Chicago; Carole Reinhart of New Jersey; Robert Schramm of the US Air Force Band in Washington, D.C.; and Pat Cairnes Wadenpfuhl and her husband Ken of Ft. Lauderdale.[39]

The New York and Chicago Staff Bands continue to give service of a reliably high order, filling a rigorous schedule of public performances, playing the latest and most challenging Army compositions (often in manuscript form), and making recordings. The Army maintains a num-

ber of regional bands that do much the same—the National Capital
Divisional band, the Pendel Brass and Singers of Philadelphia, the
Carolinas Divisional Youth Band, and until 1972 the New Jersey Youth
Band. Some bands are gathered together for special events, like those
that march every year in the Tournament of Roses, and Cotton Bowl
parades, and the Thanksgiving Day parade in Detroit, or the excellent
instructors' bands at Star Lake, CMI, Western Music Institute, and the
South's Territorial School of Music. The Asbury College SASF Band is
unique both for its affiliation with national headquarters and because it
is made up entirely of Salvationists from one college.[40]

These bands have a three-fold purpose: serving public relations, per-
forming at ceremonial functions, and offering a religious ministry. The
main burden of the Salvation War is still carried, however, by the
Army's corps bands, which accompany religious services on the congregational level, both indoors and outdoors, and play for corps weddings,
funerals, and the annual Christmas appeal. The Army's official defini-
tion of a "band" remains what it was in the Founder's day: "A group
of not fewer than four senior [at least fourteen years old] Salvationists
who voluntarily serve together to further the purposes of The Salvation
Army by means of instrumental music." Not every Salvation Army band
is as small as this, but the Army has done wisely in making careful
provision in regulation and in music for the quartet: many corps have
little more, and most corps have no band at all. Despite enormous and
sustained effort on the part of officers and soldiers, the number of corps
bands has declined since 1950. In 1979 there were 398 of them in the
United States, for 1,074 corps, which means that sixty-three percent of
American corps do not have a band.[41]

On the bright side, the thirty-seven percent of the corps that still have
bands show no signs of giving them up. The Army has published a
wealth of music for the small band, including The Salvation Army *Brass
Ensemble Journal* (1960, 1964) and a book of regional tunes published
in Atlanta called *Songs of the South* (1975), which can be played with
"a good harmonic balance" using just four musicians. In 1979 the
Army's international music department in London ordered a revision of
the classic 1928 *Band Tune Book* so that its contents can also be played
adequately by just four instruments. Ninety-six percent of those corps
with bands have "junior bands" as well, made up of younger players who
insure a supply of future bandsmen. Most bands are small, it is true—
the average size of a corps band in 1978 was not quite eleven players

—but there are perhaps seventy-five corps bands of twenty pieces or larger, many of them generations-old and exceptionally proficient: a single example for each territory might be Cambridge, Massachusetts, Silver Band; Atlanta Temple Band; Chicago Mont Clare Band; and a fine new band, the Santa Ana, California, Citadel Band.[42]

The Army's willingness to adapt its music to the taste of contemporary ears has not left it. The twenty years after 1960 witnessed a multiplication of efforts by Salvationists both to write innovative music for the traditional brass band and to form small "gospel-rock" groups of instrumentalists and singers, to carry the Good News to youthful hearers hitherto indifferent to the Army's brass-band evangelism. Officers like Captain Ernest A. Miller were committed in the sixties to broadening the Army's musical appeal, and reminded their fellow officers that, after all, it was still the "function of music to communicate." Jim Curnow and a group of talented young Salvationists from the Royal Oak, Michigan, corps formed the "Royalheirs" in 1965, followed by the "Second Destiny," which toured the Central territory for two summers in 1969 and 1970 playing in parks and camps. Other groups appeared, sponsored by corps and divisions, to play in the crop of coffee houses that sprang up briefly in the late 1960s, and at youth rallies, high schools, beaches, and New Jersey boardwalks.[43]

In some areas, however, no amount of innovation, no degree of willingness to move with the times could save the Army's ministry. A significant casualty was the Women's Social Service department. Officers of the department made an effort to adapt to the rapid changes that come over them in the 1960s: "service is not static," declared the official *Handbook* for home and hospital administration in 1962. "Policies and programs must be reviewed and reassessed periodically to insure their effectiveness in meeting the needs of people." The Army's kindhearted service to unwed mothers had always been been one of its most effective social programs, but in the sixties it began to die, the victim at last of changed public morals, steeply rising costs, and ever more stringent governmental and professional standards, which small private hospitals are hard-pressed to meet. Officers watched in despair as social acceptance of teenage and single-parent pregnancy, the easy availability of public medical care, and—hardest of all to bear—abortion emptied their little hospitals. Occupancy in Salvation Army homes and hospitals has declined sharply since 1969; from 1970 to 1978, for instance, total bed capacity has fallen by fifty-five percent to 874, and the number of newborn infants provided for has fallen by almost forty percent, to 3,667. Many maternity homes closed, and continue to close. In October, 1978, the Women's Social Service Department of the East was itself closed. Because the pioneer rescue home officers did not keep accurate records of their work, it is not certain how many thousands of babies have been placed by the Army in the arms of childless couples since 1887 when the first home was opened, nor how many women have left these places of refuge, convinced in their hearts that Christ loved them. It is certain that the number of homes has declined drastically in the past ten years, and it is sad to reflect that the time may be coming when there will be no more.[44]

This is a defeat, and the best efforts of public relations cannot make it otherwise. But there have been victories as well for the Army's social welfare in the 1970s. Even the Women's Social Service Department has had its triumphs: there were ninety-seven conversions to Christ in its operations in 1977, for instance, and several of its facilities have been adapted to meet contemporary needs. In Cincinnati the Catherine Booth Home has opened a mother/baby after-care program, a residential day-care center where young single mothers learn to care for their babies, and in Philadelphia the Army converted its hospital to the Booth Maternity Center, which offers a program in midwife-training that has gained national attention. Other defunct maternity homes have been converted to day-care centers and senior-citizen facilities. The Army has expanded in the general hospital field. Ground was broken in 1955 for the Booth Memorial Hospital in Flushing, New York, which was joined in 1979 by another in the suburban area south of Cincinnati.

The ministry among alcoholics has become professional and sophisticated with programs in several stages, leading through detoxification to long-term counseling and rehabilitation. The Founder's "Darkest England" scheme, adapted again and again to meet evolving social conditions, is triumphantly alive in Salvation Army Harbor Light corps. Among the most innovative and successful of these programs are Chicago's Freedom Center; the enormous Cleveland Harbor Light Complex, whose veteran director, Major Edward V. Dimond, has pioneered several advanced rehabilitative techniques, including musical therapy; and the three-stage Harbor Light Center in St. Louis, commanded by Captain Jack Bennett, himself a Trophy of Grace, whose efforts produce two genuine and lasting converts out of every hundred "intakes"—a remarkably successful record for rescue work among transient alcoholic men.[45]

The Men's Social Service centers have likewise adapted successfully, not only to changing conditions of urban life, but to the findings of a proliferation of sociological and medical research on alcoholism, and even to such worrisome developments as the neighborhood garage sale. Careful study revealed, for instance, that most homeless drunkards are not actually "addictive" drinkers; they drink simply to fill their time, as a compensation for "social deprivation," or for companionship—not from uncontrollable physical need. This revelation naturally raised the hopes of officers that such men might be more amenable to spiritual rehabilitation than they would be if their problem were entirely, or even primarily, physiological.[46]

At the same time, the very pronoun "he" became inappropriate to describe the Army's beneficiaries, as an increasing number of alcoholic women appeared, many of them working-class wives and mothers. Army centers wished to offer solace and counseling to married couples, too. As a result of these trends, and to avoid the stigma that professional social welfare personnel now attach to single-sex programs, The Salvation Army decided in 1977 to change the name of its social institutions from Men's Social Service to Adult Rehabilitation centers (ARCs); the territorial departments, however, retain the traditional names. Even so, the great majority of clients are still men, and among these the Army has achieved mighty results in recent years. In the West Commissioner Richard E. Holz, territorial commander since 1974, encouraged long-term ARC residents to enroll as "adherents" of The Salvation Army, as a formal recognition that they were transients no longer and the movement that had rescued them was their spiritual "home." (An adherent is defined a person who attends The Salvation Army regularly, as one would attend any church, but does not become a formal member—a soldier; often this is because soldiers must not smoke.) In 1978 fully 425 center beneficiaries had joined up as adherents, the more experienced men taking on the new converts as "disciples" in the new life.[47]

Programs directed at homeless alcoholics were not alone in experiencing beneficial change in the last twenty years. The decades have been a time of rapid and far-reaching change throughout The Salvation Army. The Army has not been sentimental about facilities that have outlived their purpose, and many cherished landmarks of the old-time Salvation War have been sold or demolished; the few soldiers remaining in these facilities managed to rescue some precious mementos of victories long past, such as a beautiful stained glass portrait of President William McKinley—a gift to the Army from his widow—saved when the old corps in Canton, Ohio, was razed. A few old halls were rejuvenated for service in a new part of the war: just as some ex-maternity hospitals became day-care centers, so the venerable Oakland Citadel became a Harbor Light mission when the corps moved to a new sanctuary on Sixth Avenue; and Los Angeles Congress Hall, once the largest corps west of Chicago, opened a mission to the Korean population that now surrounds the old hall on West Ninth.

Some change has been internal, innovations that serve mostly to improve administrative efficiency. The Army's territorial leaders, concerned over the increasing complexity and expense of the bureaucracy that implemented their decisions, commissioned a management analysis in 1968 by Booz, Allen & Hamilton, a New York consulting firm. Many of their recommendations were acted upon over the next several years. The main result of these reforms was that the four territories adopted a uniform, streamlined command structure. The territorial commander, a commissioner, is chief executive. His second-in-command, the chief secretary (a full colonel) supervises the heads of the three main administrative branches, under lieutenant–colonels: personnel (officers' appointments, records, pensions), program (music, youth, women's organizations, social service activities), and business. One major recommendation, that the Army establish a national training college in order to pool training staff personnel and avoid expensive duplication, was not adopted; but the Army has made large efforts since to improve the quality of the four territorial training-school programs.[48]

Another effort at national centralization was more successful: in 1965 the four territorial editions of *The War Cry* were partially merged into a single version; each territory retained control over the last eight pages of the twenty-four-page edition circulated within its own region. In 1970 the vestiges of territorial editorial control were eliminated, and a truly national *War Cry* emerged, published from national headquarters in New York. In 1973 two more Army ranks were eliminated: lieutenant–commissioner and brigadier (always a puzzler to the American public, which naturally mistook it for the rank of brigadier–general, when in fact the Army's "brigadier" was one rank lower than lieutenant–colonel.) A new national system of accounting and recordkeeping was introduced in 1977, designed to speed the analysis of statistics from the field; the system has yet to prove itself to hard-pressed corps officers, however, who shrink in alarm from the new pile of ledger forms. The Mexico division was detached from the Southern territory and became the heart of a separate territorial command of its own in 1976.[49]

The long and convoluted legal history of the American eagle version of the Army crest played itself out at last in 1976, when the copyright on the crown-topped model (the Army's international symbol, expropriated by Major Thomas Moore when he decamped in 1884) was discovered to have expired irrevocably. The American commissioners, in a spirit of international camaraderie, promptly ordered the reintroduction of the crown-crest on a massive scale; the eagle had disappeared from the last bit of stationery, drumhead, and building-front in the country by 1980.[50]

Of far greater interest to the public has been the diversification of Salvation Army social welfare services. Some Salvationists have developed new programs in fields long occupied by the Army, while others have carried the flag into new areas. The Salvation Army provided both on-the-spot practical relief and coordinated the channelling of personnel and resources on a national scale in the earthquakes in Alaska in 1964, in Peru in 1970, and in Guatemala in 1976. The last enterprise was unique in that the Army's Southern territory, represented on the scene by Major Harold Hinson, not only provided short term relief but built 521 permanent blockhouses and a community center in Tecpan. The Army was present in full force at every major domestic disaster as well, from the Gulf Coast hurricanes of 1969 to the floods along the Kentucky, Ohio, and Mississippi rivers in 1978 and 1979. In 1970 the Army joined other emergency service organizations in providing "disaster liaison officers" on a regional basis under the auspices of the Federal Disaster Assistance Administration. In 1975 Lt.–Colonel Ernest A. Miller was made "primary liaison" for the FDAA when he was placed in charge of the Army's new National Public Affairs and Disaster Services Office in Washington, D.C.[51]

From 1968 to 1971 a team of energetic Salvation Army officers served four civilian refugee camps near Saigon, in South Vietnam. The Salvation Army Medical and Social Welfare Services in Vietnam, guided by Major and Mrs George Collins and Captain and Mrs Erich Hamm, helped nearly two thousand refugees per week—half of them children —with medical attention, food distribution, remedial primary education, and spiritual counseling. Much of the bounty distributed by the

Army team came from individual contributors in America, the US Red Cross, and from the US Department of State's Agency for International Development (USAID). This was but a small part of the financial assistance provided by the federal government for various Salvation Army welfare programs in the 1970s.[52]

Brigadier Leslie Hall energetically directed a special bureau for the development of federal grants in the Southern Territory in 1978–1979. Governmental agencies have helped to finance "juvenile delinquency prevention services" in five Southern cities, a large-scale feeding program for the elderly in the Kentucky-Tennessee division, and a high-rise senior citizens' apartment building in Orlando, Florida. The trend to increased federal funding and to programs like these in the South is nationwide. In Manhattan the Department of Housing and Urban Development is financing the construction, under Army auspices, of a large low-cost housing unit in Harlem; a small corps facility on the premises will be built entirely with Army funds. There are federally funded nutritional programs, day-care, juvenile court probation, and drug rehabilitation plans from coast to coast. Some Harbor Light services are dependent on federal funds. There is a growing reliance on "purchase-of-service" contracts, by which the public agency pays only for certain parts of the Army program (such as floor space, use of kitchen, utility bill, janitorial service, vehicles, and professional staff time); often these contracts are joined to the employment of beneficiaries of the Federal Comprehensive Education and Training Act (CETA). These persons provide the Army—or the part of the Army program that is being funded by the governmental agency—the benefits of their labor, but they are not responsible to the Salvation Army officer nominally in charge of the local facility.[53]

All of this has been a mixed blessing to the Army. General William Booth was convinced in his day that the British government should pay for his plan to transport the country's urban poor to farm colonies abroad, and in 1904 Frederick Booth-Tucker sought federal endorsement and financing for his own version of the farm-colony scheme. Yet many modern officers are troubled by the recent increase in government funding of Army programs. Their concern is concentrated on two problems: federal agencies exert considerable control over the administration of programs that they finance; this threatens the Army's long-cherished independence to carry out its own unique combination of social and religious enterprise in its own way. Secondly, the First Amendment to the Constitution has been interpreted by both the executive and judicial branches of government to forbid federal funding of religious activity. This means not only that there can be no obviously evangelical purpose to any Army program that receives substantial federal money to support it, but also that officers must calculate what proportion of their own time, that of their staff, the utility bill, building costs, office supplies, and so on is devoted to religious work, and deduct a like proportion from any budget presentation for funds. This requires officers to divide their programs for budget purposes into "religious" and "social" activities, which is distasteful to them and to the Army's long-standing tradition that its social and spiritual work cannot be divided. Worse still, some officers have been ordered to remove Christian pictures and mottos from rooms in Army buildings being used for funded welfare programs. A number of federated-fund programs—including the United Way (a new name for the Old Community Chest)—are making similar demands on The Salvation Army.[54]

Officers have dedicated their lives to evangelism. Although they are aware that the role of a corps officer is somewhat more complex than that of the minister of a mainline denomination, they see themselves as pastors, spiritual counselors, and ministers of the gospel of Christ. They do not look lightly upon programs, bearing the beloved name of their crusade, but only nominally under their control, that are merely good works—charity—not given in the Savior's name, and with no clearly redemptive purpose. Army leaders share this concern, and have officially reaffirmed that the "primary purpose" of the Salvation Army officer "is to reach the spiritually and physically impoverished with the gospel of Jesus Christ." Yet leaders also recognize that the Army's reputation for scrupulous accounting and efficiency, and the affectionate trust in which many of the disadvantaged continue to hold it, will attract increasing sums of government money for a variety of welfare programs that are often well-intentioned, innovative, and helpful, and which bring large numbers of people into Army buildings, a number of whom may become interested in its religious work. Some of these projects are large with promise: in 1978, for instance, USAID bestowed a grant on the Army that enabled it to set up the new Salvation Army World Service Organization to assist in the training of indigenous officer leadership around the world. The first director of the new organization, Lt.–Colonel Ernest Miller, is a firm believer in the Army's evangelical purpose and views his new office as a continuation of the purposes of the old Founder himself.

The Army's official position on governmental funding is a careful one: the Army must be watchful, it must retain control of programs administered in its name, and it must not waver on its traditional stand that no distinction can be drawn between its religious and social programs. The commissioners' conference stated the official position in 1972, as part of new guidelines for American corps officers: "There is nothing inconsistent about the Army's receiving governmental funds so long as it would require neither a denial of its Christian incentive nor a compromise of its evangelical intention."[55]

The impact of federal funding, however, is great only upon those welfare programs that depend upon it; if the funds should evaporate only those programs, almost all of them recent, would suffer. Traditional corps programs, and most of the Army's own long-established welfare enterprises, would not be seriously affected. The same is true to a lesser extent for United Way funding. The percentage of the Army's income that comes from United Way allocations differs widely from division to division, and from corps to corps within divisions, but The Salvation Army is not dependent on United Way funds for its existence. Large, well-established corps are less dependent on the United Way than are small, struggling ones. These differences are reflected on the divisional level. In the Southern California and Eastern Michigan divisions, for instance, the overall Army program receives perhaps twenty-four percent of its total revenue from the United Way; in the Louisiana-Alabama-Mississippi division, on the other hand, the percentage is just over forty percent, which is slightly less than the aggregate percentage for all divisions in the Eastern territory. Nor does the Army dominate United Way budgets: in 1976 The Salvation Army nationwide received only five percent of the United Way's total allocations to all agencies.[56]

The remainder of the money for the Army's evangelical and charitable endeavors must be raised directly from the public through mail appeals, special project campaigns, and the vitally important annual Christmas kettle collections, which have become a national tradition with tinkling handbells and brass quartets playing happily through Leidzen's *Carolers' Favorites.* These methods, and the fact that funds left to the Army in wills are applied to the acquisition or improvement of permanent facilities in order to provide a lasting memorial to the generosity of the departed friend, are made a part of every formal agreement between The Salvation Army and the United Way. There is also "internal giving"—the "cartridges" of the soldiers and the cash collections taken up in meetings—although few corps in the United States at present support themselves in this way. In fact American Salvationists are, on the average, poor givers to their own cause. This is partially due to the fact that most Salvationists are literally poor; most are women, single or widowed; the majority of the complete families are from the working class; many Salvationists are elderly; and one third of the Army's active membership is under the age of fourteen. Nevertheless, the anxiety of officers that the Army is becoming dependent on outside funding would be eased if soldiers gave more sacrificially, as the example of Christ and the record of members of other evangelical denominations require. The Salvation Army wisely requires that every corps become self-supporting as soon as possible, but only a handful of very large corps have so far achieved it.[57]

It is important that the corps become financially independent, because it is at the corps level that The Salvation Army still maintains the longest part of its front lines in the war for souls. Large-scale jubilees and congresses, with massed bands and hallelujah excitement yet marked with a certain grand dignity, as though the participants moved every moment to the thrill of leading forward a still-great crusade, continue to punctuate the Army calendar, but it is in the corps that the evangelical work of the Army takes place. In 1977 General Arnold Brown presided over thunderous public meetings in Atlanta as the Southern territory celebrated its Golden Jubilee of fifty years of service, and Chicago and New York welcomed new territorial commanders Commissioners John Needham and W.R.H. Goodier with great pageantry. In February 1979, the South greeted its new leader, Commissioner Arthur Pitcher, and in March Commissioner Ernest W. Holz was installed in New York as the Army's seventeenth national commander, in the time-honored flamboyant style that thrills Salvationists today as much as it did when Evangeline Booth presided over much the same kind of scenes for their parents. But Salvationists know, even as the Army's leaders know, that it is only when the troops have returned to the weekly routine of the corps that the Great Salvation War can be pushed forward again. The corps remains, as it was in 1880, the "heart of the Army's evangelical mission."[58]

The corps are not free of problems. The most pressing of these is attendance. If not actually declining, membership in The Salvation Army is not keeping pace with the increasing population of the country as a whole. There was no intent to deceive when the Army reported a five percent increase in membership in 1975, which caused religious periodicals to hail it as "the fastest growing US religious body"; the Army decided in 1975 to begin recording everyone who makes use of its community-center youth programs and corps facilities. The figures for actual members—soldiers, recruits, and adherents—are less encouraging. In 1979 the Army had 78,132 senior soldiers (full adult members) and another nearly eleven thousand recruits and adherents. The much larger figure of "total membership" of nearly 400,000, which is given to religious publications like the *Handbook of Denominations*, represents every name on the corps rolls, most of whom attend irregularly, or not at all, and who contribute nothing to the work. (Officers cannot easily remove names from the roll; it can only be done if the person is dead, or requests in writing that his name be removed, and every removal that is not matched by a new enrollment reflects adversely on an officer's record.) The totals for 1979 are hardly more—perhaps twelve percent more than they were in 1936, although the national population has increased by seventy percent. In the Eastern territory, membership has actually declined in absolute numbers since 1927, and attendance at Army religious services has been decreasing in the Central territory since 1947. Returns on the national level are even more disquieting: the number of corps has declined steadily since 1950 (1,380 to 1,074), the number of bandsmen since 1960 (6,097 to 4,149 [1978]), and the number of adult local officers (the most active category of adult member: the sergeants, treasurers, musicians, Sunday school teachers) since 1970 (15,217 to 14,346 [1978]).[59]

Salvationists at every level are naturally alarmed at these unhappy developments. Nor are they always compensated by cheery reports of the Army's many good works. A national soldier's commission, meeting in 1967 at the request of the commissioners, declared their concern: "Without the continuing development of healthy corps spiritual life, all of the splendid, manifold social, community and welfare activities are stripped of their vitality insofar as soul-saving is concerned because of a lack of committed Christian leadership." Those who looked for causes for the long-term decline in The Salvation Army corps found that some of them are general, and do not affect the Army alone: the decline of urban areas, which alienates churchgoers from the neighborhood of the building, causes them to drive long distances from their new suburban refuges, and makes them reluctant to come downtown after dark at all; a long, national decline in Sunday school attendance, which afflicts other churches as well as the Army; and the development of alternative forms of social activity, especially in the evenings and on weekends, such as television, shopping malls, and for the more affluent, boats and summer houses.[60]

Other causes bear uniquely upon the Army: its image as a social welfare agency sometimes works at cross-purposes to its evangelical ministry; persons with spiritual troubles usually seek out a minister and a church that they recognize for what they are. It is sad to note that the open-air ministry that clearly establishes the Army's evangelical posture has declined through the decade of the 1970s from 23,000 per year in 1970 to 13,000 in 1978. Problems exist inside the hall as well. The pressure on a corps officer to maintain the full range of welfare, public relations, and business activities is very great. Major Herbert Luhn, a successful and experienced corps officer, spoke for many of his comrades when he told a national Army conference in 1978 that the corps officer "cannot possibly function effectively in all areas of his responsibility." This has been part of the cause of the "declension" of the corps' "Spiritual Mission." Other officers are concerned that some of their colleagues who do have adequate time for their pastoral duties fail to discharge them. Captain Philip D. Needham warned his fellow officers in 1972 that many soldiers were "dying spiritual deaths" from a steady diet of shallow and ill prepared sermons. Others point to research on church growth that suggests there is a close relationship between the length of pastoral tenure and the size of the congregation; they denounce the Army practice of transferring officers frequently from corps to corps, and the inevitable promotion to staff positions of many of the most able and dedicated.[61]

Even the smallness of the Army congregation works against further growth, throwing a heavy burden on the few regular members who do attend and causing newcomers to feel conspicuous and awkward. And the Army *is* small, making up only four-tenths of one percent of all churchgoers in the United States. A Sunday morning congregation of seventy-five persons is considered good for most corps. Even if every man, woman, and child on the roll were to show up which would require many to travel hundreds and thousands of miles—there is only an average of 103 soldiers (senior and junior) per corps in the United States. The number of corps with as many as two hundred in regular attendance is very small, perhaps three dozen at the most nationwide. It is hardly surprising, then, that a staff officer like Major David Baxendale could announce in 1971, when these trends were already apparent, that the corps had "come to a crossroads, a time for agonizing reappraisal."[62]

Yet there are reasons for hope: even those officers who are most knowledgeable and concerned about the Army's problems are the most optimistic about the ability of the movement to adapt to them and to move on into a future bright with promise. The Salvation Army has enormous strengths, which other religious and charitable organizations rightly envy. Its fundamental Christian principles have not wavered in the United States, either in doctrine or in practice, since the courageous Shirleys unfurled the flag on a Philadelphia street corner in 1879. The Army is first and foremost a branch of the Church of Christ on earth. Twice in recent years the Army has stated to the Internal Revenue Service, in official and unequivocal terms, that its leaders claim tax exemption for their organization not because it is a charity but because it is a denomination of the Christian church. The Army's aggressive and unwavering commitment to its "Eleven Doctrines," which are a straightforward statement of Wesleyan theology, has earned for it a large role in the current affairs of the nationwide Christian Holiness Association, out of all proportion to the Army's small size as a denomination. Its firmly orthodox Christianity bestows great strength on the Army's members, who share a sense of divine purpose, a missionary zeal, and an abiding and warm-hearted loyalty to Christ, Whom they regard as their Friend, their Brother, their great Commander, Who overlooks and encourages them in every forward step in His cause. All this is wonderful to the distracted leaders of mainline denominations that wander aimlessly from theological schisms to identity crises and back again.[63]

The Army is as firmly committed to noble practice as it is to high principle, and its high standards, like its orthodoxy, are a potent source of its high morale. Its accounting and auditing procedures are exemplary. The Army will compromise on nothing. The Salvation Army is formally affiliated, in this complex society, with forty-one major organizations—so many that in 1977 the Army helped to organize a national council to coordinate them all, the Coalition of National Voluntary Organizations. Yet the Army belongs to none that require it to surrender a single moral principle. It officially resigned from the USO, which it had helped to found, when the USO began to serve alcoholic drinks in its clubs in 1976. The Army likewise suspended its membership in the World Council of Churches in 1978 after that body authorized a grant of funds to guerrilla organizations in Rhodesia-Zimbabwe, members of which were implicated in the murder of unoffending Salvation Army missionaries in that country.[64]

This decision by the Army's international leaders does not reflect any lack of concern for the problems of the developing parts of the world. The Salvation Army carries on its evangelical and social ministries in eighty-one countries besides the United States, a work to which American Salvationists are devoted. The Army in the United States raised $3,748,756 from internal sources in 1977 to support overseas projects. These "self-denial" funds from the United States are the largest single source of funds for the Army's foreign missions, and in addition eighty-five American officers are serving in appointments outside the United States.

Standards set for soldiers, both in the service required of them and in their daily lives as well, are uncompromising. The life of a Salvationist is a strict one. The Army's *Orders and Regulations for Soldiers* originally written by the Founder, was finally revised in 1977, making large allowance for changed social conditions. But it makes no concessions on fundamental Army principles: soldiers are expected to avoid every sort of immorality, vulgarity, and dishonesty, and to treat everyone they encounter in a straightforward, kindly, and brotherly way. The "Articles of War" that soldiers must sign has changed from Victorian times only to be made more strict: in 1975 the Army made it a rule that soldiers must not use tobacco. Soldiers are expected to obey their officers in every lawful thing, and to support the Salvation War with their time and money, heart and soul. For their part, Army leaders have made repeated efforts to demonstrate that they recognize and value the vital role of the lay Salvationist in The Salvation Army. This recognition has led on the national level to the annual Soldiers' Seminar, which was launched in 1967 at Glen Eyrie, Colorado, and to a number of commissions, committees, and planning councils on the territorial and divisional levels— so many by 1975 that the national chief secretary had to remind the territorial commanders to use the "current names" for them when corresponding with headquarters. These commissions function in every territory; among the best-organized of these are the Territorial and Divisional Laymen's and Officers' Councils (Terloc and Divloc) of the Western territory, appointed in 1970.[65]

The capacity of its soldiers for service in the corps is one of the Army's most valuable resources. No less is true for the dedication of its field officers. The amount of time that the average Salvationist donates to corps duties is amazing. While officers are tempted to sink beneath the time consuming business and welfare parts of their assignments, and leaders try one expedient after another to relieve or encourage them, the prodigious evangelical and social activity of the corps goes on, carried by officers who somehow find the strength they need and by the soldiers, for whom the Army is not merely a church but a way of life. The typical Salvation Army corps community center—the new official name indicates the broad role of the modern corps—is a busy place all through the week, indoors and out: just over 250 corps still valiantly carry on the open-air ministry every week. Weekly schedules selected at random, from corps, for instance, in Danville, Kentucky, Kittanning, Pennsylvania, Columbus, Ohio, Anderson, Indiana, and Sunnyvale, California, reveal a dozen different meetings; most soldiers attend at least half of these, and some attend them all—along with the officer or his wife or the assistant officer. These schedules could be reproduced literally a thousand times; taken collectively they represent quantities of time and energy expended weekly in behalf of the religious work of The Salvation Army that must encourage the most discouraged observer of the Army scene. And what is even more striking is that Salvationists are willing to do more: the capacity for sacrifice and the zeal for souls that marked the early-day Army crusaders is not dead in many hearts; such feelings wait only to be rekindled by a renewed sense of the movement's high evangelical purpose to produce the great revival for which officers and soldiers have so long yearned.[66]

The Salvation Army benefits from its past. The Army has a glorious history—whimsical, humorous, exciting, and inspiring—and the present generation of Salvationists is made aware of it in many ways. Few denominations are prouder of their past, nor more eager to celebrate its milestones and keep alive its traditions. Very little that is noble or redemptive is ever entirely lost in the Army. Everyone has a scrapbook, a box of letters, a favorite story. The Army loves to reminisce—but the Army's long memory is not merely nostalgic; rather it gives today's soldiers a sense of collective responsibility, as though the departed pioneers have laid a claim upon the lives of those who follow after. Old songs, old sermons, even old advice, do not strike Salvationists as old-fashioned; they are as eager to be inspired by these bequests from long-dead comrades as their fathers were by the originals. They are willing to follow the orders of General Albert Orsborn, to put the Army's history to usury, and to reinvest its spiritual capital.[67]

But The Salvation Army must look to the future if it is to fulfill the trust it yet bears from God, from its zeal-consumed forebearers, and from those outside who still look to it as a living embodiment of much that is noble and generous in the American spirit. If the Army can attract the best of its youth to its service in the future, as it has in the past, no problem will prove insurmountable. The pioneer Army was a young Army—sixteen-year-old officers were common—and it faced discouragements as great as those of today and overcame them, or learned to do God's work despite them. Many of today's problems—small corps, a shortage of internal funds, of officers, and soldiers, the public's benign indifference to outdoor evangelism, and its confusion about the Army's welfare and religious ministries—are in fact old problems, with which the Army has lived for a hundred years. They are worse today only in degree; whether or not they will overcome the Army lies in the hands of those who will deal with them.

In 1978 a number of high-ranking officers of The Salvation Army were interviewed in connection with the preparation of this book; included among them were three national commanders, four territorial commanders, and six chief secretaries. Each of these officers declared, without knowing the statements of any of the others, that the dedication, talent, and zeal of the Army's current generation of young people were together the single most encouraging thing about the movement today. If history has a message for these young people, the Army of the future, it is this: that zeal for Christ, a willingness to bear all things that some might be saved, and a quick, hospitable spirit open to every means to the great end, are sovereign. No obstacle can stand in the way of an Army led by hearts like these, as it still marches to Glory.[68]

Epilogue

The staff-captains, ensigns, and adjutants have gone now, the energetic methods of an earlier day have vanished from the land. There are no more drives on the devil, sermons from coffins, or papier-mâché whiskey bottles. The high-collar uniform and the bonnet, now endangered species, may soon disappear. Yet The Salvation Army remains very much as it began, a common man's crusade for the redemption of lost souls. The din of battle is now more subdued, but the Great Salvation War rages on in many places.

The Army has been in the United States for 100 years. It has fulfilled at least some of the wild prophecies of its pioneer officers, who came to the shores of America confident that their movement would spread from coast to coast, sweeping sin and the devil before it. The Army has braved the dangers of adversity and popularity in turn, and has triumphed; it has become secure in the affection of the country, yet it is officially as firmly committed as ever to its Biblical doctrines and its evangelical purpose.

Throughout its century-long history in the United States, the Army has displayed great strengths, which have become characteristic of it and which overshadow the few weaknesses that have also become part of the movement. The Salvation Army is still driven by a sense of clear purpose; its members on every level feel that they are part of a high and noble crusade: to rescue the lost souls of the world. The loyalty of many Salvationists to the Army is remarkably high, and most of them are energetic workers in its behalf. The Army still possesses a large reservoir of talent and energy.

The confidence in which the American people hold the Army has enabled the movement to provide a range of community services far beyond what the meager resources of the soldiers themselves could support. It is true that its traditional reliance on public and governmental funding for its welfare operations has caused a certain confusion in the public mind as to the true purpose for which The Salvation Army exists. Many Salvationists are disappointed that the majority of welfare statistics are not translated into spiritual returns; the annual reports of the Army's religious statistics in the past decade have caused concern.

The Salvation Army has nevertheless secured for itself an important place in the religious life of the nation. It must affirm that place in the way it has always done so: by proclaiming its high evangelical purpose in every activity that it sponsors. Acts of kindness, done in the Name of Christ, have always been the hallmark of Salvation Army social service. There are signs that the Army's traditional open air ministry is being revitalized: officers and bandsmen are taking the street-corner meeting to new places, at new times, so that there are listeners to profit from that still-precious means of propagating the Gospel. Army leaders are aware that the increased burdens on the soldiers require more rigorous training for field officers, with special emphasis on ministerial aspects. The soldiers regard the corps officer as their pastor, and naturally look to him for the same spiritual solace, and to each other for the same Christian fellowship, that people like themselves enjoy in other doctrinally conservative denominations. For their part, the soldiers have shown a willingness to increase the burden of their financial support of the corps, and to follow them when Army leaders determine that the demands of the salvation war require a change of location. Many soldiers are becoming involved in the community services offered by their corps, and drawing new people into an awareness of the claim of Christ upon their lives.

What, after all, has been the one constant factor in the history of The Salvation Army in the United States over the past 100 years? How did the Army flourish in its early days, and what has sustained it all the years thereafter? The pioneer officers and soldiers had no abilities or opportunities that are denied their successors today. Salvationists are very much what they have always been, except that the present generation is more full of ability, talent, and high promise than past generations have been. Salvationists, however, have always made up for every lack with courage; they have never abandoned all thought of their own comfort and well-being, but they have lived as though their lives had no higher purpose than to love and serve God, and to get others to do the same. The Salvation Army has always been willing to do anything that a precious soul may be saved. That has been its glory. That is its glory now.

APPENDIX I

The Ranks of The Salvation Army, 1878–1980

Rank	Adopted	Current/Discontinued
General	gradually assumed from 1878	Current
Chief of the Staff (not formally a rank but a position held by a Commissioner)	1880	Current
Commissioner	1880	Current
Lieutenant–Commissioner	1920	1973
Colonel	1880	Current
Lieutenant–Colonel	1896	Current
Brigadier	1889	1973
Senior–Major	1948	1959
Major	1879	Current
Staff–Captain	1881	1931
Field–Major	1923	1931
Commandant	1916	1931
Adjutant	1888	1948
Ensign	1888	1931
Senior–Captain	1948	1959
Captain	gradually assumed from 1877	Current
Lieutenant	1879	Current
Second Lieutenant	1948	1959
Probationary Lieutenant	as early as 1917	1973
Cadet	1880	Current

Clearly, these ranks were not all in use at the same time. For many years some ranks were reserved only for staff officers, or if employed for officers "in the field" (i.e., corps work) were still considered "staff" ranks. An example of the Army rank structure for various years is given:

1890	1950	1980
General	General	General
Chief of the Staff	Chief of the Staff	Chief of the Staff
Commissioner	Commissioner	Commissioner
Colonel	Lt.–Commissioner	Colonel
Lt.–Colonel	Colonel	Lt.–Colonel
Brigadier	Lt.–Colonel	Major
Major	Brigadier	Captain
Staff–Captain	Senior–Major	Lieutenant
Adjutant	Major	Cadet
Ensign	Senior–Captain	
Captain	Captain	
Lieutenant	Lieutenant	
Cadet	Second Lieutenant	
	Cadet	

National Commanders of The Salvation Army in the United States, 1880-1980

Commander	Years in Command	Disposition
George Scott Railton	1880–1881	Transferred
Thomas E. Moore	1881–1884	Deserted
Frank Smith	1884–1887	Transferred
Ballington Booth, the Marshal	1887–1896	Deserted
Maud Ballington Booth		
Frederick St George de Lautour Booth-Tucker		Transferred
Emma Moss Booth-Tucker, the Consul	1896–1904	
Evangeline Cory Booth, the Commander	1904–1934	Elected General
Edward Justus Parker*	1934–1943	Retired
Ernest I. Pugmire	1944–1953	Retired
Donald S. McMillan	1953–1957	Retired
Norman S. Marshall	1957–1963	Retired
Holland French	1963–1966	Retired
Samuel Hepburn	1966–1971	Retired
Edward Carey	1971–1972	Retired
Paul J. Carlson	1972–1974	Retired
William E. Chamberlain	1974–1977	Retired
Paul S. Kaiser	1977–1979	Retired
Ernest W. Holz	1979–present	

* National Secretary, 1934–1943; appointed National Commander 1943.

The Doctrines of The Salvation Army (as set forth in the Deed Poll of 1878)

1. We believe that the Scriptures of the Old and New Testaments were given by inspiration of God; and that they only constitute the divine rule of Christian faith and practice.

2. We believe there is only one God, who is infinitely perfect—the Creator, Preserver, and Governor of all things—and who is the only proper object of religious worship.

3. We believe that there are three persons in the Godhead—the Father, the Son, and the Holy Ghost—undivided in essence and co-equal in power and glory.

4. We believe that in the person of Jesus Christ the divine and human natures are united; so that He is truly and properly God, and truly and properly man.

5. We believe that our first parents were created in a state of innocency but, by their disobedience, they lost their purity and happiness; and that in consequence of their fall all men have become sinners, totally depraved, and as such are justly exposed to the wrath of God.

6. We believe that the Lord Jesus Christ has, by His suffering and death, made an atonement for the whole world, so that whosoever will may be saved.

7. We believe that repentance toward God, faith in our Lord Jesus Christ, and regeneration by the Holy Spirit are necessary to salvation.

8. We believe that we are justified by grace, through faith in our Lord Jesus Christ; and that he that believeth hath the witness in himself.

9. We believe that continuance in a state of salvation depends upon continued obedient faith in Christ.

10. We believe that it is the privilege of all believers to be "wholly sanctified,"

and that their "whole spirit and soul and body" may "be preserved blameless unto the coming of our Lord Jesus Christ" (I Thessalonians 5:23).

11. We believe in the immortality of the soul; in the resurrection of the body; in the general judgment at the end of the world; in the eternal happiness of the righteous; and in the endless punishment of the wicked.

Bibliographical Review

The following brief remarks are intended only to supplement the more complete bibliographical information cited in the notes. The major sources of primary materials for this book were the collections housed in the Salvation Army Archives and Research Center in New York City; the Circle "M" collection, deposited by Major John Milsaps in the Houston Metropolitan Research Center; Houston Public Library; the valuable and extensive private collection of Colonel Paul Seiler, Ocean Grove, New Jersey; and the private collections of Commissioner Ernest W. Holz the national commander, Major John Busby in Atlanta; and Mr Harry Sparks of Los Angeles. The Salvation Army archives also contain many formal reports from various Army commissions, meetings, and officers, and a complete set of the annual reports of The Salvation Army Historical Commission, Eastern territory, which has a national purview.

The Salvation Army archives also has a complete set of the American, and later Eastern territorial, *War Cry*, and a nearly complete set of the Moore edition of *The War Cry* as well. The archives also holds sets of *The Conqueror, All the World, The Young Soldier, Social News, The Staff Officer's Review, The Field Officer,* and *The Officer* magazines; and the Army's wartime publications, *The War Service Herald* (August 1917 to September 1919), and *The Red Shield* (January 1942 to December 1943), which became the *War Service Bulletin* (January 1944 to December 1945). The national publications office at national headquarters contains complete sets of the four territorial *War Cry* editions on microfilm, and a continuing set of the new national *War Cry*. The four territorial Schools for Officers' Training have complete sets of their territory's *War Cry* editions, and their libraries also contain collections of old books, pamphlets, and memorabilia; the Schools in the East and South have started formal museum programs as well, and the other Schools have many items available for consultation.

There have been several dissertations and theses on The Salvation Army, all but one of them recent. Lamb's excellent dissertation of 1909 has been joined by those by Bosch, Wisbey, and Magnuson, which place the Army in a historical context; those by Green, Lorenzen, and Needham on Army theology; those by Verner and Nelson on Army hospital work; by Mehling, Wrieden, and Thompson on social case work; and by Dexter on officer training programs. Hodder has done extensive work on Frank Smith. All of these scholarly works were of great value to the present author.

The published writing of Salvationists about themselves and their work is vast in quantity and of uneven quality; much of it is cited in the text. Ballington Booth was a fine writer, and many other early-day officers had great hearts and a vivid prose style. The later work of Watson, Chesham, Sandall, Frederick Coutts, Barnes, Hall, Pitt, and the *War Cry* articles of these and Brindley, Harris, Cunningham, and the Booths, are valuable. Careful reporting on the Army by those outside its ranks has found its way into print, and some of this material is of great value. The two volumes by Ervine have not yet been surpassed, and the more narrow work of Lamb, Lee and Pettit, and the report by Booz, Allen and Hamilton, were indispensable. Two works deserve special notice: Nora Marts' *Facts About The Salvation Army: Aims and Methods of the Hallelujah Band* (Chicago, 1889) is based on the author's observations of the Army in 1888, taken down by her while studying the Army (disguised as an officer) to collect material for articles in the *Chicago Tribune;* it should be required reading for anyone interested in the early-day Army. The same is true for a perceptive and sympathetic description of the Army in its very early days, "Red Cross Knights—A Nineteenth Century Crusade," by Agnes Maule Machar in *The Andover Review,* August, 1884.

In addition to an amazingly large number of allusions and references in novels, short stories, motion pictures, television programs, and magazine cartoons, The Salvation Army was featured as the object of two modern novels, *Salvation Johnny,* by Natalie Anderson Scott (Garden City, 1958) and Astrid Valley's *Marching Bonnet* (New York, 1948).

The following notes should be sufficient for the purposes of this volume. However, it should be remarked that these published notes represent a condensation of the exhaustive listing of references and sources supplied by the author. Scholars and other parties interested in obtaining a more complete set of bibliographic information for each reference should write to the Archives and Research Center, The Salvation Army, 145 West 15th Street, New York, New York 10011.

LIST OF ABBREVIATIONS USED IN NOTES

Seiler Coll.   The collection of Salvation Army memorabilia, artifacts, and papers of Colonel Paul Seiler, Ocean Grove, New Jersey.

Busby Coll. The collection of papers and documents relating to Salvation Army history owned by Major John Busby, Atlanta, Georgia.

Holz Coll. The private collection of Salvation Army documents owned by Commissioner Ernest W. Holz, national commander.

Milsaps Coll. The Milsaps Collection, Circle "M" Collection, housed in the Houston Metropolitan Research Center, Houston Public Library.

> Houston RC   Houston Research Center
>
> Milsaps WCC, then volume number   Milsaps *War Cry* clipping scrapbooks, 5 vols., numbered by volume and page.
>
> Milsaps SB, then volume number   Milsaps scrapbooks, 3 vols., numbered by volume and page.
>
> Milsaps Diary   4 volumes Old Series (O.S.) cover years 1880-1883, 69 volumes New Series, 1896-1930.

AWC The American *War Cry* published by national headquarters, 1881-1921; it reported on all SA activities in the country except those in the far west; after January, 1921, it became *The War Cry*, Eastern edition.

B/F Biographical file.

Conq *The Conqueror*, published by The Salvation Army, 1892-1896; complete set SAA.

G/F General file

LD *The Literary Digest.*

SA The Salvation Army.

SAA The Salvation Army Archives and Research Center, 145 W. 15th Street, New York, New York 10011.

SANHQ The Salvation Army national headquarters; various addresses; from 1896 to the present, 120 West 14th Street, New York, New York 10011.

SATHQ/ The Salvation Army territorial headquarters; letter indicates location as for SFOT below (SATHQ/E is New York City).

SFOT/ Salvation Army School for Officers' Training; letter indicates location, as follows: E—Eastern, Suffern, New York; C—Central, Chicago; W—Western, Rancho Palos Verdes, California; S—Southern, Atlanta, Georgia.

WC/C *The War Cry*, Central edition, 1921-1970

WC/E *The War Cry*, Eastern edition, 1921-1970

WC/S *The War Cry*, Southern edition, 1927-1970

WC/W *The War Cry*, Pacific Coast edition, 1883 to 1921; from 1921 to 1970, Western edition.

WC *The War Cry*, National edition, 1970-present.

Notes

CHAPTER I

1. Bernard Watson, *Soldier Saint: George Scott Railton, William Booth's First Lieutenant* (London, 1970), 59; the quotation is from a private letter, shown to Watson by a member of the Railton family.
2. Comr. Frederick de L. Booth-Tucker, *The Life of Catherine Booth: The Mother of The Salvation Army* (2 vols; London, 1892), II, 81, 85-86, 88-89; William Booth, "To the Officers and Soldiers of the Salvation Army," *The Salvationist,* October 1, 1879, 254, in Seiler Coll.; [George Scott Railton], *Twenty-One Years Salvation Army* (London, [1888]), 7-23, 44; St. John Ervine, *God's Soldier: General William Booth* (2 vols.; New York, 1935), I, 64, 93, 194, 213, 233-254, 292-94.
3. Watson, *Railton,* 43; Ervine, *God's Soldier,* I, 480-81; Herbert A. Wisbey, Jr., *Religion in Action: A History of The Salvation Army in the United States* (Ph.D. dissertation, Columbia University, 1951), 22-26, hereafter cited as Dissertation; Wisbey, H.A., *Soldiers Without Swords: A History of The Salvation Army in the United States* (New York, 1955), 21; Railton, *21 Years SA,* 133; Comr. Edward Carey, *It Began in Cleveland, Ohio! The story of The Salvation Army's first pioneering venture outside the British Isles,* SAA; Dorothy Hitzka, *The James Jermy Story or the Earliest Inception of The Salvation Army in America* (Cleveland, no date), SAA; *The Christian Mission Magazine,* August 1870, 112; January 1873, 15; April 1873, 63; September 1873, 144; November 1873, 164; August 1874, 204, in SAA "James Jermy" file.
4. AWC, August 25, 1888, 6-7, 9.
5. AWC, August 4, 1888, 1-2; AWC, November 28, 1908, 11; December

5, 1908, 1, 16; October 16, 1909, 1, 9; "How the Salvation Army Came to America," WC/C, September 12, 1925, 12; September 19, 1925, 14; September 26, 1925, 14-15; interview with Mrs Russell Crowell [née Everald Eliza Knudsen, granddaughter of Eliza Shirley], Garden Grove, California, December 8, 1978; photocopy of AWC July 9, 1881 [Philadelphia], 1, SAA "Shirley family" file; Wisbey, Dissertation, 28-36, 42, 72, 119, *Soldiers*, 11-16; Booth-Tucker, *Catherine Booth*, II, 162-163.

6. George S. Railton, "Salvation Beginnings in America," WC/C, March 14, 1925, 4, 15 [written in 1892]; AWC, December 24, 1892, 2.

7. Watson, *Railton*, 43-45; Ervine, *God's Soldier*, I, 481-85; Eileen Douglas and Mildred Duff, *Commissioner Railton* (London, [1920]), 68; Railton, *21 Years SA*, 36, 73.

8. Ensign William G. Harris, "Looking Back," WC/E, July 7, 1928, 11; Hugh Leamy, "Tambourine," *Colliers*, September 8, 1928, 12.

9. Holograph note in Railton's hand, in SFOT/E Musuem G/F, "Railton;" Douglas & Duff, *Railton*, 70; Booth-Tucker, *Catherine Booth*, II, 164.

10. [George S. Railton], "Our American Landing," AWC, April 11, 1896, 12; WC/C January 10, 1925, 11, quoting from first AWC [St Louis], January 15, 1881; Harris, "Looking Back," July 14, 1928, 11.

11. New York *World*, March 11, 1880, 5; Railton, *21 Years SA*, 135; Harris, "Looking Back," July 21, 1928, 11; Wisbey, Dissertation, 26-27, 42.

12. New York *World*, March 11, 1880, 5; Railton, *21 Years SA*, 135; Railton, "Our American Landing," 12; AWC, March 19, 1887, 1; "The Army of Salvation," *Harper's Weekly*, April 3, 1880, 214; *New York Times*, March 15, 1880, 8; March 16, 1880, 8; March 19, 1880, 8 (clippings SFOT/E Museum G/F Railton; AWC, November 26, 1892, 12; AWC, March 3, 1900, 12.

13. [George Scott Railton], *Heathen England* (London, 1879), 61-79; Railton, "The Army's Advent in the States," AWC, December 24, 1892, 2; Leamy, "Tambourine," 12.

14. New York *World*, March 15, 1880, 5; "Army of Salvation," 214.

15. Harris, "Looking Back," July 21, 1928, 11; WC/W, July 1, 1933, 12; Colonel Wm. H. Cox, "The Salvation Army Around the World," *Missionary Review of the World*, August, 1919, 586-87; Sgt. B.A. Richardson, "Victorious Veterans: The Pioneer Corps of the Central Division," AWC, January 29, 1898, 2, states that Railton opened New York No. 1 only after he returned from Philadelphia, and only then was Ash-Barrel saved. Railton, *21 Years SA*, 135-137; AWC, March 27, 1886, 1; "The First of a Mighty Multitude: Or, The Capture of Ash Barrel Jemmy, the First

Convert in the U.S.," AWC, April 22, 1893, 4; Kemp was made a lieutenant after one year and seven months as a faithful soldier; he was sent to
Jersey City No. 1, then promoted to Captain and sent to Boston, where
he served until he died on March 11, 1895: AWC, April 6, 1895, 10, and
December 21, 1895, 11.

16. One account, for instance, suggests that Atlantic City was not opened until
     May. See "45 Years in America: A Brief Historical Sketch," WC/C,
     September 12, 1925, 16; Richardson, "Victorious Veterans," 2; Wisbey,
     Dissertation, 53-54; *The Salvation News*, Philadelphia, July 10, 1880, 2
     SAA.

17. New York *World*, March 17, 1880, 8; Railton, *21 Years SA*, 135; Robert
     Sandall, *The History of The Salvation Army* (6 vols.; London, 1950), II,
     App. E contains entire ultimatum, 317-318; New York *Daily Graphic*,
     March 25, 1880, quoted in Wisbey Dissertation, 51, 59; Crowell interview;
     "Army of Salvation," 214; AWC, December 9, 1893, 10; SFOT/E Mu-
     seum G/F "Brooklyn," has typed mss material on Lewis Pertain, who died
     on March 23, 1922.

18. Railton, "Advent," 2; AWC, February 27, 1892, 3; AWC, March 2, 1895,
     12; Douglas and Duff, *Railton,* 75-77; *The Salvation War, 1884, Under
     the Generalship of William Booth* (London, [1884]), 61; Crowell inter-
     view.

19. Railton, in a letter to William Booth, quoted in Douglas and Duff, *Railton,*
     74.

20. *The Salvation News,* July 10, 1880, 1-2; WC/W January 21, 1933, 2, 5.

21. J. Evan Smith, *Booth the Beloved: Personal Recollections of William
     Booth, Founder of The Salvation Army* (London, 1949), 18-19; Railton,
     21 Years SA, 138; Douglas and Duff, *Railton,* 67-86; *The Baltimore Sun,*
     October 18, 1880, October 19, October 29, and January 14, 1881, copies
     sent to author by Brig. Evelyn Allison; the original "Hallelujah Seven"
     were Capt. Emma Westbrook, Rachel Evans, Clara Price, Mary Alice
     Coleman, Elizabeth Pearson, Annie Shaw, and Emma Eliza Florence
     Morris. When Prof. Wisbey interviewed Emma Morris Lambert in Febru-
     ary, 1949, she could trace only four of the pioneer women; three of these
     had lived and died in the US [Wisbey Dissertation, 41, 60]. In 1890 only
     two of the pioneers—Captains Price and Westbrook—were still serving as
     officers [AWC, June 14, 1890, 2]. Eliza Shirley recalled later in life that
     four of the women had returned to England and resigned as officers, and
     two remained in the US, but not as officers [Crowell interview]. The only
     pioneer who remained an officer throughout life was Capt. Emma West-

brook, who retired as a commandant (after 1931, Field–Major) and died in 1933.

22. WC/E, September 12, 1925 [orig. January 15, 1881], 12; WC/C, January 10, 1925, 11.

23. Railton, "Advent," 2; WC/C, January 10, 1925, 10.

24. WC/E, September 12, 1925, 12.

25. Douglas and Duff, *Railton*, 82-86; Watson, *Railton*, 66-68.

26. Wisbey, Dissertation, 67-70, *Soldiers*, 30-31; Ervine, *God's Soldier*, I, 519-520; AWC, March 5, 1887, 5; Aaron Ignatius Abell, *The Urban Impact on American Protestantism, 1865-1900* (Hamden, 1962; orig. 1943), 120.

27. Booth-Tucker, *Catherine Booth*, II, 165; Wisbey, Dissertation, 74-75; AWC, September 14, 1884, 1; Crowell interview; WC/E, October 8, 1932, 12; Commandant Eliza Shirley Symmonds died on September 18, 1932, in Racine, Wisconsin.

28. "Army of Salvation," 214; Prof. C.A. Stork, "The Salvation Army: Its Methods and Lessons," *The Lutheran Quarterly*, XII (October 1882), 556; AWC, December 6, 1884, 3; Columbus, Ohio, *Daily Ohio State Journal*, January 12, 1885, xerox copy sent to author by Brig. Lawrence Castagna.

29. AWC, July 4, 1885, 2-3; July 11, 3; Comr. William Peart, "How We Started in Chicago," WC/C, February 16, 1924, 8; Comr. Edward Justus Parker, *My Fifty Eight Years: An Autobiography* (New York, 1943), 9, 39, 54-55, 87-88.

30. Minute No. 12, August 2, 1890, in Busby Coll.; copies SAA.

31. WC/W, July 18, 1891, in Milsaps WCC, II, 105-106; WC/W, July 1, 1887, WCC, II, 271; Milsaps Diary, 4 (O.S.), 243-254; AWC, May 2, 1891, 1-2; Capt. Day, "San Francisco," *Conq.*, September 1893, 335; Milsaps Diary, January 15, 1897, 14; There were five issues of the Newton *War Cry* [WC/W, May 22, 1897, states but four WCC, I, 223]; they are preserved in the Milsaps material at Houston: WCC, II, 105 (November 1882), 145 (December 1882), 165 (February 1883), and 185 (March 1883) and Milsaps SB,II, 39 (May, 1883).

32. Milsaps' commission as a "Seargeant" in Newton's Army in Milsaps SB,II, 1; Milsaps Diary (O.S.), 255, 257-265, 268-269.

33. Day, "San Francisco," 335-336.

34. WC/W, March 1884, 1; October 1884, 2; December 1885, 2; February 1886, 2; March 1886, 2.

35. WC/W, November 1886, 1; January 15, 1887, 1; March 1884; Maj. Alfred Wells, "An Account of the opening and early days of the Salvation

Army on the Pacific Coast," holograph 35 pp, 21 pp typed, in Milsaps unprocessed mss, "California" file; AWC, May 2, 1891, Milsaps WCC/II, 319.

36. Comr. Frank Smith, *The Salvation War in America for 1885* (London, 1886), 149-150; [Major] Alfred Wells, "Review of the California Forces," AWC, January 10, 1885, 1; WC/W, July 1884, 1.

37. WC/W, July 1, 1887, 1; AWC, November 10, 1888, 1; WC/W, November 1886, 2; AWC, December 18, 1886, 3; WC/W, January 1, 1887, 3; June 1, 1887, 1; AWC, November 19, 1887, 13; WC/W, November 2, 1895, 2.

38. WC/W, July 1884, 1; May 1884 [3]; Railton, *21 Years SA,* 138.

39. Wisbey, Dissertation, 97-98; Crowell interview; Ensign Clifford Brindley, "Commissioner Richard E. Holz," WC/E, April 13, 1929, 11.

40. Entire statement from AWC, July 24, 1884, in Wisbey Dissertation, 103-104.

41. Brindley, "Holz," WC/E, April 13, 1929, 11, and April 20, 1929, 12; The Salvation Army, *History of Injunction Legislation: The Salvation Army vs. The American Salvation Army* (New York, 1910), 24-33, 37.

42. Brindley, "Holz," WC/E, April 20, 1929, 12; AWC, March 19, 1887, 4; AWC, November 22, 1884, 3-4 [front page missing in SAA copy]; Smith, *Salvation War, 1885,* 15-16.

43. [William Booth], *The General's Letters, 1885* (London, [1886]), 51-67, or AWC, January 24, 1885, January 31 and February 7; *The Salvation War, 1884,* 62-64; Norman Murdoch, *Salvationist-Socialist Frank Smith, M.P.: Father of Salvation Army Social Work* (New York, 1978); Kenneth G. Hodder, *Report and Catalogue for Materials Obtained during Research on Frank Smith, M.P. and of the B.B.C. Recording Archives* (New York, 1978), SAA.

44. WC [Moore edition], May 21, 1881, 1; May 7, 1885, 1, in SAA; Staff–Capt. Richard E. Holz, Diary, entry January 5, March 11-13, 1887, in SAA; Application form and instructions to Candidates, [Moore's Army], November 21, 1888, Holz Coll.

45. "Personal Reminiscences of Commissioner Gifford," address to Cadets, [orig. 1927, updated to 1930], 47 pp typed ms, in a private collection; WC/W, October 1886, 1; Brindley, "Holz," WC/E, April 20, 1929, 15; Allan Whitworth Bosch, *The Salvation Army in Chicago: 1885-1914* (Ph.D Dissertation, Univ. of Chicago, 1965), 13, 26; hereinafter cited Dissertation.

46. AWC, November 13, 1886, 1; November 20, 1886, 1-2; November 27,

1-2; December 4, 1-2; December 11, 1-2; December 18, 1-2; January 15, 1887, 5; Bosch Dissertation, 33-35.

47. AWC, October 26, 1889, 8; November 2, 1889, 5, 9; New York *World,* January 20, 1889, 2; *The American War Cry,* official gazette of the American Salvation Army, February 9, 1889, 1-3, contains explanation for deposition of Moore, in Seiler Coll.; Brindley, "Holz," WC/E, May 4, 1929, 12; Salvation Army *Disposition of Forces, November 1, 1889* (New York, 1889), 7. Twenty-five posts of Moore's Army refused to acknowledge the "Booth yoke" and follow Holz back into the worldwide ranks; these organized under Major William Grattan, then Major James William Duffin, as the American Salvation Army, which was incorporated on April 4, 1900. By means of lengthy litigation The Salvation Army forced the American Salvation Army to change its name; as a result, the American Rescue Workers was incorporated on April 12, 1913, and continues to operate a small work. On March 10, 1908, William V. Grattam, last remaining director of the American Salvation Army, surrendered the original and only legal charter of that organization to Commander Evangeline Booth. US Dept. of Commerce, Bureau of the Census, *Census of Religious Bodies, 1936: American Rescue Workers* (Washington, 1940), 1-3, and *The American Rescue Workers Constitution, Orders, Regulations and Book of Rules* (no pub. data), 3-6, both in SFOT/E Museum, G/F "Moore;" Appellate Division of the Supreme Court, First Division, *The Salvation Army in the United States, Appellant, Against the American Salvation Army, Respondent* (New York, [1908]), 454-455, 470-71, kindly loaned by Comr. Richard E. Holz, grandson of the Major Holz in the text; Broadway files Nos. 1 and 4, SAA, "American Rescue Workers" correspondence.

CHAPTER II

1. Allan Whitworth Bosch, *The Salvation Army in Chicago: 1885-1914* (Ph.D. dissertation, Univ. of Chicago, 1965), 26.

2. Agnes Maule Machar, "Theological and Religious Intelligence: Red Cross Knights—A Nineteenth Century Crusade," *The Andover Review,* II (August 1884), 205; [Col. & Mrs Howard Chesham, compilers] *Combat Songs of The Salvation Army* (New York, 1976), 4, 10, 12, 20; *The Song Book of The Salvation Army* (New York, 1955), songs 671, 798.

3. Roger Green, *The Theology of William Booth* (Ph.D. dissertation [in process] Boston College, 1980); Leicester R. Longden, *The Church Mili-*

tant and *The Salvation Army: A Theological Appraisal of William Booth and His Movement* (B. Div. thesis, Union Theological Seminary, nd); Philip D. Needham, *Redemption and Social Reformation: A Theological Study of William Booth and His Movement* (M.Th. thesis, Princeton Theological Seminary, 1967).

4. Comr. Ballington Booth, *From Ocean to Ocean; Or, The Salvation Army's March from the Atlantic to the Pacific* (New York, 1891), 102; Maud B[allington] Booth, *Beneath Two Flags: A Study in Mercy and Help Methods* (4th ed.; Cincinnati, 1894 [orig. 1889]), 17; Lt.–Col. Wesley Bouterse, "Our Holiness Foundations," read at Brengle Institute, June, 1978, 2.

5. [William Booth] in *The Salvationist,* January 1879, quoted in Cyril J. Barnes, ed., *The Founder Speaks Again: A Selection of the Writings of William Booth* (London, 1960), 45; interview with Prof. Roger Green, Wilmore, Ken., March 22, 1979; William Booth, "The Millennium: or The Ultimate Triumph of Salvation Army Principles," *All the World,* VII (August 1890), 337-343.

6. *All About The Salvation Army By Those Who Know* (New York, 1890), 16; Bouterse, "Holiness Foundatons," E. Schuyler English, *H.A. Ironside: Ordained of the Lord* (Grand Rapids, 1946), 56-58, 68-71: Ironside was one early officer who resigned over the issue of sinless perfection. Charles Edward Russell, "A Rescuer of Ruined Lives: General William Booth and The Salvation Army," *The Missionary Review of the World,* 32 (June 1909), 451 (quotation); Professor Charles A. Briggs, "The Salvation Army," *North American Review,* 159 (December 1894), 704.

7. Clarence W. Hall, *Samuel Logan Brengle: Portrait of a Prophet* (Chicago, 1933), 88-89; Comr. S.L. Brengle, *Helps to Holiness* (London, [1896]), 24-25; interview with Lt.–Col. Lyell Rader, Ocean Grove, New Jersey, June 23, 1978.

8. A.F. Marshall, "The Salvation Army," *The Catholic World,* 51 (September 1890), 739, 742-743; Catherine Booth, "Hot Saints," in *Papers on Practical Religion* (London, 1901), 174; WC/C, January 10, 1925, 10, reprinting AWC January 15, 1881; AWC December 1, 1888, 8; April 26, 1890, cover; Booth, *Ocean to Ocean,* 103-110; *SA Song Book,* 682 (1879) and 479 (1899).

9. Booth, *Beneath Two Flags,* 130.

10. "Salvation in London," *The Living Age,* August 1, 1914, 313, quoting *The Nation: SA Song Book,* 798 (1882); WC/W, February 1886, 1.

11. Capt. Vincent Cunningham, "Railton," WC/C, March 8, 1924, 7; Louisville *Courier Journal,* May 18, 1883, copy sent to author by Maj. James

Pappas; WC/W, October 1884, 1; Rev. Thomas Easton, *Blood and Fire: The Salvation Army, Its Rise, Progress and Present Standing, and Work of the Fifth N.J. Corps* (New Brunswick, 1884), 17; [William Booth], *The General's Letters* (London, 1886), 36; English, *Ironside*, 67.

12. AWC, September 24, 1892, 9; WC/W, November 1, 1890 and November 15, 1890, in Milsaps SB, II, 19-22; AWC, July 11, 1891, 1-2; Minute No. 24, June 18, 1891, Busby Coll.; WC/W, January 1886, 2.

13. AWC, August 2, 1890, 1-2; Booth, *Ocean to Ocean*, 175.

14. AWC, December 1884, 4; Macher, "Red Cross Knights," 203; interview with Sr.–Maj. Charles A. Schuerholz, Asbury Park, New Jersey, June 30, 1978.

15. William Booth, *Orders and Regulations for Staff Officers of The Salvation Army* (London, 1904), 252, 277-278; AWC, November 29, 1884, 3; December 6, 1884, 2; June 11, 1890, 10; WC/W, May 15, 1887, 1; June 1, 1887, 2; Nora Marts, *Facts About The Salvation Army: Aims and Methods of the Hallelujah Band* (Chicago, 1889), 78-79; Herbert A. Wisbey, Jr., *Religion in Action: A History of The Salvation Army in the United States* (Ph.D. dissertation, Columbia University, 1951), 78.

16. Needham, Thesis, 108-109, 157, 164-165; Longdon, Thesis, 49-51; W.T. Stead, *General Booth: A Biographical Sketch* (London, 1891), 68.

17. Booth, *Beneath Two Flags*, 128-129.

18. Minutes No. 2, July 13, 1889 and No. 23, June 16, 1891, Busby Coll.; AWC, June 29, 1889, 5; July 20, 1889, 8; "Personal Reminiscences of Commissioner Gifford," 1927, updated to 1930, in a private collection; Commissioner Edward Justus Parker, *My Fifty-Eight Years: An Autobiography* (New York, 1943), 50-52; WC/W, November 1884, 2. In the appendix is a list of Salvation Army ranks used during the history of the movement; the author is indebted to Lt.–Col. Cyril Barnes of international headquarters, Mrs Col. Paul D. Seiler and Lt.–Col. David Moulton for help in compiling.

19. [Ballington and Maud B. Booth], *The Soldier's Manual: or Piety and Practice* (New York, 1889), 33-37; AWC, July 25, 1885, 1; August 5, 1893, 1-10, see esp. 7.

20. Booths, *Soldier's Manual*, 23; William Booth, *Orders and Regulations for Field Officers of The Salvation Army* (London, 1901), 525 on "Grading of Field Officers;" WC/W, March 1884, 1; January 1, 1888, 2 ("the great Salvation War.")

21. *The Officer*, 1 (January 1893) 13.

22. The New York *World*, March 13, 1883, 1; AWC, January 3, 1885, 3;

January 17, 1885, 1; November 20, 1886, 2; June 16, 1888, 12; January 25, 1891, 1; WC/W, July 1886, 2; June 1889, Milsaps WCC/I, 5; WC/W, September 7, 1895, 9; Milsaps SB, II, pocket in back of book, identified photograph, Oakland Citadel corps in 1885; Danbury *Sun Times*, August 23, 1886, copies sent to author by Lt. William Francis; Sgt. B.A. Richardson, "Victorious Veterans. The Pioneer Corps of the Central Division," AWC, January 29, 1898, 2; *The Salvation Fight under the Stars and Stripes* (New York, [1888]), 20; The Salvation Army *Price List of Publications Outfit Goods and Musical Instruments, October, 1893* (London, 1893), 98, 102-106, Seiler Coll. String bands formed a great part of the musical ministry of the Scandinavian corps. See William Booth, *The Salvation Army Orders and Regulations for Bands* (London, 1891), 9, Seiler Coll.

23. Booth, *SA Orders & Reg. for Bands*, 6, 8, 10; Parker, *My 58 Years*, 80, 187, 190; Bosch, Dissertation, 62-64; AWC, March 28, 1891, 7; "About the World: The Salvation Army Crisis," *Scribner's Magazine*, XIX (May 1896), 657.

24. AWC, July 5, 1890, 3; Booth, *Beneath Two Flags*, 40; Staff–Captain Slater, "The Music of the Salvation Army," *Conq.*, IV (January 1895), 34; AWC, December 12, 1885 (Francis matl.); November 7, 1891, 3; Machar, "Red Cross Knights," 204; Lt–Col. Charles Skinner, "Is Any Merry? Let Him Sing!" *The Officer*, XVII (July 1966), 450-52; Captain Ernest A. Miller, "The Beat That Communicates," *The Officer*, XV (December 1964), 832, (the first "secular" tune used by the Army with Booth's permission was "Champagne Charlie.")

25. Prof. C.A. Stork, "The Salvation Army: Its Methods and Lessons," *The Lutheran Quarterly*, XII (October 1882), 557, 562; Staff–Captain Marshall, "The United States Press and The Salvation Army," AWC, February 7, 1891, 1; *All About The Salvation Army 1884* (Brooklyn, no date), 10-12; "A Salvation Army Miracle Play," *The Illustrated American*, January 23, 1897, frontispiece and 136; WC/W, July 30, 1889, 9; September 2. 1893 (Milsaps SB,II, 62-63); in Milsaps WCC/III, 3080349 an excellent collection of announcements and small posters; Lt.–Colonel T.W. Scott, "How to Advertise Army Meetings," in *Western Congress Addresses* (Chicago, [1906]), 60-62.

26. [George Scott Railton], *Heathen England* (London, 1879), 40; Machar, "Red Cross Knights," 204.

27. AWC, March 5, 1887, 1, 4; WC/W, May 1884, 1; July 1886, 1; Sep-

tember, 1886, 4; AWC, February 25, 1888, 6; May 30, 1885, 1; June 6, 1885, 2; April 24, 1886, 1; May 22, 1886, 3.

28. AWC, March 3, 1894, 5; March 28, 1885, 1-2; WC/W, April 18, 1896, 8; Bosch, Dissertation, 208-209; Parker, *My 58 Years,* 107-109, 126-127, 134-142, 144-152, 168-170; Commander [Frederick] Booth-Tucker, *The Consul* (London, 1903), 107-108; Milsaps Diary, February 12, 1897 and AWC, July 18, 1908, 16.

29. Catherine Booth, *Aggressive Christianity* (Boston, 1889), 59; SFOT/E Museum G/F, "Brengle," has letter, undated, S.L. Brengle to his daughter Mrs H. Chester Reed, about weapons at the altar.

30. Oscar Handlin, *The Uprooted* (New York, 1951), 117-143, and *Immigration as a Factor in American History* (Englewood Cliffs, 1959), 76-77, 79-84; H. Richard Niebuhr, *The Social Sources of Denominationalism* (Cleveland, 1962 [orig. 1929]), 200-235; Timothy L. Smith, "Religion and Ethnicity in America," *American Historical Review,* 83 (December 1978), 1174-1177, esp. 1176-77; Dr Smith's suggestion that many immigrants were drawn to "messianic" and millennial doctrines supports Prof. Green's contention that part of the Army's appeal lay in Booth's post-millennialism.

31. AWC, January 21, 1888, 12; February 25, 1888, 10; March 10, 1888, 1; April 14, 1888, 15; June 16, 1888, 9; July 2, 1888, 4; Major K.A. Walden, "Through 45 Years: A Review of The Salvation Army's Scandinavian Work in the United States of America, 1887-1933," trans. Lt.–Col. T. Gabrielsen, Chicago, May 1933, in SAA "Scandinavian" file, unprocessed; AWC, June 16, 1894, 13.

32. AWC, July 21, 1889, 4; February 2, 1889, 4-5; February 9, 1889, 4-5; January 31, 1891, 8; June 25, 1891, 1, 4; October 29, 1892, 7; January 5, 1895, 12; WC/W, April 1, 1944, 11; Captain Percy Soule, "Our Home Mission Work: A Talk with Lt.–Col. Holz, *Conq,* VI (July, 1897), 153; "A Short Review of the Scandinavian Work in the United States," *Harbor Lights* (June 1898), 178-179; Leo Alf, "Strang-Orkestern vid Chicago 13," *Conq,* II (April 1893), 155; Bosch, Dissertation, 47, 53, 63; Adjt. Winchell, "Chicago," *Conq* II (February 1893), 61; WC/W, January 9, 1937, 3, 14.

33. "Pushing Forward the Swedish War," AWC, August 25, 1894, 4; interviews with Mrs Lt.–Col. F. William Carlson, August 7, 1978, and Col. C. Stanley Staiger, July 28, 1978, Ocean Grove, New Jersey, and with Col. William Maltby, June 30, 1978, Asbury Park, New Jersey. See the novel by Astrid Valley, *Marching Bonnet* (New York, 1948).

34. Railton, quoted in Thomas F.G. Coates, *The Prophet of the Poor: The Life-Story of General Booth* (New York, 1906), 130; letter quoted in Eileen Douglas, Mildred Duff, *Commissioner Railton* (London, [1920]), 74; *The Salvation News*, October 16, 1880, 1-2; *The War Cry* (Moore edition), May 7, 1885, 1; July 29, 1886, 1, in SAA; AWC, October 29, 1887, 9; November 19, 1887, 11; July 7, 1889, 9; October 22, 1892, 8; December 2, 1893, 5; Ensign Jaeger, "The German-American War," *Conq*, V (August 1896), 357; Mary A. Scherer, "The German Work: Its Rapid Growth and Development in the United States," *Harbor Lights*, I (March 1898), 91; AWC, June 16, 1894, 11; June 8, 1895, 9; September 22, 1894, 2.

35. "The Stranger Within Our Gates: A Work Among Germans and Italians in the United States," *Harbor Lights*, 2 (September 1899), 334-335; AWC, May 19, 1894, 1; June 16, 1894, 5; Brig. Richard E. Holz, "Scandinavian, German and Italian Department, Notes," AWC, December 12, 1896, 3; Ensign Kupfer, "A Visit to the Italian Corps," *Conq*, V (September 1896), 420-22; AWC, March 17, 1906, 6. For a brief time there was a Russian corps in New York: founded by Envoy John Reut, a Russian Jew converted in his homeland in 1892, who moved to New York in 1907 and attended the Bowery corps. He borrowed a drum and a flag, hired a hall with his own wages, and opened a corps in the Russian-Jewish settlement in New York. The work was heavily opposed: every street meeting had two police, every indoor meeting required three. Reut even produced a crude version of the WC in Russian, German, and Yiddish. The corps opened formally in March, 1909, bur soon sank without a trace. AWC, November 13, 1909, 1, 12.

36. WC/W, October 1884, 2; January 1885, 2; March 1885, 2; April 1885, 2; February 1886, 1; December 15, 1887, 5; January 18, 1896, 6, 9; March 21, 1896, 6; April 11, 1896, 3-4, 6; July 11, 1896, 6; July 25, 1896, 9; August 15, 1896, 4; September 26, 1896, 8; October 3, 1896, 8; November 28, 1896, 7; October 18, 1924, 8-9; *Conq*, V (August 1896), 385.

37. St. John Ervine, *God's Soldier: General William Booth* (2 vols.; New York, 1935), I, 480-81; Douglas and Duff, *Railton*, 74; AWC, July 18, 1885, 1.

38. WC/W, November 1884, 4; AWC citations for 1885: July 11, 1; July 18, 1; August 22, 1; August 29, 4; September 19, 1; September 26, 2; October 3, 1; September 5, 1; October 31, 3; November 21, 3; November 28, 1 (dismissal of Braithwaite); December 5, 1; December 12, 1; December 26, 7; for 1886: January 23, 1; February 6, 1; April 3, 1; Comr. Frank Smith,

The Salvation War in America, 1885 (New York, 1886), 135-137, 11; George Scott Railton, *Twenty-One Years Salvation Army* (London, 1888), 140; AWC, January 8, 1887, 9; May 14, 1887, 1.

39. AWC, October 3, 1891, 11; May 14, 1892, 13; September 7, 1889 and WC/W April 18, 1896, 8; AWC, August 25, 1888, 4; January 31, 1891, 4; William J. Brewer, *Lifting the Veil; or, Acts of the Salvationists* (Boston, 1895), np; AWC, August 25, 1900, 7; August 20, 1887, and S.L. Brengle to Adj. David Farrar, St. Petersburg, Florida, February 12, 1936, Francis matl.; Hall, *Portrait,* 84.

40. AWC, July 14, 1894, 8; July 21, 1894, 8; July 28, 1894, 5; December 28, 1895, cover and 2; May 20, 1899, 8.

41. AWC, July 28, 1894, cover; June 23, 1894, 9; July 7, 1894, 12; WC/W, June 30, 1894, 7; "Our Apostle to the Colored People," *Conq,* V (October 1896), 474; "Colonel Holland, Our New Apostle to the Colored Race," AWC, August 22, 1896, 1-2; "Colonel Holland: An Interview," *Conq,* VI (January 1897), 13; Booker T. Washington to Maj. T.C. Marshall, Tuskegee, Alabama, July 28, 1896, *Conq,* I (October 1896), 475. See also Norris Alden Magnuson, *Salvation in the Slums: Evangelical Social Welfare Work, 1865-1920* (Ph.D. dissertation, University of Minnesota, 1968), 324-344, 459-460, and Needham, Thesis, 73.

42. Matthew 25:31-46; Maud Ballington Booth, "Salvation Army Work in the Slums," *Scribner's Magazine,* January 1895, 103.

43. *Mended Links: The Annual Report of The Salvation Army's Rescue Work in the United States 1903* (New York, nd), np, SAA: Comr. Frank Smith, *The Salvation War in America, 1885* (New York, [1886]), 126-127; Danbury *News-Times,* April 21, 1887, Francis matl.; WC/W, August 1886, 3; March 1, 1887, 1.

44. AWC, October 9, 1886, 1; February 5, 1887, 8; March 19, 1887, 5 (at that time, the rescue home was the only Army institution beyond the corps); July 2, 1887, 8; July 30, 1887, 9; April 28, 1888, 12; October 27, 1888, 4; April 16, 1892, 2 and illus; June 25, 1892; July 15, 1893, 2; WC/W, February 1, 1887, 1-2; April 1, 1887, 1; August 1, 1887, 1; finding qualified officers for these homes was a constant problem: William Evans to Maj. [R.E.] Holz, New York City, October 7, 1890, Holz coll.

45. AWC, July 5, 1890

46. AWC, August 10, 1889, 14; August 31, 1889, 8; October 12, 1889, 9; October 19, 1889, 13; November 30, 1889, 5; March 1, 1890, 2-3 [orig. New York *World*]; AWC, August 30, 1890 [orig. *Illustrated American*]; Harry B. Wilson, "Contrasting Methods of Salvation Army Warfare,"

Harper's Weekly, December 22, 1894, 1219; Maj. Bown, "Glimpses of Slum Operations," *Conq*, IV (January 1895), 19; Maud Ballington Booth, "The Church of the Black Sheep: An Article on The Salvation Army," *Harper's Weekly*, March 15, 1896, 250; Edwin Gifford Lamb, *The Social Work of The Salvation Army* (Ph.D. dissertation, Columbia University, 1909), 117-118, 120, 132; Lyman Abbott, *Christianity and Social Problems* (Boston, 1896), 20-21, held the slum sisters up as an example of the way in which Christ shared the poverty of His followers.

47. William Booth, *In Darkest England and the Way Out* (London, 1890), 26-27, 278; AWC, November 22, 1890, 2-3,8; December 6, 1890, 2; Albert Shaw, "A Year of General Booth's Work," *The Forum*, February 1892, 766-67; Commander Ballington Booth, "The Salvation Army: Its Work Among the Poor and Lowly: The Work of the Shelter Brigade," *Harper's Weekly*, December 30, 1890, 1257.

48. AWC, February 6, 1892, 1, 4-5; March 18, 1893, 11; "Our New York Lighthouse," *Conq*, I (February 1892), 11; Lt.–Col. Norman J. Winterbottom, "The Salvation Army Western Territory . . . Chronology," states that use of kettles began in San Francisco in 1893; ms in SATHQ/W, Personnel Dept.

49. Parker, *My 58 Years*, 154-155; Lyman Abbott, "The Personal Problem of Charity," *The Forum*, February 1894. 667-668; "Social Progress in the United States," *Harbor Lights*, May 1898, 142; Bosch, dissertation, 277-285; Comr. Frederick Booth-Tucker, *The Salvation Army in the United States* (New York, 1899), np, for complete survey of SA social activities in 1899; "Odds-and-Ends Charity," *Harper's Weekly*, December 2, 1899, 1220 plus illus.; Order No. 20, "The Salvation Army Special Orders to Social Officers," gold-stamped binder, SAA, all signed Edward J. Parker, dated December 1, 1910; interview Sr.–Maj. Railton F. Spake, Los Angeles, December 11, 1978.

50. AWC, June 16, 1894, 11; July 28, 1900, 5; Minutes No. 53, March 1, 1897, Busby coll.

51. Jacob A. Riis, *The Making of an American* (New York, 1902), 387-88; William T. Stead, *If Christ Came to Chicago* (Chicago, 1894), 269; William Hayes Ward, "The Salvation Army," *Harper's Weekly*, December 2, 1893, 1147; Walter Besant, "The Farm and the City," *Living Age*, January 29, 1898, 306, 314. Walter Rauschenbusch, *The Social Principles of Jesus* (New York, 1916), 5; Richard T. Ely, "The Simple Gospel of Christ," in Ely, *Social Aspects of Christianity and Other Essays* (New York, 1889), 27-29; Washington Gladden, "Religion and Wealth," *Biblio-*

theca Sacra, 52 (January 1895), 160; Henry F. May, *Protestant Churches and Industrial America* (New York, 1963 [orig. 1949]), 91-111, 121-122.

52. Winchell, "Chicago," 58; AWC, September 16, 1893; September 15, 1894, 8; October 20, 1894, 2; Bosch Dissertation, 115-116, 121-123; James E. Beane: *'That Terrible Summer:' The Salvation Army and the Great Pullman Strike of 1894* (New York, 1977), SAA.

53. *Salvation Fight under the Stars and Stripes,* 45; WC/W, July 20, 1895 (Milsaps WCC/I); September 14, 1897,6,14 (labor quotes); AWC, June 27, 1891, 6; Josiah Strong, *Religious Movements for Social Betterment* (New York, 1900),33: "Now it is very significant that the working multitudes who shun the churches flock to the meetings of the Salvation Army"; AWC, April 28, 1888, 8 (labor made tractable); The Army was remarkably frank about its value to captains of industry in this regard: "The Capitalist's Debt to the Salvation Army," LD, January 3, 1914, 24, quoting Evangeline Booth, "Why the Capitalist Should Help the Salvation Army," AWC, December 27, 1913; for developments out West, see issue of *Pacific Union Printer,* San Francisco, February 1895, in Milsaps SB/II, 71, and Milsaps Diary, November 4, 1897.

54. AWC, December 25, 1886, 1; Milsaps WCC/II, 303, 353, and *passim;* Magnuson, *Salvation in the Slums,* 124-125, 129.

55. Booth, *Orders & Regs. for Staff Officers, 1904,* 81; notarized financial statement issued by Frank Smith, December 1, 1884-July 31, 1885, in SFOT/E Museum, G/F "Moore," showing that WC sales accounted for 52 percent of all Army income. For this reason, it was practically impossible for an officer to decrease his order for *War Crys.* See AWC, February 4, 1888, 5. On Auxiliaries, see AWC, August 20, 1887, 9; WC/W, November 15, 1887; December 15, 1887, 7; March 9, 1889, 8-9; January 18, 1890, 13; October 15, 1892; Dr Lyman Abbott, "Why I Am an Auxiliary," *Conq,* IV (January 1895), 41; Major T.C. Marshall, "The Auxiliary League," *Conq* VI (May 1897), 109; *Harper's Weekly,* December 22, 1894, 1216; Wisbey, Dissertation, 94, 197-198.

56. AWC, April 3, 1886, 1, 4 (Cleveland), also in Railton, *21 Years SA,* 142; AWC, December 10, 1892, 3 (Harrison) also WC/W, May 9, 1892 in Milsaps SB/II, 28-29; WC/W, January 18, 1896, 4 (McKinley) and AWC, August 14, 1897, 8, 13.

57. Robert Sandall, *The History of The Salvation Army* (6 vols.; London, 1950), II, 241; AWC, April 7, 1894, 13; November 25, 1893, 8, 12; Gifford, "Reminiscences," 35-36; Booth, *Beneath Two Flags,* 63; "The Major of the Empire State," *Conq,* II (January 1893), 29; Ensign Roland

Hughes, "Our Heritage The Army," WC/E, May 21, 1932, 3, 15; *Salvation Fight under the Stars and Stripes,* 37-38; AWC, October 31, 1903 and May 2, 1891, in Milsaps WCC/III, 163 and 320; Milsaps Diary, May 14, 1898; AWC, July 31, 1886, 1 and March 22, 1890, 1-2 and "A Maid of Connecticut," *Conq,* IV (February 1895), 62-63; Milsaps SB/II, 25, "dina might" letter.

58. WC/W, February 15, 1887, 1; Brewer, *Lifting the Veil,* 11; WC/W, February 1, 1887 Milsaps WCC/I, 1-2; interview with James T. Stillwell, Suffern, New York, July 12, 1978; "Maid of Connecticut," 63-65; AWC, May 30, 1885, 1; July 11, 1885, 3; August 1, 1885, 1; July 24, 1886, 1; July 28, 1888, 9; August 18, 1888, 12; January 11, 1890, 1-2; Marts, *Facts About the SA,* 202-209; Railton, *21 Years SA,* 141 (quote).

59. Three saloons folded in Danbury during the Army's first two years there: Danbury *News Times,* November 12, 1887, Francis matl.; Ernest H. Crosby, "The Saloon as a Political Power," *Forum,* May, 1889, 325; Charles H. Sheldon, *In His Steps* (Grand Rapids, 1967 [orig. 1896]), 88-96, 110, 113-115; James F. Richardson, *The New York Police: Colonial Times to 1901* (New York, 1970), 182-185, 280-284; Sandall, *History,* II, 239-240; Stead, *If Christ Came to Chicago* 49-68, 303-307, 379; Herbert Asbury, *The Barbary Coast* (New York, 1933), 245; Bosch, Dissertation, 22-23; Booth, *Ocean to Ocean,* 91-92; Smith, *Salvation War in America, 1885,* 17-50; *Facts Concerning the Recent Outrage Upon Religious Liberty at Galion, O* (Cleveland, 1893), Seiler Coll.; WC/W, July 18, 1891 (Milsaps WCC/II, 106), states that it was "simply impossible" to list all of those who were arrested "because so many have suffered that way for Christ."

60. The references to Joe the Turk in Army literature and reminiscences are voluminous. Capt. Joseph Garabed, "Joe the Turk," AWC, March 26, 1892, 4; same, "In Prison Oft: Joe the Turk Still 'Moves Around:' " *The Officer,* October 1895; Adj. William Harris, "Joe the Turk," WC/E, January 6, 1934, 4; WC/W October 30, 1937.

CHAPTER III

1. Ensign [J.C.] Ludgate, "A Typical Open-Air Meeting," AWC, March 14, 1898, 13; *All About The Salvation Army, By Those Who Know* (New York, 1890), 5 (quotation); AWC, August 22, 1896, entire issue.

2. AWC, December 10, 1892, 4, 9; WC/W, February 22, 1897, 7; Commander Ballington Booth, *A Manifesto for 1895 to the Staff and Field*

Officers of The Salvation Army in the United States (New York, 1895), np, Seiler Coll.

3. "The Headquarters of The Salvation Army," *Harper's Weekly,* March 30, 1895, 293; WC/W, August 3, 1895, 7; AWC, June 17, 1893, 9; September 1, 1894, 1, 4-5; Herbert A. Wisbey, Jr., *Religion in Action: A History of The Salvation Army in the United States* (Ph.D. dissertation, Columbia University, 1951), 194-195.

4. J.J. Keppel to Booth-Tucker, Chicago, September 16, 1898, Wood Coll., SAA; Ensign William Harris, "Looking Back Long Liberty Trail," WC/E, August 11, 1928, 11; "The Reminiscences of Commissioner Gifford," [1930], private collection, 39-43; *All About The Salvation Army* (Brooklyn, 1884), 14.

5. AWC, August 27, 1887, 5; William Hayes Ward, "The Salvation Army," *Harper's Weekly,* December 2, 1897, 1147.

6. *The Musical Pioneer* (New York, 1890), 1-2, in SATHQ/E, Music Dept.; SA *Songbook,* Nos. 372, 781; AWC, September 3, 1887, 8; Maud B. Booth to Mrs R.E. Holz, New York, January 23, 1890, a note of concern about sick children, signed "Your sister in sympathy and in love of the War, which Christ is helping us to wage." Holz Coll.

7. Commissioner Ballington Booth, *From Ocean to Ocean; Or, The Salvation Army's March from the Atlantic to the Pacific* (New York, 1891), autograph inscription in flyleaf, copy in Circle "M" Collection, Houston RCC, M267.15B ("who daily yearns"); Lt.–Col. Wallace Winchell, "Shall the Saloon Come Back?" WC/E, July 9, 1932, 3; Ballington's *Herald* articles were later reprinted as: Commissioner and Mrs Ballington Booth, *New York's Inferno Explored* (New York, 1891), xerox SAA, orig. SFOT/E library, Jno. Gilmer Speed, "The Salvation Army Congress," *Harper's Weekly,* December 3, 1892, 1166.

8. J.J. Keppel to Booth-Tucker, Chicago, September 16, 1898, Wood Collection, SAA: "The Ordination of Ballington Booth," *The Outlook,* October 3, 1896, 618-619.

9. SFOT/E Museum, B/F, "Split-Ballington," statement re: resignation.

10. AWC, April 14, 1894, 5; September 22, 1894, 16; September 29, 1894, 1, 4; October 27, 1894, *passim;* on the pulpit warning, see AWC, November 17, 1894, 9; original poster and Booth's handwritten instructions to printer in Seiler Collection; "The General's Journeys in North America," *Conq,* IV (April 1895), 153-165; "The Salvation Army Jubilee," *Harper's Weekly,* November 3, 1894, 1048; William Booth to Emma Booth-

Tucker, London, April 22, 1896 ("Yankee Doodleism"), in SFOT/E Museum B/F, "Split-Ballington."

11. Susan Fulton Welty, *Look Up and Hope! The Life of Maud Ballington Booth* (New York, 1961), 90-95, 100-105; R.V. Trevel, "Maud Ballington Booth," in Warren Dunham Foster, *Heroines of Modern Religion* (New York, 1913), 242-244; printed letters from Ballington Booth, dated February 29 and March 4, 1896, Seiler Coll., binders; "Good American Salvation," *The Nation*, March 5, 1896, 191.

12. AWC, February 8, 1896, 9; WC/W, February 15, 1896,7—the last word from the Booths in the WC, contained letter to American troops announcing their farewell; there was no hint of resignation.

13. New York *Herald*, March 2, 1896, 6; "The Salvation Army Troubles," *The Outlook*, March 7, 1896, 426; "Good American Salvation," 190; WC/W, March 21, 1896, 8; Brig. E. Fielding to General William Booth, Chicago, February 23, 1896, Busby Coll., SAA: "About the World; The Salvation Army Crisis," *Scribner's Magazine*, May 1896, 658.

14. WC/W, April 11, 1896, 6; AWC, April 4, 1896, 9; supplement to AWC, May 2, 1896, following p 8; Adam Gifford to Ballington and Maud Booth, January 10, 1896, Gifford copy book, private collection; J. Garabed to Mrs Ballington Booth, Boston, May 5, 1896, in SFOT/E Museum, G/F, "Joe the Turk, Correspondence."

15. Maud B. Booth, *Beneath Two Flags: A Study in Mercy and Help Methods* (Cincinnati, 1894; [orig. 1889]), 215; New York *Herald*, March 2, 1896, 6; Major Milsaps, the California pioneer, was a mainstay of loyalty. See Milsaps Diary, January 15, 1917, April 2, 1897, April 11, 1897, May 25, 1897, March 1, 1898, April 1, 1898, June 12, 1898, October 5, 1898; A.M. Nicol, *General Booth and The Salvation Army* (London, no date), 233-249; Sallie Chesham, *Born to Battle: The Salvation Army in America* (New York, 1965), 98; interview with Lt.–Col. Edward Laity, Atlanta, November 24, 1978; Brig. Richard Holz to Ballington Booth, Binghamton, New York, July 24, 1896, and Ballington to Holz, New York City, June 22, 1896, both in Seiler Collection, binders.

16. AWC, June 11, 1887, 8; WC/W, March 21, 1896, 8; interview with Col. Bertram Rodda, Oakland, December 12, 1978; Allan Whitworth Bosch, *The Salvation Army in Chicago: 1885-1914* (Ph.D. dissertation, Univ. of Chicago, 1965), 135; Clarence W. Hall, *Samuel Logan Brengle: Portrait of a Prophet* (Chicago, 1933), 96-99; Chesham, *Born to Battle*, 98-99; Comr. Samuel Logan Brengle, *The Soul-Winner's Secret* (London, nd), 55 (last quotation).

17. AWC, March 28, 1896, 8-9; "Consul and Commander Booth-Tucker," *Conq* V (May 1896), 203-204; Commander [Frederick] Booth-Tucker, *The Consul* (London, 1903), 106-107; interview with Mrs Edmund C. Hoffman, Asbury Park, New Jersey, June 23, 1978; WC/E, January 3, 1948, 1, 3, on death of Higgins, who was in the US 1896-1905.

18. New York *Herald*, April 2, 1896, 5; AWC, April 4, 1896, 9; SFOT/E Museum, B/F, "Split-Ballington," has several pieces of important correspondence on the crisis; Mrs Col. Carpenter, "Consul Emma Booth-Tucker," in her *Some Notable Officers of The Salvation Army* (London, 1926), 26; AWC, March 5, 1904, 1, 8, on the death of Sen. Mark Hanna.

19. "Salvation by Noise," *The Nation*, June 3, 1897, 411; Milsaps Diary, March 8, March 10, 1897, and February 21, April 11, June 22, July 13, 1899; Booth-Tucker, *Consul*, 116; WC/W, April 11, 1896, 1, 6-7; May 2, May 9, 1896, *passim*; May 23, 1896, 1, 2, 6-7; Bosch, Dissertation, 133-138.

20. James E. Beane, *The Incorporation of The Salvation Army in the United States (1882-1899)* (New York, 1975), 10-11, SAA; Frederick Booth-Tucker to the Chief of the Staff, New York, December 22, 1898 ("boodlers"), in SFOT/E Museum, C/F, "Moore;" AWC, May 13, 1899, 8; *The Salvation Army Incorporated in the State of New York, Certificate of Incorporation and By-Laws* (New York, no date), courtesy Col. William Bearchell.

21. Rev. Josiah Strong, "The Salvation Army in the United States," AWC, December 22, 1900, 3; Major J.C. Ludgate, "Conducting Open-Airs Singlehanded," AWC, August 23, 1902, 5; WC/W, April 7, 1900, 3; June 15, 1897 in Milsaps WCC/I, 81; Minute No. 61, March 25, 1898, on uniform, in Busby Coll., SAA: see also No.77, October 10, 1901; brochure, *Century Advance, July 1, 1899–Dec.31, 1900, Plan of Campaign, by Commander Booth-Tucker*, Holz. Coll., xerox SAA; *Guide to the Fall & Winter Red Crusade of 1903–1904 by the Commander*, Seiler Coll. binders; Booth-Tucker, *Consul*, 139; AWC, January 29, 1898, 8 ("we met").

22. Booth-Tucker, *Consul*, 164-166, 177, 178-79 lists many of the powerful friends of the Army who paid tribute to the Consul at her funeral; on the flow of directives, Minute No. 45, December 3, 1895, Minute No. 46, August 11, 1896, Busby Coll., SAA.

23. Commander [Frederick] Booth-Tucker, *The Salvation Army in the United States* (New York, 1899), np; Bosch, Dissertation, 251-55, 302-305; *Mended Links: The Annual Report of The Salvation Army's Rescue Work in the United States 1903* (New York [1903]), 17, SAA; AWC, August 23,

1902, 1,9; August 31, 1901,9,12; September 5, 1908,cover; November 15, 1902, 4; December 13, 1902, 14; January 31, 1903, 5; February 14, 1903, 5; February 21, 1903, 4; WC/W, November 28, 1896, 1-3; Maj. [Samuel L.] Brengle, "A Few Notes on My Western Trip," *Conq*, VI (November 1897) 259; Staff–Capt. Merriweather, "A Jail Conversion," *Harbor Lights*, April 1898, 128; WC/W, August 18, 1900, 3; Booth-Tucker, *Consul*, 118.

24. Minute No. 84, June 20, 1902, Busby Coll. SAA: *The Little Soldier*, November 26, 1885, 2, 4, in Seiler Coll. binders; AWC, January 22, 1887, 8; interview with Mrs Edmund C. Hoffman, and see her testimony, WC/E, June 1, 1929, 4, 11.

25. Minute No. 28, October 6, 1891, Busby Coll.; AWC, June 16, 1894, 13; *The Salvation Army Band of Love International Music Drills* (London, 1899), SFOT/E Museum, G/F, "Band of Love;" Staff–Capt. Winant, "The American Junior Soldier War," *Conq*, V (January 1896), 10-11; Minute No. 64, May 13, 1898, Busby Coll; Brig. William Halpin, "The Children for Jesus," *Harbor Lights*, April 1898, 124-125; AWC, June 3, 1899, 2-3.

26. AWC, November 12, 1904, 10; G.D. Whelpley, "Salvation Army Colonies," *Harper's Weekly*, September 7, 1901, 902; AWC, August 27, 1898, 11; photographic album of Lytton Boys and Girls Home, SATHQ/W Property Dept., SAA: AWC, October 6, 1900, 4, 8; October 13, 1900, 4; October 20, 1900, 7, on Cincinnati fire.

27. AWC, May 23, 1896, 1-2; New York *Herald*, April 24, 1896, 12; April 29, 1896, 5; "Salvation by Noise," 411; WC/W, August 15, 1896, 4; Aaron Ignatius Abell, *The Urban Impact on American Protestantism, 1865-1900* (Hamden, 1962 [orig. 1943]), 135, WC/W, July 18, 1896, 8; Minute No. 47, October 21, 1896, allowing divisional officers to staff corps with persons who had not completed the "usual six months' training," Busby Coll., SAA.

28. Booth-Tucker, *SA in the US;* Milsaps Diary, November 4, 1897; Minutes No. 52, November 30, 1896, No. 54, June 7, 1897; No. 70, October 10, 1898, No. 74, October 20, 1900, No. 81, June 20, 1902, all on Mercy Box league; for attitude on appeals, see No. 80, February 20, 1902; Adj. Maltby, *The Poor Man's Church: Report of The Salvation Army (Incorporated) in Meadville, for the Year Ending March 25, 1900* (Meadville, Pennsylvania 1900), courtesy Col. Maltby.

29. William Booth, *In Darkest England and The Way Out* (London, 1890), 100-159.

30. Lyman Abbott, "The Personal Problem of Charity," *The Forum*, February 1894, 663-665; Josephine Shaw Lowell, "The True Aim of Charity Organi-

zation Societies," *The Forum,* June, 1896, 495; Norris Alden Magnuson, *Salvation in the Slums: Evangelical Social Welfare Work, 1865-1920* (Ph.D. dissertation, Univ. of Minnesota, 1968), 283; Marvin E. Gettleman, "Charity and Social Classes in the United States, 1874-1900," *The American Journal of Economics and Sociology,* 22 (April, 1963) and (July, 1963), 327-29, 417-418; Commander [Frederick] Booth-Tucker, *The Social Relief Work of the Salvation Army in the United States* (Washington, 1900), 28; Staff–Capt. Wm. H. Cox, "At the Lighthouse," AWC, February 6, 1892, 4.

31. Booth, *In Darkest England,* 70, 83, 136; AWC, October 10, 1896, 8; February 20, 1897, 8; Frederick de Lautour Booth-Tucker, "The Farm Colonies of the Salvation Army," *The Forum,* August 1897, 752, [William H. Cox], "The Proposed Colonization Scheme: The Substance of an Interview with Commander Booth-Tucker," *Conq,* VI (September 1897), 201-202.

32. Booth-Tucker, *Social Relief Work,* 29-37; WC/W, August 25, 1900 cover; "Draft Outline for Regulations for Vacant Lot Farms," no pub. data, Holz Coll., AWC, March 27, 1897, 14; May 8, 1897, 10-11; December 18, 1897, 2-3.

33. AWC, January 21, 1899, 5; Whelpley, "Salvation Army Colonies," 902; Booth-Tucker, *Social Relief Work,* 35-36; Milsaps Diary, January 1, 1898; Frederick Booth-Tucker, *Farm Colonies of The Salvation Army* (Washington, 1903), 983-984; Dorothy Hitzka, *Farm Colonies of the Salvation Army and in Particular the Ft. Herrick Colony, Mentor, Ohio* (Cleveland, 1976), 6; SFOT/E Museum G/F, "Farm Colonies (General);" on the bill, see AWC, April 9, 1904, 8; May 14, 1904, 5; *The Congressional Record,* 3454-3455 (1904), information courtesy Lt.–Col. Ernest Miller.

34. Staff–Captain (Jay Bee) Burrows, "Fort Amity, Col.," *Harbor Lights,* June 1898, 172-173, AWC, July 9, 1898, 5; March 29, 1902, 4; August 12, 1905, 13; "Successful Farm Colonies," *The Outlook,* July 11, 1903, 640-41; Whelpley, "Salvation Army Colonies," 902; interview with Mr James T. Stillwell, Suffern New York, July 12, 1978; SFOT/E Museum, G/F, "Farm Colony—Amity;" H. Rider Haggard, *The Poor and the Land: Being a Report on the Salvation Army Colonies in the United States and at Hadleigh England with Scheme for National Land Settlement* (London, 1905), 67-72; Edwin Gifford Lamb, *The Social Work of The Salvation Army* (Ph.D. dissertation, Columbia Univ., 1909), 99-116; Marie Antalek, *The Amity Colony* (M.A. thesis, Kansas State Teachers' College, Emporia, 1968), 37-76.

35. AWC, September 17, 1898, 9; Hitzka, *Farm Colonies,* 10, 12-13, 25, 30;

Church of the Black Sheep: Annual Report of The Salvation Army in Cleveland, 1898-1899, np; Haggard, *Poor and the Land,* 115-116, 119; Antalek, *Amity Colony,* 34-36; R.E. Holz, national social secretary, to Commander Booth-Tucker, New York, March 8, 1899 ("grumbling"), in Holz. Coll.; AWC, September 27, 1913, 1, 9.

36. AWC, October 16, 1897, 4; WC/W, October 23, 1897, in Milsaps WCC/I, 297 and WC/W, October 9, 1897, in same 101-102; Haggard, *Poor and the Land,* 38-66; WC/W, August 11, 1900, 7; August 18, 1900, 3; July 28, 1900 in Milsaps WCC/I, 3; Milsaps Diary, March 22, 1897, May 16, 1897, October 20, 1897, February 10, 1898; Antalek, *Amity Colony,* 30-34.

37. C.C. Carstens, "Shall Salvation Army Take the Public Into its Confidence?" *Charities,* April 27, 1907, 118; same author, "The Salvation Army —A Criticism," *The Annals of the American Academy of Political and Social Science,* 30 (November 1907), 126-127.

38. Booth-Tucker, *Consul,* 9, 155-157, 176; AWC, November 14, 1903, and November 21, 1903, *passim;* February 20, 1904, 1, 9; interview with Mrs Edmund C. Hoffman, who attended the funeral; SA *Songbook,* no. 457; Seiler Coll. binders contains one of the purple-trimmed funeral programs.

39. AWC, August 27, 1904, 8; Harry Edward Neal, *The Hallelujah Army* (Philadelphia, 1961), 12-13.

40. Commission issued to Evaline Cory Booth by General William Booth, November 9, 1904, in Busby Coll.; Milsaps Diary, January 6, 1905; AWC, November 26, 1904, 9; December 3, 1904, 16.

41. AWC, March 7, 1903, 6, 8; April 23, 1904, 7; William Hamilton Nelson, *Blood and Fire: General William Booth* (New York, 1929), 228-230; Brig. Ashley Pebbles, "Our Responsibility for those who have failed Socially," Salvation Army, *Western Congress Addresses* (Chicago, [1906]), 105; Bosch dissertation, 232-233.

42. Lamb, *Social Work of the SA,* 69-70; Comr. Edward Justus Parker, *My Fifty-Eight Years: An Autobiography* (New York, 1943), 152-53; Henry Jarvis, "A People's Palace," *The Outlook,* June 2, 1906; AWC, February 4, 1905, 7; May 1, 1915, 11; Bosch Dissertation, 255; Ernest A. Bell, *Fighting the Traffic in Young Girls: Or, War on the White Slave Trade* (Chicago, 1910), 442-445, 475.

43. AWC, August 23, 1902, 2; October 20, 1906, 5; October 27, 1906, 6-7; July 31, 1909, 1-8; August 26, 1911, 1, 8-9; Bosch, Dissertation, 242-248; "Brief on Ohio, Pittsburgh & Southern Province, 1908, Colonel R.E.

Holz, P.O.," large brown binder, SAA, np, account of Euclid Park trip, July 9, 1908; AWC, July 25, 1908, 3.

44. AWC, August 14, 1897, 7; November 8, 1913, 8.

45. W.J. Ashley, "General Booth's Panacea," *The Political Science Quarterly,* VI (September 1891), 549-550; WC/C, November 5, 1927, 13; Bosch, Dissertation, 192-196; William Booth, *Orders & Regulations for Field Officers, 1901* (London, 1901), 401, 525.

46. Brig. W.F. Jenkins, "The Making of Soldiers," *Western Congress Addresses,* 36-37; Holz, "Brief, O.P.&S. Province;" WC/W, October 1884, 1-2.

47. "A North-American 'Hard Nut.' How Shall it be Cracked," *The Field Officer,* November 1902, 187; Jenkins, "Making of Soldiers," 38, 41 42.

48. Harold Begbie, *Life William Booth: The Founder of The Salvation Army* (2 vols.; London, 1925), II, 163 ("better sort"); Interviews with Lt.–Col. William Bearchell, Asbury Park, New Jersey, June 30, 1978, with Lt.–Col. Wesley Bouterse, Atlanta, November 28, 1978; Mrs Col. Norman S. Marshall, *History of The Home League in the Eastern Territory* (New York, 1976), SAA; AWC, February 20, 1915, 9.

49. SFOT/S Museum, book of papers relating to Brengle, carbon of "An Open Letter to a Troubled Young Officer;" AWC, February 21, 1903, 8; February 28, 1903, 4; October 31, 1903, 2; April 19, 1913, 12; Holz, "Brief, O.P.&S. Province."

50. AWC, April 23, 1887, 6; Mrs Brig. Cozens, "Our Invasion of Kentucky," *Conq,* IV (June 1895), 259; AWC, August 22, 1896; clipping Philadelphia *Sunday Press,* November 3, 1903, 6, in SFOT/E Museum G/F, "USA History;" AWC, March 5, 1904, 7; William E. Barton, "The Church Militant in the Feud Belt," *The Outlook,* October 10, 1903, 351-352; see also Ensign Clifford Brindley's long and helpful biography of Richard Holz, "Commissioner Richard E. Holz," WC/E, April 13-August 31, 1929.

51. AWC, January 30, 1904, 5; March 2, 1907, 1-*passim;* WC/W, November 8, 1941, 13.

52. AWC, May 25, 1889, 8, cited in Bosch Dissertation, 72-73; AWC, June 29, 1889, 1; March 10, 1900, 16; WC/W, October 13, 1900, Milsaps WCC/I, 6; AWC, September 22, 1900, 8; September 29, 1900, 9; October 6, 1900, 1, 8-9; October 13, 1900, 9, 12; October 20, 1900, 5.

53. AWC, May 19, 1906, 1, *passim;* June 2, 1906, 3-4, 6-7.

54. AWC, May 5, 1906, 1, 9, 12; May 26, 1906, 4-5, 13; June 16, 1906,

4; June 30, 1906, 4-5, 8-9; July 14, 1906, 8; April 13, 1907, 5; April 20, 1907, 2.

55. AWC, June 16, 1906, 8; June 23, 1906, 2, 8, 12; May 11, 1907, 9, 13.

56. AWC, March 16, 1907, 6; August 31, 1907, 12; September 28, 1907, 1, *passim;* October 12, 1907, 8-9, 12; November 16, 1907, 13; November 23, 1907, 9.

57. *All About the SA,* 1884, 22; AWC, August 20, 1892, 5; September 3, 1892, 8; *Orders & Regs. for Field Officers, 1901,* 242-244.

58. AWC, December 11, 1909, 12; SFOT/E Museum G/F, "Boozers' Convention;" Clarence W. Hall, *Out of the Depths: The Life-Story of Henry F. Milans* (Westwood, New Jersey, 1930), 126-138, illus. fac. 132, 139-148; broadside song sheet, "Jim and Me," undated, Holz Collection.

59. AWC, December 26, 1908; WC/S, April 23, 1927 cover; fine example of Falk portrait loaned to author by Mr Tom McMahon, Ocean Grove, New Jersey. See illustrations, this volume.

60. Comr. Frank Smith, *The Salvation War in America for 1885* (New York, [1886]), 74; SA, *Certificate of Incorporation,* 4, lists value of all Army property in 1899; the only sizeable piece of property was NHQ; the farm colonies were owned by the colonists—the Army held on leases and mortgages.

61. Minute No. 77, October 10, 1901, Busby Coll, and Field Minute No. 3, January 1, 1911, in SAA; Catherine Baird, *William McIntyre: God's Harvester* (London, 1948), 30-32; AWC, May 25, 1907, 8 ("lofty pedestal"); Holz, "Brief, O.P.&S. Province;" Col. W.A. McIntyre, *Twenty Years Housing The Salvation Army* (New York, 1920), 9; Agnes L. Palmer, *The Time Between: 1904-1926* (New York, 1926), 19-28, 10; AWC, February 25, 1911, 1, 6-7 (Flint); SATHQ/W, Property Dept. files (Oakland).

62. Holz, "Brief, O.P.&S. Province."

63. Lamb, *Social Work of the SA,* 25, 133, 137; Carstens, "Salvation Army —A Criticism," 117-120; AWC, November 27, 1909, 8, 13; December 11, 1909, 1, 8-9, 12; Peter W. Stine, *Loaves and Fishes in Boston: A Modern Holiday Miracle* (New York, 1978), SAA.

64. Booth quote in Chesham, *Born to Battle,* 133; WC (London), August 31, 1912, 5 ("kiss him for me"); Nicholas Vachel Lindsay, "General William Booth Enters Into Heaven," *Poetry: A Magazine of Verse,* I (January 1913), 101-103; see also LD, March 8, 1913, 541-542.

65. AWC, June 6, 1914, 10; June 13, 1914, 11, 13; June 27, 1914, 8-9, 12; *The Salvation Army Congress of the Nations 1914. Celebration at the*

Crystal Palace, Tuesday, June 23rd. Official Programme, Seiler Collection, binders.

CHAPTER IV

1. *You Should Know These Things* (New York, 1915), 6.
2. *Where Shadows Lengthen: A Sketch of The Salvation Army's Work in the United States of America* (New York, 1907), 52-53; J. Stanley Sheppard, *The Prison Work of The Salvation Army* (New York, 1948), 29-30, 77-80; *Close-Ups from Humanity's Scrapheap: Being the Annual Prison Report of The Salvation Army, 1921-1922* (New York, 1922), 87; AWC, February 3, 1917, 8-9.
3. *Service: An Exposition of The Salvation Army in the United States* (New York, 1941), 12-13; Charles Edward Russell, "A Rescuer of Ruined Lives: General William Booth and The Salvation Army," *Missionary Review of the World,* 32 (June 1909), 456; Raymond Arthur Dexter, *Officer Training in The Salvation Army: An Institutional Analysis* (Ed.D. dissertation, Stanford University, 1962), 16-17; "The Salvation Army's Campaign," *The Outlook,* April 26, 1916, 943; Theodore Roosevelt, "The Salvation Army," *The Outlook,* August 23, 1913, 892-93.
4. Holz Diary, August 15, 1892, SAA; correspondence on these "spurious concerns" in two Broadway files boxes, "No. 4," and "C," in SAA, which also has catalogued the complete correspondence of Brig. Madison J.H. Ferris; Nels Anderson, *The Hobo: The Sociology of the Homeless Man* (Chicago, 1961 [orig. 1923]), 250.
5. AWC, August 29, 1914, 8; September 12, 1914, 8, 12.
6. AWC, November 14, 1914, 8-9, 12; January 2, 1915, 9; George Taggart and Wallace Winchell, *A Yankee Major Invades Belgium* (New York, 1916), 7-12.
7. Taggart and Winchell, *Yankee Major,* 25-27, 43-44, 49, 71, 134-135, 144-146, 172-173, 194, 108-109.
8. Evangeline Booth, "The Salvation Army and the War," AWC, April 21 1917, 9.
9. William Howard Taft, chmn, Ed. Board, *Service With Fighting Men: An Account of the Work of The American Young Men's Christian Associations in the World War* (2 vols.; New York, 1922), I, viii, 26, 38, 48-50, 130; II, 499, 627-629; Herbert A. Wisbey, Jr. *Religion in Action: A History of The Salvation Army in the United States* (Ph.D. dissertation, Columbia University, 1951), 326.

10. Taft, *Service*, II, 44; I, 96 footn. 1; II, 409, 504, 511-519; *The War Service Herald*, IX, April 4, 1919, 8-9, SAA; Weldon B. Durham, " 'Big Brother' and the 'Seven Sisters:' Camp Life Reforms in World War I," *Military Affairs*, XLII (April 1978), 58.

11. Evangeline Booth, "Mothering the Boys at the Front," *The Forum*, September 1918, 305; Durham, "Big Brother," 59-60; Taft, *Service*, I, 387; AWC, August 4, 1917, 16; *War Service Herald*, November 11, 1917, 7; "Salvationist 'Soldiers of the Soil,' " LD, June 6, 1917, 1784; AWC, May 12, 1917, 9; The Salvation Army, *Soldiers of the Soil* (New York, 1918), pamphlet, SFOT/E Museum, G/F, "Farm Colonies/General."

12. Evangeline Booth and Grace Livingston Hill, *The War Romance of The Salvation Army* (Philadelphia, 1919), 44, illus f. 48.

13. Booth and Hill, *War Romance*, 45-47; materials on the Lee-Pershing incident, covered by letter Maude D. Dart to Comr. Holland French, Los Angeles, October 19, 1964, SANHQ/ chief secretary's office.

14. Booth and Hill, *War Romance*, 55-56, 82, AWC, August 25, 1917, 1, 9; SFOT/E Museum, G/F, "World War I," has special war commissions; Wisbey, Dissertation, 330.

15. *Akron Beacon Journal*, November 11, 1976, B-10; Sr.–Major Helga Ramsay, "War Service in France and Army Occupation in Germany," typed on dictation, both in SFOT/E Museum, G/F, "World War I;" Taft, *Service*, I, 147-148; II, 505; *War Service Herald*, July 6, 1919, 8-9, key 14, and August 7, 1919, 8-9, key 12, for officer and non-officer SA personnel in WW I.

16. Booth and Hill, *War Romance*. 59-61, 91, 97; Ensign Lydia Margaret Sheldon, Diary, autograph and photograph albums, in SFOT/E Museum horizontal drawer case "World War I"; see diary, October 1, 1917; Taft, *Service*, I, 127, 560-561, 571; "Salvation Army Pie and Prayers at the Front," LD, October 19, 1918, 67; Booth, "Mothering the Boys," 305; Commandant Joseph Hughes, "A Salvationist in the War," WC/C, August 4, 1923, 13.

17. AWC, July 6, 1918, 4; February 23, 1918, 16; Booth and Hill, *War Romance*, 109, fac. 228, 259; Frank Freidel, *Over There: The Story of America's First Great Overseas Crusade* (New York, 1963), 293-297, 300-302; "Imperfect Religion in the YMCA," LD, November 16, 1918, 32-33; Taft, *Service*, I, 249-250; interview with Mr James Stillwell, Suffern, New York, July 12, 1978.

18. Booth, "Mothering the Boys," 309; clipping Omaha *Daily News* Magazine, no date, no p, and letter, Comr. Thomas Estill to Martha Porter,

Chicago, June 16, 1919, on grave decoration, both in SFOT/E Museum, G/F, "WW I;" Adjutant Helen Purviance, "A Doughgirl on the Firing Line," *The Forum*, December 1918, 654; Booth and Hill, *War Romance*, 51-52; Taft, *Service*, I, 100-101.

19. Booth and Hill, *War Romance*, 13; Evangeline Booth, "Around the World with The Salvation Army," *National Geographic Magazine*, April, 1920, 347. Purviance, "Doughgirl," 649; Wisbey, Dissertation, 332; Booth and Hill, *War Romance*, 76-78; "SA Pie & Prayers," 63-64; interview with Col. Florence Turkington, Asbury Park, New Jersey, August 9, 1978, who also provided author with list of WW I personnel, SAA; [Adjutant Raymond C. Starbard], "Pies and Doughnuts: A New Kind of War Munitions Furnished by the Salvation Army: Special Correspondent of the Outlook," *The Outlook*, June 5, 1918, 220; Freidel, *Over There*, 295; Ramsay, "War Service," 2.

20. Starbard, "Pies & Doughnuts," 220-221; "SA—Pies & Prayers," 64; Purviance, "Doughgirl," 650; Ramsay, "War Service," 3, 6; AWC, May 4, 1918, 4; Hughes, "Salvationist in the War," WC/C, June 30, 1923, 16; interviews with Stillwell, Col. Turkington.

21. Starbard, "Pies & Doughnuts," 220; Booth and Hill, *War Romance*, 258-259, 66-67, 75.

22. AWC, August 4, 1917, 9; February 16, 1918, 12-13; March 22, 1919, 2; see above, Chapter II [47-48]; "SA—Pies & Prayers," 64; Booth and Hill, *War Romance*, 100-106; Wisbey, Dissertation, 339-340.

23. Freidel, *Over There*, 293; "SA—Pie & Prayers," 63; Craig Hamilton and Louise Corbin, eds., *Echoes from Over There* (New York, 1919), 31-32, 176; AWC, March 23, 1918, 9; June 8, 1918, 9; June 29, 1918, 9; August 17, 1918, 2; Booth, "Mothering the Boys," 307; "What the Salvation Army has Done," LD, March 16, 1918, 38-39.

24. Booth and Hill, *War Romance*, 35-40; Herbert Adams Gibbons, *John Wanamaker* (2 vols.; Port Washington, New York, 1971 [orig. 1926]), II, 420-421.

25. AWC, June 30, 1917, 9; February 16, 1918, 8-9, 12-13; June 2, 1917, 9; August 4, 1917, 16; July 6, 1918, 5; Durham, "Big Brother," 59.

26. AWC, December 22, 1917, 21; May 18, 1918, 8, 9, 16; May 25, 1918, 4; Sheldon autograph album; AWC, April 19, 1919, 2, 12; May, 3, 1919, 4, 16; May 17, 1919 entire ("Home Service Campaign" number); *War Service Herald*, August 1, 1917, 15; May 5, 1919, 1-2, 4-5, 10; *Stars and Stripes*, May 2, 1919, clipping in SFOT/E Museum G/F "WW I'"; "The Motherly Salvationists," LD, May 11, 1918, 32; "Salvation Army Drive

for a 'Home-Service Fund,'" LD, April 26, 1919, 30; "The Salvation Army Drive," *The Outlook,* May 28, 1919, 140; program, Salvation Army Home Service Meeting, Madison Square Garden, May 18, 1919, SFOT/E Museum, B/F, Evangeline Booth.

27. AWC, November 30, 1918, 8; January 15, 1919, 9; March 22, 1919, 16; August 14, 1920, 12, 14.

28. "Salvation Army has fought Satan Fifty-Four Years," LD, July 19, 1919, 34; WC/S, October 27, 1928, cover; AWC, August 14, 1920, 12; "Millions for the Salvation Army," LD, June 7, 1919, 39; J. Ray Johnson, "Campaigning with The Salvation Army," AWC, July 5, 1919, 10-11; *Now We Are Sixty: Anniversary Greetings to The Salvation Army* (New York, 1940), np, letter from Bruce Barton.

29. AWC, August 22, 1896, 6; WC/W, July 16, 1898, 1-3, 4-5; Capt. Masasuke Kobayashi, "The Salvation Army Among the Japanese of the Pacific Coast," AWC, September 25, 1920, 4.

30. AWC, September 25, 1920, 8-9; WC/W, April 9, 1921, 12-13; "The Romance of the Japanese Work in America: An Interview with Staff-Captain M. Kobayashi," WC/E, April 7, 1928, 11, 13; General Bramwell Booth to Comr. Adam Gifford, London, April 28, 1921, Gifford collection, SAA; interview with Brig. Masahide Imai, Santa Clara, California, December 12, 1978.

31. WC/W, November 19, 1921, 2, 5, 8-9, 10-11; November 26, 1921, 5; May 12, 1923, 11; June 16, 1923, 8-9, 13; September 1, 1923, 3; April 5, 1924, 5; September 13, 1924, 10; September 27, 1924, 8-9; Imai interview; Brig. Masahide Imai, "The Salvation Army," in Rev. Sumio Koga, *A Centennial Legacy: History of Japanese Christian Missions in North America, 1877-1977,* Vol. I (Chicago, 1977), 62-65.

32. AWC, August 7, 1920, 8-9; August 14, 1920, 1; October 2, 1920, 1, 8; The Memorandum of Appointment, Lt.–Comr. Adam Gifford, Territorial Commander of the West, February 3, 1921, Gifford collection, SAA; Porter R. Lee, Walter W. Pettit, *Social Salvage: A Study of the Central Organization and Administration of The Salvation Army* (New York, 1924), 11, 33-34.

33. Norris Alden Magnuson, *Salvation in the Slums: Evangelical Social Welfare Work, 1865-1920* (Ph.D. dissertation, Univ. of Minnesota, 1968), 429-431, 434; Mr Phil Collier, asst. ed. WC, kindly provided information on WC, April 2, 1979.

34. WC/C, April 16, 1923, 4; Sigmund A. Lavine, *Daughter of Salvation* (New York, 1970), 93 (BPOE cable); New York *World,* September 9,

1922, 1, 6; September 12, 1922, 8; "The Recall of Evangeline Booth," LD, October 7, 1922, 34; "An Army, Not an Association," *The Outlook*, September 27, 1922, 134-136; New York *World*, September 14, 1922, 5.

35. Evangeline C. Booth [ECB] to Adam Gifford, New York, September 28, 1922; Gifford to E. Higgins, San Francisco, October 14, 1922; ECB to Gifford, White Plains, telegram, November 4, 1922, in which she describes herself as "nearly distracted," the situation with Bramwell "intolerable"; Col. Walter Jenkins to Gifford, New York, November 14, 1922, mentions danger of "brain fever" in ECB, that she has "broken down" by ordeal, suggesting that Gifford send a "heartening wire." Gifford collection, SAA, closed.

36. Brig. Richard Griffith to Gifford, White Plains, New York, November 14 [1922], with "Brown-Cory" code; Gifford collection, SAA, closed.

37. There is an interesting exchange of letters on the Manifesto No. 1 in Gifford collection, SAA; Commissioner Edward Higgins, the chief of the staff, wrote to the territorial commanders stating that these manifestos had been received all over the Army in America and Britain, that the General had decided not to make any public comment, and that he, the Chief, would be glad to know what "effect," if any, the manifestos were having on American officers. On April 6, 1925, ECB telegraphed the American commissioners, instructing them as to how they should respond to inquiries from London: they were to equivocate, to avoid saying that the manifesto was simply being ignored or that nobody was taking it seriously. Rather they were to say that it was being "fully discussed" by officers, that it was too early to know what their reaction would be. They were to use their "own language" in these responses. As a result, Adam Gifford wrote to Higgins that there was "no question" in his mind that the manifesto was "being fully discussed," but a "large majority" of the officers remained "dead silent." To date, he offered, there had been no statements of "disloyalty," but in his judgment "many minds" were "somewhat disturbed." Higgins to Gifford, London, March 24, 1925, ECB to Gifford, New York, April 6, 1925; Adam Gifford to ECB, San Francisco, March 8, 1925, and to Edward Higgins, San Francisco, April 9, 1925, all in Gifford collection, SAA, closed. On "Atwood" writings, see F.A. MacKenzie, *The Clash of the Cymbals: The Secret History of the Revolt in the Salvation Army* (New York, 1929), 72-73; Lee & Pettit, *Social Salvage*, 71; " 'Wilful Will' Booth and His Salvation Army," LD, February 9, 1929, 38-50; "An American Salvation Army," *The Outlook*, November 24, 1926, 392-393; interview with Col. Wm. Maltby, Asbury Park, New Jersey, June 30, 1978: before

Maltby went to London in 1925 on business, the Commander instructed him to answer any questions there about her status in the United States by saying that the American people loved her. See for praise of General Booth from the all unsuspecting rank and file, WC/C, March 27, 1926, 7, 10-11; May 1, 1926, 8-9; E. Irena Arnold, *Poems of A Salvationist* (New York, 1923), 19.

38. WC/S, February 5, 1938, 13; WC, December 30, 1978, 12-13; WC/E, February 3, 1923 pictorial section; WC/S, December 17, 1927, 15; WC/C, December 12, 1925, 3; Dr Charles Wheeler, "Through the Hole in the Doughnut," WC/C, January 29, 1921, 7; Edward Justus Parker, *My Fifty-Eight Years: An Autobiography* (New York, 1943), 176-177; Agnes L. Palmer, *The Time Between: 1904-1926* (New York, 1926), 50-51.

39. AWC, April 19, 1919, 3; see "Shall We Forget the War?" WC/C, November 10, 1923, 6; Virginia Mack, "Redeemed," WC/C, June 30, 1924, 13; "45 Years in America: A Brief Historical Sketch," WC/C, September 12, 1925, 12; *Ten Talks on The Salvation Army*. The Sesqui-Centennial International Exposition, Philadelphia, June 1-December 1, 1926 (New York, 1926), 74-75; WC/S, March 26, 1927, 3; WC/S, April 23, 1927, 5; WC/S, July 30, 1927, 2; Evangeline Booth, *Let Us Live: An Address Delivered to the American Legion Convention, Trocadero Palace, Paris, September 21, 1927* (New York, 1928), 5-7; on clubs, see WC/C, July 30, 1921, 13; WC/W, September 10, 1921, 11; WC/C, January 23, 1926, 5; WC/C, February 23, 1929, 10; WC/W, July 14, 1923; Lt.–Col. C.W. Bourne, "Thirty-Three Years in Uniform" WC/C, September 13, 1924, 11; Minutes of the Territorial Trade Board, January 7, 1927 to December 17, 1932, in Transfer Trade Finance Board Minutes, SATHQ/S, office of Maj. Houston Ellis, Trade secretary, see for February 9, 1927 (officer's dues).

40. Salvation Army *Orders & Regulations for Officers, 1925*, 149; Sallie Chesham, *Born to Battle: The Salvation Army in America* (Chicago, 1965), 179-181; Damon Runyon, "The Idyll of Miss Sarah Brown," in his *Runyon A La Carte* (Garden City, 1945), 94-96, and his *Guys and Dolls* (New York, 1931); ECB to Gifford, New York City, October 30, 1922, Gifford collection, SAA; interview Brig. Christine McMillan, June 26, 1978.

41. WC/W, February 3, 1923, 5; WC/C, October 29, 1922, 9.

42. WC/C, November 18, 1922, 2; ECB to Adam Gifford, telegram, New York, November 4, 1922, Gifford to ECB, San Francisco, November 6, 1922, in Gifford collection, SAA; WC/C, July 26, 1924, 8.

43. Ensign W. W. Bouterse, "The Salvationist in High School," *The Young*

Soldier, February 11, 1928, 2; Southern Territorial Staff Council, Memoranda of Decisions and Suggestions, Bryson City, North Carolina, June 22-27, 1927, transcript copy, p 9, Holz collection.

44. On conditions in corps in the 1920s, author interviewed the following: Col. Frank Guldenschuh, June 16; Brig. Fred Crossley, June 30; Sr.-Major Charles A. Schuerholz, June 30; Sr.–Maj. and Mrs Carl Blied, July 14; Mrs Annie Breen, same date; Brig. and Mrs Ernest Baxendale, August 7 (all in Asbury Park, New Jersey, 1978); Lt.–Col. Edward Laity, Atlanta, November 24, 1978; Sr.–Maj. Bertha Shadick, December 15, and Mrs Sr.–Maj. George Watt, same date, Los Angeles, California, 1978; Bosch Dissertation, 258; Pamela Search, *Happy Warriors: The Story of the Social Work of The Salvation Army* (London, 1956), 162.

45. WC/W, October 22, 1921, 5-9, 10, 11-12; October 29, 1921, 10; WC/C, August 12, 1922, 1, 11; Lee and Pettit, *Social Salvage*, 94 ("have little significance"), [Brigadier] Ferdinand Braun, "We Still Save Men," *The North American Review*, 227 (March 1929), 316-317.

46. Captain Karl E. Nelson, *The Organizaton and Development of the Health Care System of The Salvation Army in the United States of America* (Thesis, Fellowship in American College of Hospital Administrators, 1973), 24, SAA; *Ten Talks*, 52, 54-56; Lee and Pettit, *Social Salvage*, 25-26, 80; interview with Sr.–Maj. Magna Sorenson, Los Angeles, December 15, 1978, with Brig. Emma Ellegard, Asbury Park, June 16, 1978.

47. Parker, *My 58 Years*, 160-162; "The Salvation Army's 'Lost Drunks,' " LD, September 18, 1920, 38; "A Salvation Army Report on Prohibition," LD, October 8, 1921, 32; Anderson, *Hobo*, 27-28, 261-262; Evangeline Booth, "Results of Prohibition in the United States," WC/C, September 3, 1921, 11; Evangeline Booth, *The Salvation Army Appraises Prohibition* (New York, 1929), SFOT/E Library.

48. AWC, June 26, 1920, 3; WC/W, July 30, 1921, 16; articles by Evangeline Booth on prohibition in WC/C, August 27, 1921, 4; September 3, 1921, 11; September 10, 1921, 13; WC/E, January 20, 1923, 16; WC/C, January 20 to March 10, 1923, later printed as a 30 pp booklet; appeared also WC/C, November 1—December 20, 1924; WC/W, August 1, 1925, 9; WC/W, July 7, 1928, 3; July 14, 1928, 3; "Salvation Army Report on Prohibition," 32; see pro-prohibition statements in *The Salvation Army Yearbook, 1922*, 71, *1924*, 80, *1926*, 108; WC/S, July 16, 1927, 8, 10; July 23, 1927, 5; *Bridging the Gulf: Being a Description of the Prison Work of The Salvation Army, Coupled with the Annual Report for 1924-1925* (New York, 1925), 12-13, 24, 46; WC/C, July 14, 1923, 8; WC/C, July

7, 1928, 3 (Republicans); WC/C, February 14, 1931, 10 (Hoover); Evangeline Booth, "The Army's Jubilee in the United States: Address to Staff Officers," *The Staff Review,* XI (January 1931), 5-7; Arnold, *Poems,* 22; WC/W, August 18, 1923, 10; WC/C, November 28, 1925,8; October 25, 1930, 7, 15.

49. WC/C, August 27, 1921, 2; *Close-Ups,* 26.

50. AWC, October 30, 1920, 3, WC/C, March 26, 1921, 5; December 3, 1921, 8; July 10, 1924, 11; May 17, 1924, 5; *What Is The Salvation Army?* (New York, 1924), 66-67; *Bridging the Gulf,* 56-58; *Broken Souls: Being the Report of Prison Welfare Work during the William Booth Centenary Year* (New York, 1929), 32; *Close-Ups,* 27.

51. *Broken Souls,* 3-5, prelude by Commander Booth.

52. *Broken Souls,* 23, 16-18, 26-27; *Bridging the Gulf,* 26-27, 33, 73-80, 104; "Our Prison Work," WC/C, February 2, 1924, 5, 15; Palmer, *The Time Between,* 96-102.

53. WC/C, December 15, 1923, 11; WC/W, September 20, 1924, 8-9, 10; Captain Ray Steadman-Allen, "The Evolution of Salvation Army Music," *The Musician* (London), July 24, 1965, 471.

54. WC/C, May 5, 1928, 13; letter to author, Lt.–Col. Ray Steadman-Allen, London, February 2, 1978; interviews with Comr. Richard Holz, Rancho Palos Verdes, Calif, December 13, 1978, with Lt.–Col. Wm. Bearchell, Asbury Park, June 30, 1978; James Neilson, "The Salvation Army Band," *The Etude,* 67 (February 1949), 122-123.

55. "Salvation Limited," *The Nation,* January 30, 1929, 124; Lt.–Cmdr. John Philip Sousa, USNRF, "Why the World Needs Bands," *The Etude,* 48 (September 1930), 657; WC/C, September 1, 1928, 9.

56. Lee and Pettit, *Social Salvage,* 95-97; Comr. W.A. McIntyre, "Story of the Southern Territory, USA," typescript 50 pp [1930], kindly lent to author by Mrs Col. William Noble, Atlanta, November 27, 1978; hereafter "Southern Story," see p 8 for community chest reference.

57. Interviews with Sr.–Maj. Charles Schuerholz and Sr.–Maj. Bertha Shadick; letter to author, M.C. Tunison, Saratoga Springs, New York, April 16, 1979.

58. WC/W, January 20, 1923, 5; *What is the SA,* 71-74; Lee and Pettit, *Social Salvage,* 91-97, 72-73; *Ten Talks,* 90; Southern staff council memorandum, June 1927, 13-17, Holz collection.

59. Palmer, *The Times Between,* 6; WC/C, July 10, 1926, 3-5; "Samptown, A 100 Per Cent Army Village," WC/C, November 22, 1924, 5; "A Whole Community at the Drumhead," LD, October 25, 1924, 33-34.

60. WC/C, October 23, 1926, 5, 8, 13 (map, announcement); WC/E, October 23, 1926, 4, 6, 9, 13; "Draft of Material in re: Birth and Re-Birth of Southern Territory," Col. Bertram Rodda, no date, 5 pp typescript, SATHQ/S, Publications Dept.; The Salvation Army *Disposition of Forces, Southern Territory, Feb. 1927*, 10-20 for breakdown of new divisions; interview with Col. Bertram Rodda, December 12, 1978, Oakland, California.

61. Interview with Mrs. Col. Lillian Hansen Noble, Atlanta; see also McIntyre, "Southern Story," and Comr. William A. McIntyre, *Christ's Cabinet: Character Stories of the Twelve Apostles* (Chicago, 1937), an engaging little book that tells one as much about McIntyre as it does about the Apostles.

62. Interviews with Col. Rodda, Lt.–Col. Laity; McIntyre, "Southern Story," 12-13.

63. WC/S, March 26, 1927, 3 (inaugural issue); WC/S, October 1, 1927, 8-9; Catherine Baird, *William McIntyre, God's Harvester* (London, 1948), 38-39.

64. WC/S, July 9, 1927, 7; Program, "Inaugural Program, Southern Territorial Staff Band, Thanksgiving Day, November 24, 1927," SATHQ/S, publications dept.; McIntyre, "Southern Story," 7 and WC/S, April 9, 1927, 10 (weak corps); Southern Trade minutes, November 28, 1928, 2; WC/C, May 26, 1928, 10.

65. Col. Richard E. Holz, "The Salvation Army and the Negroes of the Southern States of North America," *The Officer*, XXII (July 1914), 479; AWC, August 14, 1920, 12, 14; on integration of large meetings in South in 1920s, interview with Comr. Ernest W. Holz, Atlanta, November 23, 1978, with Col. Bertram Rodda, and with Lt.–Col. Laity; Southern *Disposition of Forces*, February 1927, 18, listed Washington No. 2 Corps, in Potomac Division, as "colored," as was the Serviceman's Hotel, Seventh and P Streets.

66. Col. W.A. McIntyre, *Twenty Years Housing The Salvation Army* (New York, 1920), 13, SAA; WC/C, June 11, 1921, 2; WC/E, November 25, 1922 pictorial section; WC/E, November 17, 1923, pictorial section; Brig. Hester Dammes, comp, "The Salvation Army Eastern Territory, Opening Dates of Women's Social Institutions," SAA, interview Brig. Emma Ellegard.

67. "The Salvation Army Soars," *The Survey*, June 15, 1930, 259; WC/C, July 12, 1930, 6. SANHQ is still housed in this building, which stands unaltered at 120 West Fourteenth Street.

CHAPTER V

1. St. John Ervine, *God's Soldier: General William Booth* (2 vols.; New York, 1935), II, App. III, 1046-1049, for Deed Poll of 1878.
2. Ervine, *God's Soldier*, II, App. VI, 1078-1090, Supplementary Deed Poll of 1904; Salvation Army *Orders & Regulations for Officers*, 1925, 11-12.
3. Lt.–Col. J. Morgan, "General Bramwell Booth 'Behind the Scenes,' " *The Officer*, VII (March/April 1956), 83.
4. Frederick Booth-Tucker to Samuel L. Brengle, London, June 21, 1927, in Gifford collection, SAA, closed; F.A. MacKenzie, Booth-Tucker: *Sadhu and Saint* (London, 1930), 233-35, 238, 249; F.A. MacKenzie, *The Clash of the Cymbals: The Secret History of the Revolt in the Salvation Army* (New York, 1929), 90-91, 122; interview with Comr. Richard E. Holz, Los Angeles, December 13, 1978.
5. An American Salvation Army," *The Outlook*, November 24, 1926, 392; "The Salvation Army Revolution," LD, December 4, 1926, 31-32; "Why the Salvation Army Revolted," LD, February 9, 1929, 25; "Colony or Dominion?" *The Outlook*, March 13, 1929, 421; MacKenzie, *Clash of Cymbals*, 64, 115-117, 164-168; for correspondence containing specific statements about the feelings of Evangeline and her circle against Bramwell, and their plans to alter the Army structure, see: R. Griffith to Comr. Henry Mapp, New York, November 22, 1927; Lt.–Col. [Richard Griffith] to [Comr. Adam] Gifford, New York, December 5, 1927; Evangeline Cory Booth [ECB] to Gifford, New York, February 17, 1928 conveying Exhibits "A" "B" and "C" her "Notes for an Interview with the General," his response to her, November 24, 1927, and her 21 pp response to him, February 9, 1928; William Peart to Gifford, New York, May 14, 1928, same, May 28, 1928; Peart to Gifford, New York, June 13, 1928; same, September 19, 1928 (if the chief refuses to call the Council, Evangeline wished to know what the reaction would be of the American commissioners if she organized a meeting between all of them and the General to "consider the whole situation"; if he refused, and if the chief of the staff were still "unfavorable" to calling the Council, "there is still the possibility of the Commander calling together the High Council. . . ."); telegram [undated] from Gifford to all Western divisional commanders, urging them to wire the Commander with their honest personal views "change of method of successorship." All this correspondence in Gifford collection, SAA, closed. Comr. William McIntyre to all officers in the South, Atlanta, December 12, December 14, 1928, urging them not to make comments

to the press and to support "our beloved Commander, Evangeline Booth," who was "fully capable" of leading US branch of the Army "in the right direction in this important matter," owned by Lt.–Col. Edward Laity, Atlanta.

6. Frank Smith, *The Betrayal of Bramwell Booth: The Truth about the Salvation Army Revolt* (London, 1929), 51-65, 89, 92-93; Comr. Catherine Bramwell-Booth, *Bramwell Booth* (New York, 1932), 474-476, 484-499, 500-503, 509, 517; MacKenzie, *Clash of Cymbals*, 64.

7. Ervine, *God's Soldier*, II, Apps. VIII-XI, 1100-1120, Atwood bulletins; W.L. Atwood to Adam Gifford, Wichita Falls, Texas, December 1, 1927, and a form soliciting articles for a new magazine, the "International Salvationist" to be published by Atwood, in Gifford collection. There is no record of Atwood in the corps record of the Wichita Falls corps, which are "reasonably complete" back to 1928. Two elderly soldiers remember that Atwood attended services at the corps occasionally in the 1920s, but was never a soldier. Lt. Marshall Gesner to author, Wichita Falls, June 22, 1979.

8. MacKenzie, *Clash of Cymbals*, 181-184; Ervine, *God's Soldier*, II, 905-906; Bramwell-Booth, *Bramwell Booth*, 485-86.

9. Bramwell Booth to ECB, London, November 24, 1927, Gifford collection.

10. ECB to Bramwell Booth, New York, February 9, 1928, 13, 15 for quotes, in Gifford collection; Bramwell-Booth, *Bramwell Booth*, 489, 521.

11. Telegram, Comr. W.A. McIntyre to Col A Kimball, Atlanta, November 14, 1928, announcing that General is "dying," and that Commander has invited all American commissioners to accompany her to London, and also inviting the divisional commanders to express their views on successorship to her directly by wire—just as Gifford asked his officers to do [see note 5 above], in Seiler collection, binders; WC/S, December 1, 1928, 8.

12. WC/C, February 23, 1929, 8; MacKenzie, *Clash of Cymbals*, 137.

13. WC/C, January 19, 1929, 8; January 26, 1929, 8-11; February 2, 1929, 9-10; February 9, 1929, 9; February 16, 1929, 9; WC/S, January 26, 1929, 6, 8-9; February 2, 1929, 4; February 9, 1929, 4; "Religious Dynasty," *The Outlook*, January 9, 1929, 60; Bramwell-Booth, *Bramwell Booth*, 489, 521; Colonel W.S. Barker, [chief sec'y, West, 1926-1930] to ECB, San Francisco, December 17, 1928 (urging her not to run for the office), Gifford collection; interview with Mrs Col. William Noble, Atlanta, November 27, 1978, who recalled that McIntyre broke his heart over the Bramwell crisis; interview with Col. Bertram Rodda, Oakland, December 12, 1978, whose father-in-law was Col. Jenkins, the national chief sec'y during the crisis;

Rodda believes that ECB allowed herself to be deceived into counting on her own election as Bramwell's successor; Ervine, *God's Soldier*, II, 1000-1001 conveys the same version; Colonel John Waldron, "Brengle and the Future of the Army," *The Officer*, XXVII (July 1976), 302-303 on Brengle's role in the crisis of 1929.

14. WC/E, March 9, 1929, 4; March 23, 1929, 9; "Why the Salvation Army Revolted," 25; Charles T. Hallinan, "The Overthrow of General Booth," *The Survey*, March 1, 1929, 712; "General Booth Goes to Court," *The Commonweal*, February 13, 1929, 413-414. An adequate, unbiased, and complete account of the overthrow of General Bramwell Booth has not yet appeared in print. It is interesting to note that there were predictions of serious trouble about the succession after Bramwell even before General William Booth died. See Agnes Maule Machar, "Red Cross Knights—A Nineteenth Century Crusade," *The Andover Review*, II (August 1884), 208; see also "General William Bramwell Booth and the Salvation Army," *The Outlook*, November 15, 1913, 562.

15. WC/C, January 5, 1929, 8-9; December 28, 1929, 9; February 22, 1930, 6; April 5, 1930, 9; May 10, 1930, 3; WC/C June 7, 1930 was "Jubilee Number"; WC/W, January 21, 1933, 5; interview with Lt.–Col. Wm. Bearchell, Asbury Park, New Jersey, June 30, 1978; *The Musical Salvationist*, July 1938, 74-75.

16. Herbert A. Wisbey, Jr., *Religion in Action: A History of the Salvation Army in the United States* (Ph.D. dissertation, Columbia University, 1951), 378 (700 percent); WC/E, November 17, 1934, 8-9; WC/S, Christmas issue, 1936, 21, 25; interviews with Col. Frank Guldenschuh, Asbury Park, June 28, 1978, with Lt.–Col. Charles Southwood, New York City, August 3, 1978, with Lt.–Col. Wesley Bouterse, Atlanta, November 28, 1978.

17. Interviews with Brig. Emma Ellegard, Asbury Park, June 16, 1978, with Sr.–Maj. Magna Sorenson, Los Angeles, December 15, 1978; Brig. Hester Dames, "The Salvation Army. Eastern Territory. Opening Dates of Women's Social Institutions," SAA, np.

18. Edward Higgins to Adam Gifford, London, June 15, 1931, Gifford collection; interviews with Lt.–Col. Bearchell, with Col. C. Stanley Staiger, Ocean Grove, July 28, 1978, with Mrs Col. William Noble, Atlanta, with Lt.–Col. Bouterse, with Lt.–Col. Norman Winterbottom, Santa Rosa, California, December 13, 1978; "Southern Trade Minutes," transfer file, SATHQ/S, trade dept., for May 14, 1931, 1.

19. Interviews with Col. C. Emil Nelson, New York City, October 24, 1977,

with Brig. Fred Crossley, Asbury Park, June 30, 1978, with Sr.–Maj. Charles Schuerholz, same, with Lt.–Col. Laity, with Mrs Col. Noble, with Sr.–Major Railton Spake, Los Angeles, December 11, 1978, with Mrs Sr.–Maj. George Watt, Los Angeles, December 15, 1978; WC/C, May 9, 1931, 13; WC/S, December 11, 1937, 5; WC/W, January 28, 1933, 5, 14, 16; US Department of Commerce, Bureau of the Census, *Census of Religious Bodies, 1936: The Salvation Army* (Washington, 1940), 1.

20. John Steinbeck, *The Grapes of Wrath* (New York, 1972 [orig. 1939]), 349-350; quoted by permission of Macmillan Publishing Co.

21. WC/E, November 22, 1930, 9; WC/C, January 10, 1931, 13; January 17, 1931, 4, 13; November 29, 1930, 8; WC/E, November 14, 1931, 8-9; WC/S see volume for 1933 *passim;* WC/E, June 17, 1933, 8; interview with Col. Wm. Maltby, Asbury Park, June 30, 1978, with Mrs Col. Noble, with Sr.–Maj. Bertha Shadick, Los Angeles, December 15, 1978; "Nostalgem" WC, May 19, 1979, 6.

22. WC/E, October 24, 1931, cover, 7, 14; WC/C, November 29, 1930, 4.

23. WC/E, October 24, 1931, 3; July 23, 1932, 8.

24. WC/C, November 29, 1930, 1; December 10, 1932, 12-13; Maltby and Bearchell interviews; Brig. Edwin Clayton, "The Glory of Hard Times," WC/C, August 13, 1932, 8; Adj. Vincent Cunningham, "Stop Talking Depression," WC/C, May 21, 1932, 5; Comr. S.L. Brengle, "What This Country Needs is a Revival," WC/C, December 3, 1932, 8, 12.

25. Interviews with Brig. Crossley, Sr.–Major Spake, Comr. Richard E. Holz; "Salvation Plus Music," *Newsweek,* December 15, 1941, 69; interview with Sr.–Maj. Carl Blied, Asbury Park, July 14, 1978; WC/W, January 9, 1937, 3, 14.

26. WC/S, December 26, 1936, 4, pict. no 2; interview with Col. Giles Barrett, Asbury Park, August 10, 1978; Lt.–Col. Charles Southwood, "Deployment of Officer Personnel in the Eastern Territory, December 2, 1976," Chart "G," in SATHQ/E, office of Field Secretary for Personnel.

27. Brief, "The Salvation Army Motorcade, Adjutant William Harris," [July 2—July 7, 1931], SFOT/E Museum, B/F, Evangeline Booth; WC/E, July 18, 1931, 13; Bearchell interview; Laity interview (nose story).

28. "Presenting Leidzen and the Metropolitan Ensemble," WC/E, November 22, 1930, 7.

29. B/M Eric Leidzen, " 'Songs of the Evangel': A Review," WC/S, April 30, 1927, 5 ("handmaiden"); account of Leidzen vs Eva episode from: private diary of Lt.–Col. Wm. Bearchell, interviews with Comr. Richard Holz, Lt.–Col. David W. Moulton, Wilmore, Kentucky, May 15, 1978; pro-

gram, "Friday Evenings at the Temple, October to May, 1932-1933," and separate program for Friday, May 26, 1933, in Busby collection; Leslie Fossey, *This Man Leidzen* (London, 1966), 24-26.

30. "Briefs, Star Lake Music Camp, 1935-1977," SATHQ/E, Music dept.; WC/W, December 14, 1940, 13.

31. On Brown, see WC/S, December 18, 1937, 5; July 3, 1948, 8, 15; January 3, 1948, 8 (Order of Founder); January 3, 1959, 6 (obit.); SATHQ/S publications bureau has file on "Mountain Mission," contains retirement program, pamphlet *Maid of the Mountains* (Atlanta, 1947); on Mexico, see WC/S, October 2, 1937, 16; October 16, 1937, 6; October 23, 1937, 8; March 5, 1938, 3; December 3, 1938, 8; December 10, 1938, 8, 11, 13, 15; May 8, 1948, 13; interview with Comr. Ernest W. Holz, Atlanta, November 23, 1978; Brief, "Inauguration of Mexico and Central America Territory, Commissioner Ernest W. Holz," no date, Holz Collection.

32. WC/W, October 30, 1937, 3, 14 (Joe the Turk); on Army ranks see Appendix I, WC/C, January 10, 1931, 9.

33. WC/E, September 22, 1934, cover, 8-9; Ervine, *God's Soldier*, II, 1017-1018; on Higgins-ECB quarrel, see exchanges between Higgins and ECB and both with Gifford, June 12, 1930, and January-April, 1931. ECB to seven international commissioners who had cabled her, her cable New York City April 20, 1931 ("My concern is that my dependence upon International respecting myself and America is worn threadbare. Records hold proof of repeated slights. Think possibly my ideas of loyalty have reached exaggerated degree.") On the Bill itself, WC/C, January 10, 1931, 9; on necessity of calming fears of divisional officers, Gifford to all Western divisional commanders, San Francisco, March 5, 1929, telegram, "Not an atom of truth in published reports that Commander intends seceding and establishing independent organization." She supports Higgins. "Perfect harmony and unanimity exists." All correspondence in Gifford collection, SAA.

34. Wisbey Dissertation, 385; program, "National Tribute of Farewell to Evangeline Booth, General-Elect of The Salvation Army, New York City, October 31-November 2, 1934," Seiler coll, binders; WC/E, September 22, 1934, cover, 8-9, 10; September 29, 1934, 9, 13, 15; in brief of appointment as territorial commander of the South, Comr. William Arnold, March 27, 1939, p 3, Busby coll.; "Evangeline Booth Commands The Salvation Army," *Christian Century*, September 12, 1934, 1132; "Greatest Army: Evangeline Booth Inspecting Outposts of 3,000,000 Salvationists," LD, November 21, 1936, 20; on lack of reform, see "Army

Now Obeys 'General Eva,'" *Christian Century*, September 26, 1934, 1221, and "Electing a Successor to Evangeline Booth," *Current History*, June 1939, 49.

35. "Scrap Book, 1937 American Tour of General Evangeline Booth. The Voice of the South," compl. Russell R. Whitman, P.R. counsel for Southern tour, October 1, 1937, in SFOT/E Museum; WC/S, October 29, 1938, 9.

36. WC/S, June 4, 1938, 8-9, 13; June 18, 1938, 15 (quote), 14.

37. WC/W, March 22, 1937, 9, 14; November 2, 1940, 13.

38. The Salvation Army, *The Nineteen Hundred Forty-Four Institutes of The Men's Social Service Department* (New York, 1944), 137; interview with Lt.–Col. Peter J. Hofman, Asbury Park, August 1, 1978; "The Salvation Army Carries On," *Newsweek*, September 25, 1939, 32 (quote).

39. *What is The Salvation Army?*(New York, 1945), 13-15; interview with Col. Giles Barrett; "Militant Christians," *Time*, November 9, 1942, 64; Parker, Comr. Edward Justus Parker, *My Fifty-Eight Years: An Autobiography* (New York, 1943), 283-298, 300-305; Sallie Chesham, *Born to Battle: The Salvation Army in America* (Chicago, 1965), 221-222, 227.

40. Interview with Comr. R.E. Holz; Wisbey Dissertation, 406-407; WC/W, November 9, 1940, 9.

41. WC/W, December 6, 1941, 9.

42. *The Red Shield*, February 1943, 1, SAA.

43. WC/W, November 9, 1940, 8; Lt.–Col. Norman J. Winterbottom, "Territorial Chronology, Western Territory, USA," no pages, "Japanese Division," in SATHQ/W, personnel dept.; SA, *Disposition of Forces, Western Territory, October 1940*, 36, *April 1941*, 11-13, *October 1941*, 11-13, 22-24; interview with Brig. Masahide Imai, Santa Clara, California, December 12, 1978, with Lt.–Col. R. Eugene Rice, Los Angeles, December 7, 1978.

44. Interviews with Col. Orval Taylor, New York City, August 4, 1978, with Lt.–Col. Rice, Lt.–Col. Winterbottom.

45. Interview with Brig. Imai.

46. *What is The Salvation Army?* 13-15; SA *Disposition of Forces, Southern Territory, December 1942*, 14, *September 1943*, 16, *November 1944*, 16, *November 1945*, 16, *October 1946*, 14; interviews with Col. Maltby, Lt.–Col. Winterbottom, Comr. R.E. Holz.

47. *1944 Institutes, Men's Social*, 3, 61, 115, *passim;* interviews with Col. Frank Guldenschuh, Lt.–Col. Hofman.

48. Interview with Brig. Ruth E. Cox, RN, Los Angeles, December 11, 1978,

with Sr.–Major Sorenson; letter Dr Alvin H. Darden to Mr Gerald White, Cincinnati, Ohio, September 30, 1968, covered by Capt. Israel Gaither to Maj. Dorothy Breen, New York City, May 25, 1979, in "Black Salvationist" research, SAA.

49. WC/W, January 31, 1942, 3; WC/E, December 27, 1941, 10, 15; *Red Shield*, January 1942, 1; interview with Brig. Henry Dries, Asbury Park, July 3, 1978.

50. WC/W, December 27, 1941, 10; February 14, 1942, 9; Comr. Samuel L. Brengle, "Killing in Battle: Is it Murder?" WC/W, January 31, 1942, 5.

51. WC/W, January 9, 1943, 10; interviews with Brig. Dries, with B/M Alfred V. Swenarton, Asbury Park, July 10, 1978, with Brig. Crossley; *Red Shield*, February 1942, 1-2; March 1942, 1; *What is The SA*, 35-36; Chesham, *Born to Battle*, 226; *Red Shield*, October 1942, 2-3; *Worker's Index for the 1943 Salvation Army Campaign for Wartime Activities and Welfare Needs* (New York, 1943), SFOT/E Museum, G/F, "WW II."

52. WC/W, January 3, 1942; April 17, 1943, 9, 12; March 18, 1944, 10; *Red Shield*, January 1942, 1; WC/W, February 20, 1943, 12; interview with Lt.–Col. Eric Newbould, Los Angeles, December 6, 1978; Winterbottom, "Territorial Chronology," np, "Hawaii Division;" interview Brig. Olive McKeown, Asbury Park, August 2, 1978.

53. WC/W, April 15, 1944, 3; May 27, 1944, 11; April 28, 1945, 13; [Lt.–Col.] Chester O. Taylor, "Nah-Kee-Ahn-Sa-Kol-Neek: A Northland Story," typescript, SFOT/W Library, 10-30, 34-40; interview with Lt.–Col. Chester O. Taylor, Hayward, California, December 12, 1978; O.M. Salisbury, *The Customs and Legends of the Tlinget Indians of Alaska* (New York, 1962 [orig. mid1920s]), 99-106, photos fac. p 20; WC, August 5, 1978, 13-14, and a cassette tape "Beginnings of The Salvation Army in Alaska," Lt.–Col. Walter Carruthers, SATHQ/W, chief secretary's office.

54. In a letter to Prof. Wisbey, the Chief of Chaplains, USA, September 27, 1948, the total of Salvation Army chaplains in WW II is given as thirty (Wisbey Dissertation, 406, note 2); Comr. R.E. Holz states that it was thirty-two (interview).

55. Interviews with Comr. R.E. Holz, with Col. Giles Barrett; Comr. Richard E. Holz, "Bombed Out on Christmas Eve: An Actual World War 2 Adventure," WC, Christmas, 1978, 8-9.

56. WC/E, December 22, 1945, cover; "New General: Salvation Army's world leader is a straight-talking preacher from street corners of London," *Life*, November 4, 1946, 85-88; [Gen.] Albert Orsborn, *The House of My Pilgrimage* (London, 1958), 146-148, 185-186.

57. *The Salvation Army Social Service for Men: Standards and Practices* (New York, 1948), 5.

58. James Neilson, "The Salvation Army Band, Part One," *The Etude*, 67 (January 1949), 20 (quotes); "Part Two," (February 1949), 123; WC/W, June 29, 1946, 9, 15 (first in the air); Flint Citadel Band has a claim to be the first band to fly to an engagement, based on a 1950 trip. See WC, April 22, 1978, 6.

59. Neilson, "Salvation Army Band, Part Two," 81, 123; interviews with Comr. R.E. Holz, B/M Alfred Swenarton; "Brief, Star Lake Camp, 1949," SATHQ/E Music Dept; Vernon Post, comp. *An Index to the Compositions of Erik Leidzen by Title* (New York, no date).

60. Interview with Lt.–Col. Laity, incl. seeing program for 1st Brengle Inst.; WC, April 8, 1978, 8 (obit. Col. Albert Pepper).

61. *Red Shield*, July, 1943, 1; *War Service Bulletin*, March 1945, 2; July 1945, 4; WC/S, January 10, 1948, 15; January 31, 1948, 4; May 29, 1948, 11; interviews with Comr. Ernest W. Holz, with Lt.–Col. Laity; Linda B. Murray, comp, "The History of Sherman Avenue Corps (Including No. 2 and Central Corps) Washington, D.C.," for Capt. Allan Wiltshire, Sherman Ave. Corps, December 4, 1978, 2–3, 4, SAA.

62. WC/S, April 24, 1948, 8–9, 13; May 15, 1948, 7; June 12, 1948, 5; June 19, 1948, 5; July 3, 1948, 11; July 24, 1948, 6; August 14, 1948, 13, September 25, 1948, 15; interview with Lt. Col. Laity; Arnold's appointment Memorandum as territorial commander of the South included these instructions: "The needs also of the large population of coloured people must not be overlooked." March 27, 1939, 4, Busby collection.

63. Interview with Col. Nelson, with Col. Guldenschuh, and with Lt.–Col. Lyell Rader, Ocean Grove, New Jersey, June 23, 1978.

64. Evangeline C. Booth to Ensign Wm. Maltby, New York City, January 16, 1928, ECB to Brig. Wm. Maltby, Hartsdale, Nov. 29, 1948, both in Col. Maltby's possession, who kindly provided much of the information for this episode. "Program, Musical Festival Featuring the Compositions of Evangeline Booth, Friday Evening at the Temple, November 19, 1948," in SFOT/E Museum, B/F, Evangeline Booth.

65. "Evangeline Booth Is Promoted to Glory," *Life*, July 31, 1950, 72–73; Maj. Christine E. McMillan, "The Founder's Daughter," WC/E, August 12, 1950, 7; see the entire issue, *passim.*

CHAPTER VI

1. *Time*, December 26, 1949, cover and 38-41.
2. *Guys and Dolls*, story by Damon Runyon, music and lyrics by Frank Loesser, book by Jo Swerling and Abe Burrows.
3. Sr.–Capt. Don Pitt, *Pilgrim's Progress: 20th Century. The Story of Salvation Army Officership* (New York, 1950), 19.
4. Paul Robb, "Cap'n Tom—The Other Side of Skid Row," *Reader's Digest*, April, 1952, 95-96; "Shock Troops," *Time*, January 26, 1948, 71; Albert Orsborn, *The House of My Pilgrimage* (London, 1958), 188-190; *Time*, December 26, 1949, 39; interview with Brig. Olive McKeown, Asbury Park, New Jersey, August 2, 1978.
5. Interviews with Col. Frank Guldenschuh, Asbury Park, New Jersey, June 16, 1978, with Col. Giles Barrett, Asbury Park, July 10, 1978, with Lt.–Col. Peter J. Hofman, Asbury Park, August 1, 1978; Howard J. Clinebell, Jr., *Understanding and Counseling The Alcoholic Through Religion and Psychology* (New York, 1956), 83-93.
6. Leonard Blumberg, Thomas E. Shipley, Jr, Irving W. Shandler, *Skid Row and Its Alternatives: Research and Recommendations from Philadelphia* (Philadelphia, 1973), 148-149; *The Salvation Army Yearbook, 1956* (London, 1956), 135 ("trophy").
7. Interview with Lt.–Col. Hofman; "Bargain Buys from the Salvation Army," *Good Housekeeping*, January 1959, 95.
8. Interview with Lt.–Col. Hofman; *Minutes of the Men's Social Service Secretaries' Conference, October 3, 4, 5, 1956* (New York, 1956), 6, 9-11, 34, 39-45, 58-59, 69, 73, *passim;* The Salvation Army Men's Social Service, *Handbook of Standards, Principles and Policies* (New York, 1960), 7-14, 61-62, 249-254, *passim.* Blumberg et al., *Skid Row*, 19-20.
9. Herbert W. Wisbey, *Soldiers Without Swords: A History of The Salvation Army in the United States* (New York, 1955), 209; same author, *Religion in Action: A History of The Salvation Army in the United States* (Ph.D. dissertation, Columbia University, 1951), 412, hereinafter cited as "Dissertation;" Sr.–Major Jane E. Wrieden, "To Strengthen Maternity-Home Service for Unmarried Mothers, II," *The Officer*, V (March-April 1954), 86-87; *The Salvation Army Services to Unmarried Parents and Their Children. Maternity Homes and Hospitals: Handbook of Information* (New York, 1962), 56-57, 18-21, 23-29 (quotations pp. 19 and 24), hereinafter cited as *Homes and Hospitals Handbook;* interview with Brig. Ruth E. Cox, R.N., Los Angeles, California, December 11, 1978

10. J. Stanley Sheppard, *The Prison Work of The Salvation Army* (New York, 1948), 23; SFOT/E Library, pamphlet files, "Penology," for reports of Salvation Army Congress of Corrections, 1959-1967; WC, March 4, 1978, 15; interview with Lt.–Col. Chester Taylor, Hayward, Calif., December 12, 1978

11. *Testament to Youth: The Salvation Army's Report to the Mid-Century White House Conference On Children and Youth* (New York, 1950), 9-16, 36, 37-39, all four WC editions for October 28, 1950; Lt.–Col. Charles Southwood, "Deployment of Officer Personnel in the Eastern Territory, December 2, 1976," charts F and G; for the figures of the decline, see *The Salvation Army Yearbook, 1955* (London, 1956), 121, and The Salvation Army *Disposition of Forces, Southern Territory, October, 1978* (national statistics), 133.

12. "Brief: Eastern Territory Public Relations Department" compiled by Lt.–Col. H.E. Weatherly, March 28, 1963, 2-3, SAA; *Action! The Salvation Army Manual for Emergency Disaster Service* (New York, 1972), 7 (quote); Wisbey, Dissertation, 315; *The Salvation Army Definitive Statement of Services and Activities* (New York, 1960), 19.

13. Orsborn, *House of My Pilgrimage*, 191; Pitt, *Pilgrim's Progress*, 15; *SA Yearbook 1955*, 122; Major David Baxendale, "These Are My People!" *The Officer*, XXIV (December 1973), 542.

14. Herbert Newton, "Is the Army Policy Scriptural?" *Conq*, II (February 1893), 55 ("pigeon-holed"); Capt. John Waldron, "Statistics Tell A Story," *The Officer*, IV (September-October 1953), 294; Wisbey, Dissertation, 410-411, *Soldiers*, 208.

15. Wisbey, Dissertation, 385-388, *Soldiers*, 194-196; "The New Army," *Time*, June 30, 1958, 68.

16. Wisbey, Dissertation, 172, *Soldiers*, 82; Lt.–Col. Norman J. Winterbottom, "Territorial Chronology: The Salvation Army Western Territory, USA," 1963-1967, "Divisions discontinued, No. 5: Scandinavian Division;" "Eastern Scandinavian" file, SAA; The Salvation Army, *Disposition of Forces, Eastern Territory, November 1960*, 64-66; *October 1961*, 6; *Central Territory, November 1963*, 50-52; *November 1964*, 42-45; *October 1965*, 48-52; WC/E February 18, 1961, 10; WC/E January 21, 1961, 15.

17. *Time*, December 26, 1949, 41; "Booth Led Boldly with His Big Bass Drum," *The Christian Century*, July 14, 1965, 886; Pitt, *Pilgrim's Progress*, 50.

18. Sr.–Maj. Henry Koerner, "Candidates: An American Contribution to an ever-relevant discussion," *The Officer*, VII (March-April 1956), 116-117;

Raymond Arthur Dexter, *Officer Training in The Salvation Army: An Institutional Analysis* (Ed.D. Dissertation, Stanford University, 1962), 139-140; "The Salvation Soldiers," *Newsweek,* June 6, 1960, 85; SA *Definitive Statement,* 11.

19. Dexter, *Officer Training,* note on p. 150; Morton Yarmon, "About The Salvation Army," *The New York Times Magazine,* November 28, 1954, 20; "The Hallelujah Army Observes Its 75th Christmas," *Life,* December 27, 1954, 10; Gilbert Millstein, " 'Sinner, Will You Let Him In?' " *The New York Times Magazine,* May 21, 1961, 30; Richard Armstrong, "An Army of Gentle Warriors," *The Saturday Evening Post,* December 15, 1962, 20; Southwood, "Development of Officer Personnel;" interview with Comr. Ernest W. Holz and Colonel John Paton, Atlanta, November 23, 1978.

20. James Francis Cooke, "Pennies in the Tambourine: An Editorial," *Etude,* July, 1953, 59; Vernon Post, comp., *An Index of the Compositions of Erik Leidzen by Title* (New York, no date), Salvation Army Eastern Territorial Music Bureau, *Catalog and Price List for Instrumental Music and Vocal Music* (New York, 1977).

21. Sallie Chesham, *Born to Battle: The Salvation Army in America* (Chicago, 1965), 254; Wisbey, Dissertation, 129, *Soldiers,* 62; *Testament to Youth,* 37-38.

22. Interview with Comr. Ernest W. Holz; Salvation Army *Disposition of Forces, Southern Territory, June 1952,* 26, *November 1952,* 26; *April 1951,* 23; *November, 1951,* 24; Helen G. Purviance to Brig. Edward Carey, New York City, March 24, 1949, filed with Capt. George H. Evans, " 'The Black Salvationist' (Work in Progress) Regarding the Cleveland (Central Area Corps), Ohio," part of material on Black Salvationists presented by Capt. Israel Gaither to the SAA.

23. WC/S January 8, 1955, 4; WC/S January 15, 1955, 10; WC/S, February 5, 1955, 9; WC/E January 21, 1961, 8 and interview with Brig. Emma Ellegard, Asbury Park, June 16, 1978; interview with Sr.–Maj. Railton Spake, Los Angeles, December 11, 1978.

24. *"A Position Statement: The Salvation Army and Inter-Group Relations* Approved by the commissioners' conference, May, 1964; Chesham, *Born to Battle,* 253-54.

25. WC/E May 18, 1963, 20-21; WC/E, September 10, 1966, 20; Baxendale, "These Are My People!," 359.

26. Lt. John Merritt, "The Salvation Army in the Inner City," *The Officer,* XX (August 1969), 565; Brig. Christine McMillan, "Opportunity Unlim-

ited at the Harlem Temple Corps," WC/E, March 11, 1967, and "The Harlem that Doesn't Make the Headlines," WC/E February 11, 1967; Capt. David Holz to Maj. Carl Hansen, Richmond, Virginia, May 31, 1968, in SATHQ/S Publications Bureau files, "SA and Blacks;" WC, March 10, 1979, 12-13; *The Musician* (New York), May 1979, 11.

27. Maj. Dorothy E. Breen, "The Army and Deprived Children," *The Officer*, XXII (June, 1971), 367; Maj. Henry Gariepy, *Urban Challenge and Response*, for presentation to the divisional commanders conference, March 22, 1973 (New York, 1973), 9-13; WC/E November 22, 1969, 19, December 6, 1969, 14-18; September 5, 1970, 12-13; interview Col. Giles Barrett.

28. Interview with Mrs. Col. William Noble, Atlanta, November 27, 1978; Breen, "Salvation Army and Deprived Children," 367-68; WC/E, March 9, 1968, 16-17; Salvation Army *Disposition of Forces, Central Territory, November 1976*, 29-30.

29. Maj. Robert A. Watson, *Report. Services to Minorities and the Inner City. The Salvation Army Eastern Territory, July, 1973* (New York, 1973) *passim* (quotes 6,8,10) and, same author, *Urban Conditions and the Leadership Challenge* Territorial Leadership Conference, November 7-8, 1973, Ocean City, New Jersey (New York, 1973), 3, 8-9, *passim*, SAA.

30. Maj. Dorothy A. Purser, *Report on the Meeting of Active Black Officers Serving in the Eastern Territory, The Salvation Army Territorial Congress, June, 1969* (New York, 1969), 3-4; Brig. B. Barton McIntyre to Col. J. Clyde Cox, New York City, May 26, 1969, "Black Salvationists" file, SAA.

31. WC March 10, 1979, 12-13; March 31, 1979, 12-13; June 16, 1979, 12-13; WC/S June 1, 1968, 2; "Black Salvationist" files, SAA, SFOT/E Library; interviews with Brig. Emma Ellegard, Col. Frank Guldenschuh, Brig. Fred Crossley, Col. William Maltby, Brig. Henry Dries, Asbury Park, with Comr. William E. Chamberlain, Comr. Paul J. Kaiser in New York, with Comr. Ernest Holz, Lt.-Col. Edward Laity, Mrs Col. William Noble, Lt.-Col. Wesley Bouterse in Atlanta, with Col. Bertram Rodda, Oakland.

32. WC/W August 17, 1940, 8; interview with Maj. Leroy Pedersen, Los Angeles, December 15, 1978.

33. WC/E January 21, 1961, 13; March 25, 1961, 10; Gariepy, *Urban Challenge*, 8-9; Watson, *Service to Minorities*, 2, 4, 6, 8, 9-10.

34. WC/W March 21, 1896, 6; May 5, 1923, 1, 8, 13; August 23, 1924, 10, 13; April 20, 1940, 8; Capt. Check Hung Yee, "Songs Under the Lanterns," *The Officer*, XVII (November 1966), 744-45, same author, "Preaching Christ in the Chinese Way," *The Officer*, XIX (January-February 1968), 11; WC March 4, 1978, 12-13.

35. Lt.–Col. Olof Lundgren to author, New York City, June 19, 1979.

36. AWC August 12, 1893, 8; Wisbey, Dissertation, 409, *Soldiers,* 208; Booz, Allen & Hamilton, *General Survey of Administration and Operations: The Salvation Army in the United States* (New York, 1968), 15; "Crisis for Salvationists," *The Christian Century,* September 23, 1970, 114; "Salvation Army Officer Ousted in Dispute over Book," same, November 4, 1970, 1312; "Memorandum: Mrs Billie B. McClure vs The Salvation Army," Atlanta, January 5, 1973, Comr. W.E. Chamberlain, SAA.

37. Porter R. Lee, Walter W. Pettit, *Social Salvage: A Study of the Central Organization and Administration of The Salvation Army* (New York, 1924), 85-86 (quote); Pitt, *Pilgrim's Progress,* 22-24; "The New Army," *Time,* June 30, 1958, 67-68; Dexter, *Officer Training,* 13, 25-27, 83, 196-205; interview with Mrs Lt.–Col. F. William Carlson, Ocean Grove, August 7, 1978.

38. E.H. McKinley, *A Preliminary Report, on the Relationship Between Asbury College and The Salvation Army, 1924-1973,* May 11, 1973, SAA; Comr. William E. Chamberlain, *Relationships Between Asbury College and The Salvation Army, Southern Territory* (Atlanta, 1973), SAA; Kenneth Baillie, Lyell Rader, *Statistical Study to Determine the Effect of Attendance at Asbury College on Commitment to Officership in The Salvation Army, 1957-1965* (New York, 1965), SAA; interview with Comr. William Chamberlain; *Education Into the Second Century: The Salvation Army School for Officers' Training, Chicago, Illinois-Asbury College, May 23, 1979* (Chicago, 1979); WC, June 17, 1978, 6; The *Salvation Army Yearbook, 1978* (London, 1978), 173; "Student Witness," *The Officer,* XV (August 1964), 574-576; Col. Dorothy Phillips, "Education in the United States (2)" *The Officer,* XXII (April 1971), 248-49.

39. *The Musician* (New York), November 1978, 6; December 1978, 3; January 1979, 6; February 1979, 7; March 1979, 12; April 1979, 8; *The Musician* (London), February 4, 1978, 73.

40. WC October 15, 1977, 12-13; February 25, 1978, 12-13; *The Musician* (New York), November 1978, 5, 11; December 1978, 6-7, 11; *The Musician* (London), February 4, 1978, 72.

41. SA *Definitive Statement* 1960, 14.

42. Statistics from national composites, *Disposition of Forces, Southern October 1978,* 133; *The Salvation Army Band Tune Book Supplement* (London, 1954) [iv] quote; see *The Musician* (New York) from first month of publication onward (October 1978).

43. WC/S February 3, 1968, 12-13; Capt. Ernest A. Miller, "The Beat That

Communicates," *The Officer,* XV (December 1964), 833; Maj. David A. Baxendale, "Blueprint for Teenage Evangelism," *The Officer,* XXII (November 1971), 602-603.

44. *Homes and Hospitals Handbook,* forward (quote); Captain Karl E. Nelson, *The Organization and Development of the Health Care System of The Salvation Army in the United States of America* (Thesis, Fellowship, American College of Hospital Administrators, New York, 1973), 57; interviews with Comr. W.R.H. Goodier, New York, August 3, 1978; with Comr. Ernest W. Holz, Col. John Paton in Atlanta, November 23, 1978, with Brig. Ruth E. Cox, R.N., with Col. Florence Turkington, Asbury Park, New Jersey, August 9, 1978; telephone interview, Lt.–Col. Mary Verner, July 10, 1979; Lt.–Col. Mary E. Verner, *Analysis of Decreased Utilization of Salvation Army Maternity Homes and Hospitals 1967-1975 and Contributing Factors* (Thesis, Fellowship, American College of Hospital Administrators, 1976), 11-18, 32-34, 42-45, 99-100.

45. Author visits to Chicago Freedom Center, May 1976, to St. Louis Harbor Light Center, May 19, 1979; Maj. Edward V. Dimond, "Syncopated Salvation," WC/C January 18, 1969, 12-13.

46. SA Men's Social Service *Handbook,* 65-68.

47. Minutes, Commissioners' Conference, May 25-27, 1977, 201, SATHQ/E; interview Comr. W.R.H. Goodier, with Comr. Richard E. Holz, Los Angeles, December 13, 1978, with Lt.–Col. Hofman; Blumberg et al, *Skid Row,* 12.

48. Booz, Allen & Hamilton, *General Survey,* 5-14, 19-21 w/chart, 38-39, 42; on national training college, see 17, 1943-50, Dexter, *Officer Training,* 188, interview with Col. Orval Taylor, New York City, August 4, 1978; *Progress Report Territorial Headquarters Reorganization. The Salvation Army Eastern Territory August 29, 1973* (New York, 1973), SAA.

49. The Salvation Army chain of command as of 1980 is nearly equivalent to that of the US military: lieutenant, captain, major, lt.–colonel, colonel, commissioner, the General; along with the rank changes of 1973, quotas for command ranks were fixed for each territory at, say, one commissioner, one full colonel and eight lt–colonels, so that most officers will rise no higher than major, and will retire at that rank.

50. Col. John D. Waldron, Chief Secretary, New York City, to divisional commanders and department heads, June 20, 1975, in SFOT/E Museum, Gen. files, "SA Symbols;" interview with Comr. Goodier.

51. Mrs Lt.–Comr Winifred Gearing, "Though Mountains Shake . . ." *The Officer,* XXI (November 1970), 730-42; *Action,* 13, 53, 55-61; Vincent

W. Erickson, "Doers of the Word in Today's Congregations," *The Luth-eran Quarterly*, 17 (August 1965), 261; "Biting the Hand That Feeds You," *Trans-Action*, April 1970, 4, and in reply, [Major Edward Fritz], "More Than Coffee and Dougnuts," *Trans-Action*, October 1970, 60-63; interviews with Maj. Don Pack, Los Angeles, December 13, 1978, with Commr. Holz, Atlanta, with Lt.–Col. Hofman, with Brig. Henry Dries, Asbury Park, July 3, 1978, with Maj. Harold Hinson, Atlanta, November 29, 1978.

52. Research material files, "Viet-Nam," in SAA, unprocessed [1978], under covering letter Colonel Norman S. Marshall to Major Dorothy Breen, New York City, September 6, 1977.

53. Interview, Comr. Ernest Holz, Col. John Paton, Atlanta, with Comr. W.R.H. Goodier, Comr. William Chamberlain,, Comr. Paul Kaiser, Col. Orval Taylor, Maj. Leroy Pedersen; letter to author, Capt. Stanley Jaynes, Jackson, Mississippi, March 28, 1978; Sheila B. Kamerman, Alfred J. Kahn, *Social Service in The Unites States: Policies and Programs* (Philadel-phia, 1976), 18-19, 532.

54. H. Rider Haggard, *Regeneration: Being an Account of the Social Work of The Salvation Army in Great Britain* (London, 1910), 13; see above, Chapter III, 27-28; Chesham, *Born to Battle*, 264; *Chicago Tribune*, July 5, 1979, 6:1-2.

55. Letter to author, Lt.–Col. Ernest A. Miller, Washington, D.C., July 20, 1978; WC July 29, 1978, 6-7; *The Role of the Corps Officer in the United States of America: Guidelines for Corps Officers of The Salvation Army in the United States of America.* Approved by the Commissioners' Confer-ence, USA, October 1972 (New York, 1972) 8, 11, 12, 19, 41.

56. Jaynes letter, March 28, 1978; *Report on Realignment of Divisional Boundaries* [Eastern territory, Nov. 1971], schedules 1-13, ff p 12, SAA; American Association of Fund-Raising Counsel, Inc., *Giving USA: 1977 Annual Report*, 39.

57. *Working Together: Principles of Cooperation for Salvation Army Participa-tion in United Appeals.* Adopted by commissioners' conference, October 1975 (New York, 1975); WC, December 31, 1977, 12-13; "Mercenaries for Christ," *Newsweek*, December 27, 1971, 50; "United Way: Are the Criticisms Fair?" *Changing Times*, October 1977, 31; The Salvation Army National Soldiers' Commission, USA, *Report and Recommendation to the Commissioners' Conference, May 22-25, 1967* (Chicago, 1967), 15-19.

58. WC, November 19, 1977, 12-13, 18-19; April 21, 1979, 19; May 12, 1979, 12-13; *Role of the Corps Officer*, 11.

59. *The United Methodist Reporter*, June 17, 1977, 5; US Department of Commerce, Bureau of the Census, *Census of Religious Bodies, 1936: The Salvation Army....* (Washington, 1940), 1-2; Douglas W. Johnson, Paul R. Picard, Bernard Quinn, *Churches and Church Membership in the United States: An enumeration by region, state and county* (Washington, 1974), ix-xi, 1-2; Salvation Army *Yearbooks, 1951*, 90; *1961*, 128, *1971*, 191; figures for 1978, *Disposition, South, October 1978*, 133; WC/E, November 17, 1934, 9; Southwood, "Deployment of Officer Personnel;" Leo Rosten, ed., *Religions in America: Ferment and Faith in an Age of Crisis. A New Guide and Almanac* (New York, 1975), 437 441, 478 460; Baxendale, "Blueprint," 601; Maj. Herbert Luhn, *Diminishing Corps and the Way Out. A Paper delivered to The Salvation Army National Social Services Conference* (Dallas, 1978), 2; Current statistics supplied by NHQ, July 19, 1979.

60. National Soldiers' Comm., *Report*, 23 (quote); Booz, Allen & Hamilton, *General Survey*, 16; Col. Paul S. Kaiser, "Our Evangelistic Outreach," *The Officer*, XVII (November 1966), 731; interviews with Brig. Ellegard, Lt.–Col. William Bearchell, Asbury Park, June 30, 1978, with Col. William Maltby, Comr. Goodier, Comr. Chamberlain, Comr. Kaiser, Col. John Paton, Comr. Richard Holz.

61. Luhn, *Diminishing Corps* 2, 4; Captain Philip D. Needham, "Preach or Perish," *The Officer*, XXIII (July 1972), 314-315, 319; T.J. Carlson, *A Viewpoint Concerning Goals and Objectives of The Salvation Army as it enters its Second Century. Submitted to a national conference of officers* (New York, 1966), 11.

62. Johnson, Picard, Quinn, *Churches*, xi, 1-2, 229-233; Baxendale, "Blueprint," 601, quotation.

63. Memorandum for the Ruling Division, IRS, submitted in behalf of the Salvation Army by Cadwalader, Wickersham & Taft, August 1, 1955, 9; "The Salvation Army as a Religious Organization," Memorandum by William J. Moss, Cadwalader, Wickersham & Taft, for the commissioner's conference, October 19, 1978, both from E. Holz collection.

64. Minutes, commissioners' conference, May 1977, 368-73; Memorandum of Appointment to Comr. William E. Chamberlain as National Commander of The Salvation Army in the United States, November 20, 1974, lists the 41 organizations, 3; filed with *National Headquarters Manual*, SATHQ/W, Personnel Dept; Comr. William E. Chamberlain to Gen.

Michael S. Davison, USA, New York City, December 8, 1976, resigning from USO, in Chief Secretary's office, NHQ, New York City.

65. Articles of Organization and By-Laws, Laymen's and Officers' Councils, SATHQ/W; interview, Col. Orval Taylor, New York City; *Chosen to be a Soldier: Orders and Regulations for Soldiers of The Salvation Army* (London, 1977), 3, 32-38; Col. W.R.H. Goodier to territorial chief secretaries, New York City, January 30, 1975, filed with *National Headquarters Manual.*

66. Brigadier Maro Smith, "The D.C. as Pastor (2)," *The Officer,* XXIV (November 1973), 495.

67. Orsborn, *House of My Pilgrimage,* 181.

68. These officers were Commissioners Goodier, E. Holz, R. Holz, Needham, Chamberlain, and Kaiser, and Colonels Albert Scott, John Paton, Will Pratt, Andrew Miller, Emil Nelson, and Orval Taylor.

Index